SCHOOLING CORPORATE CITIZENS

How Accountability Reform Has Damaged Civic Education and Undermined Democracy

Ronald W. Evans

Routledge
Taylor & Francis Group

NEW YORK AND LONDON

First published 2015
by Routledge
711 Third Avenue, New York, NY 10017

and by Routledge
2 Park Square, Milton Park, Abingdon, Oxon, OX14 4RN

Routledge is an imprint of the Taylor & Francis Group, an informa business

© 2015 Taylor & Francis

The right of Ronald W. Evans to be identified as author of this work has been asserted by him in accordance with sections 77 and 78 of the Copyright, Designs and Patents Act 1988.

Library of Congress Cataloging-in-Publication Data

Evans, Ronald W. Schooling corporate citizens : how accountability reform has damaged civic education and undermined democracy / by Ronald W. Evans.
    pages cm
    Includes bibliographical references and index.
    1. Social sciences—Study and teaching—United States.   2. Citizenship—Study and teaching—United States.   3. Civics—Study and teaching—United States.   4. Education—Standards—United States.   5. Educational accountability—United States.   6. Educational evaluation—United States.   I. Title.
    LB1584.E946
    2015300.71—dc23
    2014025767

ISBN: 978-1-138-78842-8 (hbk)
ISBN: 978-1-138-78843-5 (pbk)
ISBN: 978-1-315-76558-7 (ebk)

Typeset in Bembo
by Apex CoVantage, LLC

Printed and bound in the United States of America by Publishers Graphics, LLC on sustainably sourced paper.

For my students

CONTENTS

LIST OF ILLUSTRATIONS

ACKNOWLEDGMENTS

As I send this book to press I would like to acknowledge all those who provided assistance in various ways. This work could not have been completed without the helpful assistance of many archivists and access to the materials they provided. I received generous assistance from Alan Walker and others at in the Civilian Records Unit at National Archives II in College Park, Maryland; Ray Wilson and other archivists at the Ronald Reagan Presidential Library, Simi Valley, California; Rachael Altman and others at the George Bush Presidential Library, College Station, Texas; Carol Leadenham and other archivists at the Hoover Institution Archives, Stanford, California; Sarah Traugott at the Dolph Briscoe Center for American History, Austin, Texas; and Brian McNerney at the Lyndon Baines Johnson Presidential Library, Austin, Texas.

I also received a great deal of assistance in procuring images from archivists and others. For their help in procuring photographs I would like to thank Bonnie Burlbaw at the George Bush Presidential Library; Stephanie Stewart and Rachel Bauer at the Hoover Institution Archives; Melissa Mead and Melinda Wallingtron at Special Collections, Rhees Library, University of Rochester; Gary B. Nash and Marian Olivas at the National Center for History in the Schools; and William G. Spady at Breakthrough Learning, Dillon, Colorado.

I would also like to thank those who offered their comments, questions, and insights on presentations from this work I made at conferences during 2013 and 2014. Among these were presentations at the annual conferences of the Society for the Study of Curriculum History, the College and University Faculty Assembly of the National Council for the Social Studies, and the American Educational Research Association. I would especially like to thank Gregg Jorgensen, the late William Watkins, William Wraga, and William Schubert for their comments, questions, and suggestions.

My colleagues at San Diego State University have been supportive of my research for many years. I received consistent and invaluable support in the form of research assigned time, small grants to fund archival visits, and a sabbatical leave, which provided ample time for writing. I would also like to thank President Elliot Hirschman of San Diego State University for a grant from the Presidential Leadership Fund, titled "Origins and Development of Accountability Reform," that helped fund travel for archival research and made this work possible.

I owe a debt of gratitude to the Men's Fellowship of the First Unitarian Universalist Church of San Diego. I would especially like to thank the men in my men's group for listening to me talk endlessly about this work and for their friendship and support. Finally, I would like to thank my wife, Mika, and my children, Katie, Mira, and Kai, my son-in-law James Humphrey, my parents, Hugh and Dorothy Evans, and my late sister Linda Evans for their love and support and for sharing this journey with me. Finally, I would like to express my gratitude to my editor at Routledge, Catherine Bernard, for taking on this project and for her help, and the assistance of many others at Routledge, in bringing it to completion.

Ronald W. Evans
San Diego, California

INTRODUCTION

Classroom teaching in social studies is haunted by ghosts of what might have been. Compelling visions of inspired social studies practice in schools are continually dashed by low-level, textbook-centered classroom practice. By the early 1970s there was growing awareness of the obstacles faced by any attempt to reform the curriculum. Though the content of instruction, the subjects and topics included in courses, textbooks, curriculum guides, and taught in classrooms, was subject to shifting emphasis, the process of education was much more resistant to change. Frank Ryan raised awareness of this dilemma in an article that appeared in *Social Education* in 1973. By the early 1970s materials from the inquiry-oriented "new" social studies reform movement were "conspicuously displayed in numerous schools," he wrote, "but frequently there is no one around to 'get them off the ground.'" Ryan argued that the chief obstacle to extensive use of the new materials could be found in what he called the "hidden curriculum." Instead of the rituals of political and cultural socialization that had previously been labeled a hidden curriculum, Ryan was referring to the "mannerisms, procedures, and ways of dealing with students" that teachers employed in their daily classroom interactions:

> What kinds of questions are being posed? How are students asked to respond to questions? How does the teacher react to the students' responses? Which students do the responding? What are the non-responding students doing?

In the typical social studies classroom, he wrote:

> Students are in neat rows of desks facing the front of the classroom ... [they] take out their social studies textbooks, and the main part of the lesson usually consists of having various students ... take turns reading aloud to the

rest of the class. The day's reading is followed by a short discussion period in which the teacher asks a series of questions which are ordinarily at the recall level. The teachers' role becomes one of soliciting from the students the facts of the day's reading.[1]

What are students learning from this pattern of instruction? That "facts are the most important part of social studies; that the best way to acquire understandings, and praise from the teacher, is to 'pay attention'; that the primary usefulness of facts is recall for the teacher"; and that social studies is "a bland mixture of information" to be "swallowed unquestionably."

"Of course," Ryan wrote, "such learning outcomes are completely incompatible with the intent of the newer social studies programs." Instead, he wrote, establishment of a new set of teacher behaviors would probably lead to the spirit of learning required "for the newer social studies to flourish." The behaviors cited included:

- utilizing "higher level questions" that ask students "to think about" the topic being studied;
- "solicitation of multiple and varied ideas from students";
- students have opportunities to "express their own ideas" and "react to the ideas of others";
- students are asked to examine the reasoning behind responses;
- the teacher relinquishes "center-stage"; and
- students, as inquirers, generate knowledge, make inferences, and check on the adequacy of their understandings.

Finally, Ryan noted perceptively, implementation of these "new" instructional behaviors was "not always easily attainable," especially when it required "an erosion" of the typical behaviors employed in a "textbook-read-recite instructional environment."[2] The new set of teacher behaviors brought higher risk and a strong element of unpredictability to the classroom, partly because student behaviors would be harder to manage in classrooms that focused on inquiry and discussion. Partly as a function of the high-stakes testing environment, today's classrooms look a lot like Frank Ryan's typical social studies classroom, but they have been adversely influenced by the impact of standards and high-stakes testing. Civic education scholar Meira Levinson describes her own creative approach to classroom teaching and how it changed under these conditions:

> In the summer of 1999, I'm preparing to teach eighth-grade U.S. history. . . . I become increasingly alarmed. There are thirty separate topics for eighth-grade U.S. history . . . With a thirty-six-week school year, I quickly calculate, I have an average of just over one week to spend on each topic.

I decide to do some judicious pruning. . . . Although I'm sorry to have lost some pieces of the curriculum, I feel good about what I've planned. I'm helped in this regard by my principal's dismissive attitude toward prepping students for the standardized test.

My students and I therefore linger on the founding of the American Republic. We have passionate discussions about the proper balance between individual freedom and governmental control.

After this, we start speeding. It turns out that ignoring standardized tests is easier said than done. Over the course of the 1999–2000 school year, my eighth-grade students are subjected to standardized testing on twenty-three separate days of school . . . students are spending 14 percent of their days in school taking standardized tests—to say nothing of any teacher-developed tests . . . a more accurate estimate for the amount of time our eighth-grade students spend taking tests is probably closer to 20 percent.

Over the next couple of years . . . my administrators' emphasis on the [testing] increases. Our students need to perform well. By the 2001–2002 school year, therefore, I have eliminated all curricular content that I predict will not be tested, no matter how fascinating or important. . . . My husband [a professor] . . . is scathing when I mention shifting from the Civil War Amendments to a review of ancient China two weeks before the [state tests]. "This is ridiculous!" he bursts out. "We don't test even our graduate students on so much material in their comprehensive exams!" He is right of course, but I still feel that I have a responsibility to my students to prepare them as well as I can for the [state tests], despite the poor effect it has on my teaching.[3]

And so, teaching a curriculum already filled with topics to be covered becomes a mad race through the textbook in an effort to prepare students for state-mandated standardized tests. "Passionate discussions," student projects, brainstorming, decision making, evaluating choices and alternatives, and emphasis on the competing ideas that make social studies so interesting and important become less frequent, even rare, jettisoned in favor of mandated content coverage and preparing students for state tests for which everyone in the system will be held accountable. Multiply Levinson's experience by many thousands of teachers, and you get a sense of the impact of standards and testing on the kind of teaching that is most common in social studies classrooms. Thus, the typical pattern of instruction in social studies classrooms, described by Frank Ryan in 1973, and the focus on low-level factual content, is reified, made even more intractable by contextual pressures imposed by the movement for school accountability. How did this come to happen? Why is it this way? What might be done about it? Is there any hope for improvement?

Framing Questions

In this project, my purpose is relatively simple. I seek to answer a handful of important questions: What is happening to citizenship education in America? Why the rush to accountability in schools? How should educators and concerned citizens respond?

Of course, these questions bring up a multitude of additional questions: What were the origins of the movement for accountability in schools? When did it start? Who or what are the main people, ideas, and interest groups behind the reform? Who is framing the debate? How and why did it take root in educational policy? What impact has it had on the social studies field and on classroom practice in schools?

In seeking to understand the various influences on the origins and development of accountability reform, I consider several contexts over the course of the past century, including major trends in our nation's social history, the history of education, and the history of social studies in schools. The framework for this study is built around an argument that over time a number of key interest groups have struggled for hegemony over schooling and citizenship education, resulting in a long history of conflict and struggle over social studies. Through it all, a vision of excellent social studies practice along various curricular paths persists, tempered by the harsh realities of classroom constancy, the persistence of recitation, and low-level practice.

The Current Context

American culture has long been dominated by capitalism and rugged individualism, so it is not too surprising that schools should be influenced by these traditions. But, in recent decades, something has changed. Business domination of schooling and a number of other American institutions has reached a new and unprecedented level. Beginning in the 1970s, business began to organize and seek influence in new ways. The Powell memo challenged the business community to fight back against liberal groups and labor, to exert greater influence on policy, and led to formation of the Business Roundtable (BRT), Heritage Foundation, American Legislative Exchange Council (ALEC), and other groups. This was partly in reaction to 1960s criticisms and a low point in the public image and policy profile of business, and partly in reaction to a new humanistic curriculum in schools and campus rebellion against the establishment. Business, and the military-industrial-academic complex, bore the brunt of critique. According to many new-wave critics, schools operated in the interest of the capitalists, exerting social control and developing workers for the capitalist machine.

During the 1970s, a seedtime for the conservative restoration in schools and society, conservatives, neoconservatives, and the New Right began to get better organized and learned how to have greater influence on policy and American institutions writ large. They reacted against the counterculture of the 1960s. These trends culminated in the election of Ronald Reagan, the transfer of increasing amounts of wealth and power to an elite, and in a plan for changing and improving schools focused on improving performance in basic skills, achieving excellence, and ultimately, on using accountability and other business principles applied to schooling as a lever for reform. Business leaders argued that schools were failing to educate large numbers of students in basic skills. They argued that business was bearing the costs of remedial training for skills that should have been learned in schools. Furthermore, they argued that application of free market competition to the arena of education would lead to improved school performance. Their arguments, which developed from seeds planted in earlier decades, came to a head during the 1980s, leading to a series of business and government education summit meetings that suddenly seemed to drive school reform.

In a parallel development, a changed workplace was evolving, one in which workers were increasingly subjected to efficiency studies, their work tasks timed, and workers treated like machines. What has evolved is a workplace in which employers are consistently looking to develop greater efficiency, eliminate jobs, and boost profits, with little regard for human consequences beyond the bottom line.[4] Likewise, teachers in the workplace of schools have been subjected to efficiency-oriented trends, with standards and pacing guides keeping them on track, and tests comparing their students' performance to others. The work of teachers is managed from above like never before. Simultaneously, we live in a society increasingly connected by social media and technology, but, ironically, one in which more and more people are experiencing the social isolation that can accompany an ethos built on rugged individualism. A recent study found that the proportion of Americans who said they had no one to talk to about important matters grew from 10 percent in 1985 to 25 percent in 2004.[5]

My thesis in this book is that the origins of accountability reform in schools can be found in the confluence of business, government, conservative and neo-conservative politicians and educators, and the religious right. These groups have contributed to development of a mainstream consensus in support of reform, fueled by naïve notions of school practice and improvement. Among the collaborators in the reform are a series of presidential administrations, from the Reagan years forward, strongly influenced by business-education advocates such as Denis Doyle and David Kearns; neoconservatives such as William Bennett, Diane Ravitch, and Chester Finn; systemic reform experts such as Jennifer O'Day and Marshall Smith; outcome-based education advocate William G. Spady; and, most recently, by advocates of the Common Core, including the BRT, Achieve, CCSSO, ASCD, and other groups.

The excellence movement of the 1980s led to a business takeover by the mid-1990s, with a focus on content standards, testing, and accountability. This was followed by an extreme phase of accountability under the No Child Left Behind Act (NCLB), and then by a move for common standards seeking greater flexibility and focus on more meaningful approaches to learning. While the school reform movement has centered on a relatively consistent set of core ideas, its focus has shifted somewhat over the years. Despite these variations, the core emphasis of reformers has centered on a one-dimensional notion of schooling for human capital, the defining characteristic of the reform movement.

This emphasis, along with application of business principles to schooling, led, by and large, to the reification of low-level learning practices focused on basic skills and knowledge, to the detriment of reflective or inquiry-oriented teaching practices in schools. The reform has centered largely on socialization, with little attention to the counter-socialization or critical questioning necessary in a democracy. In recent years, the frequency of meaningful discussion and reflective thought in social studies seemed to reach a new low. As a teacher, scholar, and parent of school-age children, I am troubled by how all of this will impact the future of democracy. I worry that it is not healthy and that it will have troubling implications for the future of a democratic society. As I write, transition to the Common Core State Standards (CCSS), the most recent iteration of accountability reform, adds a new wrinkle with uncertain impact. The CCSS are inquiry oriented and offer teachers greater flexibility, yet they are being implemented within the superstructure of systemic reform. It is too early to tell how the CCSS and new "smarter" tests will play out in schools.

Despite this development, recent research indicates that, in social studies, excellence and accountability reforms have led to a narrowing of the curriculum, an increase in course taking and requirements in high school, the reification of a low-level focus, and increasing attention to test preparation. Reforms have led to more traditional teaching that is both content focused and teacher centered. Research suggests that accountability has led to a new grammar of schooling, largely the same as the old grammar but even more resistant to change due to the influence of testing on teaching and on teachers' curriculum decisions and choices.[6]

The literature on democratic education is, for the most part, hopeful and forward-looking. Scholars seeking to improve civic education seem perpetually optimistic. However, in recent years, with the rise of testing and accountability, the weight of evidence suggests declining discourse in social studies classrooms mirroring declining social capital, a declining sense of community, and contributing to a society in which democracy is increasingly at risk.[7]

A Note on Sources, etc.

Prior to launching into the narrative, it may be helpful to provide a few comments on how this work was created. In each portion of the book, I gathered evidence where I could find it, from archives, reports, media stories, and the work of other scholars. My research included trips to the National Archives II in College Park, Maryland, and to a number of presidential libraries and other repositories. In writing the narrative, I consciously tried to concentrate on primary sources as much as possible, though after the year 2000 archival sources are more limited due to a time lag in their availability. Materials from the George W. Bush Library are not yet available, beyond public papers, and the Obama Library is, at this time, a distant vision. Yet public sources are readily available. I wish to acknowledge that several secondary sources were especially helpful in conceptualizing and writing this volume. Among these were works by Larry Cuban, Patrick McGuinn, Diane Ravitch, and William Hayes.

Chapter 1 provides an opening essay and extended introduction relating to the themes and thesis of the book and the organizations, institutions, and interest groups that have influenced the origins and development of school accountability, posing alternative ways of seeing the rise of accountability in schools. Chapter 2 and chapters 4 through 7 are broadly chronological, sequenced by presidential administration. Each chapter follows policy turns, major trends, and key actors, while tracing the rise of the excellence and accountability reform movement and its impact on schools. Chapter 3 documents the neoconservative influence on social studies, describing the revival of history and geography. In the conclusion, I briefly examine evidence on the impact of excellence and accountability reforms on trends in social studies curriculum, course offerings, and instructional practices, and link these trends to questions about the future of democracy.

I would also like to add a brief note regarding my personal views on the accountability movement. My thoughts were perhaps most succinctly expressed in a paper written in the mid-1990s, published in 2000, titled, "Thoughts on Redirecting a Runaway Train: A Critique of the Standards Movement."[8] I have been skeptical of the standards and accountability movement from the start. However, in writing this history of its origins and development, I have tried to approach the task with a sense of balance. In researching and writing the narrative, there were moments when I had to reassess my own shallow thinking and limited knowledge, looking again and again at the evidence. Throughout, I have endeavored to present the actions, views, and statements of various figures and players in their own voices and in a way that each would say is fair.

In *The Social Studies Wars*, I wrote that my work on the history of the social studies field included elements of alternative genres: "aspects of the Western, with a full cast of heroes and villains, myth and legend"; ingredients of the "mystery, especially around key questions"; and a measure of "tragedy." In the introduction to that book, I wrote: "On the whole, I have written this history largely as the story of a civil war, with competing armies of American educators clashing on the battlefield of curriculum development and their recommendations breaking over the anvil of classroom constancy."[9] Among the camps as I portrayed them were traditional historians, advocates of social science inquiry, social meliorists, and social reconstructionists, along with those supporting a consensus or eclectic approach. While those groups are still present, there are new and dissonant influences.

In this volume, the narrative also contains aspects of new and disturbing genres. My description of accountability reform is partly a horror story, especially for teachers and students, as the tentacles of control reached deep inside classrooms. It includes some characteristics of science fiction: a brave new world controlled by increasingly intrusive forms of surveillance, with new roles for computers, often uncritically accepted, and new means for controlling the behaviors of teachers and students with little consideration of what's lost. In the new era of accountability reform, social efficiency and scientific management are dominant paradigms, shaping much of what has evolved.

The story also contains elements of industrial fiction, like the Horatio Alger story, but without the happy ending. As William G. Spady has argued, accountability reform has led to industrial-era schooling on steroids, putting children and teachers into stronger, smaller, tighter, and more confining "boxes." Moreover, the reform has largely served to reify the cultural reproduction of social strata despite the rhetoric of equity, of "No Child Left Behind," and considerable focus on eliminating the achievement gap. In the end, as Jules Henry suggested in 1963, schooling continues to be dominated by a process of socialization, where children are drilled in cultural orientations.[10]

Notes

1. Frank L. Ryan, "Implementing the Hidden Curriculum of the Social Studies," *SE* 37, no. 7 (November 1973): 679–680.
2. Ibid., 680–681.
3. Meira Levinson, *No Citizen Left Behind* (Cambridge, MA: Harvard University Press, 2012), 250–253.
4. Alana Semuels, "How the Relationship Between Employers and Workers Has Changed," *LAT*, April 7, 2013.
5. Geoffrey Mohan, "Social Isolation Increases Risk of Early Death, Study Finds," *LAT*, March 26, 2013; Robert D. Putnam, "Bowling Alone: America's Declining Social Capital," *JD* 6, no. 1 (1995): 65–78.
6. Levinson, *No Citizen*, 250–252.
7. Jeffrey Gates, *Democracy at Risk: Rescuing Main Street from Wall Street* (Cambridge, MA: Perseus, 2000).
8. Ronald W. Evans, "Thoughts on Redirecting a Runaway Train: A Critique of the Standards Movement," *TRSE* 29, no. 2 (2001): 330–339.
9. Ronald W. Evans, *The Social Studies Wars: What Should We Teach the Children* (New York: Teachers College, 2004), 4.
10. Jules Henry, *Culture Against Man* (New York: Random House, 1963), 283.

1

ORIGINS OF ACCOUNTABILITY REFORM

During the past one-third of a century, since at least the mid-1970s, the business of schooling has changed significantly due to an increasing focus on accountability. This has occurred, ostensibly, in the belief that a system of standards and testing will help advance what schools are doing and lead to improved performance by all concerned: teachers, administrators, and students. This approach to school reform is rooted in the notion that it will lead to improved outcomes for society, better prepared workers, and development of a more educated citizenry. Over the years, the business sector has been one of the dominant groups demanding and inspiring reform, though not the only influential group. Moreover, an overall approach and many key strategies for implementation and management of the reform have come from the business sector, and have applied business principles to schools. Business involvement in educational policy has a long history from at least the mid-nineteenth century, rooted in the argument that education has important economic value, that it can make important contributions to the economic and social health of the nation, and that school has individual and collective benefits. By the late twentieth century, the notion that school could solve national social and economic problems combined with the belief that it was a key to individual economic success to form a powerful ideology fueling a business-driven approach to school reform.

Much of the literature describing, chronicling, applauding, or critiquing accountability reform has argued that business leaders were central to the reform, and with strong reason. Business groups have played a key role in the reform: demanding improvement in the preparation of workers; contributing to school improvement through partnerships with schools and districts in the 1970s and 1980s; leading the push for systemic reform that emerged in the 1980s and 1990s; and playing a key role in the lobbying push for specific policies, programs, and laws that would implement accountability reform. Business involvement is perhaps rightly viewed as the dominant force driving accountability reforms in schools. Historian Larry Cuban describes the logic of the reform. Key assumptions include:

- Strong economic growth, high productivity, long-term prosperity . . . depend upon a highly skilled workforce.
- Public schools are responsible for equipping students with the knowledge and skills necessary to compete in an information-based workplace.
- All public schools are doing a poor job of preparing high school graduates for college and the workplace, with urban schools doing the worst job of all.
- Schools are just like businesses. The principles that have made businesses successful can be applied to schools to produce structural changes that will improve academic achievement as measured by standardized tests . . .
- Higher test scores in school mean better performance later on in college and the workplace.[1]

As Cuban points out, these beliefs did not spring entirely from corporate leaders but were shared among a broad consensus of elected officials, parents, and educators, and evolved unevenly. Sometimes stated explicitly, most were implicit in the framing of the problem and solutions. From these assumptions, a specific formula developed for fixing schools:

- Set clear organizational goals and high standards for everyone.
- Restructure operations so that managers and employees who deliver the services decide what to do.
- Reward those who meet or exceed their goals. Shame or punish those who fail.
- Expand competition and choice in products and services.[2]

Belief in what came to be called "systemic reform" crossed political party lines, took root in virtually every state in the nation during the 1990s, and became de facto national policy with passage of NCLB in 2002. Business involvement in schooling gained new popularity during the mid-1970s due to an economic downturn and a shortage of workers with the necessary skills. Businessmen turned to schools to solve national problems, just as they had in the 1910s and the 1950s. A gradual consensus emerged among business and civic elites, shared by many educational leaders, that the nation should use the schools to improve the economy by improving student achievement.

Business influence not only set broad policies, but a range of influences began to appear in the day-to-day work of schools: superintendents became "CEOs" and their deputies "chief operating officers" and "chief academic officers"; schools set standards and measured performance against "benchmarks"; they "outsourced" services to private firms; they inserted performance clauses in contracts and established "bonuses" and sanctions to reward and punish. Failure to reach "proficiency" could mean break up of a school or worse. In many districts, teachers were required to post standards for each day's work and were ordered to follow "pacing guides." All of these innovations were consistent with the principles of "scientific management."

While a dominant role for business is undeniable, in tracing the origins of accountability reform one is inevitably drawn in multiple directions. Prior to the 1980s, the role of business, while important, was not the dominant force that it would later become. In this essay, I will argue that several other key factors contributed to the direction of school reform. While business influence, including both a human capital orientation and a business model for reform centering on standards, measurement, and accountability linked to consequences has come to dominate educational policy and strongly influenced many school practices, tracing the origins of the reform necessarily involves examining other important factors and trends.

The movement for accountability in schools had origins in several key influences that can be traced to the 1950s and before. Each of these strands developed over time, some with roots in the nineteenth century. A rising conservative movement developed in the United States from the 1940s and 1950s that, by the 1970s, began to exert a much stronger influence on both schools and society. Combined with the growth of the religious right, conservatives had increasing influence on education policy. At about the same time, there was a burgeoning business influence in schools. At least part of the growing support for a conservative restoration took root in the "back-to-basics" movement, a 1970s trend similar in tone to the postwar "crisis" over progressive education. During the 1950s, critics charged that schools were soft and blamed progressive educators such as Dewey, Kilpatrick, Counts, and Rugg for their permissive practices and left-leaning politics. Another factor may be seen in the increasing influence of efficiency and accountability trends in schools over the course of the twentieth century, particularly in the 1970s. These trends combined with the long history of testing and measurement in education, making common cause with some educational psychologists and "effective schools" researchers who applied testing in new and increasingly rigorous ways. Organizational trends also lent support to increasing accountability and provided the institutional mechanisms to enforce new accountability measures. Moreover, a growing federal and state role in educational policy and governance has contributed in powerful ways since the late 1950s. Beginning in the 1970s there was a gradual but significant shift in social studies curricula. The 1980s revival of history in schools resulted in more emphasis on history and geography and less attention to other social sciences, inquiry, and social issues—amounting to a reframing of educational purposes by refocusing pedagogy and curricular content. This shift mirrored a general movement toward more traditional teaching and away from progressive educational practices.[3]

Ways of Seeing

Accountability reforms have origins in ongoing struggles over schools and their curriculum. Advocates for school reform from a variety of perspectives have long struggled over control of schools.[4] In the history of education we have a long legacy of reform, reaction, and ideological battles over schooling, over whose vision of the future will be dominant. The history of social studies education has been especially impacted by ideological conflict.[5] Social studies curricula and textbooks have served as a lightning rod, attracting comment and criticism regarding the nature of the field and the purposes of schooling, and reflecting competing visions of the worthy society, as if the curriculum is a screen on which critics of various stripes project their vision of a preferred future, often inspiring acrimonious, colorful, and dramatic rhetoric. Curricular struggles of past and present are fought over issues of curricular hegemony, over whose version of "the American way" will be taught in schools. Thus, these battles might be seen as a struggle over values, over competing visions of the future and of the good society.

Moreover, disagreements over education reflect the nation's cultural divide: red states versus blue states; Democrats versus Republicans; conservatives and cultural fundamentalists versus liberals and moderates. These are deep fractures, a reflection of long-term trends, and are not easily healed. Which side are you on?[6]

Social studies education has a long history of millennial battles over the curriculum: the Rugg and Nevins controversies in the 1940s; the controversy over progressive education in the 1950s; and reactions to the "new social studies" reforms of the 1960s and the academic freedom cases it spawned. From a contemporary vantage point, each of these episodes could be seen as part of a long-term struggle against progressive social studies and progressive education writ large. In examining the origins of accountability reforms, these battles cannot be ignored. They exemplify ongoing conflict over the purposes of education. For example, the Rugg controversy centered on Harold Rugg's avant-garde social studies textbooks, attacked as "un-American" and discarded by schools; the Nevins controversy involved a prize-winning historian who charged that schools were no longer teaching American history and the patriotism needed during a time of war; the inquiry-oriented new social studies encountered criticism and controversy centered on MACOS (Man: A Course of Study) that brought an end to funding for social studies reform.

Rhetorical battles of the 1960s and 1970s are especially relevant because they helped shape and generate accountability reform. Critics of the 1960s curriculum reforms, which were generally progressive or inquiry oriented, included an array of conservative and ultraconservative groups who gained considerable momentum during the 1970s, including the John Birch Society, the Heritage Foundation, Dr. Onalee McGraw, textbook reviewers Mel and Norma Gabler, conservative columnist James J. Kilpatrick, the American Party, and the Council for Basic Education, which was, ironically, an early supporter of "new social studies" reforms.[7]

A growing conservative juggernaut got its message across to the public, pol-icymakers, and a wide network of activists through newsletters, press releases, position papers, monographs, books, the tireless efforts of volunteers, donations, grants, and money from benefactors. Conservative groups made innovative use of new·media through direct mail, talk radio, Christian broadcasting, fundamentalist churches, and Christian bookstores.[8]

Over the years the nation has witnessed continuous criticism of progressive forms of education combined with repeated calls for basic skills instruction and improved accountability. While these battles over the schools were largely rhe-torical, intellectual exchanges that occurred somewhere in the ether above the day-to-day experiences of teachers and students in schools, they did capture pop-ular sentiment and, at times, the public imagination.

To what extent do these intellectual battles help explain the rise of account-ability reform? Though these were not the specific events leading to establishment of an accountability regime, they did represent a trend away from progressive innovation and contributed to movement in the direction of control, toward more traditional and conservative forms of education. Many themes trumpeted by conservative critics have appeared again and again in the recent school reform movement, emphasized by intellectual leaders such as Diane Ravitch, Chester Finn, William Bennett, and E.D. Hirsch. Moreover, they expressed doubts, even hostility, toward progressive education, support for the back-to-basics movement and "effective schools" research, and were deeply connected to a rising conserva-tive movement.

Ideological Origins

One way of explaining the rise of accountability reforms would focus on the larger sociopolitical and cultural context and its impact on educational rhetoric. From the mid-1970s to the mid-1980s and beyond, social studies, especially the progressive issues-centered approach, experienced a decline, paralleling a con-servative restoration in politics, schools, and American culture. The conservative restoration in schools and society, a backlash against the legacy of the 1960s, grew out of 1970s concerns over declining standards during a period of experimenta-tion and turmoil. It followed a generally conservative shift in public mood regard-ing the perfectibility of humankind, the role of science in helping us understand society and life, and a shift in attitudes regarding the proper role of government in curricular reform. Major episodes of the era included back-to-basics, the literacy crisis, the excellence movement, and the revival of history.

Although many of the trends of the 1960s had begun to erode by the early to mid-1970s, they were subjected to direct attack in the years leading up to and following the election of Ronald Reagan. By the early 1980s, the liberal consensus on schooling had begun to unravel, and two related but distinct forms of educational conservatism gained favor. The first of these came in the form of the New Right, led by the Heritage Foundation, a Washington-based think tank consisting of several conservative scholars including Onalee McGraw, Eileen Gardner, Russell Kirk, E.G. West, David Armor, Thomas Sowell, and George Gilder. Other important voices in the new right movement included Senators Orrin Hatch and Jesse Helms, fundamentalist ministers Jerry Falwell and Tim LaHaye, textbook critics Mel and Norma Gabler, and Arthur Laffer, the supply-side economist. The New Right called for a much smaller federal government role in education, championed an extremist position against "secular humanism," and favored active censorship and teaching of creationism. A larger and less cohesive group of neoconservative educators, politicians, and businesspeople, who could be described as "centrist conservatives," called for a shift in federal policy away from equity to an emphasis on excellence. Though the two groups overlapped on a number of issues, they had basic differences regarding the mission of schooling and the role of government in education.[9]

From the perspective of the New Right, most of the schools' problems could be linked, ironically, to over-centralized decision-making caused by rising federal power. In resistance to the mainstream, the New Right supported educational free choice and diversity. Many New Right advocates believed that vested interests were leading the nation toward a unified curriculum based upon principles of secular humanism. The New Right sought to promote its agenda and to counter the spread of secular humanism in schools and society through interlocking organizations, think tanks, and political action committees with extensive mailing lists; a network of nationally circulated magazines, tabloids, and newsletters; and through an "electronic church" composed of nearly forty television stations and over a thousand radio stations. Its agenda included "model" legislation for states, prayer and creationism in schools, censorship, ending unionism, promoting Christian schools, cutting taxes, "nurturing conservative ideas," fighting "secular humanism," and "channeling" corporate money . . . to colleges that promote "free enterprise."[10]

Leaders of the New Right used propaganda skillfully, making scapegoats of the National Education Association (NEA), the public school system, "secular humanism," the US Office of Education (USOE), and textbook writers. Moreover, their attacks came at a timely moment, when public education was at a low point—ravaged by inflation, declining student enrollment, increasing costs, and fading public confidence. Many critics charged schools with nearly total failure, citing a lack of discipline, lack of serious study, teachers unprepared in their subject matter, social promotion, subjective grading systems, and "too much pedagogical faddism."[11]

The New Right sought to achieve their objectives through three main approaches: searching out and destroying those elements in the schools that promote free inquiry through attacks on secular humanism; limiting and controlling learning materials in classrooms and school libraries via censorship; and injecting into classrooms the essence of the Christian Bible, with creationism as the initial vehicle. The first of these had direct ramifications for social studies instruction. The term "secular humanism" was used by the New Right as a code word with which to brand offenders, in an attempt to eradicate the person or practice from schools. For hard-core Christian fundamentalists, humanism was viewed as an evil so insidious as to be at the heart of most of what was wrong with humankind.

The New Right critique of humanism was expressed clearly in a pamphlet produced by the Fort Worth, Texas, Pro-Family Forum, titled: "Is Humanism Molesting Your Child?" The pamphlet charged that humanism "denies the deity of God, the inspiration of the Bible, and the divinity of Jesus Christ . . . believes in equal distribution of America's wealth to reduce poverty . . . Humanism is being inculcated in the schools." Humanism was viewed as "destructive to our nation, destructive to the family, destructive to the individual."

In one tract circulated by a Moral Majority-related group, students were urged to follow a list of commandments:

- Don't—discuss values . . .
- Don't—confide in teachers, particularly sociology or social studies or English teachers . . .
- Don't—take "social studies" or "future studies." Demand course definitions: history, geography, civics, French, English, and so on . . .
- Don't—role-play or participate in sociodramas . . .
- Don't—get into classroom discussions that begin:
  What would you do if . . .?
  What if . . .? Should we . . .?
  Do you suppose . . .? Do you think . . .?[12]

New Right critics also engaged in a widespread movement to ban, remove, and occasionally burn materials designed for student use. Censorship efforts focused on textbooks, works of literature, poetry, films, school dramas, records, comic books, magazines, reference works, and coloring books. For censors, the targets frequently involved "dirty words," but also included alternative images of family life, evolution, race relations, religion, politics, patriotism, free enterprise, communism, or other topics that may have been improperly treated. The censors proclaimed themselves to be Christian, patriotic Americans. Perhaps the most well known were Mel and Norma Gabler and Phyllis Schlafly's Eagle Forum, but there were many others.[13]

The overall plan of the New Right included infusing education with Christian/ Protestant religion, injecting large doses of the Bible; transmitting the rightness of Victorian morality, free enterprise, and militarism; minimizing student inquiry or investigation; and isolating educational theory and practice from experimentation and innovation. The ultimate goal was to weaken and eventually eliminate the public system of education by creating rival Christian schools that would bleed the public schools of financing, students, teachers, and community support.[14]

Centrist neoconservatives, on the other hand, were a more diverse and thoughtful group, though their activities lent credence and support to the conservative cause. Their intellectual core was made up of individuals with ties to the American Enterprise Institute, *The Public Interest*, and *Commentary*. This group included Nathan Glazer, James Q. Wilson, Chester E. Finn, Daniel P. Moynihan, James Coleman, Joseph Adelson, Diane Ravitch, and columnist George F. Will. Neoconservatives argued that the basic causes of educational problems in the 1980s were the social experiments of the 1960s and 1970s, which made too many demands on the schools in the name of reform, and excessive federal intervention to promote educational equity.

Neoconservatives posited three overarching missions for the schools: promoting economic development for the nation; preserving a common culture; and promotion of educational equity through color-blind access and improved quality. They generally agreed on the need to strengthen educational standards, establish a more limited and selective role for the federal government, increase the amount of homework, reduce nonacademic electives, abolish social promotion, and strengthen requirements for admission and graduation. They also agreed on the need to impose traditional classroom discipline, to improve the quality of teachers, and to promote business/education cooperation.[15]

The neoconservative centrist philosophy lay behind much of the educational agenda of the 1980s and 1990s, and it was the driving force behind many of the reports on educational reform during the time. Much of this conservative activism was a backlash against the legacy of the 1960s for its political sins, or against a perceived decline in standards. Behind this was a conservative intellectual movement that had been brewing at least since Friedrich Hayek's *The Road to Serfdom* in 1942.

Back-to-Basics

Accountability reforms also had roots in the back-to-basics movement of the 1970s that was itself, in part, a replay of the criticisms of progressive education that occurred in the 1950s, and in part a reaction to the inquiry-oriented curriculum reform movement of the 1960s. The neoconservative movement, combined with the New Right, found expression in the back-to-basics movement. Many reforms of the 1960s, including the new and newer social studies, flew in the face of traditional demands for order and content coverage. This emerging sentiment, and reactions describing open education as a "fad," was expressed in 1974 in school districts across the nation. In 1975 the College Board revealed that Scholastic Aptitude Test (SAT) scores had declined steadily since 1964. Public concern about declining test scores combined with complaints about lax standards and charges that students were doing less reading and writing, and led to calls for instruction in the basics: reading, writing, and arithmetic. By 1977, in response to this demand, thirty-eight state legislatures had passed laws requiring minimum competency tests in the basic skills.[16] In most instances, the movement focused on a single objective, improvement in the three R's. In other's, it expanded to include a wide range of aims including patriotism and puritan morality. The Council on Basic Education (CBE) seemed nominally in the forefront. However, its leaders held a broader definition of "the basics" than did many latter-day proponents.[17]

What did back-to-basics advocates want? Because they had no single organization, spokesperson, platform, or declaration of principles, the closest we can come is a composite. According to one educational writer in the late 1970s, with a good deal of regional and temporal variation, advocates of back-to-basics wanted the following policies implemented:

1. Emphasis on reading, writing, and arithmetic in the elementary grades. Most of the school day is to be devoted to these skills. Phonics is the method advocated for reading instruction.
2. In the secondary grades, most of the day is to be devoted to English, science, math, and history, taught from "clean" textbooks, free of notions that violate traditional family and national values.
3. At all levels, the teacher is to take a dominant role, with "no nonsense about pupil directed activities."
4. Methodology is to include drill, recitation, daily homework, and frequent testing.
5. Report cards are to carry traditional marks (A, B, C, etc.) or numerical values (100, 80, 75, etc.) issued at frequent intervals.
6. Discipline is to be strict, with corporal punishment an accepted method of control. Dress codes should regulate student apparel and hairstyles.
7. Promotion from grades and graduation from high school are to be permitted only after mastery of skills and knowledge has been demonstrated through tests. Social promotion and graduation on the basis of time spent in courses are out.
8. Eliminate the frills. The *National Review*, a conservative journal, put it this way: "Clay modeling, weaving, doll construction, flute practice, volleyball, sex education, laments about racism and other weighty matters should take place on private time."
9. Eliminate electives and increase the number of required courses.
10. Ban innovations (a plague on them!). New math, new science, linguistics, instruction by electronic gadgets, emphasis on concepts instead of facts—all must go (the new social studies would also go).
11. Eliminate the school's "social services"—they take time from the basic curriculum. "Social services" may include sex education, driver education, guidance, drug education, and physical education.
12. Put patriotism back in the schools. And love for one's country. And for God.[18]

The most extreme advocates of the new back-to-basics approach wanted to purge the school of its impurities. Most did not support all of these planks, yet a consensus was emerging around several of the main ideas, and others were tacitly supported by centrist conservatives, if not openly advocated.

Behind the rapid growth of the various conservative groups were a number of factors, not the least of which was the growth of conservative ministries during the 1960s and 1970s, the expansion of the ministries via radio and television, and dissemination of literature through churches and a large network of Christian bookstores.[19] Much of the activity, and development of the broad infrastructure of their network, was instigated by specific issues of the time. Just as the antiwar and civil rights movements had inspired liberal and radical activism on a host of related issues, something similar happened on the conservative side, especially as the liberationist movements of the 1960s led to changes in the everyday lives of more and more Americans. Those who reacted with anger or fear organized their own movements and organizations to counter busing, oppose abortion, eliminate sex education, counter feminism, stand up for a traditional, conservative version of American patriotism, and to act as a watchdog over the schools, making sure that any materials that undermined their values and point of view were met with resistance. On this, they were relentless and very successful.

Among protesters there were at least two or three elements—the ultraconservative evangelical Christians of the New Right; the traditional conservatives, perhaps best represented in education by the CBE; and the think tanks and conservative foundations (Heritage, AEI, etc.)—that were a growing force, giving the burgeoning conservative movement its formidable base of economic and political clout. Put together, these elements represented a potent political force and would soon remake the educational landscape.

Educators responded in a variety of ways. Because back-to-basics covered a range of convictions, many educators embraced some of them while rejecting others. Some argued that the schools had never left a focus on the basics. Others opted for an expanded version of the "basics" with inclusion of teaching children to think and analyze problems. Still others viewed the back-to-basics movement as "a simplistic solution for complex educational problems" with the potential to "throw us back 100 years." There was, by many accounts, a good deal of disagreement over what "basics" were to be included.[20]

On the whole, schools responded to these demands with movement toward a new educational trinity: minimal competency, proficiency testing, and a performance-based curriculum. These were the early stages of a movement to establish a system in which no student would go from grade to grade or graduate from high school unless he or she could prove, via test results, mastery of at least a minimal body of skills and information. Most school administrators and school boards lent support to the idea of a back-to-basics approach by stressing greater emphasis on reading, writing, and arithmetic, though relatively few districts restructured their policy statements or made wholesale changes in instructional programs. More common were a range of efforts from the cosmetic to the new initiative designed to satisfy the demand for more emphasis on the basics, a traditional approach that had continued uninterrupted in the vast majority of school classrooms throughout periods of reform. State legislatures and state departments of education generally jumped aboard the back-to-basics and minimal competency movement.

A number of prominent educational researchers joined the movement with a focus on "effective schools" research. They extracted key principles from low-income and predominantly minority schools in which students were scoring higher on standardized achievement tests: clearly stated academic goals; a principal's instructional leadership; concentration on basic academic skills; safety and order in the school; frequent monitoring of academic achievement; and connecting what is taught to what is tested. One effective schools advocate, Ron Edmonds, developed four key principles that were later embraced by school reformers: all children can learn and achieve results that mirror ability, not family background; top-down decisions wedded to scientifically derived expertise can improve individual schools; measurable results count; and the school is the basic unit of reform.[21] These trends toward competency, effectiveness, and basic skills were 1970s forerunners of full-blown accountability.

Other histories of the period have found support for these countertrends. According to Angus and Mirel, curriculum differentiation remained the overriding characteristic of the high school, even though tracking and other forms of ability grouping had been severely criticized by new wave critics such as Jonathan Kozol and were no longer considered politically correct. As evidence they cite what they describe as a "neo-efficiency or accountability" movement that ran concurrently with the new wave or humanistic trend in education during the 1970s but captured less attention from most scholars and the media. "Under the accountability umbrella," they wrote, "was a conglomerate of old and new reform ideas: programmed instruction, individualized instruction, differentiated staffing, behavioral or performance objectives, competency-based instruction, teaching machines, instructional systems, computer-managed instruction, team teaching, behavioral modification, performance contracting, and career education." Ironically, as they point out, many of these innovations, most of which were plainly at odds with the new wave of progressivism in schools, were rooted in the "education for social efficiency" championed by administrative progressives of an earlier era.[22] By the late 1970s, two-thirds of the states had mandated minimum competency testing for graduation.[23]

Despite a strong level of public support for the neo-efficiency movement, many educators feared the growth of state power over the schools that it signaled, along with the spread of testing. "What worries me most," said one curriculum director in the 1970s, "is that we shall actually be asking teachers to teach to the test—a practice already condoned." The overwhelming worry of many educators appeared to be the possibility that schools were moving toward producing a generation of "minimal mediocrity," stressing student progress in rote mechanical skills of communication and computation and neglecting critical thought, social criticism, and creativity.[24]

Behind the back-to-basics movement lay the nation's periodic pendulum swing, from liberalism to conservatism and back. This paralleled a strong public appetite for accountability, a high divorce rate and disintegration of the family, demands for discipline, and a curb to the excesses of permissiveness. These were combined, for many critics, with a bundle of causes ranging from Dr. Spock and the passive influence of television to creeping socialism. Of course there were many more immediate causes. Parents were taking a larger role in school affairs and frequently tried to reshape policies and programs. Many African Americans and Latino Americans believed that their children were being shortchanged with respect to basic skills and became strong advocates for the basics. For years, teachers had been urged to focus on creativity and the development of independent thinkers. It was not always clear whether this focus was in addition to or instead of instruction in basic skills. Employers had long complained that high school graduates could not read instructions and lacked computational abilities. To the slogan, "Johnny can't read," industrialists added, "And Johnny can't work, either." Many college professors lodged longstanding complaints about the declining level of student preparation. Moreover, public perception held that schools would benefit from beefed-up standards. In 1975, when the Gallup poll asked a sample of parents the reason for declining student test scores, a significant number of respondents said, "Courses are too easy; there is not enough emphasis on basics." All of this coincided with a financial crunch during which a bare-bones, low-cost school program had a certain appeal to taxpayers.[25]

To some extent the back-to-basics movement was a media construction. Articles appeared in countless national publications extolling the move "Back to Basics in the Schools." Typical was an article from 1975 that alleged, "Willy-nilly, the U.S. educational system is spawning a generation of semi-literates."[26] *Newsweek* reported, in October 1974, that "all across the nation, parents, school boards, and often the pupils themselves are demanding that the schools stop experimenting and get back to basics—in reading, writing, arithmetic and standards of behavior to boot." Open classrooms, "relevant" topics and course materials, permissive discipline, and lax standards had been introduced at the expense of work in the traditional disciplines like English composition, history, the hard sciences, and foreign languages. Professional educators were clearly held responsible. *Newsweek* concluded, "the growing call for a return to the basics seems a healthy signal that masses of Americans are no longer willing to accept a pharmacopoeia of educational nostrums that has been handed them by a relative handful of well-meaning, but sometimes misdirected innovators."[27]

Social studies was one of the targets of the movement, as critics charged that secondary educators had stressed the "fun and the relevant" in the social sciences with the result that students were "quite conversant with local, national, and international problems, but they can't write three consecutive declarative sentences in the English language." By and large the response among social studies educators was to argue that instruction in basic skills and content was already a major part of the curriculum, and that infusion of work explicitly focused on reading and writing skills could help improve student learning.[28]

By 1980, the National Council for the Social Studies (NCSS) had joined with a number of other leading educational organizations to support the essentials of education, acknowledging that "Public concern about basic knowledge and the basic skills in education is valid," but arguing that society should avoid the easy tendency to limit the essentials to the three R's. NCSS held that teachers should resist pressures to concentrate upon "easy-to-teach and easy-to-test bits of knowledge." Despite these disclaimers, an NCSS statement titled the "Essentials of Social Studies" revealed the profound influence that the conservative restoration was having on the field. In its description of the content knowledge of social studies, the statement gave priority to the academic disciplines and implied a more traditional focus on content, along with inculcation of democratic beliefs. In hindsight, it was a curious document, melding a response to the basics movement with social efficiency and critical thinking skills. In a sense, it signaled the co-optation of social studies by a rising conservatism.[29]

There were critics of the movement as well. One noted detractor, Richard Ohman, a professor of English at Wesleyan, charged that the literacy crisis was "a fiction, if not a hoax." Ohman wrote, "the available facts simply do not reveal whether young Americans are less literate than their counterparts in 1930 or 1960." Other surveys of reading test results found "no solid evidence of a decline in reading ability," and concluded: "We are now convinced that anyone who says he knows that literacy is decreasing . . . is at best unscholarly and at worse dishonest." Moreover, Ohman charged that the literacy crisis was a "media-created event." The decline in test scores was, he argued, due to other factors including a drop in enrollment in English courses; a reduced dropout rate resulting in more students taking standardized tests; and a dramatic increase in the percentage of women test-takers. Thus, the "literacy crisis" was partly a result of increasing social justice.

A larger explanation for the back-to-basics movement might suggest that each time the American educational system has rapidly expanded, admitting previously excluded groups to higher levels, the trend has been greeted by a chorus of voices charging a decline in standards. Moreover, in this instance, much of the fuss came from members of the cultural and educational elite and focused on the "grammatical, stylistic, and conceptual abilities" of an elite group, college students. In addition, a conservative spin was plainly apparent, including a tendency to indict the movements of the 1960s both within and outside education.[30] In succeeding years, the literacy "crisis" and the charge that our schools were failing would become an underlying and central premise for accountability reforms.

This history illustrates the rise of a conservative political and educational movement that was gradually gaining traction and influence in a changing political landscape. This rising influence was aided, abetted, and deepened by the rise of religious fundamentalism. Deeper causes might be found in a plethora of troubling developments during a time that one historian labeled the "nightmare decade." "Watergate, a changing set of values, Vietnam, inflation, and a host of other confusing trends in the social order . . . brought about a situation in which people [were] frustrated, confused, angry and fearful. When such conditions exist . . . there is a desire on the part of human beings to seek simple solutions to complicated problems, react to change with hostility, and meet authority . . . with . . . lack of trust . . . [Schools and] textbooks [became] a convenient scapegoat," and back-to-the-basics became a battle cry.[31] In the larger picture, the growing conservative movement and the rise of the religious right suggest the burgeoning of a strong and dedicated segment of the populace committed to turning back the clock on the revolutions of the 1960s in schools and society, restoring a sense of order. While this provides some background understanding of the general context of school reform out of which the accountability movement would grow, it is less helpful in guiding us to a deeper understanding of the growth of a larger government role in education.

A Political Construction

A second way of seeing the growth of accountability reforms in schools is by examining the growing role of state and federal governments in what was once historically viewed as a local concern. As Tyack points out, compulsory public education has long been justified on explicitly political grounds, and associated with nationalistic impulses. The modern national educational system, in effect, exists to create citizens and legitimize the power of the state. Families from frequently divisive subgroups send their children to state-run schools to learn a common language, to get along with peers, to take orders, and to absorb a national history and identity. Not that this is equally effective with every student, but that the institutional process is designed, in part, to create citizen-workers. In a similar fashion, advanced education in college and graduate schools may be seen as legitimizing elites. In sum, educational institutions help institutionalize the authority of the state.[32]

Historical examples illustrate this point. Many of the founding fathers explicitly supported this function. In the period following the American Revolution, a number of thinkers, notably Thomas Jefferson, Benjamin Rush, and Noah Webster argued that schools should strive to transform attitudes to support the new nation. Rush projected a uniform state system of schooling that would develop children into "republican machines." Webster suggested that schools should teach a uniform language, and wrote a "Federal Catechism" so that all schoolchildren would learn "republican principles." Jefferson argued for creation of state primary schools to create loyal citizens.[33] Moreover, using schools to develop nationalistic sentiment has cut across countries and time. The Prussian system had loyalty to the state as a central goal.[34]

In the United States, the political construction of education has coincided with a growing role for the state and federal government in educational matters. Though the federal government has long played a role in schooling, that role has grown exponentially since the mid-twentieth century, with increasingly complex state-federal interactions in the realm of educational policy. Despite this expansion, it is important to note that federal aid to education is nearly as old as the nation. In the late eighteenth century, the Northwest Ordinances reserved 1/36th of the land allocated each western township for schools.[35] During the Civil War, Congress passed the Morrill Land Grant Act of 1862, extending land grants for higher education. After the war, the government devoted significant resources to support the Freedmen's Bureau, which helped provide educational opportunities.

During World War I, labor demands led to passage of the Smith-Hughes Act in support of vocational and technical education along with job training. A short time later, government provided educational aid to the disabled, deaf, and blind. During the depression, both disabled and disadvantaged students received attention. Though bills providing general aid to education were defeated on the grounds that education remained a state responsibility, by the late 1930s Congress created the National Youth Administration and the Works Progress Administration, both of which expanded job-training programs. In addition, the Agricultural Adjustment Act authorized the Department of Agriculture to purchase surplus food for school lunch programs. By 1946 several laws were consolidated into the National School Lunch Act, which provided free meals to low-income children.[36]

The federal role in support of education expanded again during the depression and World War II, with passage of the Lanham Act, supporting education for children whose parents worked for the government, and the G.I. Bill of Rights, technically known as the Servicemen's Readjustment Act, in 1944, providing financial support for the education of veterans. Despite growing federal involvement in education, during the postwar era the political climate changed, and fears of "federal control" resurfaced, leading to defeat of several attempts at passing general aid bills, with opponents raising the specter of "communistic" federal involvement in local schools. In 1949, Dwight D. Eisenhower wrote, while president of Columbia University, "unless we are careful, even the great and necessary educational processes in our country will become yet another vehicle by which the believers in paternalism, if not outright socialism, will gain still additional power for the central government."[37]

In hindsight, Eisenhower's comments were especially ironic because his term saw the most dramatic expansion of federal aid to education to date, with the creation of the new cabinet-level Department of Health, Education, and Welfare; increasing involvement in special education; an expanding federal role in desegregation efforts after the *Brown* decision; a gripping national crisis in Little Rock; and, following Sputnik, passage of the National Defense Education Act (NDEA), which unleashed an unprecedented level of federal funding for the improvement of education. Still, federal aid and programs for school curriculum improvement during the next few decades were almost entirely voluntary. Teachers were free to adopt or reject new materials or approaches as they saw fit, with little consequence for those who chose to ignore reform initiatives.[38]

The Kennedy and Johnson years saw even greater attention to the needs of disadvantaged students with the Council of Great City Schools, passage of the Civil Rights Act (1964), and the Elementary and Secondary Education Act (ESEA) in 1965.[39] Title I of ESEA focused on the needs of poor and disadvantaged students, and it allowed for funds to be spent on instruction, including textbooks, ancillary materials, teachers, and technology. Compensatory education efforts such as Title I were bitterly debated as an obstacle to racial integration and equality. In 1966, James Coleman and others were commissioned by U.S. commissioner of education Harold Howe to examine issues impacting poor and minority students. Coleman's study, *Equality of Educational Opportunity* (1966), concluded that neither racial integration nor compensatory education were strongly related to school achievement, but that achievement was strongly related to family background and socioeconomic status. The work of Coleman, Christopher Jencks, and other researchers suggested that the best way to improve school achievement might be to raise family income. Despite these findings, policies continued to focus primarily on narrow school-based reforms.[40]

During the Nixon years, studies of the "effectiveness" of federal programs such as Title I led to new calls for greater measurement and accountability, and to creation of the National Institute of Education (NIE) and the National Assessment of Educational Progress (NAEP), which would track student progress in inner cities and throughout the nation, similar in purpose to collection of health statistics as a window on areas of need.[41] Aid to special education increased dramatically during the 1970s, highlighted by passage of the Education for All Handicapped Children Act (P.L. 94–142) during the Ford administration.[42]

The latter 1970s saw creation of more steps toward a growing federal role in holding schools accountable. Making good on a campaign pledge, President Jimmy Carter won passage of the Department of Education Organization Act (1979), which raised education to cabinet-level status amid continuing controversies over special education, court-ordered busing, school finance reform, broad issues of school accountability, and concerns over the effectiveness of federal programs. Congress also authorized establishment of the Office of Educational Research and Improvement (OERI), with the purpose of sponsoring research on school effectiveness. Concerns over low student achievement levels at a time of economic strain led to increased reliance on standardized testing and taxpayer calls for efficiency. Attention focused on student achievement resulted, in part, from media hype over SAT test score declines, and it led to many calls for more work in the area of "basic skills competency." By 1978, several states began to implement mandates for basic skills instruction and testing, hoping to assess overall effectiveness and hold teachers and administrators accountable, while other states, such as

Massachusetts and New York, had been using such accountability measures for some time. By 1980, all fifty states had established some type of minimum competency testing program. Backing the new "accountability" trend was the increasing involvement of business leaders in school reform, growing in part out of federal grants supporting business–school partnerships.[43]

As we have seen, the political construction of accountability is inexorably linked to a rapidly expanding federal and state role in school policy. Moreover, all of this took place in the context of a nation in which wealth, income, and power are shared unequally, complicating and undermining reform.[44] While a political lens sheds light on the rapid growth of government size and power, it may omit other important factors that have impacted education. Race, class, gender, and disability have each had an impact on the politics of schooling. Thus, a modified political model emphasizing *ethnocultural politics* may provide additional insights and help further refine the political construction of education.[45] In school accountability reforms, appeals to the need to educate urban youth, especially African American and Latino youth, played a key role. Likewise, *media politics* have had a profound impact on debates over educational policy in a variety of arenas, just as they have impacted discourse and decision-making on other aspects of our lives. Media coverage of SAT score declines in the 1970s whipped up public sentiment for new forms of accountability. In more recent years, mainstream media attention to school performance, international comparisons, and business-led calls for rigorous standards and testing have lent support to public acceptance of the notion that our schools are failing, largely muted the protests of many scholars and teachers, and manufactured consent for accountability reforms.[46] Though the growth of government at state and federal levels has led to a shift in the locus of policy, most day-to-day decisions are still made and implemented by local bureaucracies. This fact makes it imperative that we examine an organizational perspective.

An Organizational Interpretation

An organizational interpretation would argue that school accountability has grown partly because it is the nature of bureaucracy in modern societies to create rules and take on greater and greater authority.[47] Over the history of education in the modern era, the corporate model of governance has strongly impacted the nature of school administration. At the turn of the last century, school governance was transformed by a powerful movement shifting schools to corporate-style governance. Decisions that were once made in the rough and tumble of pluralistic politics were shifted to administrators. Organizational reform during the early decades of the twentieth century led to centralized control in elected boards of education and "scientific" management by administrators. City and state departments of education grew in size and influence, consolidating many rural schools, and enforcing uniform educational standards. Advocates of these reforms argued that educational decisions were best made by experts. As decision-making shifted to school superintendents, the number of specialists and administrators multiplied. School systems gained size, added new tiers of staff, and were segmented into new divisions: elementary, junior high, and high school; vocational programs; handi-capped education; counseling services; bureaus of research and testing; and other departments, seemingly ad infinitum. After 1890, a new focus on what was called "educational science" evolved, helping educators collect and process information, and, it was hoped, make better decisions.

Administrative progressives had a profound and continuing influence on the growth and development of the comprehensive high school during the twentieth century. Social efficiency educators, steeped in principles of "scientific manage-ment," created schools modeled on the ideas of efficiency experts. Curriculum experts such as Franklin Bobbitt, W.W. Charters, and David Snedden, and admin-istrative progressives such as Elwood P. Cubberley called for the application of Taylorism to schools with a ruthless efficiency, resulting in the emergence of what one observer described as an "orgy of efficiency" to create a giant "sorting machine," with students assigned to various levels and receiving differing treat-ments.[48] In overcrowded city schools, administrators developed plans for full and efficient use of facilities, with students attending school in shifts, and every nook and cranny of the building and grounds put to full use. In the curriculum Bobbitt posited, the goal was to "Work up the raw material into that finished product for which it is best adapted. Applied to education this means: Educate the individual according to his capabilities."[49] Thus, it was thought, some are better suited for manual labor, others for managerial or scholarly pursuits. Raymond Callahan and others have illustrated the ways that educational administrators consciously bor-rowed administrative approaches from the corporate model.[50]

During the course of the twentieth century, virtually all aspects of schooling were influenced by scientific management, from the physical plant and the atten-dance office to the curriculum. Textbooks were no longer simply the creation of authors and publishers but were subjected to a codified adoption process, readabil-ity formulas, and review by committees composed of citizen-experts, what has been called the "great textbook machine."[51] Testing was the handmaiden and chief tool of the movement for efficiency in schools.[52] Testing was viewed by most Americans as authoritative and scientific. And, as we have seen, by the 1970s, the neo-efficiency movement was asserting a strong influence, leading to minimum competency test-ing and a variety of other trends.[53] In sum, the accountability movement must be seen as a logical extension of efficiency trends over the course of time.

An organizational interpretation calls attention to the fact that large-scale institutions with business-like qualities have exerted a profound influence on the lives of most Americans for at least a century. The accountability phase of school reform is the most recent episode in a long history that has generally moved in the direction of greater supervision and surveillance of teachers and students via administrative control. Organizations have developed the means to implement and enforce various kinds of accountability measures and have privileged certain kinds of curricula over others: textbooks over ancillary materials; literacy, mathematics, and science, over social studies and other subjects; and traditional forms of education over progressive. An organizational perspective also calls attention to the tendency for power to be concentrated toward the top of the pyramid, a trend that has gained increasing influence during the accountability era.

While an organizational interpretation offers important insights related to the nature of educational institutions, it is not without flaws. It may be unsound to generalize the tendency toward bureaucratization as a uniform movement toward ever increasing control. The concreteness that we may associate with terms like "efficiency" and "standardization" is seldom played out in absolute terms. There are often differences in application to state and local environments, with a multitude of variations. Moreover, though the accountability movement has touched schools in every state in the nation, it has taken somewhat different form in different areas. One virtue of the economic interpretations we take up next is that they provide powerful explanations of the interests and motivations of people who inhabit organizations.

Economic Interpretations

Two major economic theories are useful in discussing interpretations of school accountability and its origins. The first of these is human capital theory, the notion that investment in schooling and higher education pays off as investment in the human capital necessary for economic development, both individually and societally. Long advanced by both mainstream and conservative thinkers as a justification for improving schooling, human capital theory is the primary underlying justification for the recent movement for school accountability. The second relevant economic theory takes a critical or neo-Marxian analysis of society and education as its starting point, emphasizing the tendency of schooling to perpetuate and reproduce inequalities of wealth, income, and power. According to this interpretive theory, schools embody the characteristics of capitalist society and function largely as a giant sorting machine.

Human Capital Theory

In the years after World War II, economists interested in economic growth began to analyze the effects of human capital on economic development and noticed that education had considerable impact. Scholarly work on investment in human beings included general studies of the contribution of knowledge to economic growth but increasingly shifted to a focus on the financial returns of education for individuals. Economists have developed increasingly sophisticated ways of measuring rates of return on investment in education, including the costs and benefits of schooling for individuals. Despite a range of estimates on specifics, most analysts agree that schooling has significant benefits for individual earnings.

Notions regarding the economic benefits of education to society have been prevalent since the founding of the common school. Horace Mann, secretary of the Board of Education of Massachusetts, devoted his *Fifth Annual Report* to this theme in 1842. Mann presented an economic justification for schooling, arguing that it not only produced good character and knowledge, but that "it is also the most prolific patent of material riches."[54] He claimed that money spent on primary schooling brought an aggregate rate of return to society of about 50 percent, and argued that it enabled people to become better decision-makers by "comprehending the connections of a long train of events and seeing the end from the beginning."[55] Moreover, he argued that schooling created workers who were punctual, industrious, frugal, and too rational to cause trouble for their employers. Mann's report, while highly biased and lacking in scholarly rigor, was used as ammunition to support school reform: in New York, the legislature ordered 18,000 copies printed and distributed; in Boston, businessmen cheered him and added that the common school was not only a "nursery of souls, but a mine of riches."[56] Businessmen over the years have tended to agree with the idea that schooling increases the productivity and reliability of workers, and strongly supported vocational education on that basis. During the second half of the twentieth century, Americans became increasingly comfortable with the idea that schooling is linked to success and that schools help determine the eventual occupational roles of students. By the 1970s, a Gallup poll reported its respondents viewed education as "extremely important" to "one's future success."[57] From that time to the present, advocates of accountability reform have generally cited some variation of the human capital argument in lobbying for school improvement.

A Marxian Analysis

An alternative economic view of schooling and accountability reform rejects the "individual choice" model as a way to understand the rise of institutions of mass education. As Bowles and Gintis wrote in 1975:

> The model is not wrong—individuals and families do make choices, and may even make educational choices roughly as described by the human capital theorists. We reject the individual choice framework because it is so superficial as to be virtually irrelevant to the task of understanding why we have the kinds of schools and the amount of schooling we do.[58]

They went on to explain that the individual choice model and human capital theory offer little useful insight into basic questions related to the functions of schooling—reproducing the capitalist class structure. Perpetuation of a society marked by gross inequalities in wealth and income has not resulted from the aggregate of individual choices, but rather from the impact of schooling in reproducing the hierarchical social structure of a capitalist economy. Instead of seeing society as a marketplace of individuals who seek to maximize their potential guided by Adam Smith's "invisible hand," they viewed American society as one in which choices are often determined by the class structure, by limited and unequal access to wealth and power. In essence, Bowles and Gintis argued that while it may appear that the American educational system has developed in response to the "investment" decisions of individuals, mediated by local school boards, in actuality the system has developed in response to changes in production (industrialization; the information and service economy) "governed by the pursuit of profit and privilege by those elements of the capitalist class which dominate the dynamic sectors of the economy." Thus, the capitalist class establishes the rules of the game and the range of acceptable choices in a way that reinforces its status.[59] They argued, further, that school reforms have largely been engineered by those who control leading sectors of the economy, citing corporate leaders who, at the turn of the twentieth century, sought to "stabilize and rationalize the economy and supporting social institutions."[60] More recent critical theorists have enhanced this interpretation and applied it to the latest reforms.[61]

In recent accountability reforms, one can observe frequent reference to human capital theory, along with a disingenuous tightening of the sorting function. Schools have become an increasingly competitive system from kindergarten through graduate school. Students are routinely identified as "basic," "proficient," "advanced," "below basic," or similar labels, and sorted by their performance. Movements to eliminate ability grouping have made only scant progress. Despite the rhetoric of reform, and an ethic of success for all, most schools continue to label and track students in a system that is largely segregated by social class and neighborhood.[62]

Critical perspectives on schooling provide powerful explanations of reformers' motives and school realities. They connect business involvement over the history of schooling with increased corporate leadership of school reform from the 1970s through the move for "systemic reform" in the late 1980s to the creation of the accountability system that is now in place. While the logic of recent reforms is rooted in a business model, business did not create school accountability systems on its own but had strong accomplices in government and among school administrators, conservative activists, back-to-basics advocates, and "effective schools" researchers.

Conclusion

So what can one learn from exploring alternative ways of interpreting the origins of school accountability reform? Why is the question of origins important? By examining the origins of accountability reform we can see that while the logic of reform is centered on a business mentality, conditions were ripe for business-driven reforms to take hold and have a major influence. As we have seen, the movement for accountability reform was well underway by the middle of the 1970s, with increasing emphasis on basic skills, minimum competency testing, and research on school effectiveness. The conservative restoration in schools and society meant that significant changes were ahead for schools and their governance. Gradually, during the 1980s, a broad critique of the schools embodied in the notion that the schools were "failing" came to be accepted as an act of faith and led to increasing efforts to improve schools by making them more accountable. Reforms gained their greatest traction during a period of prosperity and economic expansion, from the mid-1990s through the first decade of the twenty-first century. Ultimately, the accountability movement was a logical outgrowth of the conservative restoration in schools and society, and it has served to make the economic purposes of education paramount, making the well-prepared worker its chief product and largely neglecting the social and aesthetic dimensions of schooling.

Notes

1. Larry Cuban, *The Blackboard and the Bottom Line: Why Schools Can't Be Businesses* (Cambridge, MA: Harvard University Press, 2004), 27.
2. Ibid., 30.
3. Ibid.
4. Herbert M. Kliebard, *Struggle for the American Curriculum, 1893–1958* (London: Routledge and Keegan Paul, 1986); Jonathan Zimmerman, *Whose America? Culture Wars in the Public Schools* (Cambridge, MA: Harvard University Press, 2002).
5. Ronald W. Evans, *The Social Studies Wars: What Should We Teach the Children?* (New York: Teachers College, 2004).
6. Ibid.
7. William W. Goetz, "The Rise and Fall of MACOS: A Blip on the Historical Screen?," *TRSE* 22, no. 4 (Fall 1994): 519.
8. Richard A. Viguerie and David Franke, *America's Right Turn: How Conservatives Used New and Alternative Media to Take Power* (Chicago: Bonus Books, 2004).
9. Fred L. Pincus, "From Equity to Excellence: The Rebirth of Educational Conservatism," *SP* 14, no. 3 (Winter 1984): 50–56.
10. Ben Brodinsky, "The New Right: The Movement and Its Impact," *PDK* 64, no. 2 (October 1982): 87–94.
11. Connaught C. Marshner, *Blackboard Tyranny* (New Rochelle, NY: Arlington House, 1978); Sally D. Reed, *NEA: Propaganda Front of the Radical Left* (Washington, DC: National Council for Better Education, 1984).
12. Brodinsky, "New Right," 90.
13. Ibid., 91–92; Fred L. Pincus, "Book Banning and the New Right: Censorship in the Public Schools," *EF* 49, no. 1 (Fall 1984): 7–21.
14. Brodinsky, "New Right," 94.
15. Pincus, "From Equity to Excellence," 52–53.
16. *Report of the Advisory Panel on the Scholastic Aptitude Test Score Decline: On Further Examination* (New York: College Entrance Examination Board, 1977), 27.
17. Ben Brodinsky, "Back to the Basics: The Movement and Its Meaning," *PDK* 58, no. 7 (March 1977): 522.
18. Ibid.
19. Brodinsky, "New Right," 88.
20. Brodinsky, "Back to Basics," 523.
21. Cuban, *Blackboard*, 56.
22. David L. Angus and Jeffrey E. Mirel, *The Failed Promise of the American High School, 1890–1985* (New York: Teachers College Press, 1999), 135.
23. Cuban, *Blackboard*, 54.

24. Brodinsky, "Back to Basics," 527.

25. Ibid., 523.

26. Merrill Sheils, "Why Johnny Can't Write," *NW*, December 8, 1975, 58.

27. Merrill Sheils, "Back to Basics in the Schools," *NW*, October 21, 1974, 87–93.

28. Special Issue, "Teaching Basics in Social Studies," *SE* 41, no. 2 (February 1977): 96–121; Barry K. Beyer, "Teaching Basics in Social Studies," *SE* 41, no. 2 (February 1977): 96–104; John P. Lunstrum, Ed., Special Issue, "Improving Reading in the Social Studies," *SE* 42, no. 1 (January 1978): 8–31; John P. Lunstrum and Judith L. Irvin, "Integration of Basic Skills into Social Studies Content," *SE* (March, 1981): 169.

29. NCSS, *Essentials of Education Statement: Essentials of Social Studies* (Washington, DC: National Council for the Social Studies, 1980).

30. Richard Ohman, "The Literacy Crisis Is a Fiction, if Not a Hoax," *CHE*, October 25, 1976, 32.

31. John Mathews, "Access Rights to Children's Minds: Texts of Our Times—Problems in Kanawha County, W.Va.," *NRP*, January 4, 1975, 19–21.

32. David Tyack, "Ways of Seeing: An Essay on the History of Compulsory Schooling," *HER* 46, no. 3 (August 1976): 365.

33. Ibid., 366.

34. Ibid.; John Taylor Gatto, "Against School," *HA*, September 2003.

35. New York State Education Department (NYSED), *Federal Education Policy and the States, 1945–2009: A Brief Synopsis* (Albany: New York State Archives, 2006, revised 2009), 5.

36. NYSED, *Federal Education Policy*, 6. See James T. Patterson, *The New Deal and the States: Federalism in Transition* (Princeton, NJ: Princeton University Press, 1969).

37. NYSED, *Federal Education Policy*, 7–13.

38. Ibid.; Barbara Barksdale Clowse, *Brainpower for the Cold War: The Sputnik Crisis and National Defense Education Act of 1958* (Westport, CT: Greenwood Press, 1981). See John L. Rudolph, *Scientists in the Classroom: The Cold War Reconstruction of American Science Education* (New York: Palgrave, 2002), and Ronald W. Evans, *The Hope for American School Reform: The Cold War Pursuit of Inquiry Learning in Social Studies* (New York: Palgrave, 2011).

39. "Bill, H.R. 2365, Elementary and Secondary Education Act of 1965" folder, Box 26, Cater Files; "ESEA" folder, Box 1, ED, LBJ Papers; LBJ Remarks, Education Bill Signing, April 11, 1965, LBJPP.

40. NYSED, *Federal Education Policy*, 13–22; James S. Coleman, et al., *Equality of Educational Opportunity* (Washington, DC: Government Printing Office, 1966); Christopher Jencks, *Inequality: A Reassessment of the Effect of Family and Schooling in America* (New York: Basic Books, 1972).

41. See documents related to education policies, Executive Education Files, Boxes 1–4, Nixon Papers.

42. NYSED, *Federal Education Policy*, 23–39.

43. Ibid., 40–44.

44. G. William Domhoff, "Wealth, Income and Power," http://www2.ucsc.edu/whorulesamerica/power/wealth.html (2006, updated 2013).

45. Tyack, "Ways of Seeing."

46. Edward S. Herman and Noam Chomsky, *Manufacturing Consent: The Political Economy of the Mass Media* (New York: Pantheon, 1988); Ronald W. Evans, "A Fickle Lover: Experiences with the Media in Historical Context," in Margaret Smith Crocco, Ed., *Social Studies and the Press: Keeping the Beast at Bay* (Greenwich, CT: Information Age, 2005); David Berliner and Bruce J. Biddle, *The Manufactured Crisis: Myths, Fraud, and the Attack on America's Public Schools* (Reading, MA: Addison-Wesley, 1995).

47. Max Weber, *Economy and Society: An Outline of Interpretive Sociology* (Berkeley: University of California Press, 1978, original 1922).

48. Joel Spring, *The Sorting Machine Revisited: National Education Policy Since 1945* (New York: Longman, 1989).

49. Franklin W. Bobbitt, "The Elimination of Waste in Education," *EST* 12, no. 6 (February 1912): 269.
50. Raymond E. Callahan, *Education and the Cult of Efficiency* (Chicago: University of Chicago Press, 1962).
51. Harriet Tyson-Bernstein and Arthur Woodward, "The Great Textbook Machine and Prospects for Reform," *SE* 50, no. 1 (January 1986): 41–45. See also Frances Fitzgerald, *America Revised: History Schoolbooks in the Twentieth Century* (Boston: Little, Brown, 1979); James Loewen, *Lies My Teacher Told Me: Everything Your American History Textbook Got Wrong* (New York: New Press, 1995).
52. Nicholas Lehman, *The Big Test: The Secret History of the American Meritocracy* (New York: Farrar, Straus and Giroux, 1999); Stephen Jay Gould, *The Mismeasure of Man* (New York: Norton, 1981).
53. David L. Angus and Jeffrey E. Mirel, *Failed Promise of the American High School* (New York: Teachers College, 1999).
54. Tyack, "Ways of Seeing," 378.
55. Ibid.
56. Ibid., 379.
57. Ibid., 382.
58. Samuel Bowles and Herbert Gintis, "The Problem with Human Capital Theory—A Marxist Critique," *AER* 65, no. 2 (1975): 78; Samuel Bowles and Herbert Gintis, *Schooling in Capitalist America: Educational Reform and the Contradictions of Economic Life* (New York: Basic Books, 1976).
59. Tyack, "Ways of Seeing," 383–384.
60. Tyack, "Ways of Seeing," 386; Samuel Bowles and Herbert Gintis, "Contradictions of Liberal Educational Reform," in Walter Feinberg and Henry Rosemont, Jr., Eds., *Work, Technology, and Education* (Urbana: University of Illinois Press, 1975).
61. E. Wayne Ross and Rich Gibson, Eds., *Neoliberalism and Education Reform* (Cresskill, NJ: Hampton Press, 2007).
62. Gary Orfield, *Schools More Separate: Consequences of a Decade of Resegregation* (Cambridge, MA: Harvard Civil Rights Project, 2001); Jonathan Kozol, *Shame of the Nation: The Restoration of Apartheid Schooling in America* (New York: Crown, 2005); John Marsh, *Class Dismissed: Why We Cannot Teach or Learn Our Way Out of Inequality* (New York: Monthly Review, 2011).

2

A NATION AT RISK?

By the early 1980s, the conservative restoration was more fully taking form. The movement garnered support from a consensus of Americans both within and outside educational institutions and received a major boost from an unprecedented flurry of reports on the status and future of schooling published in 1983 and after. The watershed for the new direction of reform came with publication of *A Nation at Risk: The Imperative for Educational Reform*, the report of the National Commission on Excellence in Education (NCE), a blue-ribbon commission appointed by President Ronald Reagan's secretary of education, Terrel H. Bell.

The context of the late 1970s and early 1980s is important to understanding the origins of what would soon become known as the "excellence movement." In a July 1979 speech to a national audience that would become known as the "malaise speech," President Jimmy Carter spoke of "a crisis in confidence ... that strikes at the soul and spirit of our national will." At the end of the 1970s, the nation "simmered with accumulated fears and frustrations" centered on economic worries marked by a unique situation labeled "stagflation," high unemployment combined with high inflation. During President Reagan's first year in office, the unemployment rate reached 10.7 percent, the highest since the 1930s, with inflation at 12.5 percent. Moreover, public support for the Great Society programs, which had spawned the rise of a large USOE, had begun to wane during the 1970s, as attention turned toward a different set of questions.

Partly reflecting these difficult times, many Americans were becoming extremely critical of the schools, complaining of inferior graduates ill-prepared to enter the workforce in an increasingly technological society. Many observers believed that an inferior educational system lay behind business losses to the Japanese, West Germany, and other nations. There were widespread popular concerns about declining standards, lax requirements, a focus on "relevance" and extracurricular activities, and decreasing time for academic instruction. Some feared that students were not being challenged academically and pointed to declining SAT scores and other indicators. For most of the century, the politics of the curriculum had swung like a pendulum between two competing ideas. Progressive-leaning educators believed that schooling should focus on student-centered learning and critical thinking, while traditionalists believed that the primary function of schools was centered on teaching basic skills of literacy, numeracy, and content in "core" subjects such as English, mathematics, science, history, and the foreign languages. Despite these concerns, education scholars believed that innovations of the 1960s and 1970s had led to only a little real change. They cited surveys and classroom observation studies indicating that teacher-centered lessons were still the norm and that most teachers taught as they had been taught. Nonetheless, the conventional wisdom in the early 1980s was that schools had swung too far in the direction of innovation and nonacademic activities, and that we needed to get back to the basics of traditional education.[1]

Ronald Reagan ran for office on a promise, included in the Republican Party platform in 1980, to dismantle the Department of Education (DOE) as a cabinet-level office and cut its funding as a way of cost saving and reducing bureaucracy, in keeping with the aim of limiting big government. The platform called for "deregulation by the federal government of public education" and noted that "parents are losing control of their children's schooling" and that Democratic policies had led to "huge new bureaucracies to misspend our taxes."[2] Carter had created the DOE as a cabinet-level department in 1979 with the purpose of giving public education a more prominent position in the nation's agenda.

The Reagan administration's domestic policy goals were to reduce the federal budget deficit, attack inflation, cut taxes, and decentralize and deregulate a wide array of federal social programs. As Reagan stated in his inaugural address, "In this present crisis, government is not the solution to our problem; government is the problem."[3] During his first year in office, Reagan met with top business people, who were also leaders in private-sector nonprofit activities, for the purpose of "enlisting their aid in stimulating private takeover of much of what govt. has tried to do in Social programs that are costly & not as effective as voluntary efforts can be."[4] Decentralization, deregulation, and privatization were key elements of the "New Federalism," partly traceable to the Nixon administration. In education, Reagan's top priority was to scale back federal aid and give control back to states and local districts, while maintaining the appearance of concern about education. During 1981, the administration persuaded Congress to cut federal aid to schools by more than 15 percent by passage of the Educational Consolidation and Improvement Act (ECIA). The legislation, converting many grant programs from categorical aid to block grants with no strings attached, marked a sudden federal retreat after decades of expanded aid and regulation.[5] The administration used block grants to reframe the federal role in education—from policy directives to general assistance, deregulating many programs and defunding others. While conservatives generally approved, to others the policy represented a major retreat from equity goals and the aim of making the federal role "more effective."[6] In keeping with his philosophy of reducing government, Reagan's proposed budgets generally sought to reduce federal spending on education during his years in office, but Congress passed budgets that actually raised federal aid to schools.[7]

Reagan appointed Terrel H. Bell, a moderate Republican and Utah commissioner of education, to the post of secretary of education. The choice of Bell as secretary was somewhat surprising given the makeup of what some journalists referred to as the "millionaire's cabinet." Bell, a former school superintendent and professor, rented a U-Haul to move to Washington and was regularly badgered by conservatives in the administration. Unlike many Reagan appointees, Bell was an experienced Washington hand who had served as acting commissioner of education during the Nixon and Ford administrations. Moreover, he considered himself "a zealot . . . a missionary ready to preach the gospel of education to all the Reaganites."[8] Nixon's influence in suggesting Bell is a distinct possibility, given his advice to Reagan in other areas.[9]

The electoral win for Reagan was large: he carried forty-four states and received 50.7 percent of the popular vote to Carter's 41 percent, a landslide interpreted by many as a mandate for conservative change and for reducing the size of government.[10] The Reagan presidency is often cast as the "Reagan revolution" because of social conservatives and the cultural shift that his presidency represented. In the election, education was given little priority, with voters ranking it as the twenty-third most important issue.[11] In 1981, by most accounts, the nation was not in very good shape. Inflation and interest rates were high, and unemployment was widespread. Moreover, American prestige abroad was at a low point after the fall of Saigon and the Iran hostage crisis. The national mood of continuing "malaise" and self-doubt was evident in media and opinion polls, and a search for scapegoats was underway. In the context of what was viewed as a "pervasive decline," frequent complaints were aired about the schools. The link between education and the economy was a perennial refrain, and it captured the thinking of Secretary Bell:

> If we were to become more competitive and increase the nation's productivity, education had a significant role to play. . . . Our loss of zest and drive and spirit would not be regained until we renewed and reformed our schools.
>
> We needed some means of rallying the American people around their schools and colleges. Educators also needed to be shaken out of their complacency. More than two decades ago the Soviet Sputnik had spurred us into action to improve educational standards and performance. We needed an equally powerful spur today.[12]

Bell wanted to "stage an event that would jar people into action" to improve the educational system. He began to contemplate asking the president to appoint a "first-rate panel" to study the problems of education, but his colleagues were dubious. When he took the idea to the White House, it was met with "diffidence or scorn." Federal commissions were ineffective, he was told. Education is a local and state responsibility. For the president to appoint a national panel would imply support for a significant federal role, which ran counter to the Reagan philosophy. When it became clear that a formal proposal to the president would be rejected out of hand, Bell decided to appoint his own cabinet-level commission, seemingly his only option.[13] In his letter proposing the commission, Bell made clear that the commission would review and synthesize data on "educational quality," draw comparisons with the educational systems of other countries, and hold hearings to define barriers to "attaining greater levels of excellence in American education." The commission would then report and offer practical recommendations for action and launch a drive to persuade school boards and other agencies to adopt policies that will "raise the levels of expected achievement" through "changes in state and local standards." His letter also noted that the commission would not report to the secretary of education but to those in general control and supervision of schools and colleges, including the academic community, governing boards, and state legislative bodies. The federal role would be one of "advocacy, encouragement, coordination, and discrimination of information" and would not "in any way focus on or ask for" increased federal expenditures or control.[14] After considerable wrangling and discussion, a charter, and approval from the Office of Management and Budget (OMB), the commission received official approval on August 26, 1981. The White House was not sponsoring the commission and some staffers at the White House and OMB considered Bell's decision to appoint his own commission an act of insubordination.[15]

The Commission

Appointing members to the commission became equally contentious. Mid-level White House staffers, and some in the DOE, wanted a conservative membership. Donald Senese, assistant secretary designate, nominated several well-known political conservatives and educators including *National Review* columnist Russell Kirk, Chicago teacher Marva Collins, literacy expert Paul Copperman, and George Weber of the CBE, and included background material on each. The materials Senese submitted with his nominations included back-to-basics tracts along with an article depicting the CBE as, "The slayers of Dewey-eyed educational dragons."[16] However, Bell wanted a commission whose membership would "command respect . . . beyond reproach . . . balanced" with "liberals and conservatives, Republicans and Democrats, males and females, minorities, educators and non-educators." Despite some rough sledding as White House staffers vetted his selection, Bell was largely able to accomplish this goal.[17]

Bell selected his friend David Pierpont Gardner, then president of the University of Utah, to chair the commission, and Milton Goldberg, a senior staff associate at the National Institute of Education and a seasoned bureaucratic professional, to become executive director, coordinating data gathering and support. Bell, Gardner, Goldberg, and the administration collaborated in selecting the membership, including one from each of the national education associations housed in Washington.[18] Among its members were school and university administrative leaders including A. Bartlett Giamatti, president of Yale University, a national teacher of the year, a parent, and two leading scientists, Glenn Seaborg and Gerald Holton. The commission represented a range of people with knowledge of the educational system and its problems.[19] When enlisting Gardner, and again at the NCE's initial meeting, Bell assured members of the commission that "there would be no interference of any kind" and that the results would be distributed and discussions held across the land with those empowered to implement changes in education via a series of dissemination conferences with governors, state education agencies, legislators, school boards, administrators, teachers, and parents.[20]

Its first meetings were held in Washington, DC, on October 9–10, 1981. On the first day, the group traveled to the White House for the full commission's only meeting with the president. In his remarks, Reagan highlighted key principles of his presidency: that education begins in the home, and schools exist to help families; that "excellence demands competition" because "Without a race there can be no champion." He stressed the importance of character education and "allowing God back in the classroom." He urged the commission to "help America get back to stressing the fundamentals in schools." His most revealing comment was that "some people insist there are no simple answers to any of the problems that plague our society. I disagree. Many of the answers are simple—they're just not easy."[21] Later, in his diary, Reagan expressed confidence in the commission, and wrote, "It is a wide ranging, solid group & I'm convinced it will set out & make an improvement in the quality of ed."[22]

During eighteen months of deliberation, with a budget of $785,000, the commission held hearings in numerous sites, gathering testimony from scholars, practitioners, teachers, students, administrators, public officials, business leaders, parents, and ordinary citizens.[23] It solicited papers on topics of concern from scholars recognized as authorities in their fields.[24] The commission held eight general meetings of its members, and the staff gained additional input from a wide array of sources, including educators, professional groups, parents, public officials, and scholars. It held public sessions in various states addressing specific topics: science, math, and technology education; language and literacy; performance expectations; teaching and teacher education; college admissions and transition; the student's role; college curriculum; education for a productive role; and education for the gifted and talented.[25] Along with testimony given at these meetings, there were twenty additional authorities who made presentations to the commission, and forty-four commissioned papers providing additional research.[26]

Once the "data" was gathered, the staff prepared summaries and began studying possible solutions. Commission members considered various proposals with the aim of reaching consensus on all aspects of the final report. Though the members of the commission reached general agreement on the main thrust and structure of the report, there were four or five who disagreed with the majority, and the report's release was postponed for a month, until late April 1983, amid the threat of one or more minority reports. Gardner was certain he could mediate differences and get a full consensus. Negotiation over details delayed release of the report and continued right up to the end. The final holdout was Seaborg, a longtime veteran of educational reform efforts, who believed strongly that the report had to be "dramatic to get people's attention." After all the meetings and discussion, the commission's staff drafted a report that "surprised" him with its blandness. On the evening before the report was due, he continued to hold out for language that he found acceptable. Exasperated, Gardner pleaded, "Glenn, you sound as if you are negotiating with the Russians." Later, Seaborg wrote, "To me it was every bit as important as if I were negotiating with the Russians . . . [because of] the importance of education to national well being and national security." Accordingly, the final text of the report contained "strong, militaristic phrases" such as "an act of war" and "unilateral educational disarmament."[27]

The Report

The NCE report was unveiled to the nation at a special ceremony in the State Dining Room of the White House on Tuesday, April 26, 1983. A draft was transmitted to the president a week prior to the unveiling. Though the report was in general agreement with Reagan's recommendations to Congress in the State of the Union address, it either contradicted or omitted other parts of the administration's agenda. The report called for a major new reform movement to improve schooling, along with greater financial support and higher salaries for teachers, but did not address the level from which additional funding should come. It emphasized "the basic purposes of schooling." It described "Knowledge, learning, information, and skilled intelligence" as the "new raw materials of international commerce" needed as the "indispensable investment required for success in the 'information age.'" While the administration was in general agreement with these goals, it did not support more funding from the federal level, and it seemed more concerned about school prayer, tuition tax credits, vouchers, and the value of private schooling. Consequently, the "mismatch" between the report and an initial draft of the president's remarks led to more than a little scheming among White House staffers, along with back and forth discussion and rewriting with Secretary Bell, over just what the president would say.[28]

As it turned out, in his remarks Reagan praised the work of the commission, mentioned a few highlights from the report, emphasized the importance of education, and supported general implementation of the commission's recommendations.

Toward the end of his speech, however, Reagan followed those remarks by prais-ing the report for its support for "tuition tax credits, vouchers, educational savings accounts, voluntary school prayer, and abolishing the Department of Education," none of which the report actually endorsed. He stated that the administration's agenda was "to restore quality to education by increasing competition and by strengthening parental choice and local control," with the overall aim "to restore excellence in America's schools."[29]

The report's strident tone and strong conclusions sparked a frenzy of media attention far beyond what Bell and the commission expected. Stories on the report appeared on the front page of virtually every major newspaper in the country, evening newscasts featured stories on the report, and editorials of sup-port appeared in countless newspapers. Both Bell and Gardner instantly received numerous invitations for interviews and speaking engagements. Seemingly over-night, the condition of education became a major issue in the media and began to rise on the public agenda. As a result, Reagan and his staff sought to get "the greatest possible mileage from the commission report." Reagan began to talk more about education and encourage state and local school reform, engaging in a rhetorical campaign that reinforced the sense that education was a national issue.[30]

Though the report contained no new research and was based on a compilation of findings, its timing and the language in which it was written created a heated atmosphere, attracted a great deal of media attention, and spawned a secondary literature of reaction and critique from scholars.[31] This report, and a flurry of others with similar themes, set the agenda for schooling, signaling the official, U.S. government-supported stance. The central thesis of the report was that our nation was "at risk." The commission blamed U.S. schools for the nation's decline in international economic competition, alleging that the position of the United States in commerce, industry, science, and technology was overtaken by "a rising tide of mediocrity in our schools which threatens our very future as a nation and a people." The report went on:

> If an unfriendly foreign power had attempted to impose on America the mediocre educational performance that exists today, we might well have viewed it as an act of war. As it stands, we have allowed this to happen to ourselves. We have squandered the gains in student achievement made in the wake of the Sputnik challenge. . . . We have, in effect, been committing an act of unthinking, unilateral educational disarmament.[32]

The commission supported its inflammatory thesis with a section captioned "Indicators of Risk," citing the poor performance of American students on inter-national comparisons made in the 1970s. The report found that scores on the SAT had shown a "virtually unbroken decline from 1963 to 1980." The report also noted high rates of "functional illiteracy" as high as 40 percent among minority youth, a "steady decline in science achievement," and a lack of "higher order" intellectual skills such as drawing "inferences from written material" and writing a persuasive essay.[33] Yet the report contradicted this evidence later, acknowledging that no other nation approaches the United States in the proportion of youth completing high school and going on to higher education. The report also included references indicating that the test scores of the top 9 percent of American students compared favorably with their peers in other nations.

Key findings of the report included the conclusion that the secondary school curriculum content had been "homogenized, diluted, and diffused"; that expectations for homework and serious academic coursework in science, mathematics, and geography were minimal; that students were given too many choices; that minimum competency was becoming the maximum; that classroom materials and textbooks were "written down" to ever-lower reading levels; and that colleges and universities had lowered admission requirements, contributing to the decline in standards. The commission found a lack of time available for instruction and that "poor classroom management" was often wasting student time that could be spent studying. On teaching, the report argued that the profession was not attracting the best and brightest, and that teacher training programs overemphasized "educational methods courses" and failed to include sufficient content area preparation.[34]

Based on its inflammatory introduction, "Indicators of Risk," and "Findings," the report made several key recommendations for change. In its first and central recommendation on "Content," the commission proposed strengthening graduation requirements by establishing a "core" of studies as the "Five New Basics" for the high school. The core included four years of English, three years of math, three years of science, three years of social studies, and one-half year of computer science, all required for graduation. Two years of foreign language in high school were highly recommended. Health and physical education went unmentioned, and the arts were clearly relegated to secondary status.[35]

In the area of social studies, the report stated in an "illustrative description" that the curriculum should:

> (a) enable students to fix their places and possibilities within the larger social and cultural structure; (b) understand the broad sweep of both ancient and contemporary ideas that have shaped our world; and (c) understand the fundamentals of how our economic system works and our political system functions; and (d) grasp the difference between free and repressive societies. An understanding of each of these is requisite to the informed and committed exercise of citizenship in our free society.[36]

Though it said little, these were remarkably traditional aims for social studies, implying an emphasis on history, economics, and civics. Asking students to "fix their places and possibilities" implied a social efficiency orientation, with emphasis on the ultimate goal of finding suitable employment.

In its second major recommendation, on "Standards and Expectations," the commission proposed that "schools, colleges, and universities adopt more rigorous and measurable standards, and higher expectations, for academic performance and student conduct." Among the specifics was the following:

> 3. Standardized tests of achievement (not to be confused with aptitude tests) should be administered at major transition points from one level of schooling to another and particularly from high school to college or work. The purposes of these tests would be to: (a) certify the student's credentials; (b) identify the need for remedial intervention; and (c) identify the opportunity for advanced or accelerated work. The tests should be administered as part of a nationwide (but not Federal) system of State and local standardized tests. This system should include other diagnostic procedures that assist teachers and students to evaluate student progress.[37]

This recommendation on standards and expectations, calling for regular use of standardized achievement tests, would become a cornerstone of the accountability movement. Other proposals included devoting more time to academic learning, requiring more homework, emphasis on effective study skills, lengthening the school day and year, merit pay and an eleven-month contract for teachers, and creation of more rigorous textbooks and curricular materials. The report was widely circulated, destined to have a major impact on educational rhetoric. Five years after *A Nation at Risk* was released, more than 200,000 copies had been distributed by the DOE, along with an estimated 5 to 6 million copies through newspaper and magazine reprints.[38]

Reactions

Reactions to the report were swift. The National Education Association (NEA), the nation's largest and most powerful teachers' union, was one of the first groups to criticize the report, and viewed it as an attack on teachers and public schools. On the other hand, the American Federation of Teachers (AFT) and its president Albert Shanker supported the general findings of the report and offered constructive criticism. Media coverage served to support the report, and cemented in the public mind the notion that schools were "at risk" and generally in poor condition. Moreover, many of the nation's governors and legislative leaders supported the report and became involved in what quickly became the "excellence" reform movement.[39] Bell met informally with the nation's governors in the summer of 1983 while they were holding their annual meeting in Kennebunkport, Maine, at the home of Vice President George H.W. Bush, for a "lobster feast and clambake." A few attacked the Reagan administration's record on education. Others, including Richard Celeste of Ohio and Bill Clinton of Arkansas, insisted that it was unfair for the administration to support a report admonishing the states for declining educational quality while pressing for more budget cuts. Several others were vigorous in support, including Richard Riley of South Carolina, Lamar Alexander of Tennessee, Robert Orr of Indiana, Bob Graham of Florida, Tom Kean of New Jersey, and Scott Matheson of Utah. Over the next few years, these and many other governors lent their support by pressing for adoption of tough academic standards for "excellence" in public schools.[40] The governors also made a pointed criticism of the DOE, saying that they had little valid information indicating where their states stood in terms of educational achievement in relation to other states. Bell acted on this suggestion "as quickly as possible," using college entrance exam scores to create an extensively footnoted wall chart ranking the states. The "wall chart" was first presented at a press conference on January 5, 1984, an unveiling of data that continued during the second Reagan administration and became an annual media event.[41]

A Flurry of Reports

Following publication of *A Nation at Risk*, there were other similar reports. Virtually all shared the central thesis of *A Nation at Risk*, that the U.S. decline in international economic competition was to be blamed on a mediocre educational system. Most prominent among the other national reports on education published in 1983 were *Action for Excellence*, the report of the Education Commission of the States (ECS), and *Making the Grade*, the report from the Twentieth Century Fund Task Force. *Action for Excellence*, the work of a panel of business and industrial leaders, echoed the thesis of *A Nation at Risk* and offered similar remedies for regaining our preeminent position in global industrial competition. In clear and unabashed language, the report called for a broadened definition of education to meet the demand for "highly skilled human capital" in the "new era of global competition." It outlined what it called "Basic Skills and Competencies for Productive Employment," which included reading, writing, speaking, listening, math, and science, along with "competencies" in reasoning, economics, computer literacy, and basic employment. "Good" citizenship was listed under basic employment. *Making the Grade* offered a similar message, specifying the components of a new "core" to insure the availability of workers to sustain a "complex and competitive economy."[42] As Joel Spring observed, these reports called for businesses to hook up with the public high school system "to ensure an adequate and docile supply of unskilled labor." However, he lamented, "the resulting distortions of education would condemn many to a life of low wages and limited career advancement."[43]

Beyond these institutional reports, a number of important scholarly works on education were also published in the early 1980s from mainstream, perennialist, and critical perspectives. In each case, these works reflected either primary research in schools, theoretical or philosophical musings, or both. A report from a group of perennialist educators published in 1982, before release of *A Nation at*

Risk, called for a "back to basics" approach to curriculum. Written by Mortimer Adler and titled *The Paideia Proposal*, the report was a philosophical defense of a liberal arts curriculum, and it called for a uniform, "one-track system of schooling" whether or not students were college bound. The report shared a general orientation with *A Nation at Risk* by calling for the need to provide a challenging education for all students along with emphasis on basic skills in reading, writing, mathematics, and science. It also called for a broad education in the liberal arts and a mix of didactic instruction with Socratic questioning and discussion.[44]

Among the works comprising what could be called a "researcher's agenda" were John Goodlad's *A Place Called School*, Ernest L. Boyer's *High School*, and Theodore R. Sizer's *Horace's Compromise*. In contrast to the commission reports, these were research reports with recommendations for school practice, and their findings were both more accurate and more soberly presented. The Boyer study found that one in ten students received an education as fine as any in the world, and that two in ten were condemned to schools that mock the name. The vast majority of students "glide" through with the understanding that they won't demand too much from school, if the school doesn't demand too much from them. More positive than the "at risk" reports, Boyer found that education was slowly improving. He called for a core curriculum, the elimination of tracking, and creation of an interdisciplinary vision with room for electives, in which content would extend beyond the specialties to touch larger societal issues. In *Horace's Compromise*, Sizer's insightful essay of the same name described English teacher Horace Smith's compromise of quality for efficiency, a compromise that many teachers were forced to make.[45]

In the most extensive research study of schools among these works, Goodlad, in *A Place Called School*, found that only 75 percent of class time was devoted to instruction, that the overwhelming proportion of instruction was in the mode of teacher "telling," and that students were rarely involved in making any decisions about their learning. Tests and quizzes stressed the recall of specifics and narrow mechanical skills. Through the practice of tracking or "ability grouping," upper groups received a rich curriculum while lower groups were taught largely through drill and rote. Instruction for mixed groups resembled that of the high groups. Goodlad called for a restructuring of the educational system and attempts to improve pedagogy by gaining active involvement of students, providing more personal attention, and using a greater variety of teaching methods.[46]

On the whole, the report of the National Commission and its sister reports expressed a corporate agenda for schooling. Their publication came on the heels of the back-to-basics movement, and they demanded more traditional schooling for human capital development. This was a new version of education for social efficiency, a turn away from the progressive vision, and another step back from the potential redemptive power of schooling. Moreover, calls for change were more than empty rhetoric. They reflected the anxieties and aspirations of the time and offered an image of a preferred future. In conservative times, the 1890s, the

1950s, and the 1980s, the keynotes have been a focus on the talented with hopes of outperforming the Russians or the Japanese, calls for greater emphasis on basics and the disciplines, and concern about incoherence in the curriculum and a lack of student decorum. In more liberal eras, the 1930s, the 1960s and early 1970s, the focus has shifted to equity for the disadvantaged, a broadening of the function of schools, and greater flexibility and innovation in teaching. From a long-term perspective, competing values such as equity and excellence are often in tension while schools have continued to go about their business largely in traditional ways, changing only slowly over time.[47] In the end, the NCE, the administration's support, and the flurry of reports reinforcing its thesis provided a strong foundation for a prolonged movement toward "excellence" reform.

Critics

Though the intent of the commission may have been to convey the message that "inattention to our schools puts the well-being of the nation at risk," and the goal may have been to awaken schools from encroaching "mediocrity" and tilt them toward excellence, these reports were not well received by many educators.[48] If the nation did have an educational crisis of the parameters described by these reports, it was a crisis manufactured by business and political leaders.

Critics had a variety of reactions. In a measured response to the central premise of *A Nation at Risk*, that our schools were to blame for the nation's decline in international economic competition, historian Lawrence Cremin wrote:

> American economic competitiveness with Japan and other nations is to a considerable degree a function of monetary, trade, and industrial policy and of decisions made by the President and Congress, the Federal Reserve Board, and the Federal Departments of the Treasury, Commerce and Labor. Therefore, to conclude that problems of international competitiveness can be solved by educational reform, especially education reform defined solely as school reform, is not merely utopian and millenialist, it is at best a foolish and at worst a crass effort to direct attention away from those truly responsible for doing something about competitiveness and to lay the burden instead upon schools. It is a device that has been used repeatedly in the history of American education.[49]

Other critics did not accept the premise that our schools were "failing." These critics would debate the data used in the reports and challenge their recommendations. A second group of critics argued that the primary problem was a lack of equal opportunity in the current educational system, and that improvement would come only through more equitable funding and reform of school finance. A third group of critics disagreed with the emphasis on "back to basics" and traditional teaching, and called for developing students as critical thinkers.

Perhaps the most thoughtful analysis, and one of the most scathing critiques written in the immediate aftermath of the reports, was an article by Lawrence C. Stedman and Marshall S. Smith, policy analysts based in Madison, Wisconsin. Stedman and Smith charged that the reports contained "weak arguments, poor data, and simplistic recommendations," and described them as political documents, which made polemical arguments rather than offering a reasoned and well-documented case. On the whole, Stedman and Smith argued, the reports had a pronounced tendency to regard schools rather narrowly as instruments for training human capital and regaining U.S. dominance over world markets. Each of the commission reports supported reckless accusations making a scapegoat of the public education system in the United States. The arguments in the reports were based on inaccurate, incomplete, and misleading data centered around a faulty thesis.[50] For example, Stedman and Smith wrote, the "problem of illiteracy for young adults is very heavily concentrated in the poor and minority (particularly male) population, a fact that goes unmentioned." They charged that international comparisons were muddled, because comparisons of an open system in the United States with selective systems in other nations were inherently flawed. The decline in SAT scores, they wrote, could largely be explained by the larger pool of college-bound seniors taking the test, many from a lower socioeconomic background. They argued that the case for a serious "decline" in our educational system was weak, and that the commissions used

> weak arguments and poor data to make their case. Neither the decline in test scores, the international comparisons, nor the growth of high-tech employment provided a clear rationale for reform. By ignoring their background reports and carelessly handling data, their reports further lost credibility. In particular, the commissions made simplistic recommendations and failed to consider their ramifications.[51]

Another reviewer, Daniel Tanner, argued that the commissions revealed "an appalling lack of understanding of the function of general education in a free society."[52] Others were critical of the commission reports for different reasons. An article in *Fortune* complained that the National Commission failed to address "the systemic cause of U.S. education's inefficiency: monopoly," meaning the virtual monopoly of public education.[53]

Given the makeup of the NCE, perhaps their findings were understandable. The commission was composed primarily of administrators from universities and K–12 schools, along with school board members. Together they accounted for eleven of the commission's eighteen appointed members. The group also included a former governor, a business leader, and one public school teacher. Perhaps the most famous commissioners were David P. Gardner, then president-elect of the University of California, and A. Bartlett Giamatti, president of Yale University and a well-known neoconservative critic of the schools. Notably missing from the commission were scholarly experts in the field of education. It is also important to keep in mind that these were political appointees negotiated with White House participation. Regardless, the makeup of the commission did not include sufficient representation from the various constituencies involved in determining school policy and in the best position to influence classroom teachers.

In the main, the voices of critics made little impact on the American public. Most of the articles written by the most thoughtful and knowledgeable critics appeared in scholarly journals and books that seldom caught the public eye. Moreover, most Americans accepted the general premise of the reports, that the U.S. decline in international economic competition was real, that schools were to blame, and that they needed to be improved. Despite an array of choices in education, the "back to basics" argument and a focus on instituting higher standards and more rigorous accountability measures seemed the reasonable and appropriate solution. However, there were many citizens who questioned the new direction in school reform.

Among responses to the reports were letters from concerned citizens received by the Reagan administration in response to the NCE report. A number of letters expressed support for the report and the new education agenda. One of these, from Chester Finn at Vanderbilt University, expressed hope that the president would give up "rattling on about tuition tax credits and school prayer," and instead, "invite serious educators in to talk about how to improve public schools . . . and *make this your issue!!!!*"[54]

Another letter, from the president of the National Parent Teacher Association (PTA), expressed a mix of support and criticism, stating: "We are glad that the power of the office of the President of the United States is behind the move to provide quality and excellence in the public schools of this nation." However, the letter enclosed a copy of the National PTA's booklet, *Looking in Your School: A Workbook for Improving Public Education*, which stated in its preface that the National PTA believes "most of the charges against public schools are unfounded" and stated, "public education is strong" and "most public schools provide a quality education for our nation's youth." Nonetheless, the authors admitted, this might be a good time to "build upon strong points" and "improve weaknesses" in public education.[55] Other writers were critical of the report and countered that "public schools ARE important, and . . . most of us are doing an excellent job!"[56]

A group of twenty-one House Democrats, all of whom were former teachers and school administrators, wrote to the president expressing concern for the integrity of public education. Those who signed, including Bill Richardson, Geraldine Ferraro, Lindy Boggs, and Carl D. Perkins, wrote: "Unfortunately, you appear to be using this opportunity to exploit the education of our children as a partisan political issue for the 1984 campaign. . . . Your recent misstatements and simplistic generalizations on education issues already threaten to undermine public confidence" in educators and schools.[57]

A notable contrasting position statement regarding the improvement of education came from the directors of the American Orthopsychiatric Association, formed in 1924 and the earliest established professional, educational, interdisciplinary membership organization in the mental health field. The statement is notable because it involved several leading scholars in education, including Seymour Sarason, Maxine Greene, Sara Lawrence Lightfoot, and James P. Comer. In a scant five pages of double-spaced type, "Education at the Crossroads: A Call for Educational Reform That Makes a Difference," the authors wrote that education reform presented an "important opportunity to clarify issues, raise questions, expose myths, and move in new directions. Will we take advantage of this opportunity or will we again forget the past, reinvent unusable wheels and shortchange present and future generations?" The report went on:

> The fact is that much of what is currently being said and recommended today was voiced after the Soviet Union orbited the first Sputnik in 1957. But today's discussion is notable for its near total amnesia about what happened and why over the past twenty-five years. The issues are often posed in simplistic ways. Complicated problems are too often given facile answers . . . all one has to do is reward some good (not defined) teachers, raise expectation levels, adhere to "standards" (also not defined), make certain specified changes in curriculum or organization and all desirable goals will be achieved. However well intentioned, this response will not work any better today than it has in the past.[58]

Unfortunately, this thoughtful counterpoint to the rhetoric of reform went largely unheeded.

Follow-Up Activities

In promoting the reform agenda of the NCE, the education directorate planned a series of regional forums, stretching from June through October and from Maine to California at cities within each of ten DOE education regions. Invitees included high school principals, superintendents, school boards, governors, state and legislative leaders, media, and representatives from the private sector including business, industry, and foundations. The typical pattern for the meetings was to include a keynote address by an administration official on the "Need for Excellence" followed by commission members (four or five) reporting on findings. The presentations would then be followed by responses, comments, panel discussions, and implementation ideas.[59]

A report prepared by the DOE, *The Nation Responds: Recent Efforts to Improve Education*, released in May 1984, detailed the state-by-state response to administration efforts to improve education, along with a chart summarizing activities.

During 1983, the authors noted, "deep public concern about the Nation's future created a tidal wave of school reform which promises to renew education." This follow-up report described a broad array of groups contributing to reform, including professional educators, the nation's governors, corporate leaders, and the public, rallying around "the ethic of excellence." In terms of public response, polls showed that education had "vaulted to the forefront of the national agenda" amid widespread agreement that "the erosion of public education threatens 'our future as a nation.'" Business and corporate leaders in chambers of commerce, statewide Business Roundtables, and local business organizations had also "taken the lead" promoting corporate financial contributions and support for educational reform.

The Nation Responds described a comprehensive school reform effort involving a wide array of initiatives: performance-based pay, incentives for outstanding achievement, career ladders, new teacher preparation programs, revised graduation requirements, increased college admission requirements, longer school days, and new extracurricular and athletic policies. In addition, the authors noted that forty-eight states were considering "new high school graduation requirements"; twenty-one reported "initiatives to improve textbooks and instructional materials"; eight states approved "lengthening the school day, seven lengthening the school year"; eighteen states instituted mandates affecting "time for instruction"; twenty-four were considering master teacher or career ladder programs; thirteen were "considering changes in academic requirements for extracurricular and athletic programs"; and five had "already adopted more rigorous standards."[60] In sum, the report described a nation embracing the new excellence reform agenda and implementing initiatives in a wide array of school categories. Notably, the emphasis was on state and local developments; federal government involvement in implementation activities was not a primary focus.

One of the main ways that the federal government continued to spur reform was through the School Recognition Program. In the years following the NCE report, the DOE held regular events at which specific "excellent" schools were recognized, often with a presidential appearance and certificate. Another way the DOE continued to support reform was through support for corporate and school partnerships in education (PIE). A booklet describing *Partnerships in Education* encouraged businesses to adopt a school, forming unique and wide-ranging partnerships in which businesses would share expertise, tutor students, serve on advisory boards, establish extracurricular clubs in such areas as math, computers, or electronics, establish a scholarship fund, donate surplus materials and equipment, present awards for outstanding achievement, and engage in a wide variety of other activities which would support mastery of basic skills and excellence in education.[61] The program, established on October 13, 1983, was championed by the Reagan administration because it was a voluntary public-private initiative and did not require federal involvement.[62]

The Reagan administration's emphasis on reducing costs and federal control is exemplified by appointment of the Grace Commission, also known as the "President's Private Sector Survey on Cost Control," conducted by business executives and a leading economic forecasting firm. J. Peter Grace submitted a letter to President Reagan on January 12, 1984, that detailed findings of the commission and recommended changes, following the president's directive to "identify and suggest remedies for waste and abuse in the Federal government." The document projected massive deficits ($13 trillion by the year 2000) "if fundamental changes are not made in Federal spending," and listed "2,478 cost-cutting, revenue enhancing recommendations" that could be made without raising taxes, without "weakening America's needed defense build-up," and "without in any way harming necessary social welfare programs." In their review of the DOE, they found an "unnecessarily complicated" organizational structure, "ineffective utilization of human resources," and "fiscal mismanagement." The Grace Commission recommended significant changes and restructuring for the DOE and greater sharing of responsibilities with the states, in consonance with the general direction of administration policies.[63]

Business and Government

Though some observers characterized the business community as "late to react" to calls for "excellence" reform in education, there is strong evidence of continual and steadily growing business involvement with the aim of establishing a corporate agenda for schooling.[64] Business was deeply involved in the educational issues of the time, but not at the forefront of reform efforts. Its leading role would develop gradually over time. A series of reports bearing the imprint of business organizations appeared during the early 1980s. *Action for Excellence*, published in 1983, a product of the ECS, spelled out a business-driven approach to reform. The ECS, made up of prominent business and industrial leaders in collaboration with governors and legislative and administrative leaders and underwritten by large corporations, was created in 1965 as an interstate compact to help state political and education leaders improve the quality of education. Its National Task Force on Education for Economic Growth, chaired by Delaware governor Pierre S. du Pont, was charged with helping with the "transition from national recommendations on education renewal to action and change at the state and local levels." Its report called for "leaders in every sector to join forces to help implement the many good recommendations of recent months."[65]

Another report from a business perspective, titled *America's Competitive Challenge: Need for a National Response*, was released on May 16, 1983. This report, prepared by the Business-Higher Education Forum (BHEF), focused on the subject of U.S. industrial competitiveness. The task force that produced the report was co-chaired by R. Anderson, CEO of Rockwell International and chair of the BHEF, and David Saxon, president of the University of California, reflecting the general makeup of the BHEF. The group met with the president on May 26, 1983, to present its findings. The central conclusion of the report was that Americans must recognize that the nation's social and economic well-being depends on how well our industries compete worldwide, and that all sectors of society share responsibility. The report advocated coordinated effort—by government, business, labor, and education—to build on the nation's industrial strengths.[66] Other reports from the business community echoed these sentiments and called for school improvement if the United States was to remain competitive in the world economy.

The CED

Though partnerships would remain a strong focus, during the 1980s the emphasis began to shift, with a growing number of reports calling for stronger business involvement. An important report from the Research and Policy Committee of the Committee for Economic Development (CED), titled *Investing in Our Children: Business and the Public Schools*, appeared in 1985.[67] The report was the result of a million dollar, three-year research effort detailing a comprehensive strategy for improving education, upgrading curriculum and standards, redeploying educational dollars, and improving the quality of the teacher workforce. This would be the first of a series of reports from the CED that would help to transform the reform movement from excellence to accountability through implementation of a business approach. It received financial support from a number of philanthropic foundations and large corporations including the Pew Freedom Trust, MetLife Foundation, Exxon, Ford, Procter & Gamble, and others.[68]

Investing in Our Children, directed by Denis Doyle of the American Enterprise Institute (AEI), stressed implementation of the four basic principles set forth in *A Nation at Risk* and received strong support from the Reagan administration and then Secretary of Education William Bennett.[69] It was endorsed by a prestigious business group, both major teachers unions, several college presidents, and other prominent educational leaders, and received funding to support seven regional conferences involving teachers, administrators, and other groups involved in education. It stressed "improving schools from the bottom up; i.e. local control and local improvement." Furthermore, it prioritized character education, good work habits, and fluency in English for "economically productive lives." It also called for spending more money on teachers and the disadvantaged at the local and state levels, and involvement of the business community in "helping the schools improve their management practices and their preparation of students for the work place."[70]

The report called for a bottom-up strategy focused "in the individual school, in the classroom, and in the interaction between teacher and student." It called for a curriculum that would combine knowledge and skills with strong work habits. It advocated policies and practices that encourage "self-discipline, reliability, and perseverance."[71] It supported tougher standards and performance measures, emphasis on developing strong academics skills for all students, and redefining vocational education by limiting it only to those programs "specifically designed" to prepare students to enter a field on graduation. The report's findings and recommendations echoed many earlier reports, but added a few notable "imperatives" that would gradually become more prominent, including calls for:

- Greater trust in "the initiative of individual schools."
- "States should refrain from excessive regulation . . . but they should set standards, monitor achievement, and intervene if schools fail to perform."
- "A new coalition to support public schools is needed—one that joins business, labor, and civic leaders with parents, educators, and school boards."
- Greater emphasis on "education research and development and its effective utilization."[72]

Given the corporate investment and participation in this report, and the agenda it put forward, this was a seminal piece, a major building block establishing a foundation for school accountability reform. It urged continued emphasis on business partnerships with individual schools and a much stronger role for business in helping to set educational policy. By the mid-1980s, the Committee for Economic Development, self-described as a "business-academic partnership," was creating research and policy tracts in support of business-friendly policies that would, "contribute to preserving and strengthening our free society, achieving steady economic growth . . . [and] improving the quality of life for all" through the "successful functioning of the free enterprise capitalist system."[73] The CED report on schooling was deeply linked to its *Strategy for U.S. Industrial Competitiveness* from 1984, which included a focus on how to "provide individuals with the skills" to adapt to the labor markets of the future by investing in human capital through education.[74] Moreover, since its origins in 1942, the CED had long been involved in policy research on major economic and social issues with the mission of achieving "economic growth . . . increased productivity . . . and improving the quality of life for all."[75]

The Intergovernmental Advisory Council on Education also developed a report to the president on its 1986 conference held in Washington, DC, titled *Educating the Workforce for the 1990s*. The conference focused on job training and retraining, and it captured much of the mainstream thinking of the time: "Job training begins in kindergarten and should continue as a life-long process . . . for the development of literary and employability skills necessary for an individual's successful participation in the workforce."[76]

The Governors' Summit

Many important elements in the emerging consensus on the direction for reform, including emphasis on preparation of the workforce, were embodied in the 1986 report of the National Governors Association (NGA), *Time for Results: The Governors' 1991 Report on Education* (1986). The report was named the Governors' "1991" Report because "it looks ahead for five years," though needed

improvement will take "longer than that." The NGA met in August 1985, forming seven task forces for the purpose of in-depth examination of crucial problems
in education. The work involved several governors who had emerged as leaders in
school reform, including Lamar Alexander of Tennessee, who chaired the effort,
and Bill Clinton of Arkansas and Tom Kean of New Jersey, who played key roles
as co-chairs. Alexander, in his summary, provided a key rationale for the effort in
simple and direct language: "Better schools mean better jobs. Unless states face
these questions, Americans won't keep our high standard of living. To meet stiff
competition from workers in the rest of the world, we must educate ourselves and
our children as we never have before."

Among their recommendations for state-led reforms were the following:

- Now is the time to work out a fair, affordable career ladder salary system
  that recognizes real differences in function, competence, and performance of
  teachers.
- States should create leadership programs for school leaders.
- Parents should have more choice in the *public* schools their children attend.
- The nation—and the states and school districts—need better report cards
  about results, about what students know and can do.
- School districts and schools that don't make the grade should be declared
  bankrupt, taken over by the state, and reorganized.[77]

In addition, the report called for improved early childhood education, better
use of technology, and more rigorous assessment of what students learn in college.
The report also held out the promise of less regulation if "schools and school districts will produce better results." Several of these themes were to become key elements of the accountability reform movement, notably, some form of career ladder
or salary for performance for teachers; public school choice; accountability for
results; and the threat of closure for schools or districts declared "bankrupt."[78] The
governors' summit was important both in its strong recommendations for state
and local reform and its contribution to the emerging emphasis on accountability.

ALEC

Another group that would have a profound impact on state-by-state education
reform was the American Legislative Exchange Council (ALEC), formed in 1973
by a small group of conservative state legislators who believed in limited government, free market principles, and federalism. Founding members included Paul
Weyrich of the Heritage Foundation. In the mid-1980s, after the release of *A
Nation at Risk*, ALEC got seriously involved in school reform by publishing its
Education Source Book: The State Legislator's Guide to Reform (1985). The *Source Book*
offered more than a dozen model state statutes that would gradually implement a
massive shift of public, tax-generated funds for the support and encouragement of
private education. This was a right-wing plan to spend public money for private

education. From the mid-1980s ALEC and similar groups, such as the State Policy Network and the State Government Affairs Council, would create a "trickle down echo chamber" that would have a major influence on school reform by lobbying for statutory change and succeeding in putting forward the New Right's education agenda in many states.[79]

According to its literature, ALEC was "dedicated to limiting the excessive growth and power of government" and was founded "to support the preservation of individual liberties, basic American values and institutions, productive free enterprise, private property rights, and limited representative government."[80] ALEC is a key state-by-state change wing of a corporate lobbying operation aimed at making American institutions more market driven and corporate friendly.[81] ALEC's *Education Source Book*, funded by the Olin Foundation, included model legislation on parental choice including tuition tax credits and vouchers; alternate certification and merit pay for teachers, with points for "the progress of students"; school discipline; and private school accountability measured by standardized tests. It also included a "Citizenship Education Resolution" containing planks promoting moral and character education and railing against "values clarification."

Since the 1970s, ALEC has established a strong record of success influencing government policy in a number of areas, generally promoting deregulation and use of market mechanisms. In education reform, its work was the lynchpin in the state-by-state work of passing legislation that would move the states toward choice, privatization, standards, testing, and strong accountability funded by corporate money from Charles and David Koch and other wealthy donors.[82]

"Right Wing Extremists"

Terrel H. Bell, in an article that appeared in the March 1986 *Phi Delta Kappan*, detailed his struggles with "right wing extremists" within the Reagan administration during his tenure at the DOE, and implied that after he left, they had taken over. Bell described the six major goals for education that the president had in mind at the start of his tenure: reduce federal spending for education; strengthen state and local control, and dramatically reduce federal responsibility for education; maintain a limited federal role to "enhance" state control; expand choice and "competition for students among schools in a newly created structure patterned after the free market system"; reduce judicial activity in education; and abolish the DOE and replace it with a less prominent agency.[83]

During Bell's tenure, the extreme right advanced far-reaching ideas that went far beyond the president's goals, including ideas challenging the necessity of public education. Critics often quoted Samuel Blumenfeld's classic 1982 right-wing text, *Is Public Education Necessary?*:

> Is public education necessary? The answer is obvious: it was not needed then and it is certainly not needed today. Schools are necessary, but they can be created by free enterprise today as they were before the public school

movement achieved its fraudulent state monopoly in education. Subject education to the same competitive market forces that other goods and services are subjected to, and we shall see far better education at much lower overall cost. Instead of a "crusade against ignorance" to reform the world, we shall have schools capable of performing the limited and practical functions that schools were originally created to perform.[84]

In contrast with this view and Reagan's desire to downgrade the DOE, Bell's purpose was to "preserve the traditional federal role in education." Therefore, bitter debates over the federal role in education "created a rancorous working atmosphere." Nonetheless, Bell was determined to be "an active and assertive Cabinet member" and preserve a strong federal role. Movement conservatives within and outside the administration looked on Reagan's election as the beginning of a revolution, and "every political action of theirs [was] guided by a radical, anti-government dogma." "The true movement conservatives believe that not a dime of federal money should be spent on education ... [and they would abolish] all federal responsibility of any kind." Some on the far right supported an end to state and local support for schooling, based on the rationale that "a school district is a government-operated monopoly ... Let the marketplace supply education to the consumer ... Only the poor should receive any financial assistance" for education. "Let the free enterprise system work to provide education. Let entrepreneurs establish schools and compete for the market. The marketplace will discipline and weed out the inefficient and less effective."[85]

In the latter part of Bell's tenure, the popularity of *A Nation at Risk* meant that attempts to dismantle the DOE and eliminate or greatly reduce the federal role in education met little success. Education reform was now on the national agenda, governors were pressing for reform in state legislatures, and suddenly, the president was spending a good deal of his time speaking from a bully pulpit on education reform. So, Bell wrote, "it was no longer a propitious time for slashing" education.

By 1985, the report and the widespread calls for education reform had led governors and legislators to submit reform proposals to their state legislatures and state boards of education. This flurry of activity led to stiffened graduation requirements in more than forty states; use of standardized tests for graduation or promotion in thirty-three states; and legislation to upgrade teacher certification requirements in nearly half the states. Most states also imposed a longer school day or year and laws requiring demonstrated computer literacy.[86] The excellence movement was beginning to have an impact.

A Change in Leadership

Appointment of William J. Bennett as secretary of education in 1985, after Reagan won reelection with 97.6 percent of the electoral vote, was a turn to the right that "right wing extremists" in the administration were undoubtedly excited about. Bennett, a former philosophy professor, and a "movement conservative," would prove to be one of the most flamboyant and divisive persons ever to serve as secretary of education. Part of a group of neoconservatives who supplied much of the intellectual firepower for the Reagan administration, he became the point man in the Reagan revolution. Bennett, in turn, appointed another polarizing figure, Chester E. Finn, Jr., as assistant secretary for research and improvement, with the purpose of placing greater emphasis on academic achievement as measured by standardized tests. Bennett and Finn cited countless studies as evidence that "dumping money" on public schools had done little to boost results.[87]

Bennett, who previously served as chairman of the National Endowment for the Humanities (NEH), was a well-known figure in conservative circles who promised to move the Reagan agenda in the direction that conservative groups supported. Bennett believed the nation had strong traditions and a legacy that was being sorely neglected at all levels of education.[88] He traveled the country highlighting the poor condition of public schools and the urgency for reform.[89]

Shortly after his appointment, Bennett issued a memo stating his intent to focus his leadership of the nation's schools during Reagan's second term on the "three C's, choice, content, [and] character." He explained that "choice" referred to giving parents greater ability "to choose schools and educational services" through tuition tax credits, vouchers, or other market choices. "Content" referred to "subject matter, teaching and teachers" with emphasis on "solid subject matter" knowledge. "Character" included school discipline, anti-drug initiatives, restoring "a sense of order" in schools, and learning "basic right and wrong." It also included support for school prayer and "a fourth 'C'—'country'." Bennett added that schools must be "places where young Americans learn both the vices and virtues of our nation," becoming "loving critics" who "appreciate the American experiment in democracy" and the forces "that seek to undermine it."[90] Later, Bennett wrote that the Reagan administration had "seized the [education] issue and focused the debate on the issues that really matter: standards, excellence, discipline, values, parental involvement and choice." He also supported prayer and a place for religion in schools and called for eliminating "value-neutrality."[91]

What Works?

The first significant DOE publication under Bennett's leadership was release of the report *What Works: Research About Teaching and Learning*, in January 1986. Intended as a follow up to *A Nation at Risk*, the report emphasized basic themes of standards, excellence, common sense, parental involvement, and choice. Preparing the volume was the first assignment given to Chester E. Finn, Jr., assistant secretary for research and improvement, when he joined the DOE in June 1985. Finn, who had served an apprenticeship as an education policy advisor to President Nixon, had served as an aide to Daniel Patrick Moynihan, and had cofounded the

Educational Excellence Network (EEN) with historian Diane Ravitch, provided intellectual firepower for the Reagan education agenda and was one of the leading intellectual advocates for excellence reform.[92]

What Works focused on standards, discipline, parental involvement, and choice and provided a brief overview of themes from "effective schools" research. The report included sections summarizing research about teaching and learning in the home, the classroom, and the school. The sections on the classroom emphasized instruction focused upon the basics of reading, writing, and mathematics. Other sections supported phonics, direct instruction, and the value of memorization, all conservative and neoconservative whipping posts. Another section emphasized "effective schools" research, discipline, and rigor. Another focused upon "cultural literacy," an approach emphasizing acquisition of knowledge and supporting traditional teaching and learning. In a section dealing specifically with history instruction, the report charged: "Skimpy requirements and declining enrollments in history classes are contributing to a decline in students' knowledge of the past," a theme that echoed charges made by advocates of the revival of traditional history such as Diane Ravitch, and others.[93]

According to a White House staffer's memo, *What Works* was "not on the level of [the] first report."[94] However, it did provide a succinct overview of research findings the administration and DOE considered important and useful in furthering the excellence movement. By late summer 1986, more than 300,000 copies were in circulation.

What Works received a critical response from many educators. At the annual meeting of the American Educational Research Association (AERA) in 1986, William Bennett appeared and sought to promote the booklet before a largely hostile audience. A number of educators charged that its "Research Findings" were simplistic and biased, clearly aimed at supporting the excellence agenda and a conservative restoration in schools. According to one reviewer, its contents represented "an expression of conservative political philosophy and not scholarly consensus about which research findings will improve teaching and learning." The reviewer concluded that it was not a straightforward synthesis and summary of research findings, but a "political document" that "invokes" research in a "modern ritual seeking legitimation of the Reagan administration's policies."[95] Conservative staffers in the DOE also provided rhetorical leadership for the conservative cause in other ways, attacking global education—which they dubbed "globaloney" and a "maudlin one-worldism"—sex education, and other liberal educational programs, and supporting traditional history and "chastity education."[96]

Human Capital Theory

By the middle part of Reagan's second administration, the human capital approach to educating the workforce was also growing more firmly ensconced. An interdepartmental "Working Group on Human Capital" was established, including representatives from the Department of Labor and DOE, with Chester Finn as a member. By the middle 1980s, human capital theory was perhaps the center-piece among the several constructs driving reform, along with back-to-basics, excellence, and the notion that reform and improvement were possible without substantial increases in funding. Human capital theory, popular among many economists and some educators, refers to the stock of competencies, knowledge, and social and personal attributes, including creativity, embodied in the ability to perform labor. Many theorists explicitly connect human capital to education and economic development or use it as justification for government subsidies for education or job training. The concept is traceable to Adam Smith's phrase, "acquired and useful abilities" as "a capital fixed and realized" that contribute to the "improved dexterity of a workman" that makes up part of an individual and society's "fortune."[97] It came into popular use among economists and other social scientists in the 1950s and 1960s, including those in educational administration.[98]

In the Chicago school of economics, human capital is viewed as similar to the "physical means of production," such as factories and machines: one can invest in human capital, and one's output depends in part on the rate of return on the human capital one owns. Thus, human capital is seen as a means of production, and additional investment yields additional output. Therefore, investment in an individual's education and training is similar to business investments in equipment.[99] In contrast to this view, critical theorists have argued that education does not lead to higher wages by increasing human capital but to making workers more compliant and reliable in a corporate setting and to treating children as a commodity. In this view, human capital theory is a misleading framework for educational policy analysis because it ignores the social class hierarchy, the hegemony of an elite, and the cultural reproduction of capitalism.[100]

Evidence on the administration's plans for education can be found in correspondence of the Working Group on Human Capital. A 1985 memo from James Baker to the Working Group on Human Capital revealed discussion of plans for a "voucher for worker development," and a new "workplace education" focused on more traditional approaches and raising standards in K–12 schools.[101] In a lengthy 1986 memo, Chester Finn recommended using the "bully pulpit" to "frame the issues, to shape the national conversation about education . . . emphasizing the *ideas* that drive the education system." Finn listed seven objectives reflecting goals common to the excellence movement: using "effective schools" research; assisting the governors in implementing *Time for Results*; encouraging "character education and instilling traditional values of self-discipline, positive attitudes, the work ethic"; avoiding "values clarification" and other approaches that "confuse students and undermine those standards of right and wrong that students learn at home"; and support for increased "data-gathering, assessment and research."[102]

Several of Finn's points were to become central elements in the emerging accountability movement: the important role of "effective schools" research in framing what would count as knowledge about schooling; a key role for state government in implementing reform; an explicit focus on human capital development as the central rationale for schooling; an implicit return to traditional teaching along with explicit endorsement of character education and emphasis on "traditional" values; and an ever increasing emphasis on standardized testing and measurable results. Also noteworthy was his critique of "values clarification," an approach that embodied the spirit and questioning attitude of 1960s counterculture.

Making It Work

A new report titled *American Education: Making It Work* appeared in April 1988, marking the five-year anniversary of release of *A Nation at Risk* and providing an update on the excellence reform movement. The report described "undeniable progress" in restoring excellence to education and claimed that the nation had "begun the long climb back to reasonable standards." It called for "accountability" and "responsibility for results" throughout the education system as the "linchpin of education reform" and supported parental "choice."[103]

President Reagan's remarks at a presentation ceremony releasing the report highlighted improvements including "career ladders, merit pay," and "a new emphasis on quality and discipline—more homework, more attention to basic skills, more attention to what works, that is, to results." He lamented an earlier time during which "money had been the only measure of progress in education . . . while federal spending went steadily up, test scores fell steadily down, and too many schools accepted the fashions of the day—the fashions of liberal culture—that held traditional standards in scorn." Then Reagan quipped, "It reminds me of what someone once said, that if God had been a liberal, we wouldn't have 10 commandments—just 10 suggestions."[104]

Other administration voices were studying the issues of the day and issuing background papers to staffers. Policy papers by staffers and appointees of the National Advisory Council on Educational Research and Improvement (NACERI) from 1984–1988 read like a primer of conservative perspectives on education. There were policy backgrounders on private-sector initiatives in education reform, on excellence in education, on content, character education, and choice, and on developing a research agenda for privatization. Several papers were critical of common progressive practices in schools and included diatribes against values clarification, bilingual education, and the NEA.[105] For the most part, these background papers underscored and helped spread conservative perspectives on education.

Conclusion

Despite Republican efforts to limit the federal role in education, and cuts in funding to the DOE and the NIE, the trend toward a stronger federal role in education and the nationalization of educational politics continued. The public agreed that schools were in "crisis" and that school reform should be a priority. In one poll conducted in 1987, 64 percent of respondents gave public schools a grade of "C" or lower. Another poll showed that by the late 1980s, the public viewed education as a very important issue facing the federal government, ranked second to the national debt in a list of five key issues including health care, foreign competition, and national defense. This was a dramatic change from the prior decade. Polls conducted in 1987 also indicated strong support for a federal role in finding solutions to problems with the education system. For example, 84 percent believed that the federal government should require state and local school authorities to meet minimum national standards, and 74 percent supported a national testing program for students in the public schools.[106] Debate over the federal role in education policy had shifted—toward a more powerful federal role and in support of stronger accountability measures.

For most of the nation's history, the federal government had little direct role in K–12 schooling. The policy regime for most of that time assumed that schools were best controlled by state and local authorities, and that they were performing adequately. During the 1960s, concerns over civil rights and poverty shattered this placid image, and a new policy regime was established with the ESEA in 1965. As a key part of the 1960s Great Society and war on poverty, the ESEA made a commitment of federal resources to defending civil rights and promoting equality of opportunity through the schools. The common view was that, on the whole, public schools were functioning well, but that the nation had a responsibility to provide equal access and the resources necessary for all students to succeed, hence the need for a federal role in education.[107]

Complacency about the general functioning of public education began to change in the 1970s and 1980s as mounting evidence suggested that student achievement had deteriorated. A *Time* magazine cover story in 1980 reported that "like some vast jury gradually and reluctantly arriving at a verdict, politicians, educators and especially millions of parents have come to believe that the U.S. public schools are in parlous trouble."[108] Release of *A Nation at Risk* and a flurry of reports with similar findings led to heightened concern about the condition of schools and the nation's competitiveness in the international economic arena.

During the Reagan administration, efforts to advance a conservative agenda supporting choice, prayer, and a narrower federal role in schooling brought limited results. But, following the NCE report *A Nation at Risk* and a flood of other reports and studies on education, the administration's efforts led to expanded media coverage of education portraying schools in a largely negative light, thus creating increased momentum for national leadership in school reform. By the middle of the 1980s it had become increasingly clear that the liberal emphasis on equal educational opportunity had been superceded by an alternative reform vision emphasizing excellence and accountability. Embraced by a coalition composed of governors, business leaders, and lobbyists, the new policy regime centered on national leadership, state-by-state application, and reforms focused on raising academic standards.[109] Despite this shift, throughout the 1980s and into the

1990s continued opposition remained, from both liberals and conservatives, to a reformist-oriented federal role in education. Among Democrats, teachers unions and many educators opposed accountability measures, strong standards, testing, and choice. On the other hand, Republicans were heavily influenced by religious conservatives and states' rights advocates who opposed any federal role in schooling.[110]

By the end of the Reagan presidency, the "at risk" thesis was firmly entrenched—most Americans concurred with the general assessment that our schools were in poor condition. The general emphasis on the theme of excellence, emphasized by Bell, while taking a step back from equity goals, illustrated the fact that moderates and conservatives were now framing the issues. The general direction of the Reagan administration federal education policy set during Bell's term was reinforced, deepened, and shifted to the right by Bennett. Moreover, the administration had set a strong foundation for business involvement in school reform, fostering partnerships between business and local school districts, as well as collaboration between business and government in developing education policy with emphasis on development of human capital. The strategy was low cost and gave the appearance of making a major contribution, with a growing reform vision merging around the need for stronger accountability measures.

But, as the nation moved toward fully embracing the corporate reform agenda, persistent and troubling questions were raised. Was the nation really "at risk" in international economic competition? Were the schools really "failing" as critics and so many reports had suggested? Were *all* the schools failing, or did we only have a problem with a certain segment of schools? These questions, raised by a number of thoughtful and pointed critics, haunted the new reform from its inception, and would continue to do so as reform entered a second phase.

Notes

1. William Hayes, *Are We Still a Nation at Risk Two Decades Later?* (Lanham, MD: Scarecrow Education, 2004), 1–6.
2. Republican Party, "Republican Party Platform, July 15, 1980," in John L. Moore, Ed., *Historic Documents of 1980* (Washington, DC: Congressional Quarterly, 1981), 583–584.
3. Ronald Reagan, Inaugural Address, January 20, 1981, APP.
4. Douglas Brinkley, Ed., *The Reagan Diaries, Volume 1* (New York: Harper, 2009), 68.
5. New York State Education Department (NYSED), *Federal Education Policy and the States, 1945–2009: A Brief Synopsis* (Albany: New York State Archives, 2006, revised 2009).
6. Milbrey W. McLaughlin, "States and the New Federalism," *HER* 52, no. 4 (Winter 1982): 4.
7. Maurice R. Berube, *American Presidents and Education* (New York: Greenwood Press, 1991).
8. Lou Cannon, *Reagan* (New York: Putnam, 1982); Terrel H. Bell, *The Thirteenth Man: A Reagan Cabinet Memoir* (New York: Free Press, 1988), 36.
9. Catherine A. Lugg, *For God and Country: Conservatism and American School Policy* (New York: Peter Lang, 1996), 63.
10. Brinkley, *Reagan Diaries*; Heritage Foundation, *Mandate for Leadership* (Washington, DC: Heritage Foundation, 1980).

11. Patrick J. McGuinn, *No Child Left Behind and the Transformation of Federal Education Policy, 1965–2005* (Lawrence: University of Kansas Press, 2006).
12. Bell, *Thirteenth Man*, 110–115.
13. Bell to Craig L. Fuller, July 6, 1981, "National Commission on Excellence in Education" folder, Box 126, Bell Papers; Bell, *Thirteenth Man*, 116.
14. Bell to Craig L. Fuller, July 6, 1981, "National Commission on Excellence in Education" folder, Box 126, Bell Papers.
15. Bell, *Thirteenth Man*, 116.
16. Donald J. Senese to Bell, June 22, 1981, "National Commission on Excellence in Education" folder, Bell Papers.
17. Bell, *Thirteenth Man*, 116–119.
18. David P. Gardner, *Earning My Degree: Memoirs of an American University President* (Berkeley: University of California Press, 2005).
19. National Commission on Excellence in Education, *A Nation at Risk: The Imperative for Educational Reform* (Washington, DC: U.S. Department of Education, 1983).
20. Bell, *Thirteenth Man*, 119.
21. Bell to NCE, November 4, 1981, "President Reagan's Remarks to the Commission on October 9, 1981," "National Commission—At Risk—Correspondence" folder, Box 126, Bell Papers.
22. Brinkley, *Reagan Diaries*, 73.
23. Gardner, *Earning My Degree*, 117.
24. NCE, *Nation at Risk* and *A Nation at Risk: The Full Story* (Washington, DC: DOE, 1984).
25. *Nation at Risk*, Appendix B, 1–2.
26. Gardner, *Earning My Degree*.
27. Glenn T. Seaborg, *Adventures in the Atomic Age: From Watts to Washington* (New York: Farrar, Straus and Giroux, 2001), 265; Gardner, *Earning My Degree*; Bell, *Thirteenth Man*.
28. David Gergin to Ben Elliott, April 25, 1983, Box 2, (073273)-(1), Reagan Papers; Bell, *Thirteenth Man*.
29. Ronald Reagan, "Remarks on Receiving the Final Report of the NCE," April 26, 1983, APP; Bell, *Thirteenth Man*; Gardner, *Earning My Degree*; Glenn T. Seaborg, *A Chemist in the White House: From the Manhattan Project to the End of the Cold War* (Washington, DC: American Chemical Society, 1998); McGuinn, *No Child*, 43.
30. Ibid., *44;* Bell, *Thirteenth Man*.
31. See, for example, "Can the Schools Be Saved?" *NW*, May 9, 1983, 50–58; "The Bold Quest for Quality," *TM*, October 10, 1983, 58–66.
32. NCE, *Nation at Risk*.
33. Ibid., 8–9.
34. Ibid., 18–23.
35. Ibid., 24.
36. Ibid., 25–26.
37. Ibid., 27–28.
38. Berube, *American Presidents*, 113–114.
39. Gardner, *Earning My Degree*.
40. Bell, *Thirteenth Man*, 135–136.
41. Ibid., 136–139.
42. Task Force on Education for Economic Growth, *Action for Excellence: A Comprehensive Plan to Improve Our Nation's Schools* (Washington, DC: ECS, 1983); Twentieth Century Fund Task Force on Federal Elementary and Secondary Education Policy, *Making the Grade* (New York: The Fund, 1983).
43. Joel Spring, "From Study Hall to Hiring Hall," *The Progressive*, April 1984, 30–31.
44. Mortimer J. Adler, *The Paideia Proposal: An Educational Manifesto* (New York: Macmillan, 1982).

45. Ernest L. Boyer, *High School: A Report on Secondary Education in America* (New York: Harper, 1983); Theodore R. Sizer, *Horace's Compromise: The Dilemma of the American High School* (Boston: Houghton Mifflin, 1984); John I. Goodlad, *A Place Called School* (New York: McGraw-Hill, 1984).

46. Goodlad, *A Place Called School.*

47. Thomas James and David Tyack, "Learning from Past Efforts to Reform the High School," *PDK* 64, no. 6 (February 1983): 400–406; Ronald W. Evans, "Corporate Agendas for the Social Studies: A Critique," *SSR* 25, no. 1 (Fall 1985): 17–24.

48. Milton Goldberg, "The Essential Points of *A Nation at Risk*," *EL* (March 1984): 15–16.

49. Lawrence J. Cremin, *Popular Education and Its Discontents* (New York: Harper and Row, 1989), 102–103.

50. Lawrence C. Stedman and Marshall S. Smith, "Weak Arguments, Poor Data, Simplistic Recommendations," in Ronald and Beatrice Gross, Eds., *The Great School Debate* (New York: Simon and Schuster, 1985), 83–105.

51. Ibid., 102.

52. Daniel Tanner, "The American High School at the Crossroads," *EL* (March 1984), 4–13; Andrew Hacker, "The Schools Flunk Out," *NYR*, April 12, 1984, 35–40.

53. Peter Brimelow, "What to Do about America's Schools," *FT*, September 19, 1983, 60–64.

54. Chester Finn to Ed Harper, May 12, 1983, #139131PD, Box 4, Reagan Papers; enclosure, Chester E. Finn, "The Drive Toward Excellence: Moving Toward a Public Consensus," *CHG*, April 1983.

55. Mrs. A.T. Leveridge, Jr., to the President, May 13, 1983, #139361, Box 4, Reagan Papers.

56. Candace Johnson to Ronald Reagan, May 23, 1984, #229320, Box 13, Reagan Papers.

57. House Democrats to Ronald Reagan, June 15, 1983, #146028, Box 5, Reagan Papers.

58. "Education at the Crossroads: A Call for Educational Reform That Makes a Difference," attachment, Chester Pierce to Ronald Reagan, March 12, 1984, #204073, Box 11, Reagan Papers.

59. Bell to Craig L. Fuller, May 26, 1983, #147396, Box 5, Reagan Papers.

60. DOE, *The Nation Responds: Recent Efforts to Improve Education* (Washington, DC: DOE, 1984).

61. Partnerships in Education booklet, #166960, Box 7, Reagan Papers.

62. Ronald Reagan to the Heads of Executive Departments and Agencies, October 13, 1983, and John Cogan to Richard Darman, October 13, 1983, #166960, Box 7, Reagan Papers.

63. J. Peter Grace, *War on Waste: The President's Private Sector Survey on Cost Control* (New York: Macmillan, 1984), v–x, 432–434.

64. Gardner, *Earning My Degree*, 135.

65. "National Task Force on Education for Economic Growth 1984 Economic Plan," attachment, Tuesday, January 31, 1984, 3:30 Meeting with Susan Adler, #201860, Box 11, Reagan Papers; ECS, "Education for Economic Growth," Dupont and Hunt, p. 46, Box 11b, Reagan Papers.

66. Jay Keyworth to the President, May 16, 1983, #143533, Box 5, Reagan Papers; BHEF, *America's Competitive Challenge: The Need for a National Response* (Washington, DC: BHEF, 1983).

67. CED, *Investing in Our Children: Business and the Public Schools* (New York: CED, 1985).

68. Ibid., 105.

69. Owen B. Butler to Ronald Reagan, August 30, 1985, #358398, Box 18, Reagan Papers.

70. Owen B. Butler to Donald T. Regan, October 3, 1985, #358398, Box 18, Reagan Papers.

71. CED, *Investing in Children*, 5–7.

72. Ibid., 3.

73. CED, *Strategy for U.S. Industrial Competitiveness* (New York: CED, 1984), 144.

74. Ibid., 7.
75. CED, "About CED," www.ced.org/about/about-ced.
76. Intergovernmental Advisory Council on Education, "Educating the Workforce of the 1990s," Washington, DC, March 6–7, 1986, #539991, Box 23, Reagan Papers.
77. NGA, *Time for Results: The Governors' 1991 Report on Education* (Washington, DC: NGA, 1986), 2–3.
78. Ibid.
79. Nanette Barrett, *Education Source Book: The State Legislators' Guide for Reform* (Washington, DC: ALEC, 1985). See Sandra Martin, *The New Right's Education Agenda for the States: A Legislator's Briefing Book* (Washington, DC: National Center for Policy Alternative, 1985); Julie Underwood and Julie F. Mead, "A Smart ALEC Threatens Public Education," *EW*, February 29, 2012; Lee Fang, *The Machine: A Field Guide to the Resurgent Right* (New York: New Press, 2013), 206.
80. Barrett, *Education Source Book*, 80.
81. Fang, *The Machine*, 212–213.
82. Ibid.
83. Terrel H. Bell, "Education Policy Development in the Reagan Administration," *PDK*, March 1986, 35, attached to Alfred H. Kingon to the President, March 13, 1986, #366353, Box 19, Reagan Papers.
84. Samuel L. Blumenfeld, *Is Public Education Necessary?* (Boise, Idaho: Paradigm, 1981), quoted in Bell, "Education Policy," 35.
85. Bell, "Education Policy," 36, 38.
86. Hayes, *Still at Risk*, 19.
87. Dave Roediger, "Assessment: The Secretary of Education's New Clothes," *MR* (May 1988).
88. William J. Bennett, *To Reclaim a Legacy: A Report on the Humanities in Higher Education* (Washington, DC: NEH, 1984).
89. McGuinn, *No Child*, 45.
90. William J. Bennett to Donald T. Regan, Memo re: "Education in the Second Term," February 28, 1985, Box 17, Reagan Papers.
91. William J. Bennett to Alfred H. Kingon, December 23, 1985, #364113, Box 19, Reagan Papers.
92. Diane Ravitch and Gil Sewall to Network Members, September 1986, "Educational Excellence Network" folder, Box 19, Hoover ESC; Chester E. Finn, Jr., to Diane Ravitch, November 22, 1988, "Diane Ravitch" folder, Box 120, Finn Papers.
93. DOE, *What Works: Research About Teaching and Learning* (Washington, DC: DOE, 1986), 55.
94. Jean to Fred, note attached to Alfred H. Kingon to Fred Ryan, January 13, 1986, #364143, Box 19, Reagan Papers.
95. Gene V. Glass, "What Works: Politics and Research," *ER* (April 1987), 5, 9; Marshall S. Smith, "Book Review: What Works Works!" *ER* (April 1986), 29; Frederick J. Ryan, Jr., to Nancy Risque, May 7, 1987, #490323, Box 22, Reagan Papers; DOE, *Schools That Work: Educating Disadvantaged Children*, What Works [Series] (Washington, DC: DOE, 1987).
96. Chester Finn, Jr., and Gary Bauer, "Among the Educationaloids: Globaloney," *AS*, May 1986, 26. See Alfred H. Kingon to the President, April 23, 1986, #390058, Box 19, Reagan Papers.
97. Adam Smith, *An Inquiry into the Nature and Causes of the Wealth of Nations* (London: Routledge, 1900, original 1776).
98. Jacob Mincer, "Investment in Human Capital and Personal Income Distribution," *JPE* 66, no. 4 (August 1958): 281–302; Gary S. Becker, *Human Capital: A Theoretical and Empirical Analysis, with Special Reference to Education* (New York: National Bureau of Economic Research, 1964).
99. Becker, *Human Capital*.

100. Samuel Bowles and Herbert Gintis, "The Problem with Human Capital Theory—A Marxian Critique, *AER* 65 (2): 74–82.
101. James Baker to Economic Policy Council, November 15, 1985, "Human Capital Working Group" folder, Box 38, Finn Papers.
102. Chester E. Finn, Jr., to Roger Semerad, October 28, 1986, #603991, Box 25, Reagan Papers; see also Working Group on Human Capital, Boxes 38 and 95, Finn Papers.
103. "White House Talking Points," April 26, 1988, #561224, Box 24, Reagan Papers.
104. Clark Judge to the President, April 25, 1988, #561224, Box 24, Reagan Papers.
105. "Published and Unpublished Articles and Research Papers, 1982–1990," Box 1 and 2, NACERI.
106. Poll data from Roper poll conducted February 14–28, 1987, and Gallup polls conducted April 8–10 and April 10–13, 1987, reported in McGuinn, *No Child*, 47.
107. "Elementary and Secondary Education Act of 1965" folder, Box 26, Cater Files.
108. McGuinn, *No Child*, 49.
109. McGuinn, *No Child*.
110. Ibid.

3

STRUGGLE FOR THE SOCIAL STUDIES CURRICULUM

While the excellence movement was taking root and gaining a head of steam toward what would became a full-blown standards and testing machine, it seemed for a time at least that the social studies field was somehow apart. Yet there were important influences on social studies from the growing reform movement. The back-to-basics movement exerted influence on the literature in social studies and undoubtedly impacted some teachers. Moreover, the tone of the emerging excellence reform movement influenced reports and rhetoric on social studies. The conservative restoration and activities by the Reagan administration led to debate over conservative initiatives, and support for an explicitly "anti-social studies" movement aimed at the revival and restoration of traditional history. From the late 1970s, in most cases, the conservative agenda for schooling was framing debate on the direction of the social studies curriculum in schools.

Nonetheless, the ongoing struggle among competing camps for control of social studies continued throughout the 1980s and 1990s. By the mid- to late 1980s the decline of issues-oriented social studies was apparent, and a renewed interest in traditional history was the trend in vogue. Progressivism in schools appeared to be all but dead, and dialogue on education continued in the framework of a national "crisis." The power brokers who had manufactured a crisis in the early 1980s continued to find the rhetoric of "crisis" a useful way to promote their agenda, turning the clock back on progressive reforms and focusing ever greater attention on measures of educational success, calling for higher performance standards, testing, further development of high-tech innovations, and emphasis on literacy, mathematics, and science.

Not too surprisingly, given the growing national fixation on education, two books calling for higher standards became best sellers. By the early 1990s, heated debate centered upon multiculturalism. Only a few years later, proposed history guidelines would become the focus of a national furor. Meanwhile, latter-day progressives continued to develop meaningful approaches to social studies. Critical theorists, advocating an updated version of education for social reconstruction, gained increasing influence among scholars and researchers. In spite of these trends and growth in rhetoric over education, teachers and schools continued to teach students much as they had in previous years.

Dialogues of the 1980s

The educational dialogues of the late 1980s centered on continuation of themes from the conservative restoration, reaction to the leftward tilt of academia, and the growing trend toward what conservatives called "political correctness." Books on education seldom become best sellers. For two books in the same year to achieve such status was without precedent. The public success of Allan Bloom's *The Closing of the American Mind* and E.D. Hirsch's *Cultural Literacy: What Every American Needs to Know* in 1987 signaled a strong and continuing public interest in education, a prolongation of the focus on excellence, and return to traditional forms of education. Bloom's thesis was that higher education was in the process of sacrificing the monuments of a great civilization on the altar of equality. He argued that higher education, stressing openness, relativism, and seeking to overcome ethnocentrism, aimed to indoctrinate citizens who would support a democratic regime. He lamented the decline of philosophy and liberal education and called for a return to a classical Western canon and traditional history. Bloom justified his recommendations with the suggestion of Western superiority. All of this was presented amid a rhetoric of alarm, lamenting the decline of higher education in the United States, paralleling charges of deterioration in public education and the teaching of history.[1]

Cultural Literacy

In *Cultural Literacy*, E.D. Hirsch made similar charges of decline but focused on public schools. The thesis of Hirsch's book was stated in its first sentence, "To be culturally literate is to possess the basic information needed to thrive in the modern world." He asserted that cultural literacy was the only means of opportunity for disadvantaged children. He argued that children from poor and illiterate homes too often remained poor and illiterate because of a "fragmented curriculum based on faulty educational theories." He called for a break with some of the theories and practices advocated by education professors and school administrators "over the past fifty years."[2]

These theories stemmed ultimately, he wrote, from Jean Jacques Rousseau, who believed that "we should encourage the natural development of young children . . . without regard to the specific content of education." Rousseau's ideas powerfully influenced John Dewey, who emphasized "the problems of experience, not the piling up of information." Hirsch argued that Dewey "too hastily rejected 'the piling up of information.'" Only through "piling up specific, communally shared information can children learn to participate in complex cooperative activities with other members of their community."[3] Hirsch called for a countervailing theory of education that stressed the importance of learning specific information. "In an anthropological perspective," he wrote, "the basic goal of education in a human community is acculturation, the transmission to children of the specific information shared by the adults of the group or polis."[4]

The book was an expansion of ideas contained in an article titled, "Cultural Literacy," which appeared in *The American Scholar* in 1983. Hirsch wrote in his acknowledgments that "the single greatest impetus" for writing the book had come from Diane Ravitch. He also cited Ravitch and Chester E. Finn, then assistant secretary of education for educational research in the DOE, for their comments on the manuscript, and Kieran Egan for helping with the larger *Dictionary of Cultural Literacy*, which expanded an initial listing of "What Literate Americans Know."[5]

Hirsch drew criticism from a number of scholars focused on issues of elitism, and on trivialization of learning. Fred M. Newmann argued that the concept of cultural literacy contained a "bewildering ambiguity" and shortcomings in rationale. Moreover, he wrote, "It is extraordinarily difficult—virtually impossible I believe—to begin with a list of unrelated items of information and then, *after* the fragments have been selected, weave them into a meaningful message." He argued that it would produce "vapid, boring reading" and preclude the in-depth study necessary to increase the probability of long-term retention.[6]

Stephen J. Thornton argued that Hirsch's conclusions did not follow from the evidence he presented. Thornton pointed out that by fourth grade, "the overwhelming emphasis of school curricula is on the transmission of information" and that it was "the deadweight of covering information" that appeared to bore and alienate so many students. He argued that a mere listing of what ought to be taught omitted attention to the crucial questions of how and why students learn, and he suggested that motivation to learn entailed the learner seeing some relevance in the content.[7]

Hirsch shared, with Ravitch, Finn, Bennett, and other neoconservatives, an interpretation of educational history and of the failings of schools, as well as a general perspective on the necessary remedy. In regard to the social studies curriculum, he offered a description of social studies gone astray. Subjects such as history and civics, which were intended to transmit traditions and duties, had declined, he argued, into a process-oriented "social studies" aimed at developing skills for living, "learning-by-doing," and "fragmentation"—and were largely devoid of content. This was the same general argument made by Ravitch, castigating social studies as the scapegoat for the decline of historical literacy. Like Ravitch, Hirsch offered a superficial and poorly drawn interpretation driven by ideology rather than hard evidence.

Despite critics, these books captured the public imagination, at least for a time. That they became so popular was a reflection of a conservative era, a time during which appeals to tradition and a return to basics continued to generate great support. As we shall see, while the conservative restoration and a growing consensus around improving the schools through traditional content and methods may have been the main current in educational reform, it was not the only one.

Critical Pedagogy

The educational dialogues of the 1980s and 1990s contained multiple voices, from many different perspectives. One of the main camps in the long turf battles over the curriculum was the meliorist or social reconstructionist group. In the latter one-third of the twentieth century, social reconstructionism was itself transcended by critical perspectives largely imported from Europe but sharing a similar orientation. The growing influence of this trend led, in part, to charges of "political correctness." These charges were a reaction to two trends: the increasing influence of critical theory in academia and the growing mandate for multicultural education. Though they were ostensibly separate movements, the two trends had much in common and shared a similar orientation toward using education as a means for social transformation.

Critical theorists in education were far from a monolithic group and included scholars specializing in reconceptualist curricular theory, cultural studies, feminist scholarship and other forms. Critical scholarship in the United States was strongly influenced by European theoretical perspectives including the critical theorists of the Frankfurt School, neo-Marxist social theory, structuralism, and more recent developments in postmodernism and poststructuralism. Many observers saw in the growing influence of critical theory a delayed impact of the civil rights and human potential movements of the 1960s. Campus radicals had grown up and now held tenured positions at major universities.[8]

In the United States, critical pedagogy retained a strong link to the works of Dewey and forged direct links to social reconstructionist theory. Frequently, critical pedagogues drew on the works of European theorists including Gadamer, Gramsci, Habermas, Foucault, and Derrida. Their agenda was similar in ultimate goals to the social reconstructionists. However, their work seemed to focus on building a community of scholars critical of mainstream educational practice, conversant in critical theory, cognizant of the systemic and interwoven nature of educational, political, and social systems, and committed to resisting the dominant interests that control the bulk of wealth and power in America and whose interests the schools tend to serve.

Among the earliest and most influential was the Brazilian educational theorist Paulo Freire. In his seminal work, *Pedagogy of the Oppressed*, Freire drew a distinction between traditional forms of education built around the banking theory, in which knowledge is bestowed upon ignorant students by knowledgeable teachers, mirroring the oppression of capitalist society, and problem-posing education, which breaks this hierarchical pattern. "Education," he wrote, "is suffering from narration sickness." The narration at the heart of traditional educational practices "turns students into 'containers,' into 'receptacles' to be 'filled' by the teacher. . . ." Education then becomes "an act of depositing, in which the students are the depositories and the teacher is the depositor. Instead of communicating, the teacher issues communiqués and makes deposits which the students patiently receive, memorize, and repeat." Banking education maintains this dehumanizing hold "through . . . attitudes and practices, which mirror oppressive society as a whole." Problem-posing education, on the other hand, creates a dialogue of teacher-student with student-teacher through which both teacher and student teach and learn simultaneously. It is an approach through which, "They become jointly responsible for a process in which all grow." This was not simple literacy but a process of liberation or "conscientization" that would provide students with the means to challenge an oppressive social order—to transform oppressive social relations.[9]

Several other important works contributed to the growth of critical perspectives on education. One of the most influential was *Schooling in Capitalist America* by Samuel Bowles and Herbert Gintis, published in 1976. Bowles and Gintis asserted that far from being the great equalizer, public schooling fostered and reproduced social class distinctions. They introduced the terms "reproduction" and "correspondence theory" to a new generation of educators. The central propositions of the book included, first, the idea that schools prepare students for adult work roles by socializing them to function in the hierarchical structure of the modern corporation or institution by replicating the environment of the workplace. Second, that parental class and economic status are passed on by means of unequal educational opportunity. And, third, that the evolution of schooling in America was best explained by a series of class conflicts arising through the social transformation of work. They argued, in essence:

> The educational system serves—through the correspondence of its social relations with those of economic life—to reproduce economic inequality and to distort personal development, thus under corporate capitalism, the objectives of liberal educational reform are contradictory: it is precisely because of its role as producer of an alienated and stratified labor force that the educational system has developed its repressive and unequal structure.[10]

Bowles and Gintis had a profound influence on the development of critical pedagogy. To varying degrees, critical pedagogues shared an affinity for reproduction and correspondence theories, often extending them to hold that not only school structures but their hidden and overt curricula tend to mirror and reproduce the dominant social hierarchy, imposing different kinds of knowledge on different groups in accordance with their place in a stratified social order. Through intellectual and moral influence as well as direct coercion, dominant groups (the economic, political, and cultural elite) maintain the hegemony of the dominant culture and retain power over marginalized groups (women, the poor, persons of color). Somewhat more recently, resistance theorists accepted most of the insights of reproduction theory, but were more optimistic regarding the potential for education to challenge dominant interests. From this perspective, schools can best be understood as "contested terrain" and school curricula as "complex discourse that simultaneously serves the interests of domination while also providing possibilities for opposition and emancipations."[11]

Another path-breaking work was *Ideology and Curriculum* by Michael Apple, published in 1979. Among the first to establish a link between the curriculum and its implicit political ideology, Apple noted that not only the school as an institution but the curriculum itself served as a means of reproducing the social, cultural, and economic patterns of society. Thus, in his view, schools were engaged in preserving and distributing the symbolic property of cultural capital. He argued that we needed a better understanding of, "'Why and how particular aspects of the collective culture are presented in school as objective, factual knowledge.' How, concretely, may official knowledge represent ideological configurations of the dominant interests in a society? How do schools legitimate these limited and partial standards of knowing as unquestioned truths?"[12] Apple's book was significant both for its insights and for the fact that it marked the beginning of an emerging discourse among educational theorists, a critical and thoughtful discourse reminiscent of exchanges among leading educators in the journal *Social Frontier* during the 1930s. Other major contributors to the discourse included William F. Pinar, Henry Giroux, Jean Anyon, Peter McLaren, Carmen Luke, Elizabeth Ellsworth, and others.

In social studies, critical theory made a brief appearance in *Social Education* in a 1985 special issue, titled "The New Criticism: Alternative Views of Social Education." The issue included a number of articles by advocates of a critical stance, including Henry Giroux's "Teachers as Transformative Intellectuals" and contributions from Michael W. Apple, William B. Stanley, Cleo Cherryholmes, Jack L. Nelson, and others.[13] At the time, it seemed the dawn of a new period in which critical perspectives might play a prominent role in social studies theory and practice. By the mid-1990s critical perspectives were a common feature of *Theory and Research in Social Education*, but they made only infrequent forays into practitioner-oriented journals. Elsewhere, Bill Bigelow contributed to a growing understanding of what a critical approach might look like in schools through articles in *Rethinking Schools* and other publications. Amy Gutman's *Democratic Education* gave voice to a thoughtful approach to schooling built around a democratic theory of education. Despite increasing rhetorical support, some observers wondered whether critical theory was having much real impact in schools.[14]

Given its political stance, critical theory was not without opponents. Many scholars asserted that it was unrealistic, naïve, or unreasonable to expect schools and teachers to act as agents of social transformation. The majority of teachers and school administrators were mainstream in their thinking and reflected the general populace. Others charged that social reconstructionism had the potential to lead toward indoctrination of students, toward proselytizing and propaganda. In addition, a number of feminist scholars, who shared a critical orientation, accused critical theorists of being gender blind and of ignoring feminist scholarship. They accused critical pedagogues of framing their work within epistemologies that are essentially masculinist and patriarchal, and of privileging logic and rationality at the expense of emotional, intuitive, and moral ways of knowing.

Multicultural Education

Another important influence on educational dialogue during the 1980s and the 1990s came in the continuing discourse over multicultural education. An outgrowth of the civil rights movement, multicultural education became a major focus in universities and schools of teacher education, as well as in public schools. The multicultural education of the late twentieth century represented the evolution of a long trend reflecting the civil rights movement: from "intercultural education" in the World War II era, to early multicultural education in the 1960s and 1970s, to the 1990s *Handbook of Research on Multicultural Education*, and national concern over political correctness, multiculturalism, and the debate over the place of multiculturalism and Western culture in the curriculum.[15] There were new players in the curriculum game. Groups that had long been excluded were now among the power brokers struggling over the curriculum.

Articles on multiculturalism had gained space in *Social Education* since the late 1960s. NCSS endorsed a multicultural focus in the curriculum with publication of its "Curriculum Guidelines for Multicultural Education" in 1976, calling for a strong component of ethnic studies in the curriculum from preschool to twelfth grade and beyond. By the late 1980s and early 1990s, controversy over multiculturalism had reached new heights. On one side were long-term advocates of a multicultural curriculum and revised canon, scholars in education and ethnic studies and their supporters, led by James A. Banks, Henry Louis Gates, Cornel West, Molefi K. Asante, Gloria Ladson Billings, and others. On the other side were neoconservative scholars including Diane Ravitch, Arthur M. Schlesinger, William J. Bennett, Thomas Sowell, and others who wanted universities and schools to include multicultural materials but to continue emphasis on the common culture.

Supporters of multicultural education asserted that the perspectives of persons of color, women, and the working class had been excluded from the study of history, literature, and the humanities, leading students to conclude that civilization was the product of European males and their culture. They maintained that mainstream ignorance of multicultural groups' contributions and historic oppression intensified intolerance and contributed to bigotry. Multicultural education was based on the premise that the purposeful inclusion of the stories, literature, and historical perspectives of diverse groups in school curricula and textbooks could help students attain a broader perspective and contribute to creation of a more equitable society. According to James Banks, multicultural education "helps students transcend their cultural boundaries and acquire the knowledge, attitudes, and skills needed to engage in public discourse with people who differ from themselves and to participate in the creation of a civic culture."[16]

Critics of multicultural education, on the other hand, argued that multicultural education was divisive because it de-emphasized our common heritage and culture and placed undue emphasis on conflicts and differences related to race, class, and gender. Critics argued that it would "Balkanize" the nation, result in shallow exposure to multicultural content, and lead to an unfortunate de-emphasis on significant content related to the development of Western culture and general cultural literacy. Moreover, some critics charged that multiculturalism often served as cover for the indoctrination of student to leftist political ideologies. According to one critic, "the call for diversity in education too often . . . is a red herring for a radical agenda."[17]

Educational historian Diane Ravitch, who would become one of the leading intellectual architects of school reform, authored a number of articles critical of multiculturalists. She charged that in the name of multiculturalism, ethnocentric "particularists" were undermining the national culture and sacrificing "unum" in the name of "pluribus." Preferring the image of a "mosaic" of ethnic groups, Ravitch maintained that particularists neglected "the bonds of mutuality" among groups and "encourage children to seek their primary identity in the cultures and homelands of their ancestors." She argued that the United States has a "common culture that is multicultural," and that this insight was behind the evolution of a "wisely and intelligently designed . . . multicultural curriculum." Ravitch called for an education that "promotes pluralism, not particularism," and she offered the California History-Social Science Framework as a model emphasizing the common culture and "a nation that unites as one people the descendants of many cultures, races, religions, and ethnic groups." She offered the New York State report, "A Curriculum of Inclusion," as a "Europhobic" counterexample. This example of the "particularist" approach, she wrote, "teaches children to see history as a story of victims and oppressors, and it endorses the principle of collective guilt." This approach, she lamented, "encourages a sense of rage and victimization" and "rekindles ancient hatreds in the present." Behind "A Curriculum of Inclusion," she charged, lay a dubious pedagogical theory that changes in the curriculum would "raise the self-esteem" of children of color and enhance their academic performance. Ravitch questioned whether history should be used as a mechanism for instilling self-esteem and filiopietism (i.e., excessive reverence for one's ancestors).[18] On the other hand, Ravitch's assertion that multiculturalism was filiopietistic was especially ironic, given her support for what many critics labeled a white self-esteem curriculum.[19] During the New York controversy over "A Curriculum of Inclusion," Ravitch was "denounced in scurrilous terms at the meeting of the Black and Hispanic Legislative Caucus" as "racist," a charge to which she took offense.[20]

In his book, *The Disuniting of America*, historian Arthur M. Schlesinger, Jr., sounded many similar themes. Schlesinger charged that "a cult of ethnicity" had arisen to attack the common American identity, replacing the goals of integration and assimilation with fragmentation and separatism, the end result being "resegregation, and tribalization of American life." Multiculturalists, he wrote, viewed European civilization as the root of all evil, as inherently racist, sexist, classist, hegemonic, and irredeemably oppressive. Like Ravitch, he called for a "balance between *unum* and *pluribus*" and a return to teaching history "for its own sake—as part of the intellectual equipment of civilized persons—and not to degrade history by allowing its contents to be dictated by pressure groups." "Above all," he went on, "history can give a sense of national identity," and can teach us that our values "are worth living by and worth dying for." Schlesinger asserted that history had given us values, "anchored in our national experience, in our great national documents, in our national heroes, in our folkways, traditions, and standards. . . . Here individuals of all nations are melted into a new race of men."[21]

Both Schlesinger and Ravitch inspired a great deal of criticism from advocates of multiculturalism, none more pointed than the comments of Gloria Ladson-Billings, who suggested that the crux of the debate centered on Schlesinger's assertion that we were once "united" as a nation. She suggested that we were far from united, and that disunion had a great deal to do with economics and opportunity. She criticized Schlesinger for clouding his arguments with personal attacks, distortions, decontextualizations, and defamation. She wrote that Schlesinger wanted to see all Americans unified around a set of ideals, but failed to recognize that the underlying cause of disunity could be found in "the widening economic gap between blacks and whites." She noted that Schlesinger, like Ravitch, all but ignored the long history of scholarship and research on multiculturalism, and she charged that Schlesinger's attack on multiculturalism fed into "a growing climate of intolerance."[22]

There were many similar exchanges during the peak years of debate over multiculturalism between advocates and defenders of the multicultural education movement. By the late 1980s, the popular press had gotten wind of developments in both critical theory and multiculturalism, and conservative opponents had made an issue of political correctness on campus, stemming partly from critical theory. *Time* and *Newsweek* ran cover stories, of which an article titled "Thought Police" was representative. Soon, a slew of magazine articles and books made a cottage industry out of the growing controversy. Dinesh D'Souza's *Illiberal Education* charged that revolutionaries and nihilists in the form of critical theorists, deconstructionists, and multiculturalists were transforming college campuses into institutions of politically correct conformity, debunking hierarchical and Eurocentric institutions, and turning their backs on the need for a broad liberal education. Roger Kimball in *Tenured Radicals* charged that the same group of scholars, some of whom had been activists during the upheavals of the 1960s, were now in positions of power as tenured professors and were transforming universities into bastions of radical activism and critical theory.

While there may have been some truth to the charges—universities long had a liberal atmosphere—the vast majority of educators in academia were relatively untouched by the new criticism, which had achieved its greatest gains in literary criticism. Though critical theory was wielding some influence in other fields, it was far from dominant in most. On the other hand, some aspect of the debate over multiculturalism touched almost everyone. *Debating P.C.*, and other similar collections, chronicled the arguments of multiculturalists and their traditionalist opponents. A few leading scholars who had come under attack in the P.C. wars had their say in Mark Edmundson's *Wild Orchids and Trotsky*. Debates raged over course requirements and revisions on campuses across the nation, public battles before galleries. And there were debates over curriculum reform and textbook adoptions in New York, California, and a host of other states. Unfortunately, during much of the 1980s and 1990s educators were busy shouting past each other from entrenched camps, much like the camps in the protracted social studies wars.[23]

Social Studies Adrift

During the early years of the conservative restoration, the back-to-basics movement, and the business-driven push for excellence, social studies appeared to be a field adrift. The era of the new social studies had come to a close, yet no similarly powerful movement for reform had taken its place. Moreover, the failure of the new and newer social studies to have the anticipated impact on classrooms led to a great deal of hand-wringing. By the late 1970s, it seemed that social studies was a field in search of itself. The journal *Social Education* and a number of other publications reflected this soul searching. From the late 1960s, it seemed that *Social Education* had become something of a potpourri, a journal dominated by special issues with a focus on what seemed to at least one observer, "one damn thing after another." First it was an issue on Russia, then Japan, then back-to-basics, and so on, seemingly without end. Even though there were many thoughtful articles and special issues published, the journal of the late 1970s and early 1980s seemed to lack conceptual focus. Social studies, it seemed, could be whatever one wanted it to be.

Among the emerging trends were global studies, technology, multiculturalism, and gender studies. Of these, the focus on computer applications to the teaching of social studies was the only development that was really new. The major camps in the turf wars were still represented, though acrimonious public debate over the field had slipped beneath the surface for a time, hidden from public view. Profound definitional dilemmas, depicted variously as conflicting camps or alternative curricular schemes, continued to haunt the field, though the battles over the various alternatives seemed to occur mainly within the profession, signaling a profound lack of unity and direction among social studies professionals.

Methods of teaching received continued attention, though that attention was relatively low key. Much of the literature continued to focus on inquiry and reflective approaches to teaching including the use of role-playing and simulation games. While work continued on helping teachers develop innovative and inter-active approaches to teaching, the back-to-basics movement was definitely tilted in the opposite direction and served to reinforce the most traditional approaches, including textbook, lecture, seatwork, and recitation.

The major camps in the struggle over social studies were, of course, still pres-ent. The civics/citizenship education camp received a major boost from the NCE reports' focus on education for social efficiency. Civics and education for social efficiency seemed to find new life from the emerging consensus, and there were many articles addressing education for citizenship, written from a variety of perspectives.

The issues-centered, meliorist alternative seemed at low ebb in the early 1980s, and support for issues-centered approaches to social studies appeared to be on the wane. The literature evidenced declining attention to issues-centered approaches, the Problems of Democracy (POD) course had disappeared, and the Public Issues Series was out of print. Moreover, no new theorist had emerged to champion the cause. The leading progressive voices were gone and others were graying. An emerging critical perspective on social studies with a natural affinity for issues-oriented approaches seemed somewhat esoteric, distanced from schools.[24] The POD course did not so much die but was simply left behind, first in a rush toward the social sciences, then in the mini-course explosion and the conserva-tive restoration. Moreover, the long struggle by educational conservatives against liberal and progressive visions of schooling undoubtedly took its toll. During the Reagan years, critics and rebels—words that aptly described most advocates of the issues-centered tradition—were cast as outsiders, marginalized during a pendu-lum swing to the right, toward more traditionalist forms of teaching and learning. The conservative restoration, in the wake of the new and newer social studies, also brought a revival of academic freedom concerns. *Social Education* ran a special issue on "The Growing Controversy Over Book Censorship" in 1982, and another on "Academic Freedom, Censorship, and the Social Studies" in 1987. To its credit, the organization consistently supported academic freedom in its publications and through the NCSS Legal Defense Fund, established in 1970.[25]

Definitional dilemmas within the field appeared to be a major feature of social studies during the late 1970s and early 1980s, making the time ripe for initiatives from outside. In their 1977 book titled *Defining the Social Studies*, Barr, Barth, and Shermis suggested that from any theoretical perspective, "social studies is a mess." In what would become the most frequently cited source on definitional alternatives, they described three traditions: citizenship transmission, social sci-ence inquiry, and reflective inquiry. An article by Irving Morrissett on "Preferred

Approaches to the Teaching of Social Studies" suggested that there were five approaches to the field, which were listed as history, experience, critical thinking, social science, and involvement. A survey resulted in the finding that respondents preferred a critical thinking approach, with social science second, and history third. Interestingly, when asked their opinion of the most frequently used approaches in the nation, the order of responses was dramatically reversed, with 72 percent listing "history" as the dominant approach.[26]

Appropriately, given the depth of social studies malaise, a front cover cartoon accompanied a special issue of *Social Education* in 1980, titled "Discussion and Debate on New Proposals for the Social Studies Curriculum." The cartoon depicted a group of seven social studies professionals sitting at a table considering a jigsaw puzzle with pieces labeled to reflect many of the traditional and current approaches to the social studies puzzle: social sciences, history, decision making, concepts, ethnic studies, international human rights education, generalizations, social action, global education, geography, futurism, career education, consumerism, moral education, law-related education, citizenship, drug education, geography, factual knowledge, skills, socialization, and so on. One of the participants commented, "It might help if we had a picture of what this is supposed to look like."[27]

There were attempts at providing curricular guidelines, though there is little evidence that they were heeded. In 1979 *Social Education* published a revision of the NCSS Social Studies Guidelines, originally written in 1971, but with few significant modifications. The growing attention to definition and to the purposes of social studies instruction led to creation of an NCSS Task Force on Scope and Sequence, which made its report in 1983. Headed by John Jarolimek at the University of Washington and composed entirely of other Washington educators, the task force developed an illustrative scope and sequence for K–12 social studies that looked very similar in general outline to the scope and sequence that was recommended by the 1916 Report of the Committee on Social Studies.[28]

Continuing discussion of definitional dilemmas and alternatives led to publication, in 1986, of a special issue of *Social Education*, "Scope and Sequence: Alternatives for Social Studies." Several alternatives were presented by leading theorists, providing an indication of the possibilities. Traditional history was represented in an article by Matthew T. Downey, "Time, Space, and Culture," which proposed a modernized and updated history-as-core approach. Shirley H. Engle and Anna S. Ochoa presented a "Curriculum for Democratic Citizenship," which posited an issues-centered curriculum built around a number of curriculum strands including environmental, institutional, cultural studies, social problems, and special problems in citizen decision making. From a critical and reconstructionist position, William B. Stanley and Jack L. Nelson recommended "Social Education for Social Transformation" and called for curricula centered around consideration of ideologies and ethics, social problems, critical thinking, proposals for change, and social participation. The special section also included brief vignettes on social studies theorists of the past including Harold Rugg, George Counts, Rolla Tryon, Edgar Wesley, Gordon Hullfish, Alan Griffin, and Paul R. Hanna.[29]

By the 1980s there was also growing recognition of the difficulty of changing social studies, an awareness that diffusion did not necessarily equate to curricular change, and a feeling that the theory/practice split was perhaps the central dilemma of the field. One letter to the editor lamented the paradox between the "real" and the "ideal" in social studies. Another shared the important insight that "diffusion doesn't equal change." The work of Larry Cuban in *How Teachers Taught* revealed that despite repeated efforts to improve the quality of teaching in the nation's schools, traditional teaching practices relying on teacher talk, seatwork, and use of textbooks and recitation were remarkably persistent.[30]

In sum, social studies appeared to drift for a time in part because there were no new initiatives with the force or power of either the new social studies or the progressive education movement. Moreover, many scholars in the field had witnessed the demise of both these movements and had increasingly begun to recognize the difficulty of large-scale change. So there emerged, for a time, a gap in reform movements. This was combined with a retreat in the face of the conservative restoration and the return by many teachers to more traditional means of teaching. Much of the blame for the slide in the vigor of social studies reform efforts lay in the context of the times. In the Reagan/Bush years and beyond, progressives in social studies were swimming against the current.

The Revival of Traditional History

Into this vacuum of near directionlessness came a new movement more in keeping with the tenor of the times, the revival of traditional history. The origins of the revival of history may be traced to the same general concerns that motivated the back-to-basics movement. It was, in a sense, the citizenship wing of the conservative restoration. Though sentiment for traditional history had never disappeared, such predilections seemed at low ebb during the era of the new and newer social studies with their focus on inquiry and issues. At least a few critics of the new social studies had called for a return to traditional history, and by the mid-1970s an increasing number of historians were expressing alarm over the decline of history teaching in schools and the loss of students to other majors in colleges and universities.[31] Surveys began to appear that showed a decline in the number of history degrees conferred from a peak of 5.27 percent of total bachelor's and first professional degrees in 1968, down to 3.06 percent in 1976.[32]

The most well-known survey of the time was issued in 1975 by a committee of the Organization of American Historians headed by Richard S. Kirkendall. The survey reviewed the status of history in the schools and colleges and reported that "history is in crisis." Kirkendall's article was based on reports by historians in each of forty-five states plus the District of Columbia. The committee found wide variations in the qualifications required of teachers in the secondary schools:

about half the states required at least four history courses, some as many as seven; in others virtually no training in history was demanded. In several states there was movement away from the history component of teacher certification, with pressure coming from departments in the social sciences, trying to increase their number of majors by increasing their component in certification requirements. In a number of states, requirements for the certification of social studies teachers were undergoing revision, with the number of required courses in history reduced. On the whole, the situation regarding teacher certification requirements was described as "quite fluid," with the implication that history's preeminence was in danger.[33]

History's position in the curriculum was also slipping, according to the report. In many states, respondents reported stability in history offerings. Yet, most members of the committee "detected a very dynamic situation, and most of the movement was away from history, at least history as traditionally defined and taught." One respondent reported, "History has been clearly de-emphasized and is now generally incorporated into social studies units . . . the general trend is toward the multidisciplinary approach." Another reported "major changes in both content and method," and charged, "the thrust of these changes has been toward teaching less history of the traditional sort, eroding any sense of a differentiated past and unique time perspectives, and turning students away from historical study." Another stated that history had "moved from a position of dominance to that of being a partner with other social sciences in what curriculum designers call the Inquiry-Conceptual Program. This new program, which hopes to integrate all the social sciences, focuses upon understanding problems, making decisions, and taking action on social and civic problems."[34]

On the whole, Kirkendall reported, "only a small number of states do not fall into one of these two categories—stability or a move away from history." It seemed to many historians that the teaching of history was changing, with losses as well as gains. In many cases, the perception was that the chronological approach had been replaced by the "inquiry method," and efforts "to link courses to the issues facing society."[35]

Kirkendall concluded that signs of improvement in the status of history teaching were scarce, doubts about history's usefulness were rampant, and confidence and interest in history were not nearly as widespread as only a few years before. He concluded it seemed unlikely historians could "destroy the influence of presentism," but suggested they could "reduce the anti-historical consequences of it by demonstrating the value of historical perspective and historical comparisons and the importance of a sense of time and place."[36]

The report drew heavy criticism along several lines. Some charged that the committee was badly informed about the secondary schools. Others suggested that the report reflected a traditional approach to teaching history that should be discarded, an approach that dwells upon the facts about the past, plagued by problems brought by the neglect of the profession including poor teaching, narrow and useless courses, and boring textbooks. Fred M. Hechinger of the *New York Times* chided the report for implying that "'social studies' . . . tampered with history's body, flavor, and purity" and concluded that poor teaching was the source of the trouble. Others concurred, charging that history courses were too often taught by inadequately trained teachers lacking enthusiasm for teaching the subject. Too often, Kirkendall admitted, courses were "narrow and almost exclusively factual," comprised of "tedious lectures, uninformed discussions, picture shows, games." History teachers needed to improve methods, and the profession needed to attract more able people.[37]

Hechinger was correct. Kirkendall, and historians in general, were blaming social studies for failures in the teaching of history. It was an attack reminiscent of Allan Nevins, Hugh Russell Fraser, and the *New York Times* crusade against social studies of the 1940s. Moreover, the "survey" reported in the *Journal of American History* provided little in the way of hard evidence to verify a "crisis" in history teaching in the schools, and it appeared to be based almost entirely on anecdotal evidence. This was a flaw it had in common with Allan Nevins's attack on social studies in the 1940s. In an article paired with a Kirkendall article in *Social Education*, Allan O. Kownslar offered something of a counterpoint. Though he largely agreed with the report, Kownslar supported the "newer methods" and reported on an ETS study that found that students who claimed they had been exposed to the newer pedagogies in the history classroom scored slightly higher on standardized tests than those who had not. He also noted that the OAH report did not include student opinions about the reasons for declining interest in history. Kownslar reported several common student complaints: that "the criteria for successful student completion of a history course appeared to be the accumulation of data strictly for knowledge's sake"; that students were expected to be passive listeners, passive note-takers, or passive memorizers. For the disgruntled student, "memorization of everything" seemed the primary reason for endless hours of traditional history. Kownslar was a strong supporter of history, but confided, "Personally, I suspect that in many cases history courses are unpopular simply because they are taught so badly."[38] A later article confirmed that many students found little value in the study of history, that the methods of teaching were too often dull, the content irrelevant to their personal lifestyles, and that many resented the fact that they were required to take history throughout their educational careers.[39]

The critique of social studies that lay behind the "crisis" was trumpeted most pointedly by Kieran Egan, a Canadian curriculum theorist. In a provocative 1983 article titled, "Social Studies and the Erosion of Education," Egan found "a fundamental conceptual confusion inherent in social studies." He cited social studies aims focused on "attitudes and skills" for furthering the "democratic form of life" and "inculcating the ability to think critically" about the major problems of the past, present, and future. Egan charged that such aims were plagued by "vacuous generalities . . . mind-numbing vagueness . . . and ideological innocence." Such conceptual confusion, he wrote, results in a social studies curriculum that "has not worked, does not work, and cannot work." Egan went on to argue that the basis for the "expanding horizons" curriculum was psychologically flawed and that social studies was designed primarily to socialize students. He concluded that we would be better off "letting the 20th century American curriculum experiment called social studies quietly die." He argued for a revival of narrative, academic history and concluded that history and the other "foundational disciplines" of the social sciences should be separated from social studies to "preserve the disciplinary autonomy of these areas and thereby their educational value." Their educational value, he alleged, "is precisely what is eroded when they become handmaidens to the socializing purpose that pervades social studies."[40]

Following Egan's call for an end to social studies, a number of neoconservative writers contributed to a growing groundswell among historians, politicians, and more than a few teachers to support the revival of traditional history. The "crisis" served as preface to the broader revival, which was spurred by another *New York Times* involvement. In the November 17, 1985, issue of the *New York Times Magazine*, an article by Diane Ravitch appeared under the title, "Decline and Fall of History Teaching." In that article and elsewhere, Ravitch made the case that history was in trouble in the schools and that the culprit was social studies. In the years that followed, publications by Ravitch, then an adjunct professor at Teachers' College, Columbia University; Lynne Cheney, chair of the National Endowment for the Humanities; historian Paul Gagnon; Chester Finn; and others with support from political figures such as California Superintendent of Public Instruction Bill Honig and former Secretary of Education William J. Bennett contributed to a growing call for the revival of history in schools, and they made the case for a return to history and geography as the core of citizenship education. Each of these scholars made significant contributions: Cheney in *American Memory: A Report on the Humanities in the Nation's Public Schools*; Gagnon in an article titled "Why Study History?" that appeared in the *Atlantic Monthly*; and Finn, as coauthor with Ravitch of *What Do Our 17-Year-Olds Know?* and *Against Mediocrity: The Humanities in America's Schools*. By the late 1980s it was clear that Ravitch was the driving force.[41]

Ravitch, Finn, and others in this group were capable, well-positioned, and highly motivated scholars who sensed that the time for their ideas was ripe. During the 1980s, they launched what they considered a "crusade" to impose their vision on schools. Their primary vehicle, the Educational Excellence Network (EEN), was a collaborative group of neoconservative educators formed by Ravitch and Finn in 1982 to "provide an information exchange for education practitioners and scholars who share certain convictions and concerns" centered around "higher school standards, rigorous cognitive learning as the central purpose of formal education, as solid academic 'core' for every youngster, a renaissance in education in the humanities, and demanding intellectual and professional standards for teachers, principals and other school professionals."[42] The EEN served as an interest group for what could best be described as an educational essentialist reform agenda and was a leading advocate of excellence and accountability reform. The group received substantial funding from conservative foundations such as the Olin Foundation and from government sources such as the DOE and NEH.[43]

The general thesis of Ravitch's work on the teaching of history was, first, that history was in trouble. Requirements had declined as history was forced to share curricular time with the ill-defined social studies. Thus, students were, sadly, ignorant of even the most basic facts of U.S. history. Second, internal disorder within history as a discipline crowded out the idea of history as a story and replaced it with process-centered approaches through which students learn how to make investigations as if training to be historians, resulting in less attention to learning the content or facts of history. Third, "History is above all the retelling of what happened in the past," and should emphasize content knowledge, appeals to the imagination, and empathy so that students can experience a different time and place.[44]

Ravitch's work was built on an overarching desire to improve the teaching of history and increase the amount of time devoted to its study. This goal shaped her argument that social studies was the primary culprit for a decline in attention to history in schools. Apparently her work was inspired by visits to colleges and universities across the nation in 1984–1985, and personal glimpses of the sorry status of social studies in New York City schools, which she portrayed as representative. Her perspective was also strongly influenced by reading the work of educational essentialists such as William C. Bagley and Michael J. Demiashkevich, whom she apparently admired.[45] She described a "golden age" of history in schools during the early years of the twentieth century, following establishment of a history-centered curriculum by the AHA-led Committees of Ten and Seven in the 1890s.[46] She held up traditional history, centered around a textbook, chronology, and history as "a story well told," as a model curriculum, and charged that this prototype had been dislodged by a "social efficiency" oriented social studies program by the NEA's *Cardinal Principles* in 1918. She described the curriculum instituted by *Cardinal Principles* as one focused on immediate social utility, on "relevance and student interest," thus grossly oversimplifying the complexity of the compromise crafted in the 1916 Report on Social Studies. In contrast to the muddled and ill-defined social studies, she lauded the new California Framework as "a historic—step towards the national revival of the teaching and learning of history." The framework established history in virtually every grade, chronologically sequenced to develop in students a repertoire of knowledge. It stressed democratic values and principles of democratic government "throughout the curriculum."[47] The underlying purpose, the use of history to instill American democratic values, to build a sense of national identity and a common culture, was a slightly revised version of Nevins's aims of the 1940s. Above all, her work conveyed the message that we needed to reinstitute history as a central discipline in schools. If the problem was social studies, the solution, in Ravitch's view, was to turn back the clock to the 1890s and reinstitute a traditional history curriculum.[48]

Ravitch, appointed by Honig, served on a committee that developed the History-Social Science Framework for California Public Schools, and she was the leading figure on a three-person subcommittee that drafted its final version.[49] As chief architect, she extolled its virtues at every turn. The framework made history the core subject of the social studies curriculum, virtually gutting the schools of any social science content. Seen by its adherents as a "landmark document," the framework reinstituted history's monopoly over social studies in California, returning history, as "the great integrative discipline" to the core of the social studies curriculum. Moreover, the framework reflected a new organizational plan that chronologically segmented the focus of U.S. history in each of its three iterations and substantially increased the number of years devoted to the study of world history, from one to three. History became the mainstay of the elementary years. And from grades five through eleven, six of seven years were claimed by courses in history and geography.

Following development of the California Framework, Ravitch, Gagnon, and a group of prominent historians including Kenneth T. Jackson, William H. McNeill, C. Vann Woodward, Michael Kammen, and William E. Leuchtenburg formed the Bradley Commission on History in Schools, a program of the EEN.[50] Generously funded by the Lynde and Harry Bradley Foundation, the Bradley Commission released a 32-page pamphlet outlining its program in 1988, titled *Building a History Curriculum*. In a section titled "Why Study History?" the commission wrote:

> History belongs in the school program of all students, regardless of their academic standing and preparation, of their curricular track, or of their plans for the future. It is vital for all citizens in a democracy, because it provides the only avenue we have to reach an understanding of ourselves and our society, in relation to the human condition over time, and of how some things change and others continue.[51]

The commission adopted a platform of nine resolutions addressed "to all citizens who bear responsibility for designing and implementing courses of study in our schools." Among them:

1. That the knowledge and habits of mind to be gained from the study of history are indispensable to the education of citizens in a democracy . . . [and should] be required of all students.
2. That such study must reach well beyond the acquisition of useful information. To develop judgment and perspective, historical study must often focus upon broad, significant themes and questions, rather than short-lived memorization of facts without context. In doing so, historical study should provide context for facts and training in critical judgment based upon evidence, including original sources, and . . . a chronological view of the past.[52]

Additional planks included carving out more curricular time for history; a "history-centered" curriculum for K–6 social studies; no fewer than four years of history in grades 7–12; a curriculum "that encompasses the historical experiences of the peoples of Africa, the Americas, Asia, and Europe"; including "women, racial and ethnic minorities, [persons] of all classes and conditions." Another recommended a "substantial program in history" for secondary social studies teachers.[53] The list contained many useful recommendations, but took an extreme position regarding the balance of history and the other social sciences in the curriculum. Furthermore, it all but ignored one of the key problems facing history teachers in the schools, the problem of making the study of history relevant and meaningful to students, a point emphasized by many social studies veterans and previous reformers.

Following publication of the guidelines, the Bradley Commission published a book, entitled *Historical Literacy: The Case for History in American Education*, in 1989. The book was edited by Gagnon and included contributions from many members of the Bradley Commission. Most of the chapters were authored by historians. Notably, not one educational theorist or curriculum specialist was included among the authors. The few professors of education that were included were those who had clearly established that they had an axe to grind and favored a history curriculum. The book was a polemic for more and better history in schools, with little or no consideration of the place of the other social sciences in the curriculum. The argument was advanced that these would be incorporated within history because it is an integrative discipline.[54]

At about the same time, Ravitch and colleagues founded the National Council for History Education (NCHE), an organization designed to advance the neoconservative agenda. They established a newsletter, *History Matters!*, which was circulated widely. A flyer advertising the organization announced in bold letters, "Good history must be at the core of the social studies curriculum." The NCHE was working, the flyer announced, to see that good history is part of every student's education: assisting state and local curriculum review committees; testifying, writing letters, and contacting officials when history is threatened in state frameworks or local curricula; conducting teacher education meetings, programs, and summer institutes. On the whole, it was conducting a broad-based lobbying effort to advance the revival of history in schools.[55]

Critiques

The response among social studies educators was rather anemic given the challenge to their leadership of the field. Many younger scholars in social studies were educational researchers rather than philosophers or theorists. Perhaps many of the leaders of the social studies field for the past quarter-century were tired from fighting their own generation's battles, or had given up trying to change the field. Nonetheless, there was a response.

Richard E. Gross, a longtime advocate of a broad and issues-centered social studies, wrote one of the first responses to the critics, whom he described as "a small but vocal, highly motivated, well-funded, and very visible interest group . . . promoting the primacy of history and geography in the school curriculum." Gross argued that there was "little evidence from the past, when history and geography held sway, that the study of these subjects produced the results that today's proponents desire."[56]

Ronald W. Evans critiqued the revival of history and its chief proponent, Diane Ravitch. Evans argued that Ravitch was using social studies as a scapegoat and ignoring the history and purposes of the social studies movement, preferring to make facile condemnations instead. The reality, he wrote, was that, "history continues to hold a dominant position among the social studies, and that one goal of the social studies movement has been to make instruction in history and the social sciences more meaningful and relevant to the average citizen." He criticized Ravitch and her colleagues for assuming that a chronological narrative, the "tell a story" approach to history teaching, was some sort of answer, when that traditional approach had continued without interruption in most classrooms and had been failing for years to interest and educate students.[57]

In his critique of the reform movement, Stephen J. Thornton asked, "Should we be teaching more history?" Thornton questioned whether the proposed reforms were well founded and whether a renewed emphasis on content acquisition would bring us back, nostalgically, to the "golden age" that Ravitch had identified. He argued that there was "scant support in the research literature for the reformers' views, and that the substitution of history for other social studies courses will be to little avail unless entrenched patterns of instruction and learning are also changed."[58]

Sid Lester, a professor at San Jose State University, wrote a critique of the California Framework in which he criticized the short shrift given to the social sciences and the failure of the Framework Committee to be more inclusive. He wrote, "There were no professors of economics, anthropology, sociology, psychology, or political science. None! Not any! Zip! Nada! . . . According to most authorities," he countered, "the 'social studies' should be comprised of the disciplines of history, geography, anthropology, economics, political science, sociology, and psychology, with some humanities, philosophy and law thrown in." Another professor from California, Duane Campbell at Sacramento State, complained, in a letter published in *Social Education*, that the framework had been "railroaded through" the adoption process using undemocratic means and over the strong objections of many representatives from the field, a charge that the developers of the framework denied.[59] In sum, critics charged that the nascent revival of history was an attempt to turn back the clock, to overturn a decades-old attempt at a compromise position between historians and social scientists, brokered by educators with the needs and interests of students at heart.[60]

What was behind the revival of history? The movement came to fruition because of the confluence of the right persons and ideas with an appropriate national climate during which conservative notions were in ascendance, in schools and the nation. It received strong support from those in positions of power and generous funding from the Olin and Bradley Foundations, groups with a strong conservative bias and the goal of influencing policy.[61] This kind of financial support, from private foundations leaning in a particular direction, was unprecedented in the history of social studies. Moreover, there were some elements of truth in the critiques leveled against social studies. The new social studies had placed greater emphasis on the social sciences and social issues. Even the 1916 report reflected a moderate, compromise position between history and the social sciences and resulted in less time devoted to pure history instruction than was the case under the Ten and the Seven. Also, it was definitely true that social studies practice was a shadow of what was possible, regardless of the philosophy or approach taken.

Clearly, the movement touched a nerve among historians and the general public who seem always susceptible to appeals to tradition, nostalgia, and a golden age. This particular appeal came at an opportune time. On the whole, the revival of history was yet another episode in the recurring war on social studies. Yet, this new initiative was different in some important ways. It was built on logical arguments that were generally well researched. Though polemical in many of its assertions and rationale, these were much more powerfully developed than by previous critics. Moreover, Ravitch and company enlisted substantial support among respected historians, generous organizational and financial backing, and established a firm beachhead by developing a "model" curriculum in the most populous state in the nation. It was apparent that this movement to reform social studies would be around for some time.

The National Commission on Social Studies

The definitional dilemma facing social studies early in the post-new social studies era led to a sense among many within the profession that social studies had reached an impasse and that something had to be done. Major curricular change seemed impossible, wrote one former president of NCSS, "because the primary political forces affecting curricular decisions immobilize each other."[62] The idea for creation of a national commission to examine social studies curricula had been floated since the late 1970s by several prominent social studies figures.

In his 1984 presidential address to the AHA, Arthur S. Link called for a "blue ribbon" committee to study the status of history in the schools. In 1985, Donald Bragaw, president of NCSS, asked the board of directors to set up a task force to examine the entire social studies program in the schools, K–12. Thus, formation of the National Commission in 1985 grew out of these two recommendations, eventually emerging as a joint project of four organizations with an interest in improving social studies instruction: the American Historical Association, the Carnegie Foundation for the Advancement of Teaching, the National Council for the Social Studies, and the Organization of American Historians.[63] Membership on the commission, and on its Curriculum Task Force, included a mix of historians, social scientists, social studies educators, and school personnel, but it was weighted toward historians, reflecting the makeup of its sponsoring organizations. Historians in both the AHA and the OAH later endorsed the recommendations of the Bradley Commission, so there was a great deal of overlap in the philosophical orientation of the two groups.[64]

The curriculum recommendations made in *Charting a Course: Social Studies for the 21st Century*, the report of the National Commission, were generally supportive of the goals of the traditional history camp.[65] *Charting a Course* called for a great deal more history in the high school grades. In fact, the foreword to *Charting a Course* cited the Report of the Bradley Commission and applauded its effort to address "the heart of the matter—what teachers should teach and children should learn." The task force called for a social studies curriculum that would "instill a clear understanding of the roles of citizens in a democracy." It called for a curriculum providing for "consistent and cumulative learning from kindergarten through 12th grade," and replacement of "redundant, superficial coverage" with "carefully articulated in-depth studies." It argued that "history and geography should provide the matrix or framework for social studies" because they offered perspectives of time and place, and it called for integration of "concepts and understandings" from the other social sciences.[66] Perhaps the most innovative aspects of the report's proposals were the notion of integrating world and U.S. history into three courses at the high school level, allowing for in-depth global study of topics, issues, and problems from the past, and the recommendation of a middle school course focused on the local community, local issues, and neighborhood problems. Both of these recommendations were, however, a drastic departure from current practice.

Critiques of the commission's work were published in *Social Education*. Shirley Engle wondered "whether changing the scope and sequence" was a "sufficient way to go about reforming social studies," and wrote that in the commission's report, "the value of history in the development of good citizens is taken for granted." He argued that the commission needed "to shift the locus of its thinking from the declarative to the hypothetical mood." Jack Nelson charged that the report was "narrow and conservative," and "anti-intellectual in its lack of concern for contemporary issues and competing ideas." Nelson concluded that the report "deserves to be forgotten quickly."[67]

Looking behind the commission report, two of the four main sponsors were *the* major historians' interest groups in the nation. Commission members were not representative of the multiple traditions in the field but were apparently chosen with an eye toward furthering the revival of history. The impact of the commission may have been limited by its failure to create a more inclusive membership with balanced representation from various camps and stakeholders in the century-long battles over social studies. It was soon eclipsed by other developments and largely forgotten.

Explaining the Conservative Restoration

As we have seen, the excellence reform movement grew out of a pendulum swing in educational rhetoric, spearheaded by the back-to-basics movement, and launched into a major school reform movement by *A Nation at Risk*. Subsequent reports and activities from a range of individuals and organizations including business, government, and scholars were gradually moving the reform toward greater use of accountability measures. As in 1970s academic freedom battles, conservative foundations assisted the cause with funding and rhetorical support. These general trends had influence on social studies, impacting rhetoric through debate and discussion, and leading to the revival of traditional history, the citizenship education wing of the conservative restoration. The central problem set forth by this chapter is to explain the conservative restoration in schools and society that lay behind the revival of history, and declining attention to reflective, issues-centered social studies.

Several explanations can help contribute to an understanding of the conservative restoration, the revival of history, and the decline of progressive social studies. First, educational reforms of the era, including back-to-basics, the pursuit of excellence, and the revival of history, were driven by educational, political, and economic forces in the society, outside of education. This was largely a response to a manufactured crisis, based on a faulty thesis and flawed assumptions, driven by those in positions of power with considerable financial resources from both governmental and private sources. New Right and neoconservative reformers were well organized, highly motivated, visible, articulate, and well funded. In social studies, the EEN, the Bradley Commission, and the NCHE were major supporters of the neoconservative revival of history. All received financial support from conservative foundations seeking to turn back the clock on the 1960s and liberal reform.[68] A small group of neoconservative educators, led by Diane Ravitch and Chester Finn, had a great deal of influence on both the larger reform and the new direction in social studies, in part because they were in step with the times, because they were well positioned and fairly eloquent in expressing their views, and because they were highly motivated, viewing their efforts as part of a "crusade" to reform and improve schooling.[69] Ravitch and Finn wrote literally hundreds of op-ed pieces that offered a critical view of education that was what a lot of non-educators wanted to hear, supporting reform of a "failing" educational system and return to a golden age of educational essentialism and traditional approaches to learning. They were also saying the kinds of things that business leaders wanted to hear, supportive of capitalism and the American system.[70] Moreover, the political trends culminating in the conservative restoration originated in reactions to the perceived excesses and very real failures of reforms of the 1960s and 1970s. The swing of the pendulum to the right seems a perennial trend in American education, which typically follows any period of innovation.

Second, the conservative restoration was built on pervasive myths about American schooling, and creation of a mythical golden age. In the larger realm, this took the form of the injunction that the schools were failing. Not just some of the schools but the schools as a whole. Thus, proponents argued, back-to-basics, reassertion of tougher standards, and a return to more conservative traditions were in order. In the revival of history, the myth of a golden age was combined with scapegoating social studies as *the* factor that led to the supposed decline of history in schools. Return to a golden age meant a return to the familiar "grammar of schooling" based partly on the reformers' belief that the only real social studies was traditional history and geography.

Third, objections to the reforms of the 1960s and 1970s were based, in part, on the accurate assessment that the reforms were not working. The failure of reforms in the era of the new and newer social studies were a large part of the rise of the conservative restoration, creating an easy target for criticism from the New Right, neoconservatives, and historians. In large part, the earlier reforms had failed due to the reformers' shortcoming in neglecting to account for organizational barriers to school change. Barriers to the promotion of higher-order thinking in social studies classrooms seemed endemic to schools. Among these were the pervasive conception of instruction as knowledge transmission, a curriculum focused on coverage, teachers' low expectations of students, larger numbers of students per teacher, lack of sufficient planning time, and a culture of teacher isolation.[71] Additional constraints on teaching such as the number of students per class, length of class periods, lack of readily available materials, and content to be taught were typically influenced if not mandated by those outside the classroom. While teachers did have a good deal of discretion over classroom space, student grouping, classroom discourse, tools, and activities, these decisions could not escape at least two major dictates from outside: maintain order and cover the required curriculum. Despite the potential for the profound influence of teacher beliefs on what occurred in classrooms, these constraints resulted in a pattern of persistent instruction, of constancy marked by teacher-centered forms of pedagogy, especially at the secondary level.[72]

Moreover, constraints were shaped by a remarkably resilient grammar of schooling that seemed to impose structural constraints on school reform. In the high school, for example, the grammar of schooling included hourly shifts from one subject and teacher to another, teachers and subjects divided into specialized departments, instructing 150 or more students a day in five classes, and students rewarded with grades and Carnegie units. Over time we have seen little lasting change in the way schools divide time and space, classify students, allocate them into classrooms, splinter knowledge, and award grades. The standard "grammar of schooling" has proven remarkably durable, persisting partly because it enabled teachers to perform their duties in a predictable and efficient fashion: controlling student behavior, sorting students into social roles for school and life outside. Such established institutional forms take on a life of their own, becoming the expected features of a "real school." They become fixed by custom, legal mandates, and cultural beliefs until they are so ingrained that they are barely noticed. As Tyack and Cuban put it, "They become just the way schools are."[73] In practical terms, the reforms of the conservative restoration were easier to sustain because they fit the general notion among teachers, parents, and the public of what a real school should be.

Fourth, philosophically, the conservative restoration and the revival of history both served what were perceived as the traditional purposes of education. Conservative members of the school culture and the public rose up and reasserted, at least for a time, more traditional forms of schooling. During the era of the new social studies, in a significant number of schools students were being asked to question the social structures. Now, during the conservative restoration, debate over the field was framed once again as "Social Studies vs. [the] United States of America."[74] Instead of education for social criticism, the focus was on social control and creation of human capital. Many Americans, it seemed, did not want education to reform American society, but simply to restore its luster. Employers wanted the education of workers who were punctual, who would follow instructions, and who would not ask too many questions. Behind this was a system of public education that seemed to have more to do with maintaining the class structure than with opening up opportunity. As one social studies luminary, Shirley Engle, suggested, "More citizens than we would like to think are really hostile to democracy. They do not want the schools to teach their children to think."[75] It seemed that an emerging consensus of politicians and the American public viewed social studies as a means of inducting youth into the traditional values of the social order—even if it had to be done by rote indoctrination.

Notes

1. Allan Bloom, *The Closing of the American Mind: How Higher Education Has Failed Democracy and Impoverished the Souls of Today's Students* (New York: Simon and Schuster, 1987).
2. E.D. Hirsch, Jr., *Cultural Literacy: What Every American Needs to Know* (Boston: Houghton Mifflin, 1987); Diane Ravitch, "Cultural Literacy," ASCD, April 6, 1989, "Ravitch, Diane, 1989–1993 Cultural Literacy" folder, Box 32, Ravitch Papers.
3. Hirsch, *Cultural Literacy*.
4. Ibid., xiii–xvii.
5. Ibid., ix–xi; E.D. Hirsch, Jr., Joseph F. Kett, and James Trefil, *Dictionary of Cultural Literacy* (Boston: Houghton Mifflin, 1988). See also E.D. Hirsch, Jr., "Cultural Literacy and the Curriculum," Keynote Address to Staff Development Conference, California State Department of Education, Asilomar, CA, January 22–24, 1985, in "Cultural Literacy, 1982–1988" folder, Box 32, Ravitch Papers; Ravitch, "Cultural Literacy."
6. Fred M. Newmann, "Another View of Cultural Literacy: Go For Depth," *SE* 52, no. 6 (October 1988): 432–436.

7. Stephen J. Thornton, "Review of E.D. Hirsch's *Cultural Literacy*," *TRSE* 16, no. 3 (Summer 1988): 244–249.

8. Dinesh D'Souza, *Illiberal Education: The Politics of Race and Sex on Campus* (New York: Free Press, 1991); Roger Kimball, *Tenured Radicals: How Politics Has Corrupted Our Higher Education* (New York: Harper and Row, 1990).

9. Paulo Freire, *Pedagogy of the Oppressed* (New York: Continuum, 1970), 57–59.

10. Samuel Bowles and Herbert Gintis, *Schooling in Capitalist America: Educational Reform and the Contradictions of Economic Life* (New York: Basic Books, 1976), 48.

11. William B. Stanley, *Curriculum for Utopia* (Albany: State University of New York Press), 100.

12. Michael W. Apple, *Ideology and Curriculum* (London: Routledge & Keegan Paul, 1979), 14; Fred M. Newmann, "The Radical Perspective on Social Studies: A Synthesis and Critique," *TRSE* 13, no. 1 (1985): 1–8.

13. Jack L. Nelson, Ed., "New Criticism and Social Education," *SE* 49, no. 5 (May 1985): 368–405.

14. Amy Gutman, *Democratic Education* (Princeton, NJ: Princeton University Press, 1987); Ronald W. Evans, "Utopian Visions and Mainstream Practice: Essay Review on William B. Stanley's *Curriculum for Utopia*," *TRSE* 21, no. 2 (1993): 161–173.

15. See James A. Banks, Ed., *Handbook of Research on Multicultural Education* (New York: Macmillan, 1995).

16. James A. Banks, "Multicultural Education in the New Century," *SA* 56, no. 6 (May 1999): 8–10.

17. Thomas J. Famularo, "The Intellectual Bankruptcy of Multiculturalism," *USAT Magazine*, May 1, 1996.

18. Diane Ravitch, "Diversity and Democracy: Multicultural Education in America," *AE*, Spring 1990, 17–20. See also the special issue of *PDK* devoted to the controversy over multiculturalism with articles by Ravitch, Banks, and others.

19. Ravitch was condemned as "racist" by a multiculturalist after one speech during controversy in New York State over the proposal, "A Curriculum of Inclusion"; Diane Ravitch to Thomas Sobol, February 24, 1990, "Curriculum of Inclusion, 1989–1993" folder, Box 33, Ravitch Papers.

20. Ibid.

21. Arthur M. Schlesinger, Jr., *The Disuniting of America: Reflections on a Multicultural Society* (New York: W.W. Norton & Company, 1991).

22. Gloria Ladson-Billings, "Through the Looking Glass: Politics and the Social Studies Curriculum: Review of Schlesinger's *The Disuniting of America*," *TRSE* 21, no. 1 (Winter 1993): 84–92; Diane Ravitch, "Multiculturalism in the Curriculum," Manhattan Institute, November 27, 1989, "Multiculturalism 1984–1994" folder 3, Box 19, Ravitch Papers.

23. D'Souza, *Illiberal Education*; Roger Kimball, *Tenured Radicals* (New York: Harper and Row, 1990); Mark Edmundson, Ed., *Wild Orchids and Trotsky: Messages from American Universities* (New York: Penguin, 1993); Catherine Cornbleth and Dexter Waugh, *The Great Speckled Bird: Multicultural Politics and Educational Policy Making* (New York: St. Martin's, 1995).

24. NCES, *A Trend Study of High School Offerings and Enrollments: 1972–1973 and 1981–1982* (Washington, DC: NCES, 1984).

25. See NCSS Notes, "House of Delegates 1975 Annual Meeting Resolutions," *SE* 40, no. 4 (April 1976): 232; Anna S. Ochoa, "Censorship: Does Anybody Care?," *SE* 43, no. 4 (April 1979): 304–309; John Rossi, Murry Nelson, Dennis Thavenet, Patrick Ferguson, Eds., "The Growing Controversy Over Book Censorship," *SE* 46, no. 4 (April 1982); Fred M. Hechinger, "Censorship Rises in the Nation's Public Schools," *NYT*, January 3, 1984; Jack L. Nelson and Anna S. Ochoa, "Academic Freedom, Censorship, and the Social Studies," *SE* 51, no. 6 (October, 1987): 424–427.

26. Robert D. Barr, James L. Barth, and S. Samuel Shermis, *Defining the Social Stud-ies* (Arlington, VA: National Council for the Social Studies, 1977); Irving Morrissett, "Curriculum Information Network Sixth Report: Preferred Approaches to the Teach-ing of Social Studies," *SE* 41, no. 3 (March 1977): 206–209; Dale L. Brubaker, Lawrence H. Simon, and Jo Watts Williams, "A Conceptual Framework for Social Studies Cur-riculum and Instruction," *SE* 41, no. 3 (March 1977): 201–205.
27. Editor, "Discussion and Debate on New Proposals for the Social Studies Curriculum," *SE* 44, no. 7 (November/December 1980): 592, 652–653. The cartoon was critiqued for its depiction of a male-dominated social studies profession. Six of the seven persons shown around the table were male.
28. Ad Hoc Committee on Social Studies Curriculum Guidelines, "Revision of the NCSS Social Studies Curriculum Guidelines," *SE* 43, no. 4 (April 1979): 261–273; NCSS Task Force on Scope and Sequence, "In Search of a Scope and Sequence for Social Studies," *SE* 48 (April 1984): 249–273.
29. Donald H. Bragaw, "Scope and Sequence Alternatives for Social Studies," *SE* 50, no. 7 (November/December 1986); Matthew T. Downey, "Time, Space and Culture," *SE* 50, no. 7 (November/December 1986): 490–501; Shirley H. Engle and Anna S. Ochoa, "A Curriculum for Democratic Citizenship," *SE* 50, no. 7 (November/December 1986): 514–527; William B. Stanley and Jack L. Nelson, "Social Education for Social Transfor-mation," *SE* 50, no. 7 (November/December 1986): 528–535.
30. Letter to Editor, "Real vs. Ideal," *SE* (1979): 414; Letter to Editor, "Diffusion Doesn't Equal Change," *SE* (1979): 484; Larry Cuban, *How Teachers Taught: Constancy and Change in American Classrooms, 1890–1980* (New York: Longman, 1984).
31. Mark M. Krug, "Bruner's New Social Studies: A Critique," *SE* 30 (October 1966): 400–406.
32. Richard S. Kirkendall, "The Status of History in the Schools," *JAH* 62, no. 2 (1975): 557–570. See also Hazel W. Hertzberg, "The Teaching of History," in Michael Kam-men, Ed., *The Past Before Us* (Ithaca, NY: Cornell University Press, 1980).
33. Kirkendall, "Status of History," 558–561.
34. Ibid., 561–564.
35. Ibid., 565.
36. Ibid., 569–570.
37. Richard S. Kirkendall, "More History/Better History," *SE* 40, no. 6 (October 1976): 446, 449–451.
38. Allan O. Kownslar, "The Status of History: Some Views and Suggestions," *SE* 40, No. 6 (October 1976): 447–449.
39. Stuart Paul Marcus and Paul Jeffrey Richman, "Is History Irrelevant?" *SE* 42, no. 2 (February 1978): 150–151; Warren L. Hickman, "The Erosion of History," *SE* 43, no. 1 (January 1979): 18–22; Margaret S. Branson, "Introduction: Teaching American History," *SE* 44, no. 6 (October 1980): 453–460; Myron A. Marty, "Doing Something About the Teaching of History: An Agenda for the Eighties," *SE* 44, no. 6 (October, 1980): 470–473.
40. Kieran Egan, "Social Studies and the Erosion of Education," *CI* 13, no. 2 (1983): 195–214.
41. Diane Ravitch, "Decline and Fall of History Teaching," *NYTM*, November 17, 1985, 50–53, 101, 117; Lynne Cheney. *American Memory: A Report on the Humanities in the Nation's Public Schools* (Washington, DC: National Endowment for the Humanities, 1987); Paul Gagnon, "Why Study History?," *AM*, November, 1988, 43–66; Diane Ravitch and Chester Finn, Jr., *What Do Our 17-Year-Olds Know?: A Report of the First National Assessment of History and Literature* (New York: Harper and Row, 1987); Diane Ravitch, Chester E. Finn, Jr., and Robert T. Fancher, *Against Mediocrity: The Humanities in America's Schools* (New York: Holmes and Meier, 1984).
42. "The Educational Excellence Network: 1988–1991," attachment, Finn to Ravitch, November 22, 1988, "Ravitch, Diane" folder, Box 120, Finn Papers.

43. For information on the EEN, see "Status of EEN grants as of April 1, 1986," in "Educational Excellence Network (EEN), 1985–1986 and undated" folder 10, Box 18, Ravitch Papers. See also Box 56/11 and Box 60/3, Ravitch Papers. As of 1986, the EEN received substantial amounts of private funding from the Olin Foundation, Vanderbilt University, and smaller amounts from the Exxon Education Foundation, Joyce Foundation, Mellon Foundation, and member contributions. It had operating expenses of approximately $80,400 per year. It also received public funding for research projects from the DOE ($70,221) and NEH ($173,431). The EEN was later "reborn" as the Thomas B. Fordham Foundation.

44. Diane Ravitch, "The Revival of History: Problems and Progress," paper presented at the Annual Meeting of the American Educational Research Association, Washington, DC, April 24, 1987, p. 6; Diane Ravitch, "The Plight of History in America's Schools," in Paul Gagnon, Ed., *Historical Literacy: The Case for History in American Education* (New York: Macmillan, 1989); Diane Ravitch, "Tot Sociology: What Happened to History in the Grade Schools?" *ASCH* 56, no. 3 (Summer 1987): 343–354; Ravitch, "The Erosion of History in American Schools," folder 5, Box 43, Ravitch Papers.

45. "Essentialist Movement, 1937–1938" folder 4, Box 6, Ravitch Papers. See also Ravitch's favorable treatment of Bagley and the essentialists in Diane Ravitch, *The Troubled Crusade: American Education, 1945–1980* (New York: Basic Books, 1983).

46. In an exchange of letters with Stephen J. Thornton, Ravitch denied that she cited a "golden age." See Stephen J. Thornton to Ravitch, August 8, 1990, and Ravitch to Thornton, August 22, 1990, in "Correspondence, 1990" folder 1, Box 4, Ravitch Papers.

47. Ravitch, "Revival of History," 12, 18.

48. Ravitch, "Revival of History"; Ravitch, "Plight of History."

49. Bill Honig to Diane Ravitch, December 11, 1988, "Correspondence 1988" folder 6, Box 3, and Peter Kneedler to Diane Ravitch, December 10, 1985, "Undated" folder 2, Box 29, Ravitch Papers.

50. "The Educational Excellence Network: 1988–1991," attachment, Finn to Ravitch, November 22, 1988, "Ravitch, Diane" folder, Box 120, Finn Papers.

51. Bradley Commission, *Building a History Curriculum: Guidelines for Teaching History in Schools* (Washington, DC: Educational Excellence Network, 1988), 5. See also Hazel Hertzberg's internal review of *Building a History Curriculum* as a member of the Bradley Commission, in which she called for increasing history requirements, in "Comments on Guidelines Booklet Memo of 1/20/88, H. Hertzberg," in "Bradley Commission on History in Schools, 1980–1991" folder 15–16, Box 45, Ravitch Papers.

52. *Building a History Curriculum,* 7–8.

53. Ibid.

54. Paul Gagnon, Ed., *Historical Literacy: The Case for History in American Education* (New York: Macmillan, 1989).

55. *History Matters!* Flyer promoting the National Council for History Education, date uncertain.

56. Richard E. Gross, "Forward to the Trivia of 1890: The Impending Social Studies Program?" *PDK* 70, no. 1 (September 1988): 47–49.

57. Ronald W. Evans, "Diane Ravitch and the Revival of History: A Critique," *TSS* 80, no. 3 (May/June 1989): 85–88; Diane Ravitch, "The Revival of History: A Response," *TSS* 80, no. 3 (May/June 1989): 89–91; "Evans and Ravitch Square Off in The Social Studies," *History Matters!,* 1989. The Ravitch papers contain a file with both manuscripts and a few margin comments by Ravitch on the Evans manuscript. One comment was directed at Evans's citation of historian Howard Zinn, who argued that the study of history should be guided by a set of core values aimed at making the world a better place. Ravitch wrote, "Is he Jesus Christ?" Ravitch also confided in a letter, "I was recently attacked in *Social Studies* magazine as the 'guru' of the movement to revive

history, and I happily plead guilty to the charge." See Diane Ravitch to James Piereson, Olin Foundation, October 12, 1989, p. 2, "Correspondence 1989" folder 8, Box 3, Ravitch Papers.

58. Stephen J. Thornton, "Should We Be Teaching More History?" *TRSE* 18, no. 1 (1990): 53–60; see Ravitch rejoinder.

59. Sid Lester, "An Analytic Critique of the 1987 Framework," *SSR* 28, no. 2 (Winter 1989): 52–61.

60. Duane Campbell, "Letters: California Framework," *SE* 52, no. 6 (October 1988): 403; Diane Brooks to Bill Honig, November 30, 1988, and Honig to Salvatore Natoli, November 5, 1988, in "California 1986–1989" folder, Box 29, Ravitch Papers; Bill Honig, "Letters: California Curriculum," *SE* 53, no. 3 (March 1989): 143–144.

61. Vince Stehle, "Righting Philanthropy," *NAT*, June 30, 1997, 15–20; Alan Singer, "Strange Bedfellows: The Contradictory Goals of the Coalition Making War on Social Studies," *TSS* 95, no. 5 (September–October 2005): 199. The Bradley Foundation was founded by Harry Bradley, a charter member of the John Birch Society. See Lee Fang, *The Machine: A Field Guide to the Resurgent Right* (New York: New Press, 2013), 240; Diane Ravitch's scholarly work during the period was "supported by conservative foundations, principally the John M. Olin Foundation." See Diane Ravitch, *The Death and Life of the Great American School System: How Testing and Choice Are Undermining Education* (New York: Basic Books, 2010), 12; and James Piereson, Olin Foundation, to Diane Ravitch, December 20, 1989, "Correspondence" folder 8, Box 3, Ravitch Papers.

62. Howard Mehlinger, "The National Commission on Social Studies in the Schools: An Example of the Politics of Curriculum Reform in the United States," *SE* 56, no. 3 (March 1992): 149–153.

63. Fay Metcalf and David Jenness, "The National Commission on Social Studies in the Schools: An Overview," *SE* 54, no. 7 (November/December 1990): 429–430.

64. National Commission on Social Studies in the Schools, *Charting a Course: Social Studies for the 21st Century* (Washington, DC: National Commission on Social Studies in the Schools, 1989); Mehlinger, "National Commission," 150.

65. David Jenness, *Making Sense of Social Studies* (New York: Macmillan, 1990); National Commission, *Voices of Teachers* (Washington, DC: National Council for the Social Studies, 1991); *Charting a Course*, v, 3–4.

66. *Charting a Course*, v, 3–4.

67. Shirley H. Engle, "The Commission Report and Citizenship Education," *SE* 54, no. 7 (November/December 1990): 431–434; Jack L. Nelson, "Charting a Course Backwards: A Response to the National Commission's Nineteenth Century Social Studies Program," *SE* 54, no. 7 (November/December 1990): 434–437.

68. See note on EEN above.

69. See materials on the public relations campaign to promote America 2000, "PR Campaign America 2000" folder, Box 95, Finn Papers.

70. Ravitch and Finn papers contain references on America 2000 and the "crusade" to change the direction of America's schools. See Finn Box 95, and 29/1.

71. Joseph J. Onosko, "Barriers to the Promotion of Higher-Order Thinking in Social Studies," *TRSE* 19, no. 4 (Fall 1991): 341–366.

72. Larry Cuban, *How Teachers Taught* (New York: Longman, 1984).

73. David Tyack and Larry Cuban, *Tinkering Toward Utopia: A Century of Public School Reform* (Cambridge, MA: Harvard University Press, 1995).

74. Edgar B. Dawson postcard to Wilbur Murra, "Textbook Controversy" folder, Box 5, Series 4B, NCSS Papers.

75. Shirley H. Engle, "Whatever Happened to the Social Studies?" *IJSE* 4, no. 1 (1989): 51.

4

BUSINESS TAKES CHARGE

As we have seen, the era of national educational reform leading to the standards movement began in earnest during a time of political conservatism and educational retrenchment heralded by publication of the report *A Nation at Risk* in 1983. The origins of the standards movement may be readily traced to the educational agenda during the Reagan and Bush administrations. The reform movement spawned by *A Nation at Risk* continued under the America 2000 program with a top-down push for standards and testing. Furthermore, America 2000 specifically called for the teaching of "history, geography, and civics" and made no mention of social studies.[1]

The standards movement was launched amid a mythical national "crisis" in education based upon the charge that our schools were in dire condition and largely to blame for a decline by the United States in international economic competition. Many educators and the public agreed that drastic reform was required to remedy the situation. However, a general lack of meaningful discourse about the mythical crisis resulted in a national obsession with fixing the schools. This obsession was motivated, in part, by fears first raised by *A Nation at Risk* that our students were not adequately prepared to allow the nation to compete in a global economy. Proposals for fixing the schools included returning to basic subjects such as history and geography instead of the broader, more inclusive social studies, developing a national curriculum, and using standardized tests to assess student knowledge. In the broader effort for school reform, the years from 1989 through 1992 were a watershed during which reformers embraced a business-driven approach to school reform, which was morphed onto the excellence movement already underway to form a new hybridized reform movement aimed at accountability, raising standards, and returning the schools to more traditional forms of pedagogy.

"The Education President"

In November 1988, the George H.W. Bush administration was elected to continue the Reagan revolution and the conservative restoration but embraced more moderate rhetoric, a more pragmatic and mainstream agenda on social policy, and a pledge to be "the education president" made during the 1988 presidential campaign. Bush would abandon President Ronald Reagan's promise to abolish the DOE and instead called for using federal influence to improve schools by utilizing standards and testing. He would contribute to the nationalization of debate over school reform by convening an education summit with the nation's governors in 1989, introducing legislation for national goals in education, and creating the National Education Goals Panel (NEGP) and the National Council on Education Standards and Testing (NCEST) to further the work of accountability reform.

During the 1988 presidential campaign, Bush's opponent was Michael Dukakis, a three-term governor of Massachusetts who had worked on education reform in his state. As Reagan's vice president, and as a representative in Congress, Bush had little previous experience with education issues. Nonetheless, both candidates devoted a great deal of rhetoric to education during the campaign. Polling data suggests that the public saw education as an important national issue, with 87 percent of respondents to one poll indicating that the issue was "very important" in determining their vote. Moreover, respondents to a 1987 Gallup survey indicated that 84 percent of Americans believed the federal government should require schools to meet minimum national standards.[2]

Early in the campaign primary season, for the first time in American history, presidential candidates from both parties participated in a debate focused entirely on education. *A Nation at Risk*, subsequent rhetoric, public perception of schools "in crisis," and the flurry of state-by-state reform efforts during the 1980s meant that candidates felt obliged to develop more elaborate reform proposals. Moreover, public support for a stronger federal role in education and more spending had increased substantially.[3] Partly in an effort to overcome the perception that Republicans were callous on education and social welfare, Bush declared that he would work for "a kinder, gentler nation" and that he would be "the education president." In his stump speech, Bush declared:

> I'd like to be the education president. See, I believe as I look into the future—our ability to compete around the world, our ability to solve problems of poverty that are unsolved in this country . . . whatever it is, education has got to be the priority. Better schools mean better jobs.[4]

In a speech to the National Press Club in June of 1988, Bush added, "our schools are absolutely not as good as they must be . . . [and] to achieve quality results, we must set and enforce standards, provide incentives, and permit the freedom and flexibility on the local level to experiment with new ideas."[5] These remarks were generally well received by the media and the voters. Though the public, and teachers unions, generally viewed Dukakis more favorably on education, it is possible that Bush's efforts on education made him seem more moderate and compassionate and may have contributed to his victory. Unions, both the NEA and the AFT, had long allied themselves with the Democratic Party. By 1988 the unions had become a major political force, able to marshal large quantities of "political resources—money, votes, and volunteers." Yet, the unions continued to oppose standards-based reform, accountability measures, and calls for expansion of school choice.[6]

Bush sought to put a more moderate face on what was essentially an extension of the Reagan presidency under his leadership. In his speech accepting the Republican nomination, and at his inaugural, he cast government as the facilitator of private charity and individual initiative, stating that leadership could come from "a thousand points of light," thus reaffirming an open door to business influence over domestic social programs and education. In the end, presidential rhetoric on improving education helped solidify school reform as a national priority, marking a break with previous presidential elections, and insuring that President Bush would continue to make education "the cornerstone for the rest of his domestic social agenda."[7]

Once in office, Bush outlined his approach, calling education, "The most important competitiveness program of all," and highlighting "excellence," "choice," and holding "all concerned accountable."[8] In March 1989, Bush sent a modest plan for educational improvement to Capitol Hill, the Educational Excellence Act of 1989, which reallocated some DOE funds to support several initiatives Bush had touted.[9] Though the legislation failed to gain passage, it did suggest a general direction.

The Charlottesville Summit

While he was still on the campaign trail, Bush called for an education summit meeting, a gesture that would give the appearance of action without incurring significant costs on the part of the federal government, while at the same time continuing the Reagan-era focus on state-level reform with symbolic national leadership. While the administration's Educational Excellence bill lay stalled in Congress, Bush turned to the bully pulpit, much as his predecessor had done, to assert symbolic leadership. The seminal event of this effort was the convening of an education summit in Charlottesville, Virginia, in late September 1989, to discuss the prospects for education reform and further develop the notion of national standards.

Even before President Bush took office, the NGA moved quickly to make good on Bush's campaign pledge to meet with the governors to discuss continuing efforts for reform in education. An NGA staffer wrote to the president-elect in preparation for a December meeting, suggesting that the governors could work together with the administration to establish specific long-range goals for improving schooling to "establish a vision of the nature of the education system and the results it must produce by the beginning of the 21st century."[10] At that December 1988 meeting, the idea of setting long-range goals for education reform was discussed, and it was agreed to pursue the matter. Subsequent communications led to a private meeting on May 16, 1990, between the president and thirteen governors, during which tentative plans for a September education summit were agreed upon.[11]

Preparations for the summit were led by Milton Goldberg, former executive director of the National Commission on Excellence that had issued *A Nation at Risk*. In early June of 1989, Goldberg and a team of scholars at the Office of Educational Research and Improvement (OERI) developed a draft of national goals. The memo they developed, "2002: A Nation of Learners," was revised and submitted to the White House a month later. The memo focused on content goals in the K–12 curriculum and suggested that the president call for seven goals to be met by 2002. A parallel effort underway in the Planning and Evaluation Service in the Office of Planning, Budget, and Evaluation led to a somewhat similar statement of goals, but with more attention to "enabling goals" and "improvement targets" including establishing a system of public school choice, statewide achievement tests, and a system requiring failing schools to develop plans for improvement.[12] The NGA's previous work paved the way, establishing an important precedent on the road to standards-based reform with its 1986 report, *Time for Results*, which called for state-led reforms focused on measurable results, better report cards about what students know and can do, public school choice, state takeover of failing schools, and career ladders for teachers.[13]

Prior to the Charlottesville Summit, the NGA held a "summit outreach" meeting with representatives from forty education, business, advocacy, and government organizations on September 25. Governors Carroll Campbell (R-SC) and Bill Clinton (D-AR) served as co-chairs for the one-day meeting. The conferees agreed that a national crisis in education existed, that poor and minority students were most disadvantaged, and that the situation called for "a need to set national education goals, and to develop a nationwide strategy for meeting them." It seemed a consensus was emerging on the need for establishing national goals and a comprehensive and coordinated strategy to reach them.[14] During the weeks and months leading up to the summit, the president's representatives had committed the administration to follow-up meetings that included a long-range plan "to work with the governors to develop a set of national performance goals," a historic first.[15]

Chester Finn, who continued to serve in the DOE during the Bush administration, described the context for what he termed a "symbolic" effort:

> The Charlottesville summit was a public relations effort necessitated by the fact that there wasn't anything else the administration could do on education. . . . Everything was dead in the water, and nothing was happening.[16]

The standards movement had received growing support from the business community during the 1980s. Moreover, business partnerships with local schools and districts, while good for public relations, had done little to change the basic operating patterns of schooling. The business community generated a great deal of momentum for standards-based education reform at the state level, including pressure on governors and state legislators to implement reform, an obsessive focus on results, and a growing awareness that the "federal input-based strategy" wasn't leading to the desired improvements.[17]

The Business Summit

In the months leading up to the governors' summit in Charlottesville, Bush met with key leaders from the BRT to discuss education reform. On June 5, 1989, at the BRT's annual meeting, he challenged business leaders to join in the effort to improve education in the states.[18] As a former businessman, Bush was one of them, with family wealth, strong links to the oil business, and long-term ties to the Eastern establishment.[19] Bush's prodding led the BRT to devote its entire summer meeting to education reform. That meeting resulted in a statement of goals for reforming education that included key elements of what would later emerge as a consensus plan for reforming schools.

At the BRT Summit meeting, CEOs of the nation's 218 largest corporations met to discuss steps toward improving education. Drawing upon nearly a decade of concerted effort from various business groups and organizations on reforming education, the BRT Summit developed a statement of goals similar to those that would emerge from the governors' summit in Charlottesville. First, the BRT committed to a ten-year program to implement its goals for reforming education. The nine-point statement of goals from the 1989 BRT Summit included outcome-based education, strong and complex assessments of student progress, high expectations for all children, rewards and penalties for individual schools, greater school-based decision making, emphasis on staff development, readiness to learn provisions, and greater use of technology.[20] Underlying their commitment to this blueprint for reform was what business leaders saw as a perceived threat to U.S. leadership in the global economy. Edward Rust, CEO of State Farm Insurance and chair of the BRT Task Force on Education in 1999, would later offer an explanation for the economic motive behind the BRT agenda on education:

> In a global economy built on knowledge and technical skills, employees must be able to do more now than they did a generation ago. And these demands will continue to increase. In 1950, 60 percent of jobs for new workers were classified as unskilled; by 2000, only 15 percent will be. . . . The percentage of U.S. companies reporting a lack of skilled employees as a barrier to growth continues to rise—from 27 percent in 1993 to 69 percent last year.[21]

So, to increase the number of "skilled" workers needed for economic growth, the educational system would have to be substantially reformed. The BRT Summit, subsequent support for the governors' summit, and the move toward national goals further increased the pressure on governors and state legislators to move forward on standards-based reforms.

John F. Akers, then president and CEO of IBM and leader of the BRT Education Task Force, issued a memo titled "Business Roundtable Call to Action" in the spring of 1989, which was circulated within the administration. The memo stated, "Business must be concerned and involved with restructuring U.S. K–12 education because of its importance to competitiveness AND as the foundation for the future strength and vitality of our democratic society." The memo listed a three-point plan for BRT involvement with education including, first, "building and strengthening partnerships" and, second, "leadership/guidance" for BRT companies from the Education Task Force. Third, and most significantly, it read:

> Develop a systems approach to education reform. The essence of this approach is to define the "output" or measurable goals desired, then determined [sic.] the human and financial resources and other elements required to achieve these goals.[22]

As the summit was approaching, Akers wrote a letter directly to President Bush on September 18, 1989, highlighting the business community's commitment to reforming education. The letter offered a statement of support and said,

> We know that business does not have all the answers, but the Roundtable's members are prepared to make a ten-year commitment of personal time and company resources to a cooperative effort to reinvigorate our nation's education system.[23]

The memo also mentioned a meeting of the task force with the president on September 26, immediately prior to the summit in Charlottesville. The attached statement, titled "The Education Decade: A Business Commitment to America's Children," heralded "a new stage of commitment to our nation's education system" and included a pledge from the business community to work for "systemic change in education." It suggested, "America desperately needs a national vision for education. Together, our challenge is to develop that vision, which should include widely accepted goals for restructuring as well as the adoption of national standards for higher levels of achievement—for students and teachers." The memorandum continued with a statement in support of "an education system that meets the principles of excellence, accountability, and quality control," and then presented four goals:

- Develop a national consensus on the vision for a world-class education system.
- Ensure acceptance for national goals for improving student achievement and completion rates and for developing a sound measurement system.
- Develop partnerships with federal and state governments, educators, parents, businesses, and other involved groups to produce a new education system.
- Help shape public opinion to support a restructuring of the nation's schools and promote more direct communication between schools and the people they serve.[24]

And so, several months before the Charlottesville Summit, the business community, the administration, and the nation's governors made a commitment to systemic reform, to developing a new system of standards and accountability that could lead to school improvement.

Plans for the Governors' Summit

Though the original plans for the Charlottesville Summit focused on showcasing examples of exemplary practice from various states, the summit's planners instead decided to focus on development of national education goals. The administration's intention was that "the Governors and the President agree to engage in a process through which they will establish long-range goals and targets for educational improvement" so as to "establish a vision of the nature of the education system and the results it must produce by the beginning of the 21st century." The goals were to be "national" rather than federally imposed, and would encourage various levels of government and the private sector to "find ways of supporting their attainment."[25]

During the spring and summer of 1989, there was a good deal of private communications among White House staff, the NGA, and others over possible plans, along with discussion of various options, including speculation on how many governors would support the president's education initiatives. One memo listed twenty-five governors that could be "counted on to support the President's education initiatives," and eleven that could help "in selling the President's programs." The latter included Democrats Bill Clinton of Arkansas, Rudy Perpich of Minnesota, and Booth Gardner of Washington.[26] Other memos discussed holding an informal session to show "quick action" and a commitment to listen seriously to the governors; holding a series of regional forums; developing four working groups at the summit, "matching our four principles"; and including special observers from universities, business, Congress, and education.[27] In reading the memos, it is apparent that the appearance of action was a key concern.

On May 16, a private meeting took place involving President Bush and thirteen governors during which the possibility of a summit was discussed. After the meeting, the NGA announced that a summit was tentatively planned for September at the White House.[28] The location was later changed. Shortly before the summit meeting was to begin, a Summit Steering Group agreed upon three main objectives for the meeting, focused on "strengthening the Nation's educational system" through state and local-level improvement, "emphasis on results," and producing "greater flexibility and greater accountability."[29]

The Charlottesville Summit Meeting

The summit meeting was held in Charlottesville, Virginia, on the campus of the University of Virginia, on September 27 and 28, 1989. Participants included members of the Bush administration, forty-nine of the fifty governors, the president's cabinet, and a few others. There were no educators or members of Congress in attendance, other than those from Virginia who helped host the meeting.[30]

The president's welcoming remarks made it clear that he thought of the federal role as that of a supporting and coordinating partner, not a leader of the effort for school reform. President Bush stated:

> There are real problems right now in our educational system, but there is no one Federal solution. The Federal government, of course, has a very important role to play, which is why I'm here and why so many members of our cabinet are here. And we're going to work with you to help find answers, but I firmly believe that the key will be found at the State and local levels.[31]

Though there were several public occasions, partly to accommodate the media, attendance at the six smaller "Working Groups" at which the governors conducted discussion of key topics was limited to the president, governors, cabinet members, and a few high-level administration officials. Each governor was assigned to two of the breakout sessions, chaired by two governors (a Democrat and a Republican), and moderated by a cabinet member. The meetings were closed to staff and the media. Working groups for the summit focused on six areas in which the NGA and the Bush administration agreed there was a need for improvement: governance, teaching, the learning environment, choice and restructuring, developing a competitive workforce, and postsecondary education.

Along with these assignments, plans for each working group included a list of key topics. At least two groups had responsibility for questions related to accountability. The working group on "Governance: Who is in charge?" included the topic: "Ensuring that schools are publicly accountable for their performance, that there is adequate scope for innovation, and that exceptional performance is recognized and rewarded." The working group on "Choice and Restructuring" included: "Considering ways of expanding choice and strengthening accountability."[32]

Among the key players at the summit were President Bush, Roger B. Porter, his assistant for Economic and Domestic Policy, Clinton, and Campbell. Secretary of Education Lauren Cavazos was present and led a breakout session but did not attend a late-night session at the Boar's Head Inn where the final joint communiqué was drafted. According to one news report, a draft statement from the NGA proposed that the government take special responsibility for ending illiteracy and assuring drug-free schools in the District of Columbia and that it target assistance to a handful of big city and rural districts across the nation with severe problems. According to Porter, the plank "really didn't fit" with the rest of the communiqué, and was taken out during the late-night session.[33]

At the close of the summit on September 28, the president and the governors issued a joint communiqué reiterating their purposes for meeting, the aim of establishing national performance goals and creation of a panel to oversee the process of creating them. Declaring that "the time for rhetoric is past," the president and governors issued what they called "a Jeffersonian compact to enlighten our children and the children of generations to come." The statement read in part:

> The President and the nation's Governors agree that a better educated citizenry is the key to the continued growth and prosperity of the United States. . . . We believe that the time has come, for the first time in U.S. history, to establish clear, national performance goals, goals that will make us internationally competitive.[34]

By the end of the summit, the participants agreed "to establish a process for setting national education goals"; to undertake "a major state-by-state effort to restructure our education system"; and to establish "a system of accountability that focuses on results."[35] What is most striking in reviewing the statement is the overriding presence of a business-driven blueprint for reform, applying principles of free market competition to schools in an effort to improve performance. The tension between setting goals and providing the necessary resources to fulfill them remained unresolved. Moreover, the deliberate exclusion of members of Congress from the summit set a tone of confrontation that would haunt the process for some time.[36]

Media Coverage

Media portrayals of the summit were generally favorable, framing the summit as a "historic event," a "first" that could lead to important school improvements. An article in the *New York Times* portrayed the summit as historic, marking the "first time" that governors—Democrats and Republicans—had agreed to forge a national education strategy, and described it as "a triumph" for President Bush. Another *NYT* article reported, "Teachers Praise Bush's Effort to Set a New Education Agenda." While a few expressed concerns about issues of money, "overall there seemed to be little criticism."[37]

An article in the *Washington Post* noted that "accountability" and the call for "performance measures" were the key principles and portrayed the summit as "a necessary next step" toward "making American school children more competitive with those of other nations." It quoted Bill Clinton as saying, "For the first time in our history, we've thought enough of education to commit ourselves to national performance goals," and noted that the movement toward performance goals had been "gaining momentum in recent years," especially among business leaders. An article in another major newspaper called the summit "exciting," "historic," and "successful" but noted that it was "reminiscent of a campaign event."[38]

Others noted a "carnival atmosphere" of "media mania," and that the key findings of the summit, which had been agreed to in pre-summit negotiations, "ratified a pre-ordained outcome."[39] The conservative *Washington Times* astutely noted the compatibility of the governors' summit with E.D. Hirsch's *Cultural Literacy* and his push for a core curriculum, and suggested that it might "reinvigorate the faltering education reform movement."[40]

The *Christian Science Monitor* reported that "competition" was the meeting's byword, noting that governors were getting "a clear message from business" about the need to improve the "level of learning of American workers." A *Washington Post* article quoted Albert Shanker, AFT president, who said of the plan for systemic reform, "It will drive what happens in the schools," in what turned out to be a prescient and accurate prediction.[41]

Is sum, media coverage of the summit seemed swept up in the "historic" grandeur of the effort to reform schools. Only a few articles mentioned business collaboration in the design of the reform, and even fewer mentioned linkages to a conservative educational agenda and the similarities with Hirsch's cultural literacy. It seems that the media was largely a collaborator in what appeared to be an emerging consensus among Democrats, Republicans, business groups, and at least a few educators in support of systemic reform.

Follow-up

Following the summit, the NGA Education Task Force and the Bush administration continued to work on developing and refining national performance goals, and established an informal steering committee. They scheduled a December 7 meeting to move toward the final wording of the goals and ways of measuring them.[42] Staffers in the White House, the DOE, and the OERI helped in examining different ways of measuring "alternative" goals, and received "valuable advice and suggestions from a variety of sources."[43]

The December 7 meeting included a private briefing for governors, administration representatives, and education aides; two concurrent sets of public discussions with education, business, and community leaders to "explore reactions and suggestions"; a public roundtable discussion with technical experts; and a private meeting to make preliminary decisions. An NGA memo from the Education Task Force Advisory Committee laid out criteria for the National Education Goals, reflecting a consensus that the goals should:

- Be brief, memorable, and inspirational—four to six goals the public can readily remember and understand.
- Be outcome and results oriented.
- Be measurable.
- Be high but attainable; reaching the goals should substantially "ratchet up" the performance of the system.
- Make our people internationally competitive.
- Drive fundamental restructuring of the system.
- Reflect a long-term perspective: roughly a ten-year time frame.[44]

Panelists at the December 7 hearing included representatives from a wide array of education, business, and community groups—a strong representation of stakeholders. Technical experts included James Comer, Chester Finn, Marshall Smith, Marc Tucker, and others who had gotten deeply involved in "systemic" reform.[45] The plan was to have the goal statements finalized in time for the president's State of the Union address in January.

The December 7 meeting and other follow-up discussions led to agreement that the "first task is to produce roughly half a dozen simple, memorable goals that the President would articulate in his State of the Union Address on January 31."[46] These statements embodied many of the same general principles agreed upon prior to the Charlottesville Summit.

When all was said and done, the six national goals that President Bush shared with the nation in his 1990 State of the Union address were:

By the year 2000,

1. All children in America will start school ready to learn.
2. The high school graduation rate will increase to at least 90 percent.
3. American students will leave grades four, eight, and twelve having demonstrated competency in challenging subject matter including English, mathematics, science, history, and geography; and every school in America will ensure that all students learn to use their minds well, so they may be prepared for responsible citizenship, further learning, and productive employment in our modern economy.
4. U.S. students will be first in the world in science and mathematics achievement.
5. Every adult American will be literate and possess the knowledge and skills necessary to compete in a global economy and exercise the rights and responsibilities of citizenship.
6. Every school in America will be free of drugs and violence and will offer a safe, disciplined environment conducive to learning.[47]

The goals were rather general and intentionally vague. The statement left unclear what was meant by terms like "demonstrated competency" and how achievement of the goals would be measured. Though the summit and subsequent negotiating efforts laid the foundation for these goals, it had not created specific strategies to reach them. However, the statement of national goals helped sustain the steady drumbeat toward school accountability reform.

Meaning of the Summit

After the national goals were announced, the next key question became how the states and schools would be encouraged to make progress on them. Many observers believed that implementing the goals would require more specific national standards along with tests to measure performance. While the logic of the goals suggested new arrangements, it was unclear whether national standards could be created without giving power to an intrusive federal bureaucracy, and there was little consensus on difficult issues surrounding measurement and accountability. Democrats, and their allies in the teachers unions, were wary of development of accountability measures that would be punitive in nature, or that would not provide more resources enhancing student's opportunity to learn. Republicans, on the other hand, while supportive of strong accountability measures that would change the behaviors of teachers and school administrators, were generally wary of a stronger federal role in education and the prospect of increased funding.[48] Despite such differences, widespread public support for national education standards continued to give the movement significant momentum and contributed to the emerging consensus in support of systemic reform.[49]

The Charlottesville Summit was an important turning point for its symbolic meaning and specific contributions. It shifted the debate to standards and national performance goals and brought a much stronger focus on accountability. Bush and his staff were looking for ways to stimulate support for school reform without significantly expanding federal spending or control. The historic meeting was a media success and marked an important compromise in favor of bipartisan support for systemic education reform. The joint statement meant that Republicans and Democrats were able to overcome underlying differences surrounding goal setting, accountability, and funding, though tensions would reemerge later. Still, the spirit of bipartisanship at the summit set the stage for further cooperation and rekindled public attention and commitment to reform American schools. The first wave of reform during the 1980s had only limited impact on schools. The Charlottesville Summit and new national goals helped energize business involvement, led to development of a framework for systemic reform, and enhanced the movement toward applying core business principles to education. Corporate school reform was now firmly in place on the nation's agenda. Moreover, key members of the Bush DOE team viewed the reform effort as embodied in America 2000 as a "crusade" to improve and change the direction of American schooling.[50]

The Powell Memo and BRT

The extent of business support for systemic reform was reflected by the Fortune Education Summit, a parallel gathering of business leaders held in late October 1989, and sponsored by *Fortune* magazine, to which the administration sent a surrogate, Roger Porter, the president's key domestic policy advisor. While the administration and business leaders were on parallel tracks, the administration was careful to keep up appearances by making Bush "the education president" rather than a shill for business leaders.[51] The Fortune Summit, held at the Willard Hotel in Washington, DC, on October 29–31, 1989, which opened with an address by John Scully, Apple CEO, included speeches or panel participation by a number of leaders of the education reform movement from business, academia, and government including Ernest Boyer, Terry Branstad, Keith Geiger, Rudy Perpich, Roy Romer, Albert Shanker, Tom Kean, Chris Whittle, Marc Tucker, and Frank Newman (ECS). It included a dinner address by Porter, titled "Government and Business: Working Together for Education Reform," a title that seemed to encapsulate the movement, and it ended with a speech by David Kearns, chairman and CEO of Xerox, titled "Challenges of the 21st Century."[52]

Though business leaders may not have been publicly acknowledged participants at the Charlottesville Summit, they had been lobbying the governors and state legislators on education reform for some time, held business education "summits" shortly before and after Charlottesville, and may have been observer-participants. They were in close communication with Bush administration officials throughout the period. Moreover, a number of states held similar education summits at around the same time, state meetings aimed at furthering the agenda for systemic education reform.[53]

Business influence on education, which had been on a steady growth curve during the 1980s, seemed to expand exponentially during the Bush administration as an interlocking directorate of business groups got increasingly involved in education reform, including the BRT, the National Association of Manufacturers, the U.S. Chamber of Commerce, the Committee on Economic Development (CED), and others. Business gradually became the driving force behind reform and took leadership by lobbying government leaders, maintaining constant pressure for a business-like model of education, and pushing for systemic reform. Key players from the business and education communities were involved as members or affiliates of the Bush administration and lobbied for systemic reform, including David Kearns, Denis Doyle, Marc Tucker, Edward Rust, and others.

History of Business Lobbying

Business lobbies have long been a part of the American scene, manipulating politicians and policies, fighting for or against particular legislation, and broadly supporting business interests. The National Association of Manufacturers (NAM) was one of the first business coalitions to use public relations methods as a means to gain political power. Its eighty founding members were a who's who of American business power. Formed in 1895 to promote foreign trade, the NAM soon shifted its focus to opposing labor unions and supporting the rights of employers to establish working conditions and set wages without government interference. The NAM lobbied against legislation aimed at protecting workers, campaigned against pro-labor candidates in elections, and opposed limits on child labor. In the 1910s, the NAM was investigated by a congressional committee, which found that it had bribed members of Congress to promote its agenda. In the 1930s, the NAM was taken over by the "Brass Hats" of large corporations, which quickly developed a plan of "business salvation," conducted a massive campaign against the New Deal, and flooded the country with biased propaganda. The NAM played a leading role in the campaign against the social studies textbooks of Harold Rugg and other progressive-era schoolbooks that aimed at giving students a "realistic" view of American life.[54]

Business groups have historically sought to frame agendas and influence government through policy discussion and advisory groups. Groups such as the National Civic Federation, the National Industrial Conference Board, the Council on Foreign Relations, the Committee on Economic Development, and the Business Council were formed during the first half of the twentieth century, many with overlapping memberships. By and large, policy discussion and advisory groups took a more moderate stance, accepting some state welfare and accommodating the rights of labor, in contrast to the NAM and the U.S. Chamber of Commerce. However, during the 1970s, as the BRT was formed and corporate funds poured into business groups, even moderate groups supported market-driven reforms. Policy discussion groups provided a private forum where strategies and policy positions could be discussed in private and where corporate leaders could select academic experts to promote their cause and confer legitimacy on corporate executives as experts, enabling them to influence public policy.

Think tanks and research institutes are another source of business influence, frequently utilizing ideas and theories from university scholars, which are often developed into policy proposals and disseminated, then sometimes taken up by government committees and drafted into legislation. In recent years especially, conservative think tanks and foundations, funded largely by corporations and wealthy conservatives, have become very adept at promoting free market ideas and policies along with a conservative and pro-business agenda. Among the leading think tanks influencing policy discussions, including those on education, were AEI, the Heritage Foundation, the Cato Institute, and the Hoover Institution. They are funded largely by conservative foundations such as Scaife, Bradley, Olin, Koch, Smith Richardson, and a handful of others and have aimed to directly influence policy through one-on-one meetings, conferences, policy statements, research, publications, media appearances, and campaign contributions.[55]

The Business Roundtable

During recent decades, the Business Roundtable has become the single most powerful voice for corporate interests on the American scene, and the leading voice for business in education reform. During the 1960s and early 1970s, business was dealt a series of defeats by the liberal Democratic coalition that elected John F. Kennedy and Lyndon B. Johnson and whose power was embodied in the "Great Society" programs. For several decades, business groups accepted the fact that their views on policy would be contested by labor and others and that compromise was a necessary feature of public life. However, a sustained shift in climate was growing cause for alarm. The civil rights, antiwar, and counterculture movements sparked an upsurge of leftist rhetoric and activity. Businesses that were praised in earlier generations for rapidly turning out munitions were suddenly labeled as war criminals and exploiters of labor.

In 1971, Lewis Powell, a corporate lawyer and future Supreme Court justice who represented tobacco companies and served on the board of Philip Morris, authored a widely circulated memo titled "Attack on American Free Enterprise System." In the memo, Powell, then a member of the Education Committee of the U.S. Chamber of Commerce, argued vociferously, and quite convincingly, that business and the capitalist system were under broad attack and needed to organize and assert political power both to protect their interests and perpetuate the system. In a "blistering and penetrating 6,466-word analysis," he urged the business community to fight back through organized political action.[56] Arguing that strength lies in "organization," "long term planning" and "consistency," he wrote:

> If our system is to survive, top management must be equally concerned with protecting and preserving the system itself . . . to counter—on the broadest front—the attack on the enterprise system. . . . Business must learn the lesson, long ago learned by labor and other self-interest groups. This is the lesson that political power is necessary; that such power must be assidously (sic) cultivated; and that when necessary, it must be used aggressively and with determination.[57]

The Powell memo offered what others have called "A blueprint for corporate domination of American democracy" and "A call to arms for class warfare."[58] Though Powell was one of many who pushed to reinvigorate business's political clout, his memo is often credited with stimulating an era of growing corporate influence in government and education, rekindling a business agenda traceable to the New Deal era and earlier.[59] Though much of the public looked upon the landscape of corporate America in the late 1960s and saw price fixing by incipient monopolies and suspected the global collusion of military, government, and business interests, "the reality was starkly different." Big business was "on the whole, a clumsy, uncomfortable, and ineffective player" in the politics of the United States.

Mobilization by the BRT and others changed that. On every dimension of corporate activity, substantial evidence reveals the rapid mobilization of business resources to influence public policy from the 1970s to the present day. Membership and budgets in business organizations grew dramatically; corporations established public affairs offices in Washington, DC, for lobbying purposes; and business groups formed new and more powerful coalitions, establishing an interconnected web of foundations, policy discussion groups, and think tanks.[60] Though its physical presence in Washington was deceptively small, corporate America was, in fact, committing huge resources and top business and legal talent to achieving a pro-business agenda. "Almost inevitably, the plan worked," wrote Robert Monks, a longtime corporate insider:

> Through its own published and widely disseminated studies and via the assiduous courting and sometimes strong-arming of the media, Congress, and the executive branch, the BRT succeeded in changing the terms of the debate over the limits on corporate reach and self-determination. Union power and presence withered. Corporations were freed of pension obligations . . . [and] most profound . . . [they] created a new class of philosopher kings.[61]

Their activity had several important additional effects: it unleashed pay and stock options to reach astronomical new records; limited shareholder access; and increased corporate influence on politics and government. Suddenly it seemed corporate leaders such as Lee Iacocca, Ross Perot, and Donald Trump were the popular equivalent of rock stars, writing books, appearing on television, and offering advice and counsel on how to fix the schools and a range of other institutions.

Three business organizations representing many of the largest corporations in the nation merged to form the Business Roundtable in 1972, with membership restricted to top corporate CEOs. Within five years the BRT had enlisted 113 of the Fortune 200 companies, representing nearly half of the U.S. economy, and had grown into a formidable collective lobbying group. Moreover, Powell's memo suggested stronger business involvement in education, on both college campuses and in secondary education, and that business representatives should "insist on equal time." He argued that business should continually evaluate social science textbooks with the intent of "restoring the balance" needed for "fair and factual treatment" of "our enterprise system."[62]

Business Groups and Education

Business involvement seemed a juggernaut that few could resist. During the 1980s and into the 1990s, business groups and their surrogates produced a steady stream of studies, reports, books, and other publications supporting a particular vision of market- and business-driven school reform that suited their interests. Included among the groups producing policy papers and reports on school reform were the BRT, the CED, the Chamber of Commerce, the BCER, the Education Trust, the Heritage Foundation, the AEI, the Hudson Institute, and others. Though they appeared to be acting independently, there was a great deal of sharing of ideas, funding, and personnel among these organizations.

One group in particular appeared to play a prominent role in setting the theoretical and intellectual foundation for business-driven school reform. The CED, discussed in the previous chapter, issued a continuing series of studies and policy statements built around promoting and maintaining U.S. competitiveness in the global economic arena. As we have seen, during the 1980s it issued a major report, titled *Investing in Our Children: Business and the Public Schools* (1985), authored by Denis Doyle of AEI, a report suggesting a business-driven approach to school reform that was deeply linked to its global vision for industrial competitiveness as spelled out in an earlier report titled *Strategy for U.S. Industrial Competitiveness* (1984). *Investing in Our Children* was followed by a somewhat similar study aimed at educational reform to help the educationally disadvantaged, titled *Children in Need: Investing for the Educationally Disadvantaged* (1987), and another report titled *An America That Works* (1990), delineating a "human capital" approach to educational improvement.

The Hudson Institute's 1987 report, *Workforce 2000: Work and Workers for the Twenty-First Century*, was also influential in leadership circles. The volume was published by the U.S. Department of Labor and examined the forces shaping the American economy, focusing on labor market trends including projected needs and challenges. It fully embraced the notion of education for development of "human capital." In a section on improving workers' education and skills, the authors wrote, "The educational standards that have been established in the nation's schools must be raised dramatically. . . . From an economic standpoint, higher standards in the schools are the equivalent of competitiveness internationally."[63]

Creating a National Consensus

A national consensus was emerging, led by a business/government coalition and centered on the notion that market forces and business principles should drive education reform, with emphasis on results and accountability. One of the clearest statements of the underlying philosophy supported by business is expressed in an influential book by David Kearns and Denis Doyle titled *Winning the Brain Race: A Bold Plan to Make Our Schools Competitive* (1988). The book was based, in part, on a speech that Kearns gave before the Detroit Economic Council in 1987.[64] Kearns would later serve in the Bush administration as deputy secretary of education. Kearns and Doyle assumed that application of these business ideas, in themselves, would lead to improvement, with little attention to any learning theory or philosophy of education but with increased support for research on what works to raise achievement. Drawing on Adam Smith, Kearns and Doyle describe a vision of unbridled venture capitalism applied to schools.

Kearns and Doyle begin with the assumption that the nation's schools are "in crisis" and represent "a failed monopoly." Though reminiscent of Blumenfeld's *Is Public Education Necessary?*, Kearns and Doyle argue that "business will have to set the new agenda" for a "complete restructure" centered around "choice," raising "standards," and strict accountability, including annual testing and high-stakes consequences. They put forth a six-point plan favoring choice, restructuring, professionalism, standards with accountability, inculcation of democratic values, and a targeted but limited federal role, in which schools that "persist in poor performance . . . [would] be closed."[65] Built around "concepts of the market place" they develop an "economic model of education" in which measurement of "performance" is the single most important contributor.

The book, and Kearns's passion for school reform, caught the attention of President Bush, who made Kearns assistant secretary of education. As Bush recalled, "I called on him personally, more than once, and I'm not afraid to say I leaned on him pretty hard."[66] Many of the core ideas, but not all of the specific proposals, discussed in *Winning the Brain Race* became the essence of the accountability movement—which gradually moved to center stage—driving the new reform.

Another influential book supporting market-based, business-driven reform that made an indelible mark on the growing school reform movement was titled *Politics, Markets, and American Schools* (1990), written by John Chubb and Terry Moe, and published by the Brookings Institution. One of the most widely cited books on educational reform throughout the 1990s, the authors argued that good leadership, teaching, high academic standards and goals, and strong parental support combined to make for effective schools, rather than plentiful economic resources or being located in a high socioeconomic status area. Despite a great deal of hopeful rhetoric in the movement for educational reform, they argued that most reforms were destined to fail because they failed to get at the root of problems, which they located in the institutions of democratic control by which schools had traditionally been governed.

Chubb and Moe built their work around analysis of several national statistical databases in order to determine factors that lead to higher levels of academic performance in schools. They concluded that improvement would only come from building-level autonomy of principals and teachers freed from bureaucratic regulation. Hence, they argued for dramatic reform in the direction of privatization and provided the kind of research legitimation that choice advocates had been hoping for. Chubb and Moe argued that responsibility for effective schools lay with teachers and parents, not with the government. Thus, the way to make schools more effective was through market competition and more aggressive choice plans. They recommended "a new system of public education, built around parent-student choice and school competition, that would promote school autonomy—thus providing a firm foundation for genuine school improvement and superior student achievement."[67]

Their findings and arguments received an unusual amount of attention from scholars and the media. Later dubbed the "neo-liberal educational bible" by one critic, scholarly reviewers described their work as "a polemic wrapped in numbers."[68] While Chester Finn heralded their work, political scientist John Witte charged, "To suggest that we know enough from High School and Beyond to overthrow the public school system in the United States and replace it with a choice system is sheer madness."[69]

The BRT Proposal

Much of the work described above was part of a movement aimed at building a consensus around the notion of business- or market-driven reform of schooling. The emerging consensus was captured in a Business Roundtable statement on the *Essential Components of a Successful Educational System* (1989). The statement placed standards, assessments, and accountability at the center of a nine-point proposal for reform. Not long after drafting the statement, the BRT launched a "50-state initiative" in 1990 to persuade each state to adopt the BRT's nine essential components of systemic reform, which aimed to create a "performance- or outcome-based" system in which "successful schools are rewarded and schools that fail are penalized" and helped to improve, among other planks.[70]

On first glance, their nine points sound reasonable. However, the quality of accountability hinged largely on the quality of assessments. For the most part assessments relied on testing of low-level items and recall of facts, rather than "integration of knowledge, an understanding of main ideas and problem solving." The money and power behind the BRT and other corporate groups meant that the wealthiest, most powerful people in the world were deciding what kind of education children would have. It represents the educational wing of what Hacker and Pierson describe as the winner-take-all politics that has brought a steady move toward more corporate power in politics and American life including supply-side economics; financial deregulation; tax cuts for the wealthy; upward redistribution of wealth, income, and power; privatization of various public services; systemic reform in education; and unrestricted corporate spending to influence elections. Moreover, this was a global phenomenon that followed a similar pattern in other nations, part of "globalization" as advocated by a consensus of neoliberal and neoconservative reformers.[71] It was also part of a larger movement toward privatization and deregulation, toward imposing an econocentric view of social institutions and private life, a quantifiable approach in which rugged individualism is promoted and there are winners and losers. It is an approach that assumed, with some arrogance, that free market business principles would improve a host of problems.[72]

Growing corporate influence has been part of a larger pattern of business mobilization for power growing out of the Powell memo and similar concerns expressed during the 1970s. Schools provided an important avenue for the business community to "fight back" against groups and policies that did not serve their interests. During the 1960s and 1970s many schools and teachers embraced progressive or inquiry-oriented reforms that inspired students to question the worth of the capitalist system. Corporate leaders felt that they were under attack. In the final analysis, growing corporate influence in education was a subset of a larger pattern of influence and control driven not by altruism or better ideas, but ultimately by the desire for power and profit.

Systemic Reform

Supporting and coinciding with the activities of business and government was growing reference to a concept known as "systemic reform." During hearings for America 2000, the concept of systemic reform appeared in widespread public discussion.[73] The theory of systemic reform was described and popularized by Marshall Smith and Jennifer O'Day in their seminal article, "Systemic School Reform" (1991). As the national reform movement grew in the 1980s, there was growing acknowledgment that the reform would have to be comprehensive and integrated. Piecemeal or fragmented reform would not lead to realization of national goals. As the term "systemic reform" came into general use, there were somewhat different meanings. For most, the concept included expanding the role of the states in education, emphasizing content-standards-driven reform, developing closely integrated and intellectually challenging curriculum and assessments, believing that all students can learn, and providing students with the opportunity to learn.[74]

Systemic reform, and the growing movement to develop national education standards, was motivated by at least three major factors. The first impetus for reform came from the notion that American students' performance had declined and fallen behind that of students in other nations, especially in mathematics and science. Combined with the general sense that the schools were failing, this made for a powerful motive for change. A second source of pressure for systemic reform came from the activities of governors, business leaders, and educators who participated in school reform efforts during the 1980s and early 1990s and who engaged in the process of strategic planning for school improvement. A third source of the movement for national standards was the example provided by the National Council of Teachers of Mathematics, who had developed voluntary national standards in late 1989, with much support and recognition.[75] A fourth source could be found in the context of a strong and influential conservative movement that had reshaped American politics over several decades, providing initial support for what would become a consensus approach to school reform.

Systemic reform made strong connections with the groundwork that had been laid during the 1980s, by the business community, at the Charlottesville education summit, and with reform efforts already underway in a number of states, notably California, Maryland, Massachusetts, and New York.[76] It also connected strongly with neoconservative educators such as Ravitch, Finn, Bennett, and others who championed and helped design and implement systemic reform.[77]

Adding to this mix of business, government, and institutional influences was a largely unnoticed and seemingly minor mechanism for influencing state legislation, ALEC, which presented corporate-backed legislative proposals by providing model legislation for state legislators to introduce in their legislatures and various forms of support. ALEC was backed by the deep pockets of wealthy corporate benefactors, and played a key role in the trenches of state-by-state battles over school reform. Additionally, in July 1990 the Bush administration created the National Education Goals Panel (NEGP) by executive order and charged it with monitoring progress. Chaired by Colorado Governor Roy Romer, the panel served to facilitate collaboration between Republicans and Democrats around a shared set of goals and helped shape a national consensus.[78]

America 2000

On April 18, 1991, President George Bush unveiled his program for the schools, *America 2000: An Education Strategy*. In his remarks at the presentation of the plan, Bush said, "If we want America to remain a leader . . . for the sake of the future, of our children and of the nation's, we must transform America's schools. The days of the status quo are over." Earlier that day, the president met with the "Business Core Group" in the Roosevelt Room of the White House and held a luncheon attended by more than ninety business and government leaders who were briefed on the president's education reform plan.[79] President Bush, Chester Finn, Paul O'Neill (CEO of ALCOA), John Akers, and David Kearns played leading roles in the meeting. The agenda outlined the role of business groups and emphasized the "synergism" of business and government collaboration. It stressed the need for a broad "nonpolitical" and bipartisan coalition "to implement the strategy and achieve the nation's education goals." It also emphasized the key roles of the NGA, the NEGP, the BRT, and the DOE "in recruiting broader support for reform." [80]

Planning for the announcement of America 2000 had been underway for some time and involved collaboration among government, business, and education scholars who advocated and collaborated on "systemic reform." A letter from Lauren B. Resnick and Marc Tucker to Secretary of Education Lamar Alexander provided a succinct outline of their work, funded by foundations, to develop "an approach to assessment that could lead to a national examination system." The letter provides a primer on key components of systemic reform including standards, testing, and a strategy for school restructuring that would become cornerstones of the America 2000 plan.[81]

At the heart of the *America 2000* program were six education goals, which grew out of the president's education summit with the governors held in Charlottesville, Virginia, in September 1989. During the summit the nation's governors developed a prearranged consensus on a blueprint for educational reform and agreed to: establish a process for setting national education goals; greater flexibility and accountability in use of federal resources; a state-by-state effort to restructure our education system; and annual reports on the nation's progress.[82] The goals presented in *America 2000* were an enhanced, fleshed-out version of the initial goals discussed at Charlottesville. As published in *America 2000*, the goals were:

Goal 1: Readiness for School. By the year 2000, all children in America will start school ready to learn.

Goal 2: High School Completion. By the year 2000, the high school graduation rate will increase to at least 90 percent.

Goal 3: Student Achievement and Citizenship. By the year 2000, American students will leave grades four, eight, and twelve having demonstrated competency in challenging subject matter including English, mathematics, science, history, and geography, and every school in America will ensure that all students learn to use their minds well, so they may be prepared for responsible citizenship, further learning, and productive employment in our modern economy.

Goal 4: Science and Mathematics. By the year 2000, U.S. students will be first in the world in science and mathematics achievement.

Goal 5: Adult Literacy and Lifelong Learning. By the year 2000, every adult will be literate and will possess the knowledge and skills necessary to compete in a global economy and exercise the rights and responsibilities of citizenship.

Goal 6: Safe, Disciplined, and Drug-Free Schools. By the year 2000, every school in America will be free of drugs and violence and will offer a disciplined environment conducive to learning.[83]

America 2000 was described as a "national strategy," "not a federal program," which "honors local control, relies on local initiative, and affirms states and localities." The "strategy" had four parts to be pursued simultaneously: "Our vision is of four big trains, moving simultaneously down four parallel tracks: Better and more accountable schools; a New Generation of American Schools; a Nation of Students continuing to learn throughout our lives; and communities where learning can happen."[84]

Thus, the major recommendations of *America 2000* included strategies to help improve the quality of teachers; choice, in the form of a voucher system, as a strategy for school improvement; creation of new innovative schools through the "New American Schools Development Corporation"; and the creation of new "World Class Standards" and achievement tests to measure student performance in five academic subjects: English, mathematics, science, history, and geography.

Like *A Nation at Risk* and similar reports of the 1980s, *America 2000* was predicated on the assumption that the nation's schools were in "crisis," and that their failure to educate knowledgeable and skilled workers was responsible for a U.S. decline in international economic competition. Though it was never enacted by Congress into law, the program created visible national goals and set the tone for federal policy during the Bush years. Publication of *America 2000* also resulted in a seemingly endless stream of commentary in the media and academic journals.

Discussion and Debate

Dennis P. Doyle, a senior fellow at the Hudson Institute, wrote that *America 2000* was the first serious policy initiative in the nation's history to address the matter of whether the federal role in education ought to be enlarged. In a glowing assessment, Doyle called the plan "altogether different ... vigorous, optimistic, and upbeat," and noted that it embraced the private sector, but did not reject a public role. He lauded the report's application of business ideas to education, characterizing the New American Schools Development Corporation as a "venture capitalist" that could move rapidly to create innovations. Doyle openly declared his view of schools as "the social institution that creates human capital" and called for new schools "rolled out and tested, precisely as new cars, new computers, new software or new airplanes are." The issue, he wrote, was not whether schools should be treated as a production process, but "how to transform a moribund institution into a high-performance organization, an organization that works."[85]

Gilbert T. Sewall of the EEN said the report's five basics, "standard language, mathematics, science, history, and geography," provided the "mental furniture" for useful lives. He cited Arthur Bestor's call, in the 1950s, for a focus on the intellectual component of education and high academic standards. Sewall also noted that rigorous academic testing was the norm in other industrial nations. Moreover, he suggested the reform would create a "mechanism for quality control in education."[86]

Others were critical. Harold Howe II, former U.S. commissioner of education, charged that *America 2000* constituted "a bold move" by the executive branch "to exert a powerful force on the affairs of schools," which failed to address school finance, growing poverty, and cultural and racial diversity. Howe also critiqued its "highly questionable" use of testing."[87] Evans Clinchy, a veteran of 1960s reform efforts, charged that Bush had "revived the hoary notion of education vouchers" that would allow public money to go to private schooling, and he noted that rhetoric of "revolutionary reform" contradicted the organizational straightjacket imposed by a "mandated curriculum" and "mandated tests" reifying "arbitrary, unrealistic subject-matter compartments" and forcing teachers to continue reliance on traditional teaching methods. He predicted that teachers would be judged on students' performance on standardized tests, which meant a reliance on lecturing, textbook assignments, and quizzes, and would inhibit development of students' intellects. "Instead of promoting . . . restructuring," he wrote, "America 2000 may well end up freezing in place the very hierarchical, top-down, anti-democratic structure that has plagued our present system of public education ever since it was put in place in the early decades of this century."[88]

Gerald W. Bracey, an NEA analyst, charged that the assumption that our schools were not performing well constituted "The Big Lie" about education. Bracey reported, "The evidence overwhelmingly shows that American schools have never achieved more . . . some indicators show them performing better than ever." He found high school graduation rates at an all-time high, and NAEP scores very stable. He characterized *A Nation at Risk* as "xenophobic screed that has little to do with education" and concluded that the commission's "rising tide of mediocrity" simply did not exist.[89]

Other researchers reaffirmed Bracey's report on the condition of public education, including Harold Hodgkinson, Iris Rothberg, and Richard M. Jaeger. Jaeger examined international comparisons and found the nation's scores strongly correlated with variables such as the mean percentage of children living in poverty, children living in single-parent families, and youth who work, meaning that test scores were a better gauge of poverty rates than the condition of schooling.[90] Jaeger cited an editorial by Robert Carr in the *Wall Street Journal* tracing the problems of America's schools to "urban blight, drugs, the erosion of the family," and a failure to provide sufficient funding. Carr concluded, "We should stop pushing the corporate model" on schools because competition "produces losers as well as winners."[91]

The National Council

Despite the public debate, by mid-1991, while the Senate and House debated *America 2000*, President Bush submitted legislation to authorize formation of the National Council on Education Standards and Testing (NCEST). A bipartisan group, the council issued a final report in early 1992. *Raising Standards for American Education* confirmed both the desirability and feasibility of creating a system of national standards and voluntary assessments. Rather than the national tests advocated in *America 2000*, the council recommended flexibility for states.[92] The council, co-chaired by Governors Carroll Campbell and Roy Romer, had thirty-two members from government, education, and business including neoconservatives and strong advocates of systemic reform such as Lynne V. Cheney, Chester E. Finn, Jr., Keith Geiger, Orrin Hatch, David Kearns, Roger B. Porter, Lauren Resnick, Albert Shanker, and Marshall S. Smith. Its report established a working blueprint for the movement toward accountability in education.

The Condition of America's Schools

Additional support for Bracey's claims came from the findings of a major study of education commissioned by none other than the Bush administration, the Sandia Report. The Sandia National Laboratories, in New Mexico, were a component of the U.S. Department of Energy. Major findings of the Sandia Report flatly contradicted claims about education being circulated by the Bush administration, and the report was suppressed.

The saga of the Sandia Report and how it was suppressed is interesting. George Bush forcefully announced his intent to become "the education president." Because realization of this goal meant improving on the supposed failings of the schools, evidence on the conditions of schooling would be needed. Secretary of Energy James Watkins instructed the Sandia National Laboratories, formerly a wing of the Atomic Energy Commission, to conduct a comprehensive study of the status of education in the United States. The study drew from existing data sources and was originally drafted in late 1990, then circulated among various educators and researchers for comment. When administration officials discovered that many of its findings contradicted their claims about the condition of schools, officials in the DOE and others in the administration demanded that the report not be released, but that it instead be subjected to further review by personnel at the NCES and the NSF. Reviewers detected trivial "flaws" in the report and recommended that the report be rewritten and subject to further review—delaying its final release. In the meantime, photocopied drafts of the report had been leaked and were being circulated. A condensed version of the report was printed in the *Albuquerque Journal* on September 24, 1991. This prompted Secretary Watkins to issue a response, dated September 30, which stated that the findings of the report were "dead wrong."[93]

At one meeting where engineers who had written the Sandia Report presented an overview to staff from the Department of Energy, the Department of Education, and some congressmen, attended by many leading players, David Kearns reportedly said, "You bury this or I'll bury you." Diane Ravitch denied that Kearns said this, but Robert Huelskamp, one of the three engineers who authored the report, has affirmed it.[94] Moreover, an article in *Education Week* reported that "administration officials, particularly Mr. Kearns, reacted angrily at the meeting." The article also contained both allegations and denials of suppression.[95] The engineers responsible for the report were forbidden at one point to leave New Mexico to talk about their findings. The official reason given was that the report was undergoing peer review by the DOE and the NSF and was not ready for publication. The report was never published as such, but appeared nearly two years later in 1993 in the *Journal of Educational Research*. A summary article appeared in *The Kappan* the same year.[96]

The findings of the Sandia Report, like the Bracey study, were strikingly different from the administration's line and contrasted sharply with the growing national assumption that the schools were failing. Sandia researchers found strong evidence that schools in the United States were performing well, with the exception of many of the schools serving poor and minority youth. SAT scores had declined because of the much larger number of test takers. International comparisons were inherently flawed, a case of making unfair cross-cultural comparisons. When the top students in the United States were compared with top students in other countries, U.S. students performed as well or better. Moreover, in higher education, the United States was the unquestioned leader.[97] These findings, which flatly contradicted the thesis of *A Nation at Risk* and much of the reform agenda, hover like a ghost at the banquet table of school reform.

Berliner and Biddle suggest that self-interest may have been a factor in the Bush administration's program for school reform. Chris Whittle, a business tycoon with an interest in schools, was a friend of Lamar Alexander's, who had previously served on Whittle's board, acted as a consultant, and greatly profited from transactions in Whittle stock. In quick succession in 1991, the Bush administration published *America 2000*, which called for vouchers; Whittle formed the Edison Project to create a proposed coast-to-coast network of for-profit schools; and Chester Finn, former assistant secretary of education and a major architect of *America 2000*, signed on to work for the Edison project. At the least, this scenario contributed to suspicions that the administration had a conflict of interests.[98]

Regardless of the motivation behind *America 2000*, it became the Bush administration's education program, and the National Education Goals Panel was established to monitor progress. The Goals Panel quickly realized that assessing achievement of the national goals would require a clear and specific understanding of what was meant by "competency" and "challenging subject matter." Thus, in 1991 and 1992, the DOE awarded grants to selected groups for the development of voluntary national standards in science, history, the arts, civics, geography, foreign languages, and English. Mathematics standards had already been developed by the National Council of Teachers of Mathematics in 1989, pointing the way for other groups.[99]

Debate in Social Studies

Among the six national goals for schools, "social studies" was nowhere to be found, replaced instead by history and geography. This shift was a major change from the earlier reports of the excellence era, which generally included "social studies" as one of the core subjects. Now, in the 1990s, as the reform movement gathered steam, the inclusion of social studies as a broad field including history and the social sciences had apparently ended.

The evidence strongly suggests that the shift from social studies to history and geography was a result of the neoconservative revival of history and its alliance with educational conservatives in positions of power. As we have seen, during the 1980s and 1990s a revival of traditional history was led by Diane Ravitch, William

Bennett, Chester Finn, Paul Gagnon, Bill Honig, and others and supported by substantial funding from the Bradley Foundation and others.[100] The revival of history was based on the scapegoating of social studies, and the argument that the field was to blame for the poor performance of U.S. students on standardized tests in history. This move to reassert the dominance of traditional history combined with the human capital emphasis of the national commission reports to form a powerful government line in favor of a history-geography matrix in opposition to advocates of a broader, more inclusive, and progressive social studies curriculum. Diane Ravitch, chief architect of the California Framework, served as assistant secretary of education during the Bush administration. Ravitch commented in 1991 to a national meeting of state social studies supervisors who were raising questions about the national standards movement and its failure to include social studies that their protests and questions were to no avail, because "the train has already left the station."[101]

By the mid-1980s, the new and newer social studies had run their course, and advocates of a new rendition of traditional history began to assert leadership. Social studies made an easy scapegoat, floundering, with unclear definition and aims, seemingly directed by fashion. During the 1980s and 1990s the revival of history became the dominant trend in the field. Soon after the Bush administration's adoption of the *America 2000* program, the Center for Civic Education, a longtime leader in civic education under the leadership of Charles Quigley, organized a coalition of teachers of civics, U.S. government, and law-related education who lobbied hard for the inclusion of civics alongside of history and geography in goal three of *America 2000*. Over objections from officials in the administration, including the DOE and the NEH, Congress added civics to the list of subjects for which national standards would be developed. And, by 1994, the National Council for Economic Education successfully obtained federal funding for the development of national standards in economics.[102]

The response of social studies leaders to these developments was mixed. In the early 1990s, leaders of the NCSS attempted to persuade policymakers that the term social studies is a useful umbrella term, that history, geography, and the other social sciences could coexist within the social studies curriculum, but to little avail. Then, responding to frantic telephone calls from many social studies teachers and curriculum specialists, the NCSS took action. After being warned, "The train is leaving the station. Hop on or be left behind," a few NCSS leaders accepted appointments to one or another of the standards development teams and were branded traitors to the cause of an integrated social studies curriculum.[103]

While there were many critics of the developing trend, the NCSS chose to respond to the revival of history and the criticism of social studies by developing a new version of the consensus definition that it had always promoted and by participating in the standards movement by developing its own set of standards statements. The goal was to develop a set of integrated standards that would draw on content from the various social studies subjects.[104] The thinking among the NCSS leadership was that the move toward standards-based reform and high-stakes testing was the wave of the future and that not being involved would have dire consequences for the organization and for the survivability of a broadly defined social studies. So, as a response to the America 2000 initiative, NCSS leaders decided that if a move toward standards and testing was inevitable, it was better to be involved than not to be involved. This would place social studies advocates in a position to have some influence over the eventual standards and testing program, and provide teachers with assistance in implementing diverse standards statements in state and local curricula. As Nash, Crabtree, and Dunn recalled, in their work on the National History Standards Project:

> History standards were clearly on the country's agenda. . . . The matter boiled down to who would write them. Those who were at first reluctant about the wisdom of this enterprise soon decided that they might compromise their own best interests if they failed to join in. If the cards were being dealt, why would historians or social studies educators not want seats around the big table?[105, 106]

As part of its efforts toward development of standards, in the early 1990s NCSS president Margit McGuire and the board of directors launched a process by which a new definition would be crafted. The board wanted to establish a definition of social studies that was "concise, clearly stated, and consistent with sound democratic and participatory principles." At its meeting in January 1992, the board crafted a brief definition statement to be circulated for comment and review. The initial statement read:

> Social studies is the integration of history, the social sciences, and the humanities to promote civic competence.

Comments from members and affiliates on the initial definition revealed a badly divided social studies profession and a great deal of disagreement. There were a total of seventy-three responses from individuals, committees, and affiliated groups. Only nine supported the definition as written, six called for its rejection, nineteen submitted a new or revised definition, and sixteen wanted geography listed in the definition. Several recommended that history be removed from top billing. A few leading social studies theorists submitted comments and alternative definitions, including Shirley H. Engle, Anna S. Ochoa, and James L. Barth, each calling for a focus on social issues or problems, critical thinking, and reflective approaches to teaching.[107] After consideration of comments from members and affiliates, in 1992 the board of directors adopted a two-part definition:

> Social studies is the integrated study of the social sciences and humanities to promote civic competence.

> Within the school program, social studies provides coordinated, sys-
> tematic study drawing upon such disciplines as anthropology, archaeology,
> economics, geography, history, law, philosophy, political science, psychology,
> religion, and sociology, as well as appropriate content from the humanities,
> mathematics, and natural sciences. The primary purpose of social studies is
> to help young people develop the ability to make informed and reasoned
> decisions for the public good as citizens of a culturally diverse, democratic
> society in an interdependent world.[108]

As the board worked with the comments and suggestions in the summer of
1992, it developed its compromise, removing mention of any particular discipline
from its initial sentence and opting for a consensus definition that would alienate as few as possible. Also, it chose not to include any reference to social issues,
social problems, or reflective methods of teaching.[109] James S. Leming, a contrarian
within the NCSS, described it as "the sum of the problems we face." He stated
that it was "illustrative of the trend to equate social studies with the chimeric goal
of citizenship," that it "eschews the mastery of subject matter and the transmission of a shared history and cultural heritage," and that it provided a "weak and
ephemeral perspective" compared to goal statements being prepared by other
organizations.[110]

Despite a worthy effort to state a clear definition and purpose, the aim of
"civic competence" stopped far short of the long held potential envisioned by
progressive, reconstructionist, or critical educators who held goals of "social
improvement," "social justice," or "social transformation." In its earliest years the
NCSS established a consensus, "umbrella" definition, perhaps in part because the
social studies "movement" was fledgling and buffeted by critics who advocated
a discipline-based orientation. The consensus position had been challenged by
many social studies educators over the years, including Harold Rugg in the 1920s
and 1930s and by the new social studies movement in the 1960s. Nevertheless, it
appeared to have staying power.

Conclusion

By the end of the Bush presidency, at least a few things were clear. Progressive
education was at bay—and a corporate model for school reform was in ascendance. The corporate model of systemic reform would bring a more conservative
approach to schooling marked by imposition of standards, accountability through
testing, and in social studies a return to traditional history and geography, resulting
in a decline in reflective activities and discussion in classrooms. The years of the
Bush presidency were a key period in which leaders in business and government
set the excellence reform in a new direction, moving further from an approach to
education centered on inputs and toward an approach to reform focused on outcomes as measured by test scores and other forms of performance accountability,

in which market mechanisms borrowed from business would be used to change the workings of the educational system. Business leaders developed a ten-year plan for systemic reform, focused on moving the system toward privatization, rigorous implementation of standards and testing, and inculcation of corporate citizens. During this period, business influence became the dominant trend, with schooling focused more and more on economic purposes. In short, corporate America was learning to have a stronger and more pervasive influence.

The rising movement for "systemic reform" was driven by a combination of factors. The business community, which had long been active in lobbying efforts, had gotten its act together like never before in a broad effort to influence American life. Its emphasis on market-based school reform gave the BRT and other groups a tangible and positive outlet for influencing a rising generation. From the perspective of business leaders, there were serious questions about the quality of schooling and the skills of many of the system's graduates, the "human capital" needed for production. Moreover, many business and government leaders harbored deeper questions related to the philosophy of schooling that gained popularity in the 1960s and 1970s and the questioning of the establishment that it sometimes fomented. They wanted a more traditional emphasis on cultural literacy and the academic disciplines.

Ultimately, the movement for systemic reform in education was traceable to the 1960s and the reactions to issues of that time, in schools and the society, many taking form in the early to mid-1970s: the 1971 Lewis Powell memo and the subsequent rise of the Business Roundtable; the business backlash and power grab; the CBE and its sentiment for a return to traditional, basic education; the rising power of the conservative and neoconservative movements, combined with the New Right and an evangelical resurgence, including the Heritage Foundation and other influential moneyed groups. In a sense, after all the turmoil and questioning of the 1960s and 1970s, the empire was striking back, moving toward creation of a "new world order," moving toward retaking control of the schools, a central, powerful, and somewhat malleable cultural institution.[111] But, its work was not done and would continue for at least the next two decades.

Notes

1. See, for example, DOE, *America 2000: An Education Strategy, Sourcebook* (Washington, DC: DOE, July 29, 1991), 2–3.
2. ABC News/*Washington Post* poll conducted October 28–November 1, 1988, and Gallup poll conducted April 1987, cited in Patrick J. McGuinn, *No Child Left Behind and the Transformation of Federal Education Policy, 1965–2005* (Lawrence: University of Kansas Press, 2006).
3. Jennifer Hochschild and Bridget Scott, "Trends: Governance and Reform of Pubic Education in the U.S.," *POQ* 62, no. 1 (Spring 1998): 79–120.
4. "The Basic Speech: George Bush," *NYT*, February 4, 1988, B10.
5. David Hoffman, "Bush Details Proposals on Education Spending," *WP*, June 15, 1988, A8.

6. McGuinn, *No Child*, 56–57.
7. Charles Kolb, *White House Daze: The Unmaking of Domestic Policy in the Bush Years* (New York: Free Press, 1994), 126.
8. Ibid., 132.
9. Patricia M. Bryan to James C. Murr, Presidential Transmittal of "Educational Excellence Act of 1989," March 30, 1989, #021149, Box 2, Bush Papers.
10. Mike Cohen, "Governors' Education Meeting with President-elect Bush," NGA memo to Raymond Scheppach and Barry Van Lare, December 12, 1988, cited in Maris A. Vinovskis, *The Road to Charlottesville: The 1989 Education Summit* (Washington, DC: National Education Goals Panel, 1999), 26.
11. Vinovskis, *Road to Charlottesville*, 25.
12. Ibid.
13. NGA, *Time for Results: The Governors' 1991 Report on Education* (Washington, DC: NGA, 1986).
14. NGA, "Synthesis of Pre-Summit Outreach Hearings," NGA, September 1989, cited in Vinovskis, *Road to Charlottesville*.
15. Bill Clinton, "Education Summit: Preparations and Expectations," to Democratic Governors' Association, September 25, 1989, cited in Vinovskis, *Road to Charlottesville*, 35.
16. Chester Finn interview with Patrick J. McGuinn, January 7, 2003, in McGuinn, *No Child*, 60.
17. McGuinn, *No Child*.
18. John F. Akers to the President, September 18, 1989, #74477, Box 6, Bush Papers.
19. See Kevin Phillips, *American Dynasty: Aristocracy, Fortune, and the Politics of Deceit in the House of Bush* (New York: Viking, 2004). See also James J. Drummey, *The Establishment's Man* (Appleton, WI: Western Islands Publishers, 1991); Herbert S. Parmet, *George Bush: The Life of a Lone Star Yankee* (New York: Scribners, 1997); John Robert Greene, *The Presidency of George Bush* (Lawrence: University of Kansas Press, 2000); Martin J. Medhurst, *The Rhetorical Presidency of George H.W. Bush* (College Station: Texas A & M Press, 2006); and Kolb, *White House Daze*.
20. Kathy Emery, "The Business Roundtable and Systemic Reform: How Corporate-Engineered High-Stakes Testing Has Eliminated Community Participation in Developing Educational Goals and Policies" (Doctoral Dissertation, University of California, Davis, 2002).
21. Edward Rust, *No Turning Back: A Progress Report on the Business Roundtable Education Initiative* (Washington, DC: Business Roundtable, 1999), 1, cited in Kathy Emery and Susan O'Hanian, *Why Is Corporate America Bashing Our Public Schools?* (Portsmouth, NH: Heinemann, 2004), 34, and in Emery, "The Business Roundtable," 46.
22. John F. Akers, "Business Roundtable Call to Action," undated memo, "08232-001 folder," Box 1, Nelson Files.
23. John F. Akers to the President, September 18, 1989, #74477, Box 6, Bush Papers.
24. BRT Task Force on Education, "The Education Decade: A Business Commitment to America's Children," attached to John F. Akers to the President, September 18, 1989, #74477, Box 6, Bush Papers.
25. Mike Cohen, "Governors' Education Meeting with President-elect Bush"; Ray Scheppach to David Demarest, January 24, 1989, in "#08232-001 folder," Box 1, Nelson Files.
26. Lanny Griffith to Steve Studdert, March 27, 1989, "#08232 folder," Box 1, Nelson Files.
27. Confidential, "Branstad Education Initiative for NGA," July 17, 1989; Draft, "Possible Scenario," NGA Conference and Summit, undated memo; Kate L. Moore to Roger B. Porter, March 23, 1989; and Kate L. Moore to Roger B. Porter, March 28, 1989, in "80232-001 folder," Box 1, Nelson Files.
28. Reagan Walker, "Education 'Summit' Scheduled for September, Governors Say," *EW*, May 24, 1989.

29. Roger B. Porter to Governor Sununu, September 20, 1989, and Summit Program Draft, 93–160, in "08232-001 folder," Box 2, Nelson Files.

30. New York State Education Department (NYSED), *Federal Education Policy and the States, 1945–2009: A Brief Synopsis* (Albany: New York State Archives, 2006, revised 2009), 55.

31. George H.W. Bush, "Remarks at the Education Summit Welcoming Ceremony at the University of Virginia in Charlottesville," September 27, 1989, Bush Public Papers.

32. "The Summit Conference on Education Working Groups," 1989, "08232-005 folder," Box 1, Nelson Files. According to Vinovskis, Perpich did not attend the meeting.

33. Vinovskis, *Road to Charlottesville*, 38; David Hoffman and David S. Broder, "Summit Sets 7 Main Goals for Education," *WP*, September 29, 1989, "08781 folder," Box 2, Nelson Files.

34. "A Jeffersonian Compact," *NYT*, October 1, 1989, 22.

35. Ibid.

36. Vinovskis, *Road to Charlottesville*, 42.

37. Deirdre Carmody, "Teachers Praise Bush's Effort to Set a New Education Agenda," *NYT*, September 30, 1989; Bernard Weiraub, "Bush and Governors Set Education Goals," *NYT*, September 29, 1989, "08781 folder," Box 2, Nelson Files.

38. Frank Swoboda, "A First Step Toward National School Reform," *WP*, September 29, 1989, "08781 folder," Box 2, Nelson Files.

39. James P. Gannon, "Would Jefferson Believe Bush's Education Summit?" *DN*, September 29, 1989, "08781 folder," Box 2, Nelson Files.

40. Carol Innerst, "Reaction to Progress Mixed at Education Summit," *WT*, September 29, 1989; Dan Warrensford, "The Feds Can't Help Improve the Schools," *USAT*, September 29, 1989, "08781 folder," Box 2, Nelson Files.

41. Marshall Ingwersen, "'Competition' Is Meeting's Byword," *CSM*, October 2, 1989, "08781 folder," Box 2, Nelson Files.

42. Terry Branstad to Bill Clinton, October 26, 1989, "National Education Goals—Development (1) 08232-005 folder," Box 2, Nelson Files.

43. Roger B. Porter to Governors on Education Task Force and Cabinet Members, December 5, 1989, "National Education Goals—Development (1) 08232-005 folder," Box 2, Nelson Files.

44. Ray Scheppach and Mike Cohen to Governors on Education Task Force and Administration Representatives, December 5, 1989, "National Education Goals—Development (1) 08232-005 folder," Box 2, Nelson Files.

45. Ibid.

46. Roger B. Porter to Governor Campbell and Governor Clinton, January 7, 1990, "National Education Goals—Development (1) 08232-005 folder," Box 2, Nelson Files.

47. George H. W. Bush, Address Before a Joint Session of Congress on the State of the Union, January 31, 1990, APP.

48. McGuinn, *No Child*, 62.

49. Ibid., 63.

50. The Ravitch and Finn papers contain references on their PR campaign and "crusade" to change the direction of American schooling. See, especially, "*America 2000* Crusade," attachment, John Crisp to Lamar Alexander, May 28, 1991, "America 2000" folder, Box 95, Finn Papers.

51. Amy L. Schwartz to Windy White, October 13, 1989, #081455, Box 6, Bush Papers.

52. Rhea F. Stein to Roger B. Porter, attached "Program" and "Participants," October 20, 1989, #091671, Box 7, Bush Papers.

53. See, for example, documents on California Education Summit, 1989, #101316, Box 8, and Illinois Education Summit, #121298, Box 11, Bush Papers.

54. Sharon Beder, *Suiting Themselves: How Corporations Drive the Global Agenda* (London: Earthscan, 2006); Ronald W. Evans, *This Happened in America: Harold Rugg and the Censure of Social Studies* (Charlotte, NC: Information Age, 2007).

55. Beder, *Suiting Themselves*; see also William Greider, *Who Will Tell the People: The Betrayal of American Democracy* (New York: Simon and Schuster, 1992); David Ricci, *The Transformation of American Politics: The New Washington and the Rise of the Think Tanks* (New Haven: Yale University Press, 1993); Sidney Blumenthal, *The Rise of the Counter-Establishment: From Conservative Ideology to Political Power* (New York: Time Books, 1986); G. William Domhoff, *Who Rules America? Power and Politics*, 4th edition (New York: McGraw Hill, 2002).

56. Robert G. Monks, *Corpocracy: How CEOs and the Business Roundtable Hijacked the World's Greatest Wealth Machine—And How to Get It Back* (New York: John Wiley and Sons, 2007), 45.

57. Lewis F. Powell to Eugene B. Snydor, "Confidential Memorandum: Attack on American Free Enterprise System," August 23, 1971, 1, 11, 25–26, Powell Papers.

58. Charlie Cray, "The Lewis Powell Memo—Corporate Blueprint to Dominate Democracy," August 23, 2011, http://www.greenpeace.org/usa/en/news-and-blogs/campaign-blog/the-lewis-powell-memo-corporate-blueprint-to-/blog/36466/; Stephen Higgs, "A Call to Arms for Class War: From the Top Down," May 11–13, 2012, http://www.counterpunch.org/2012/05/11/a-call-to-arms-for-class-war-from-the-top-down/.

59. Kim Phillips-Fein, *Invisible Hands: The Making of the Conservative Movement from the New Deal to Reagan* (New York: W.W. Norton, 2009); Lee Fang, *The Machine: A Field Guide to the New Right* (New York: New Press, 2013).

60. Jacob S. Hacker and Paul Pierson, *Winner-Take-All Politics: How Washington Made the Rich Richer—And Turned Its Back on the Middle Class* (New York: Simon and Schuster, 2010).

61. Monks, *Corpocracy*, 61.

62. Powell, "Confidential Memorandum," 16–17.

63. William B. Johnston and Arnold E. Packer, *Workforce 2000: Work and Workers for the Twenty-First Century* (Indianapolis, IN: Hudson Institute, 1987), 116–117; Stephen I. Danzansky to Diane Ravitch, August 5, 1991, "Workforce 2000, 1991" folder, Box 32, Ravitch Papers.

64. David T. Kearns, "The United States Educational System: An Educational Recovery Plan," delivered at the Economic Club of Detroit, Detroit, Michigan, October 26, 1987, *Vital Speeches of the Day*, 150–153.

65. David Kearns and Denis Doyle, *Winning the Brain Race: A Bold Plan to Make Our Schools Competitive* (San Francisco: Institute for Contemporary Studies, 1988); Denis Doyle and Marsha Levine, "American Business and Public Education: The Question of Quality," *PJE* 63, no. 2 (Winter 1986): 17–26.

66. Tom Zeller, Jr., "David T. Kearns, Champion of Education Reform, Dies at 80," *NYT*, February 28, 2011.

67. John Chubb and Terry Moe, *Politics, Markets, and America's Schools* (Washington, DC: Brookings Institution, 1990), jacket.

68. Kenneth J. Saltman, "What (Might) Happen When Teachers and Other Academics Connect Reason to Power and Power to Resistance?" Rouge Forum Conference, April 2012, Vancouver, BC; Kenneth J. Saltman, *The Failure of Corporate School Reform* (New York: Paradigm Publishing, 2012); Gene V. Glass and Dewayne A. Matthews, "Are Data Enough? Review of Chubb and Moe's *Politics, Markets and America's Schools*," *ER* 20, no. 3 (1991): 24–27.

69. Chubb and Moe, *Politics*, book jacket; Anthony S. Bryk and Valerie E. Lee, "Is Politics the Problem and Markets the Answer? An Essay Review of *Politics, Markets and America's Schools, EER* 11, no. 4 (1992): 439–451; Glass and Matthews, "Are Data Enough?"

70. "Nine Essential Components of a Successful Education System," *Baltimore Sun*, April 24, 1991.

71. Hacker and Pierson, *Winner-Take-All*; Beder, *Suiting Themselves*; Bill Moyers, "How Wall Street Occupied America," *NAT,* November 11, 2011; Moyers, "Triggers of Economic

Inequality," January 15, 2012, billmoyers.com; see also "Asia-Pacific Education Symposium," Boxes 2–4, Bruno Manno Papers, which suggests that participants sought to create a "new world order" with a "classical education" for all.

72. Monks, *Corpocracy*.
73. NYSED, *Federal Education Policy*, 58.
74. Marshall Smith and Jennifer O'Day, "Systemic School Reform," in Susan H. Fuhrman and Betty Malen, Eds., *Politics of Curriculum and Testing* (Bristol, PA; Falmer Press, 1991); Maris A. Vinovskis, "An Analysis of the Concept and Uses of Systemic Educational Reform," *AERJ* 33, no. 1 (Spring 1996): 53–85.
75. Diane Ravitch, "Developing National Standards in Education," paper presented at the American Sociological Association Meeting, Pittsburgh, PA, August 1992, cited in Vinovskis, "Systemic Reform," 55–56; NCTM, *Curriculum and Evaluation Standards for School Mathematics* (Washington, DC: NCTM Commission on Standards for School Mathematics, 1989).
76. Vinovskis, "Systemic Reform."
77. Diane Ravitch, *The Death and Life of the Great American School System: How Testing and Choice Are Undermining Education* (New York: Basic Books, 2010); Chester E. Finn, Jr., *Troublemaker: A Personal History of School Reform Since Sputnik* (Princeton, NJ: Princeton University Press, 2008). See also Ravitch Papers, Box 29, and Finn Papers, Box 95, for evidence regarding their roles.
78. NYSED, *Federal Education Policy*.
79. "Luncheon (Education Initiatives)" April 18, 1991, Folder 1, Box 95, Finn Papers.
80. "Agenda: Core Business Group Breakfast Meeting," April 18, 1991, Folder 1, Box 95, Finn Papers.
81. Lauren B. Resnick and Marc Tucker to Lamar Alexander, February 28, 1991, Folder 1, Box 95, Finn Papers.
82. "Joint Statement, the President's Education Summit with Governors, University of Virginia, Charlottesville, Virginia, September 27–28, 1989," *America 2000*, 73–80.
83. *America 2000*, 59–72.
84. Ibid., 13.
85. Denis P. Doyle, "America 2000," *PDK* 73, no. 3 (November 1991): 184–191.
86. Gilbert T. Sewall, "America 2000: An Appraisal," *PDK* 73, no. 3 (November 1991): 204–209.
87. Harold Howe II, "America 2000: A Bumpy Ride on Four Trains," *PDK* 73, no. 3 (November 1991): 192–203.
88. Evans Clinchy, "America 2000: Reform, Revolution, or Just More Smoke and Mirrors?" *PDK* 73, no. 3 (November 1991): 210–218.
89. Gerald W. Bracey, "Why Can't They Be Like We Were," *PDK* 73, no 2 (October 1991): 104–117; Gerald W. Bracey, *Bail Me Out! Handling Difficult Data and Tough Questions About Public Schools* (Thousand Oaks, CA: Corwin Press, 2000).
90. Richard M. Jaeger, "Weak Measurement Serving Presumptive Policy," *PDK* 74, no. 2 (October 1992): 118–126, 128.
91. Ibid., 126.
92. NCEST, *Raising Standards for American Education* (Washington, DC: NCEST, 1992), 27–28.
93. Daniel Tanner, "A Nation Truly at Risk," *PDK* 75, no. 4 (December 1993): 288–297; David C. Berliner and Bruce J. Biddle, *The Manufactured Crisis: Myths, Fraud, and the Attack on America's Public Schools* (Reading, MA: Addison-Wesley, 1995), 165–168; David C. Berliner and Gene V. Glass, *50 Myths and Lies That Threaten America's Public Schools: The Real Crisis in Education* (New York: Teachers College, 2014).
94. Gerald Bracey, "Righting Wrongs," *HP*, December 3, 2007; Gerald Bracey, "Diane Does Rush," *HP*, December 6, 2007.
95. Julie A. Miller, "Report Questioning 'Crisis' in Education Triggers an Uproar," *EW*, October 9, 1991.

96. C.C. Carson, "Perspectives on Education in America: An Annotated Briefing," *JER* 86, no. 5 (May/June 1993): 259–265; Robert M. Huelskamp, "Perspectives on Education in America," *PDK* 74, no. 9 (May 1993): 718–721.

97. Carson, "Perspectives"; Huelskamp, "Perspectives."

98. Berliner and Biddle, *Manufactured Crisis*, 149–150.

99. Diane Ravitch, *National Standards in American Education: A Citizen's Guide* (Washington, DC: The Brookings Institution, 1995).

100. Diane Ravitch, "The Decline and Fall of History Teaching," *NYTM*, November 17, 1985, 50–53, 101, 117; Robert Stehle, "Righting Philanthropy," *NAT*, June 30, 1997, 15–20.

101. Judy Butler, Arkansas curriculum coordinator for social studies, in attendance at meeting, in interview with the author at AERA, 1998.

102. C. Frederick Risinger and Jesus Garcia, "National Assessment and the Social Studies," *The Clearing House* 68, no. 4 (March/April 1995): 225–228.

103. Ibid., 227.

104. Ibid.

105. Gary Nash, Charlotte Crabtree, and Ross Dunn, *History on Trial: Culture Wars and the Teaching of the Past* (New York: Knopf, 1997), 158; Kevin Vinson, "National Curriculum Standards and Social Studies Education: Dewey, Freire, Foucault, and the Construction of a Radical Critique," paper presented at the annual meeting of the National Council for the Social Studies, 1998, 9.

106. Vinson, "National Standards."

107. "Definition" folder, 1991–92, including James L. Barth to Margit McGuire, June 15, 1992, Shirley H. Engle to McGuire, March 7, 1992, and Anna S. Ochoa to McGuire, April 14, 1992, Accession #960307, File 2, McGuire Papers.

108. Ibid.

109. Ibid.

110. James S. Leming to George Mehaffy, November 1, 1993, Accession #960307, File 2, McGuire Papers.

111. There was explicit attention to the international dimensions of school reform during the Bush administration and a specific focus on a global transformation of schooling to establish a "new world order." See George Bush to Members of the Asia Pacific Economic Cooperation, August 5, 1992, and DOE, Asia-Pacific Education Symposium, "Education Standards for the 21st Century," Box 3, Manno Papers.

FIGURE 1 Terrel H. Bell, with Ronald Reagan (Reagan Presidential Library, no. C 14184-21a)

FIGURE 2 William J. Bennett, Secretary of Education, 1985–1988 (George Bush Presidential Library)

FIGURE 3 Chester E. Finn, Jr. (Courtesy of Thomas B. Fordham Foundation)

FIGURE 4 George H.W. Bush (Executive Office of the President of the United States)

FIGURE 5 Diane Ravitch, with Barbara Bush (George Bush Presidential Library)

FIGURE 6 David T. Kearns (Rhees Library, University of Rochester)

FIGURE 7 Lewis F. Powell, Jr. (Library of Congress, LC–USZ62–60140, 1976)

FIGURE 8 William J. Clinton (Bob McNeely, White House)

FIGURE 9 William G. Spady (Courtesy of William G. Spady)

FIGURE 10 Lynne V. Cheney (Defense.gov_photo_essay_090110-D-7203C-014)

FIGURE 11 Gary B. Nash (Courtesy of NCHS)

FIGURE 12 Louis V. Gerstner, Jr. (Kenneth V. Zirkel, 1995)

FIGURE 13 George W. Bush (White House photo by Eric Draper_030114-O-0000D-001)

FIGURE 14 Bill Gates (World Economic Forum)

FIGURE 15 Barack Obama and Arne Duncan (www.ed.gov: back-to-school-potus-1.jpg)

5

THE BATTLE OVER STANDARDS

During the 1990s, the growing movement for school reform would reach a new level of intensity. Rhetorical support and legislative efforts for accountability reform continued to grow at both the state and federal levels. The movement for reform would be given legal status as the "official" federal government-approved direction for change with passage of Goals 2000 and the reauthorization of ESEA in 1994. By the late 1990s, with continued lobbying and political efforts from the business community and nongovernmental organizations, in concert with the Clinton administration and many governors, a national consensus was emerging around establishment of standards and high-stakes testing, with consequences, as the primary means for implementing educational reform. By the year 2000, virtually all the states had established standards and some system of accountability, though efforts were uneven and results varied widely.

In social studies, the revival of traditional history and geography continued to wield influence, as increasing numbers of states revamped their curricula and relabeled courses. At the national level, beginning in the early 1990s, there were efforts to develop voluntary national standards by a number of social studies groups. One of these efforts, the National Standards for United States History, led to a lengthy national controversy, temporarily derailing efforts toward development of standards. Another controversy over Outcome-Based Education (OBE) and little-known educational psychologist William G. Spady further delayed movement toward national standards and tests. However, the general trend toward a national consensus in support of standards, testing, and accountability as the core of systemic reform continued almost unabated in the states, driven by the continuing "crisis" of mediocre performance of American students on international comparisons and the general sense that the nation's schools were failing. Behind what appeared to be a national consensus was an array of opposition groups on the left and the right that continued raising questions about the direction of reform.

Clinton and Standards-Based Education

On January 20, 1993, the George H.W. Bush administration was succeeded by the administration of William Jefferson Clinton, formerly the popular governor of Arkansas, and a Democrat. It was apparent early on that differences between the educational program of the Clinton administration and its predecessor's would be rather small. Clinton had served as co-chair of the 1989 Charlottesville Summit at which the general blueprint for reform and the six national goals had been developed. He was one of the key leaders of the 1986 NGA Summit leading to publication of *Time for Results*, and he was deeply committed to federal action for education reform. In his campaign and administration he drew on ideas from the Charlottesville Summit and the work of the National Education Goals Panel (NEGP) on which he served, as well as initiatives from the previous Congress and the work of the states. Moreover, as a member of the Democratic Leadership Council (DLC) he had strong ties to the corporate sector and was committed to continuation of the educational reform movement.

The DLC, founded in 1985, was built on the premise that the Democratic Party should shift away from the leftward turn it had taken in the 1960s and support more viable centrist/progressive approaches to governance. Inspired by a series of electoral losses, it advocated fiscal responsibility, shedding the party's tax-and-spend reputation and adopting more moderate social and economic policies. In 1990, the DLC issued the "New Orleans Declaration: A Democratic Agenda for the 1990s," describing its mission to "expand opportunity, not government," supporting economic growth and a new politics of reciprocal "responsibility." The declaration also supported "the free market, regulated in the public interest" and the need to "invest in the skills and ingenuity of our people."[1] Education reform and "investment" were a prominent part of the New Democrats' agenda.

Support for education reform was a centerpiece of Bill Clinton's 1992 presidential campaign. He pledged that "in a Clinton administration, students and parents and teachers will get a real Education President."[2] Clinton made an effort, prior to his election, to distinguish his approach from that of George Bush. Clinton gave greater rhetorical attention to issues of educational equity, citing Jonathan Kozol and the "savage inequalities" in school spending.[3] He complained that the Bush program had no record of following its lofty ideas for reform with money; that the New Development Schools that Bush proposed left most of our schools out of the reform process; and that it amounted to a plan "to tinker around the edges," a "trickle-down education" rather than a comprehensive plan to restructure and improve all the schools. Like Bush, Clinton called for world-class standards, national educational goals, and "a meaningful national examination system" to support their realization.[4] Clinton's credibility as an education reformer was reinforced by his record in Arkansas, participation in NGA activities, and detailed reform proposals, including implementation of standards and testing. As he later wrote in his memoir, "If our whole nation was at risk, we [Arkansas] had to be on life support."[5] Clinton's education platform was also strongly linked to his promise of "an economic plan to compete and prosper in the world economy" through better education and training.[6]

During the election campaign, the NEA and AFT supported Clinton by large majorities, in part because of his support for increasing school funding and his opposition to vouchers. However, in 1992, the teachers unions were "passionately opposed" to Clinton's call for enhanced public school choice and his support for national standards and testing. Their continued opposition served as "a brake" on school reform throughout his administration.[7] Clinton's support for school reform was a key element in the campaign and included a move "beyond the traditional democratic focus on access and resources."[8] In speeches Clinton linked education with individual and national economic development, making it what one consultant called "a bedrock economic issue."[9] A centrist, bipartisan coalition was beginning to emerge around a new policy regime in education that emphasized systemic reform, but with disagreement on specifics.[10]

Following Clinton's victory in the election, the most notable aspect of the Clinton transition to the presidency was the continuity of his policies with those of his predecessor. Not only was there a consensus on systemic reform, but many of the parts and players were interchangeable. On November 11, 1992, shortly after Clinton was elected, Marc Tucker wrote an eighteen-page letter to Hillary Clinton, a member of the board of the National Center on Education and the Economy (NCEE), which Tucker founded in 1988. Promoted as "education reform," the plans laid out in the "Dear Hillary" letter served as a timely blueprint for school restructuring, as part of a vision to "remold the entire American system for human resource development." Much of Tucker's ambitious plan would become law in the 1994 passage of three major pieces of legislation: the Goals 2000 Act, the School-to-Work Act, which was aimed at more effectively connecting schooling to employment, and the reauthorization of ESEA. The plan spelled out in Tucker's letter was developed by a group of leaders "closely associated" with the NCEE, including John Sculley, David Rockefeller, Mike Cohen, David Hornbeck, Lauren Resnick, Mike Smith, and others. It called for "Clear national standards of performance" in schools, "set to the level of the best achieving nations" that every student would be expected to reach by age sixteen, and a "national system of education in which curriculum, pedagogy, examinations, and teacher education and licensure systems are all linked to the national standards" with substantial state and local variations. It called for schools to abandon "the American tracking system" and for "school delivery standards" to assure the "quality of instruction is high everywhere." It also called for greatly expanded public school choice and recommended that the new administration advance this reform agenda via a resubmission and continuation of the education reform legislation on which Congress had already been working.[11] The vision spelled out in Tucker's "Dear Hillary" letter contained many elements similar to the recommendations of NCEE's bipartisan Commission on the Skills of the American Workforce in its 1990 report *America's Choice: High Skills or Low Wages!*[12]

Goals 2000

One of Clinton's first acts was to appoint a fellow southern governor, Richard Riley of South Carolina, an activist for education reform, as secretary of education. While Clinton was committed to New Democratic reforms, a lot of others, even in his administration, were not. Liberal Democrats were eager to expand federal programs, while conservatives argued that social welfare spending was ineffective. The public was generally positive about Clinton's education agenda and supported a stronger federal role in education reform. A large majority supported national standards (70 percent), a national curriculum (69 percent), and national tests (77 percent). However, many conservatives and liberals were still wary of national education reform—conservatives because it could lead to federal control, and liberals because it failed to address questions of unequal school funding.[13]

The New Democratic plan for national education reform was encapsulated in a 1992 book titled *Mandate for Change*. It argued that increased funding would not solve the schools' problems and called for the president to lead "a radical redesign of U.S. education" emphasizing public school choice and development of charter schools. Many of these middle-ground proposals were opposed by liberal Democrats, the NEA, and much of the education establishment.[14] In early 1994, needing a quick legislative victory after the controversy stirred up over his early policy initiative including defeat of the administration health care plan and narrow passage of a budget, Clinton revived and modified Bush's America 2000 initiative, renaming it Goals 2000. The intent was that it would serve as a blueprint to focus all K–12 federal education programs on national standards.[15]

Goals 2000 called for development of voluntary national standards and assessments based upon the six national goals described in America 2000. Many observers viewed Clinton's plan as little more than a renamed, repackaged America 2000, but there were important differences. Perhaps the most important distinction was related to the federal role in development of standards. Under Clinton's plan, states were required to submit standards to the DOE before receiving Goals 2000 grant money. Additionally, Clinton's proposal called for creation of federal oversight panels that would monitor and assist with state education reform efforts; it incorporated a different approach to school choice, supporting only public school choice; and it gave greater weight to the traditional Democratic focus on inputs by calling for an opportunity to learn commission (OTL) that would insure adequate funding levels.[16]

During acrimonious negotiations, House Democrats, under pressure from union lobbyists, continued to fight for resources over reform. In the face of opposition from both sides, the Clinton administration removed or weakened many of the reforms in its original proposal, de-emphasizing national testing and watering down OTL provisions. In the end, Goals 2000 was approved by wide margins in both the House (306–121) and Senate (63–22). Several factors may explain its passage. First, Democrats were motivated to provide Clinton with a legislative victory on one of his signature domestic policy issues. Many Republican moderates supported the bill because it had first been proposed by Bush and promised a more results-oriented policy. Perhaps most importantly, business leaders and lobbyists viewed the bill as a crucial lever for workforce improvement and economic growth and worked hard for its passage with members of both parties.[17] The final version of Goals 2000 received the support of almost all major business and education groups, but many of the proposed reforms were either eliminated or compromised, making standards and participation in "Goals 2000 systemic improvement programs" voluntary, and using incentives rather than mandates to encourage reform.

With congressional approval of the 1994 Goals 2000: Educate America Act, the six national education goals developed and agreed upon by the nation's governors and the Bush administration were formalized into law with relatively minor changes. The legislation passed Congress in February and was signed into law on March 31, 1994. Though differences with the Reagan/Bush years were evident, continuity centered on the myth of schools "in crisis" was noteworthy. Goal 3 was substantively revised, and two additional goals were inserted on teacher training and parental involvement. Goal 3 read:

> Goal 3: All students will leave grades 4, 8, and 12 having demonstrated competency over challenging subject matter including English, mathematics, science, foreign languages, civics and government, economics, the arts, history, and geography, and every school in America will ensure that all students learn to use their minds well, so they may be prepared for responsible citizenship, further learning, and productive employment in our nation's modern economy.[18]

Changes to Goal 3 were significant, with a broader array of subject areas now included. In the social studies arena these included "civics and government" and "economics." There was, again, no mention of the broader field of social studies. Moreover, the Goals 2000 Act specified that state and local school districts were responsible for creation of their own goals and standards, and that nationally produced standards statements, such as those in history, geography, and civics, were voluntary. No funds were tied to implementation of any of the nationally developed standards, yet they were given rhetorical support as representing "what teachers and scholars believe students should know." Among the social studies disciplines, standards for history, geography, and civics were specifically mentioned. The NCSS Standards for Social Studies were not mentioned, and the term *social studies* was nowhere to be found.

Goals 2000 also established a crucial enforcement mechanism, creating the National Education Standards and Improvement Council (NESIC) with the power to "certify" state standards. By the mid-1990s, virtually all of the states were developing standards statements in keeping with Goals 2000. As of spring

1995, only three states had not begun the process.[19] A grant program authorized under Goals 2000 to support state efforts for systemic reform already underway was having the desired effect. However, reliance on state-by-state initiatives meant that there was a great deal of variation by state, district, and school. The program received strong support from governors and business leaders, especially those who participated in the 1989 summit. Funding, which began at $94 million per year, climbed to $490 by 1999, and provided over $2 billion to promote standards-based reform. Though a few states initially declined funds on "states' rights" grounds, within two years of the start of funding, forty-eight states had accepted grants, and within three years the money and the reform had reached more than one-third of the nation's 15,000 school districts.[20]

ESEA Reauthorization of 1994

In parallel with Goals 2000, President Clinton proposed reauthorization and revision of the Elementary and Secondary Education Act (ESEA) but wanted it to be passed only after Goals 2000 had become law. The idea was that Goals 2000 would be enacted first and would set the agenda to establish standards and tests as the centerpiece, with ESEA funds used to support Title I programs for the disadvantaged tied to helping children in poverty meet new state standards. The proposed new law, renamed the Improving America's Schools Act (IASA), required states to use the same academic standards for all students. Prior to its passage, the Title I program allowed states to use less rigorous achievement standards for economically disadvantaged students. Funding for IASA, which reached $11 billion, was contingent on state and local development of systemic reform.[21] Because all fifty states were already accepting ESEA funds, and because the amounts were sizable, it meant that changes in the law would force states to adopt standards-based reforms. Clinton's proposal generated renewed opposition in Congress because it was seen as mandating standards and assessments. Moderates were generally supportive of the reauthorization and most Democrats came to support the bill after strong presidential lobbying.[22]

Changes to ESEA were seen by many as the most significant revision since its inception in 1965 because it required states to develop school improvement plans and challenging content standards in core subject areas in order to receive federal funds. States were also required to develop assessments, set "benchmarks" for "adequate yearly progress" by Title I students, and publish disaggregated test scores. Schools that failed to meet state targets for two consecutive years would be designated as "needing improvement." Moreover, states would be encouraged to use "corrective action" with failing schools including such actions as withholding funds, transferring and reconstituting staff, creating new governance, and transferring students. The legislation gave the DOE authority to grant waivers and offer flexibility to school districts, and boosted public school choice by providing funds ($15 million the first year) for start-up of charter schools.[23] When combined with Goals 2000, IASA largely enacted the essence of the Kearns and Doyle blueprint for systemic reform proposed in *Winning the Brain Race* (1988).

In his comments at the signing of the IASA on October 24, 1994, Clinton stated that the new law

> Represents a fundamental change. . . . For 30 years the federal government has shipped money to the states and the local school districts to try to help with problems that need the money . . . in ways that prescribed in very detailed manner the rules and regulations your schools had to follow. . . . This bill changes all that. This bill says the national government will set the goals. We will help develop measurements to see whether [you are] meeting the goals. But you will get to determine how you're going to meet the goals.[24]

Though debate on Goals 2000 had focused on "voluntary" standards, the new legislation barely six months later changed that. Standards and assessments, the essential ingredients of systemic reform, were now a mandate. Mike Smith, undersecretary of education at the time, noted that in combination, "Goals 2000 and the 1994 ESEA change imposed on the state a particular kind of reform—to play ball, states had to go along with standards-based reform."[25] Despite the new mandate, standards and assessments were controversial in many states and still being debated. Due to widespread skepticism over the new rules, many states set up minimal accountability systems to comply with the law. In many cases, very little changed. Under the new mandate states were given the freedom to design their own accountability systems, and the results varied widely.[26]

Despite sometimes weak enforcement, the Clinton administration's efforts on education, including Goals 2000 and the reauthorization of ESEA, served to further nationalize education politics and policymaking. Yet, the Clinton years "produced a very important and large legacy . . . [to] bring the country behind a new education agenda based on choice, high standards, and accountability for results."[27] Many of the reform ideas embodied in the new legislation including standards, assessments, adequate yearly progress, school report cards, and corrective action—ideas that had been trumpeted by business leaders and advocates of systemic reform for some time—found their first national mandate in the ESEA reauthorization. The policies were made possible in part by increasing support for standards-based reform among the nation's Republican governors and by lobbying from business leaders and groups such as the Chamber of Commerce, the National Alliance of Business, and the Business Roundtable. Despite increasing support for a centrist, reform-oriented position in education, political developments soon threatened to undo the emerging consensus.

Conservative Backlash

In the 1994 midterm elections, Republicans made historic gains and captured control of both houses of Congress, partly due to a backlash against Clinton's failed health care proposal. Under the guidance of Newt Gingrich (R-GA), Republicans proclaimed a new "Contract with America," which launched an ambitious attempt to roll back the size and power of the federal government, abolish several cabinet agencies, and cut taxes. Republican gains could be partly attributed to bold leadership by Gingrich and the increasingly powerful influence of the religious right. The recently passed expansion of federal power in education became a prominent item on their agenda and would remain a visible, controversial topic throughout the 1990s.

Following their historic victory in the 1994 elections, Republicans had gained control of both houses of Congress for the first time in forty years. Education was a prominent topic in the Republican campaign message, including a call for the elimination of Goals 2000, abolition of the DOE, and restoration of local control. The Christian Coalition made education a focus of its campaign, and it emphasized opposition to federal influence and outcome-based education (OBE), along with support for school prayer and vouchers. OBE meant a focus on empirically measuring student performance, requiring that students demonstrate that they have learned the required skills and content, and seemed congruent with accountability reform.[28] However, as adopted in many school districts during the time, OBE generally promoted curricula and assessment based on constructivist methods and discouraged traditional education and direct instruction. The popular movement for OBE led to controversy in many areas of the United States, stoked by the religious right. New Right resistance was reflected in a Montana newspaper headline, quoting an anti-Goals 2000 woman saying, "Goals 2000 made me into a sex slave."[29]

OBE, often known under different names such as performance-based education or standards-based education, was the brainchild of William G. Spady, an educational sociologist and curriculum theorist whose work with James Block and Benjamin Bloom on mastery learning led him to develop the theory of outcome-based education. OBE focused on systemic reform and emphasized learning outcomes, what a student could actually do at the end of their learning experiences. Spady promoted OBE as a form of systemic educational reform and restructuring during the 1980s and 1990s through the Network for Outcome-Based Schools. As the movement for OBE developed, there were various definitions and approaches, ranging from the more conservative, academic, and content oriented, to Spady's more progressive version that tended to emphasize authentic learning and performance goals related to life roles. Spady's brand of OBE was built around four principles, "focus on outcomes of significance," "expanded opportunity," "high expectations," and "design down from where you want to end up."[30] Spady's version of "transformational" OBE went well beyond content-based curriculum. While it didn't make content irrelevant, the content was no longer an end in itself. It focused instead on developing "self-directed learners, collaborative workers, complex thinkers, community contributors, and quality producers," who were "conscious, creative, collaborative, competent, and compassionate."

By the early 1990s, outcome-based education was "all the rage" as some twenty-six states in the United States had some form of OBE in their schools, influenced by Spady's work. Its popularity stemmed in part from its practical, commonsense appeal, and the fact that it combined elements of systemic reform and restructuring with accountability and a focus on results, consonant with the business-driven reform movement. In many states, the BRT was a major booster of OBE-style reforms. However, application of Spady's theories in some areas of the United States led to intense controversies stirred by the religious right, which viewed OBE as a plot for mind control, undermining Christianity.

Controversy over Outcome-Based Education

Controversy over OBE began in Pennsylvania when Peg Luksik, a parent, teacher, and fundamentalist Christian, charged that a state goal focused on the outcome of students being "tolerant of other people" was aimed at advocating homosexuality.[31] The controversy attracted national media attention and participation or comment by conservative groups and individuals from the religious right including Focus on the Family, G. Gordon Liddy, Phyllis Schlafly's Eagle Forum, Pat Buchanan, Pat Robertson's Christian Coalition, Beverly La Haye's Concerned Women for America, Rush Limbaugh, and William J. Bennett. Spady debated Buchanan on *The Pat Buchanan Show* on the merits of OBE against charges that it was some form of mind control or social engineering.[32] According to one commentator, Spady was described as "a socialist, a communist, a globalist, a one-worlder, a new-ager; as anti-Christian, anti-traditional values, anti-family, un-American, diabolical, duplicitous, [and] subversive."[33] The Christian right's campaign against OBE was part of a larger crusade to remake American society. As David Berliner points out, some members of the Christian right seek the destruction of public education. Many espoused theories of child rearing emphasizing "physical punishment, breaking children's will, and obedience to authority," practices "incompatible with the constructivist models of learning" advanced by many educators.[34] Like other curriculum dustups, the controversy reflected not only the culture wars, but deep and genuine differences over what and how children should be taught, and whose America they would inherit.

Many of the critics, according to Spady's own account, were against the state having any influence on the "beliefs of their Christian children." For some critics, anything that dealt with "the values and inner development of young people" either lacked academic weight or was "psychological mind control."[35] Within two years, OBE was anathema to many, especially in rural areas where the Christian right had most influence.[36]

Despite the controversy it inspired, Spady and OBE contributed to the foundation and practical application of accountability reform through the notion of focusing on the outcomes of schooling rather than inputs. More conservative versions, focused almost entirely on measuring student mastery of academic content, though a bastard version of Spady's OBE, became a central element of the bipartisan consensus. As Peter Schrag observed, "it fit perfectly" with the idea of school decentralization and was "a welcome answer" to the constant liberal emphasis on inputs, which usually meant more money.[37] Philosophically, OBE had much in common with Life-Adjustment Education (LAE), popular in the 1940s and 1950s, with its emphasis on "life roles" and its rationalist, structural functionalist paradigm that embodied a strong element of social control. The fact that Spady's "progressive" version of OBE came under such vehement attack, and that the controversy impacted the course of national education policy, reminds us how political school reform can be.

Despite Republican electoral gains in 1994, conservative proposals on education were at odds with most voters. Polls showed 81 percent opposed to any decrease in federal funding for schools, and more favorable ratings for the Democratic Party on education issues by a large margin.[38] Nonetheless, Republican commentators urged a focus on rolling back Clinton's education initiatives. A Heritage Foundation report called for abolition of the DOE, repeal of most of the Goals 2000 legislation (including NESIC), and overturning many provisions of the ESEA. It also advocated federal grants to fund school choice experiments and argued that "the dramatic shift in power both in Congress and in the states gives conservatives unprecedented opportunity to undo many of the harmful education programs of the last 30 years."[39] Republican attempts to reduce the federal role and Goals 2000 succeeded in passing several significant amendments, rolling back some of the most stringent requirements, and transferring much of the funding into block grants, thus giving greater flexibility and power over education reform to the states.[40]

Democrats Respond

Despite these setbacks, polls showed that the American public continued to support federal spending for an active and well-funded federal role in education, as well as key programs on the environment, Medicare, and Medicaid.[41] Moreover, the centrist DLC called for a "progressive alternative" to the Contract with America that would transfer more power to state and local levels but would continue and expand federal leadership for reform on pressing problems. Education became a focal point in the Democratic counterattack, as the administration stressed the importance of education reform for individual economic opportunity and national economic growth. They portrayed Republican positions as ideologically extreme and out of touch with the mainstream. In a series of speeches culminating in his January 1995 State of the Union address, Clinton staked out a middle ground, advocating active but limited government, a message built around what became known as "M2E2": "balancing the budget in a way that protects our values and defends *M*edicare, *M*edicaid, *e*ducation, and the *e*nvironment" (italics added). In his speech, Clinton embraced much of the Republican rhetoric while calling for continued federal activism in a number of areas, including education. "The era of big government is over," he declared, "but we cannot go back to the time when our citizens were left to fend for themselves."[42]

Democrat's defense of the education reform program was assisted by moderate Republicans who warned that killing Goals 2000 or eliminating the DOE would create a perception that the party was unconcerned about the schools. Throughout the period, influential groups from the business community such as the BRT, the Chamber of Commerce, the NAB, and the NAM, along with the NGA continued to actively support Goals 2000 and lobbied Congress to continue federal programs aimed at raising educational standards via systemic reform, urging that federal programs be modified rather than repealed. Business groups created the Business Coalition for Education Reform (BCER) and continued to lobby Congress to use federal money and power to press states to improve schools.[43]

Despite Republicans' efforts to roll back education reform, polls indicated that the public continued to view the administration's proposals favorably. Republican proposals for vouchers and block grants were portrayed as part of a broadside attack on the idea of public education and were increasingly unpopular with voters. As the 1996 election was approaching, Republicans realized that their attacks on Clinton's education agenda could hurt them at the polls, and they largely abandoned their assault. A Republican president, George H.W. Bush, had initiated the push for standards and accountability in schools, and "it proved impossible for conservatives to put that genie back in the bottle."[44]

History Standards Controversy

Meanwhile, as the Clinton administration was busy building a Republican-appearing consensus, groups of scholars and teachers were completing drafts of national standards for the schools in each core subject area. The 1994 National History Standards were an outgrowth of thinking among many historians, similar to that of NCSS leaders, that if standards were inevitable, it was best to be involved and have some influence. During the Bush administration, the National Center for History in the Schools (NCHS) at the University of California, Los Angeles (UCLA) was selected to develop standards for the teaching of history, outlining the content and processes that students would study. The two-year process for developing the standards was financed by a grant of $525,000 from the NEH and a grant of $865,000 from the DOE.[45]

The National History Standards Project was engaged in developing separate sets of standards for American history, world history, and for the K–4 elementary curriculum. Though each of these documents offered interesting and insightful recommendations on the contents and process of teaching history, it was the *National Standards for United States History*, released in 1994, that generated the most interest. Even before its release the report swirled in a storm of controversy in the media, touched off by an October 20, 1994, editorial in the *Wall*

Street Journal written by Lynne Cheney, former chairperson of the NEH during the Reagan and Bush administrations. Cheney charged that the standards were a loaded document whose "authors save their unqualified admiration for people, places, and events that are politically correct." She argued that the standards offered heavy doses of multiculturalism and obsession with such topics as McCarthyism (nineteen references), racism (the Ku Klux Klan is mentioned seventeen times), and mistreatment of indigenous peoples but gave little attention to some of the core developments and figures of American history.[46] Cheney's editorial was preceded by a letter from Diane Ravitch to Charlotte Crabtree expressing concerns over possible bias contained in many of the examples of standards-based activities, a letter that may have reached Cheney as well.[47]

Rush Limbaugh echoed Cheney's critique and extended it by defining his own approach to the study of history:

> What? . . . history is an exploration? Let me tell you something folks. History is real simple. You know what history is? It's what happened. It's no more . . . The problem you get into is when guys like this [Gary Nash, the principal author] try to skew history by, "Well, let's interpret what happened because maybe we don't like the truth as it's presented. So let's change the interpretation a little bit so that it will be the way we wished it were." Well, that's not what history is. History is what happened, and history ought to be nothing more than what happened. Now, if you want to get into why what happened, that's probably valid too, but why what happened shouldn't have much of anything to do with what happened.[48]

The Cheney and Limbaugh commentaries were accompanied by a stream of articles and editorials in the nation's media, portraying the battle over the standards largely in terms of a political debate over what history should be taught in secondary school U.S. history courses, and how those courses should be taught. Critics suggested that the standards presented young learners with a grim picture of American history that cast everything European and American "as evil and oppressive." They charged that the world history standards "give no emphasis to Western Civilization" and feared that the standards would become a form of "official history."

The majority of articles covering the controversy framed it in political terms, as part of a cultural and ideological war over schooling and the future of society. For example, one report stated, "The result was less a debate over how effective the new standards would be in inspiring school children and more an exchange of angry accusations about hidden political agendas. Both sides charged that the other was trying to create a past to correspond with their disparate world views."[49]

The storm of controversy continued into the halls of the U.S. Senate, where Slade Gorton, a Republican from the state of Washington, introduced an amendment to abolish the standards. The Senate, in a voice vote of 99 to 1, rejected the standards. In his speech, Gorton contended that "These standards are ideology masquerading as history," and declared, "In order to stop this perverted idea in its tracks and to ensure that it does not become, de facto, a guide for our nation's classrooms, it must be publicly and officially repudiated by this Congress." Senator Bennett Johnston (D-LA), who cast the only "nay" vote, did so because he thought the language of the condemnation was too weak.[50]

The standards developed at the NCHS at UCLA, headed by Charlotte Crabtree and Gary Nash, were the result of a two-year collaborative process among teachers, curriculum specialists, and historians. The directors of the project attempted to build a broad consensus of involvement by various educational and civic groups with an interest in the teaching of history. The standards they developed were of two major types: historical thinking skills and historical understandings. The reports placed a strong emphasis upon moving students beyond the passive approach of absorbing dates, facts, and concepts, toward analysis of historical issues and decision making. On the whole, the standards made a strong effort at developing a workable, inquiry-based approach. For example, students were asked to find evidence, identify central questions, examine major social issues, and address moral questions. Some standards focused on historical thinking skills, including chronological thinking, historical comprehension, historical analysis and interpretation, historical research capabilities, and historical issues-analysis and decision making. These "thinking skills" were "integrated" into various standards throughout the volumes as they related to specific historical topics.[51] The document reflected project participants' vision of good history teaching. It aimed to provide students with "opportunities to examine the historical record for themselves, raise questions about it, and marshal evidence in support of their answers."[52] Accompanying the standards were "examples of student achievement" intended to help teachers with specific, concrete models for applying the standards. The standards gave unprecedented and much needed emphasis to the new social history that had emerged from the most recent generation of historians. The materials presented a multiplicity of voices that had previously been underrepresented. In a sense, the *Standards for United States History* were a partial realization of the inclusion of multiple voices that many historians including Gary Nash, Howard Zinn, and others had called for over a number of years.[53]

Unfortunately, critics focused on the illustrative classroom activities as if they were intended to provide a comprehensive, detailed list of the content to be included. Gary Nash and Ross Dunn, lead authors of two of the standards books, charged that critics such as Cheney and Limbaugh, by counting names mentioned in the illustrative activities, made "a deliberate attempt to mislead the public that these guidelines are textbooks, which of course they are not." Instead, the standards themselves included very few names because they focused on "big ideas, movements, turning points, population shifts, economic transformations, wars and revolutions, religious movements, and so forth."[54] Moreover, Nash and Dunn responded, critics "tried to link the standards in the public mind to extreme, left-wing revisionism, hoisting them as a useful symbol of all things un-American." The critics, they wrote, had scrawled, "politically correct" across the standards. Nash and Dunn concluded that critics had conducted what they termed "campaigns of disinformation."[55]

Other reviewers offered a more balanced assessment of the standards. A focus group of educators from the National Council for the Social Studies contracted during the standards development process found the standards to be "a fairly conservative document," more inclusive but otherwise little different from what has been proposed for much of the twentieth century.[56] Compared to many alternative conceptualizations of social studies content and instruction, the standards were well within mainstream traditions. On the other hand, following release of a revised and less controversial edition, Arthur M. Schlesinger found that the original draft of the standards document that had released such a firestorm was far from "flawless," and suggested that "the slant and spin of interpretation and emphasis were sometimes dubious." He was troubled by the implication that American history was formed equally by the convergence of European, African, and Amerindian cultures. Yet, these problems, he thought, were easily remedied. Nash and his colleagues responded, he wrote, "as scholars should. They took note of objections, reconsidered various points and produced a redraft. The revised standards seem a sturdy and valuable document, sober, judicious, and thoughtful." Moreover, he warned against history as "social and political therapy," the use of the past by those on both extremes who seek to convert history into cheerleading to promote their own values.[57]

The revised *National Standards for History* combined the standards for U.S. history, world history, and K–4 history into one volume, replacing the three volumes that had stirred such controversy. In this version, the authors wisely deleted the source of so much controversy, choosing to omit most of the teaching and class activity suggestions contained in the original volumes. It was, as one reviewer saw it, a watered-down version designed not to offend.[58] Yet, it had the desired impact, blunting criticism of the earlier volumes and receiving a much more positive reception.[59]

Nash, Crabtree, and Dunn offered a full response to the controversy over the standards in *History on Trial: Culture Wars and the Teaching of the Past*. In their book, the lead developers of the standards that generated so much heat gave a thoughtful accounting of the development of the standards, the new scholarship that went into it, the charges of critics, and their own counteroffensive and attempted to put the entire episode into contextual perspective. They viewed the standards movement as positive for encouraging a new activism among historians, who were getting more involved again in collaborations with teachers. They drew parallels between their experience and the controversy over the Rugg textbooks in the 1930s, especially noting the unethical tactics used by conservative critics in both episodes. They documented development of the standards and their call for a more global and multicultural approach to history that grew out of the latest scholarship. And, they offered justification for their own actions and choices.[60] Unfortunately, the authors were not very self-critical, and they failed to probe the deeper connection between the standards controversy and the much longer war on social studies. It was especially ironic that the standards were brought down by anti-democratic demagoguery. As part of a top-down reform accompanied by the specter of enforcement via national assessment tests, the vehicle encapsulating the standards was anti-democratic at its heart. The controversy over the U.S. history standards, like a blindside tackle, temporarily stopped the standards movement in its tracks. If creating standards in history could be so controversial, was it even possible to develop workable standards in other subjects that might be politically palatable as well as practical in application?

A Multitude of Standards Statements

The NCSS Task Force for Social Studies Standards created by the board of directors in 1992 under the leadership of Donald O. Schneider, a former president of NCSS, was charged with development of a standards statement congruent with the new NCSS definition. During the years that the NCSS standards were being developed, there were three concurrent projects for the development of standards in the broader social studies arena, each receiving federal funding from the DOE. These projects included the development of standards for the teaching of civics/government, geography, and history. Development of the NCSS standards received neither federal funds nor the official sanctions that went with them.

The NCSS did play an instrumental role in getting the civics/government project established, in conjunction with the Center for Civic Education, under the direction of Charles Quigley. The NCSS also cooperated with the group developing history standards, though in a more limited way, primarily through appointment of a funded focus group, chaired by Linda Levstik, appointed to review a draft of the standards. The NCSS had a very limited role in development of the geography standards.[61]

The *National Standards for Civics and Government* were developed by the Center for Civic Education, with support from the DOE and the Pew Charitable Trusts, and were published in 1995. The document included content standards, a rationale, and a statement of standards for each relevant content area. The standards were organized around five major questions aimed to help students inquire into important concepts related to civic life, the American political system, and the roles of citizens.[62]

The work of the Geography Education Standards Project, which received support from the DOE and several geographic education societies, was published under the title *Geography for Life: National Geography Standards*. This book identified a set of voluntary benchmarks that every school and district could use as a guideline in developing its own curricula. It detailed eighteen geography standards to be included in grades K–4, 5–8, and 9–12 and addressed geographic skills and student achievement.[63] These two sets of standards received a much more positive reception from both policymakers and the general public than had the history standards. They were fewer in number than the history standards, and they were more specific regarding assessment of student learning.

As for the social studies standards, in the fall of 1993 a draft of the NCSS Standards for Social Studies was circulated by the Task Force on Curriculum Standards and received mixed reviews. The proposed standards offered ten thematic strands focused on each of the following: Culture; Time, Continuity, and Change; People, Places, and Environments; Individual Development and Identity; Individuals, Groups, and Institutions; Power, Authority, and Governance; Production, Distribution, and Consumption; Science, Technology, and Society; Global Connections; and Civic Ideals and Practices.

While many of those who worked on the standards statement felt that it offered a strong alternative to standards statements coming from the disciplinary organizations, a number of others were critical of the standards for presenting a weak compromise on the curriculum, for suggesting thematic strands that were clearly disciplinary, and for failing to develop a fully issues-centered and interdisciplinary approach. A proposed resolution at the annual business meeting of the College and University Faculty Assembly of NCSS in 1993 called on the Task Force on Curriculum Standards to "rethink its work." It read, in part:

> Rather than the compromise presented in the Task Force report, we urge that the authors develop an alternative vision for the social studies, a vision that is innovative and dynamic, proposing a unitary field of study that is fully issues-centered, interdisciplinary, and aimed toward reflective citizenship, rather than a field that is largely derivative and a compromise among discipline-based interests.[64]

After a brief discussion, the motion failed, voted down by two-thirds of those in attendance.

The NCSS standards were published the following year under the title *Expectations of Excellence: Curriculum Standards for Social Studies*. They contained excellent material on the kind of teaching the task force envisioned, in a section titled "A Vision of Powerful Teaching and Learning." That segment of the report contained the material developed early in the work of the task force, and offered a clear statement on the kind of powerful and innovative teaching that the best social studies teachers supported. This was teaching and learning that is "meaningful, integrative, value-based, challenging, and active." The volume also contained introductory segments on definition and rationale, and on the purposes and uses of the social studies standards. It was hoped that teachers and standards commissions would draw on the NCSS standards when developing curriculum standards for their own states and localities. The heart of the book was contained in its ten thematic strands, retaining the same outline as in the preliminary draft. That was followed by examples of the standards in practice, an attempt to help teachers conduct exemplary social studies lessons.[65]

So, by the mid-1990s the social studies arena had a number of national statements on curriculum standards. All of the major national organizations in social studies had, through their actions, purchased the standards mentality. Some believed that it was good to have a voice in the developments, while others argued against involvement in a reform with whose assumptions they did not agree. However, as several scholars observed, the multitude of different standards statements from the various associations masked a lack of general consensus on the content of the curriculum, leaving the field in what appeared to be a continuing state of "fragmentation" and disarray.[66] In fact, many of the recommendations made in the standards documents were in conflict. The four sets of standards available by the spring of 1995 totaled 1,292 pages. Standards in history and geography called for separate required courses in each subject in grades 5–12: historians wanted six full years of history, and geographers called for two required years of geography, as well as a senior elective. Both groups also argued that their standards should be fully integrated into the K–4 curriculum as well. Administrators, curriculum supervisors, teachers, and curriculum committees reported feeling overwhelmed by the prospects of designing a coherent K–12 curriculum based on the mass of separatist claims on the social studies portion of the school day.[67]

Clinton's Second Term

The 1996 presidential election was in many ways a referendum on federal education policy. Polls indicated that education was the issue that voters most wanted to hear candidates discuss in the campaign, not only for its own sake, but due to its relevance to debates over economic opportunity and other key domestic issues. Republican nominee Senator Bob Dole (R-KS) did not emphasize education in his campaign until August 1996, when he countered Democratic proposals with the charge that federal involvement was counterproductive. Dole hewed to a conservative line on education policy, reminiscent of early policies of Ronald Reagan supporting vouchers, school prayer, and abolition of the DOE. Moreover, Dole had voted against both Goals 2000 and the 1994 ESEA amendments. The Clinton campaign portrayed him as out of touch with the average American.[68] Meanwhile, business groups and the NGA continued their efforts to support a strong state and federal school reform program, promoting a forward-looking approach at the Palisades Summit in March 1996 that contributed to the emerging consensus.

Following Clinton's re-election, a campaign in which education had been a critical issue that Democrats won decisively, most Democrats read the results as a mandate for more federal activism on improving schooling. Republicans did a great deal of soul-searching, concluding that they could no longer afford to be viewed as anti-education. As a result, the terms of the discussion on education reform during Clinton's second term shifted from whether there should be a federal role, to a focus on what the nature of the federal role should be. What emerged was a "policy window" during which a new federal policy regime could be built. The new regime centered on a consensus view that the federal government and the states should collaborate to promote school improvement and higher levels of student achievement thorough public school choice, standards, assessment, accountability, and increased funding.[69]

In his State of the Union Address on February 4, 1997, President Clinton outlined key components of his education agenda for the next four years and called for a "national crusade for education standards":

> Tonight I issue a challenge to the Nation: Every State should adopt high national standards, and by 1999, every State should test every fourth grader in reading and every eighth grader in math to make sure these standards are met.[70]

The president's speech outlined an expansive ten-point agenda for school reform that included certifying 100,000 new master teachers, the "America Reads" literacy initiative, emphasis on early learning, public school choice, character education, safe and drug-free schools, lifetime learning, school construction, opening the doors to college for more students, and connecting every classroom and library to the Internet. Later in his speech, Clinton addressed his motives for education reform:

> We must understand the significance of this endeavor. One of the greatest sources of our strength throughout the cold war was a bipartisan foreign policy. Because our future was at stake, politics stopped at the water's edge. Now I ask you and I ask all our Nation's Governors, I ask parents, teachers, and citizens all across America for a new nonpartisan commitment to education, because education is a critical national security issue for our future, and politics must stop at the schoolhouse door.[71]

During Clinton's second term, the administration developed a strategy to promote its education agenda that kept the focus on plans for national standards and national testing while also promoting related K–12 education initiatives in support of charter schools, teacher standards, literacy, education technology, and other goals.[72]

A White House "Meeting on National Standards," held on March 5, 1997, brought together a group of key participants in systemic reform for the opportunity to "brainstorm" on strategy and "advancing your agenda of national standards and tests." The participant list of "experts in the standards field" revealed a distinct bipartisan tone and included Diane Ravitch, Don (E.D.) Hirsch, Mike Smith, Marc Tucker, Roy Romer, Secretary Riley, and others, but also suggested a strong neoconservative influence.[73] Later that year, Clinton appointed Ravitch to the National Assessment Governing Board, whose purpose was to oversee testing of basics in fourth and eighth grades.[74] The administration developed sophisticated "cross cutting strategies" in its efforts for school reform, emphasizing national legislation, a state-by-state legislative reform strategy, and constituency group support.[75] White House strategy documents reveal an emphasis on proposals that had bipartisan support as a way of building momentum, pursuit of a "multi-pronged approach to national standards and tests," and the strategy of keeping the "entire education agenda visible and [using] the bully pulpit to promote education reform."[76]

National Testing Controversy and the Goodling Amendment

As noted above, in the aftermath of the 1996 election the GOP abandoned its opposition to an activist federal role on education, and the debate shifted to questions over how to make reform more effective. Both parties embraced the notion of using national leadership to promote systemic reform but disagreed over whether the federal government or the states would set standards or install accountability. Clinton set his administration on the course of supporting national tests, but only in two core subjects, reading and math, and proposed only two required tests, in reading at fourth grade, and in math at eighth. Chester Finn observed that "if national testing goes down in flames it will be because of people on the left who hate the word 'testing' and people on the right who hate the word 'national.'"[77]

Conservatives warned that even limited national tests were a slippery slope that would lead toward "central control of all aspects of education," while liberals were concerned that tests might unfairly penalize disadvantaged students and could be used to support privatization. The conflict produced strange alliances, with liberal Democrats and conservative Republicans joining forces against the administration. Moderates from both parties, and an increasingly active and influential number of nongovernmental groups and their lobbyists, notably from the religious right, were on one side, and the business community on the other. As it evolved, the controversy, and a good deal of White House energy, centered on the Goodling amendment to an education and labor appropriations bill. The Goodling amendment was a proposal from Congressman Bill Goodling (R-PA) to prohibit use of federal funds to develop or implement tests associated with the president's voluntary national standards initiative. Goodling, a former teacher and school superintendent, opposed the "runaway train" toward imposition of national tests because its development was taking place without specific congressional authority. In an op-ed in the *Washington Post*, he offered his "commonsensical" view that more tests were unnecessary because schools already had enough standardized testing, that they could lead to "inappropriate and unfair comparisons" of schools and students, would lead teachers to "teach to the test," and could lead to a national curriculum.[78] Proponents of national testing, including William Bennett and Chester Finn, argued, on the other hand, that national testing in core subject areas was a necessary step toward imposing tough standards and that Clinton's plan should be modified by giving greater authority to a revised, bipartisan National Assessments Governing Board.[79] Controversy over the Goodling amendment and the Clinton plan served as a sort of lightning rod for various perspectives on the broader movement for systemic reform. In the end, a compromise was reached that allowed preliminary development of the tests, but at a slower pace, and stipulated that specific congressional approval would be needed before tests could be deployed. Though the movement toward national tests would continue, at least for a time, this meant that it would be delayed.[80]

Competing Plans for Reauthorization

Despite the setback over national testing, Clinton was determined to leave a strong legacy of school reform. In his State of the Union Address in January 1998, he announced several new "micro-initiatives" as part of the administration plan for ESEA reauthorization in 1999.[81] Though many in Congress supported Clinton's call for class-size reduction, an emerging coalition including the Heritage Foundation, the Progressive Policy Institute, and the Brookings Institution criticized the administration's focus on inputs in a letter to Congress, arguing that we had a problem of teacher "quality" and "distribution," with few of the best teaching the neediest kids.[82] While there was growing support for a strong federal role in school reform, it was accompanied by a shift in focus from inputs to outcomes. The editors of the *New Democrat* captured it well when they recommended a simple rule for Democrats: "never, ever talk about more spending for schools without talking about accountability for schools."[83]

Republicans issued their own proposal, the Straight A's proposal, or the "Academic Achievement for All Act," which sought increased flexibility for states and increased funding, in exchange for accountability guarantees in the form of annual public reporting on student achievement linked to performance targets. Major conservative groups supported the Straight A's proposal, including the Heritage Foundation, the Cato Institute, Empower America, the Family Research Council, the Eagle Forum, the Christian Coalition, and the Education Leaders Council—all part of a coalition of some thirty groups called EXPECT (Excellence for Parents, Children, and Teachers).[84]

Centrist Democratic senators Joe Lieberman (D-CT) and Evan Bayh (D-IN) offered a third plan, the "Public Education Reinvestment, Reinvention, and Responsibility Act," in November 1999. "The Three R's" as it was called was based on ideas developed by the DLC with input from the White House, and was an attempt to find a middle ground. The proposal called for dramatically increased funding coupled with flexibility—states would be held accountable for progress on student achievement goals and would be rewarded for success or penalized for failure.[85] The Three R's proposal encapsulated an emerging consensus that placed state and local authorities in positions of implementing change but gave the federal government increased power in the form of leadership and funding for accountability reform.

By the late 1990s, the longtime coalition of civil rights groups and liberal Democrats began to support tough standards and testing, demanding that the federal government hold states accountable for improving student achievement. Thus, pressure from the left and the right was pushing both parties toward the center and creating a new consensus around school accountability. Though none of the three plans was adopted, and reauthorization of ESEA was postponed until after the 2000 election, federal appropriations for education rose 38 percent between 1996 and 1999, and another 15 percent during 2000, illustrating the growing emphasis on improving education and reflecting a period of economic growth.[86] Debate over the three plans for ESEA reauthorization revealed that a large middle ground of agreement was developing on how to improve schools, creating what one observer called "a middle path" on accountability reform.[87] Meanwhile, during the late 1990s, standards and accountability measures were rapidly being adopted at the state and local levels with strong corporate support amid building momentum for reform. That momentum would carry over into the next administration.

Growing Corporate Influence

Throughout the years of the Clinton administration, business influence on school reform continued to grow, in consonance with the ten-year plan developed by the Business Roundtable in the late 1980s. The 1990s brought a dramatic mushrooming of what seemed at times a dizzying array of interest groups, private organizations, think tanks, and university-linked research institutes. The alphabet soup of groups included the venerable and established interest groups that had long been part of the crusade to improve schooling, such as the BRT, CBE, CED, NCEE, NAM, NAB, and the U.S. Chamber of Commerce, but also included more recently minted groups such as the BCER, the Education Trust, and Achieve Inc. Though groups were not monolithic, they often shared members, with key personnel serving on the board of directors for multiple groups, and similar funding sources from wealthy corporate and conservative donors. They also shared the distinction of supporting and lobbying for a similar and widely supported blueprint for systemic school reform built around standards, testing, and choice.[88]

By the late 1990s dozens of private organizations and think tanks were involved in the push for school reform. In the absence of a federal agency to approve state standards, several organizations began rating state efforts. The AFT, CBE, Fordham Foundation, and Achieve Inc. began publishing reviews of state standards.[89] Other groups emerged in the 1990s to sponsor systemic reform initiatives, often taking leadership or control of individual schools, a group of similar schools, or even entire school systems. Among these were the Coalition of Essential Schools, originating at Brown University under the leadership of Ted Sizer, and the Edison

Project, led by business entrepreneur Chris Whittle. Most of these groups supported high-stakes testing and accountability, but some were opposed. Conservative think tanks also became increasingly active in education reform, notably the Heritage Foundation, the American Enterprise Institute, the Cato Institute, the Manhattan Institute, and the Brookings Institution. Though they had a scholarly imprint, these groups typically advocated and lobbied for neoconservative or neoliberal positions supporting a corporate model of systemic reform, with strong support from conservative and corporate donors.[90]

The 1996 Palisades Summit on Education

Likely the single most visible and influential business-sponsored event during the 1990s was the 1996 Education Summit. The event was sponsored by the NGA and BRT, attended by governors, business leaders, and educators, and was held at IBM headquarters in Palisades, New York. In a sense, it marked the "in earnest" beginning of the standards movement and an emerging consensus among key leadership groups toward developing a national consensus—a key turning point linked with a more important role for business leaders in instigating and sustaining systemic reform.

The 1996 summit had its immediate origins after the 1995 annual meeting of the NGA held in Burlington, Vermont. The NGA invited Louis V. Gerstner, Jr., the CEO of IBM, to speak. In a 1994 book titled *Reinventing Education: Entrepreneurship in America's Public Schools*, Gerstner described a plan for improving America's schools based on his experience with the RJR Nabisco Foundation and its "Next Century Schools" program. The hallmarks of the program included encouraging entrepreneurship and innovation through decentralized power and market competition among schools, bypassing the bureaucracy, and focusing on the classroom and students. It was especially congruent and supportive of the growing emphasis on public school choice, magnet schools, and innovative use of technology.[91]

Gerstner emphasized an approach to teaching casting the teacher as "coach," "counselor," and "manager" of student "workers." The book was another in the line of treatises promoting the application of business ideas and market-driven competition to the task of reforming schools, coauthored by longtime advocate of business-driven reform Denis Doyle, who coauthored the influential *Winning the Brain Race* with David Kearns. In both cases, corporate leaders who had led restructuring of large companies such as Xerox, RJR Nabisco, and IBM applied a similar approach to reforming schools, with little attention to institutional differences and no depth of knowledge on educational theory or practice.[92]

At the July 1995 meeting with the governors in Burlington, Gerstner issued a challenge:

> You are the CEOs of the organizations that fund and oversee the country's public schools. That means you are responsible for their health. They are very sick at the moment.[93]

Gerstner told the governors that the battle for curriculum standards had to be waged state by state, not to wait for any national agreement on education standards. The day after his address, Governor Tommy Thompson of Wisconsin (R) called Gerstner and asked him "to co-host an Education Summit between the nation's governors and America's top corporate executives." Of the plans for the summit, Thompson said, "I knew this would be a powerful coalition that . . . will spark a race to the top as each community—and eventually, each state—tries to outperform others, and eventually, as each state tries to outperform the other."[94]

The summit, held on March 27 and 28 in Palisades, New York, on the wooded IBM campus, was attended by forty-one governors, forty-nine corporate leaders, and thirty education experts, with the aim of developing strategies to inspire the nation's schools to develop tough, rigorous standards. Among those in attendance were CEOs of a major corporation from each state and what had become the usual list of advocates supporting systemic reform: Lynne Cheney (AEI), Christopher Cross (CBE), Denis Doyle (Heritage Foundation), Chester Finn (Hudson Institute), Keith Geiger (NEA), David Hornbeck (Philadelphia Superintendent), Diane Ravitch (NYU), Lauren Resnick (New Standards), Al Shanker (AFT), and Marc Tucker (NCEE).[95]

The conference theme centered on an assertion made by Gerstner in the conference's opening session:

> It's time to stop pointing fingers and assigning blame. It's time to stop debating. It's time to stop making excuses. It's time to set standards and achieve them.[96]

By the end of the two-day meeting, business leaders and governors endorsed the use of standards and achievement testing and created a policy statement identifying a series of commitments including "an external, independent, non-governmental entity" to provide "leadership, benchmarking, and reporting on the progress of each state."[97]

President Clinton addressed the summit on its second day. Unlike the 1989 Charlottesville Summit, hosted by President Bush, at this summit the president was in a support role as an invited speaker, with Gerstner playing the lead, an important symbolic and substantive difference. A strong supporter of the reform, in his address Clinton endorsed a business-driven approach:

> I've heard Lou Gerstner talk about it in his, almost his mantra about standards . . . the next big step has to be to have some meaningful and appropriately high standards and then hold people accountable for them . . . In 1983 we said, "We've got a problem in our schools. We need to take tougher courses . . . In 1989 we said, "We need to know where we're going. We need goals." Here in 1996, you're saying you can have all of the goals in the world, but unless somebody really has meaningful standards and a system of measuring whether you meet those standards, you won't achieve your goals.[98]

It was an historic event and could be seen as a watershed in the effort for systemic reform of education. The summit was a renewed call for reform and an effort to get the accountability movement off and running again. The movement for systemic reform, which had been making headway in the early years of the Clinton administration, was seemingly stalled by controversy over the role of government, by those arguing for the "devolution" of federal power and increased state and local control, by renewed culture wars including attacks on outcome-based education from the religious right, and by the colorful national controversy over history standards.[99] Throughout intervening years, business support for standards-based reform coupled with tough accountability measures had been strong. In a sense, the Palisades Summit marked a sort of transition of leadership from the federal level to state-by-state reform, with national guidance and stronger business involvement. The symbolism of IBM president Louis V. Gerstner at the podium in the leading role, and the president as an invited guest, suggested that business had become the dominant influence.

Perhaps the most noteworthy "new" initiative from the summit was the proposal to establish "an external, independent, nongovernmental effort" [henceforth "the entity"] to measure and report each states' progress via "high profile" televised announcements. Following the summit, a group of CEOs and governors founded Achieve Inc. to serve as the nongovernmental "entity" charged with shepherding the process of setting and implementing state-level standards. Achieve would be a nonprofit, bipartisan effort. At about the same time, three prominent business groups, the BRT, NAB, and U.S. Chamber of Commerce announced their common agenda to help educators "set tough academic standards that apply to every student in every school . . . and use that information to improve schools and create accountability."[100]

Not everyone bought into the summit's rhetoric. As the Palisades Summit was still in session, the ongoing debate over outcome-based education simmered beneath the surface. Governors seemed to choose their words carefully, trying to keep their remarks general enough so that both liberals and conservatives could stay involved. CEOs seemed most concerned about moving schools toward "bottom line" reforms. Shortly after the summit, the Family Research Council took issue with Gerstner, offering a succinct critique:

> "The time for debate is over," declared IBM CEO Lou Gerstner. . . . Over? Since when? Look at any state in the union and you'll find heated debates over government standards, top down education policy, and—most of all—who controls the children. But parents' side of the debate was not well-represented at the summit, which closed with the passage of a document stating: "The primary purpose of education is to prepare students to work successfully in a global economy." Education is no longer for the individual's "good life," as Aristotle put it, but to serve the interests of the Nation and its employers.[101]

The 1999 Palisades Summit

The 1996 summit was followed by a continuing key role for business leaders in lobbying for and helping institute reform in the states and supporting the national reform agenda in federal policy discussions. By the late 1990s, every state but one had established academic standards in core subject areas, and most states had tests to measure student achievement, at least in English and mathematics. Most were also reporting test results publicly as the reform was nearing a "midway point."[102]

The 1999 National Education Summit repeated the model set by the 1996 summit but added more educational leaders from states, school districts, and universities around the nation among its 117 participants. The summit was held over two days, September 30–October 1, 1999, again on the IBM campus in Palisades, New York, and sponsored by Achieve Inc., "the entity" founded to shepherd reform at the 1996 summit and cosponsored by the BRT, Council of the Great City Schools, Learning First Alliance, NAB, NEGP, and NGA. Summit co-chairs included Thompson and Gerstner from 1996, and Governor James B. Hunt, Jr. (R-NC) and John E. Pepper, chairman of the board of Proctor and Gamble. Also among the participants were several intellectual architects of systemic reform, including Christopher Cross (CBE), Denis Doyle (SchoolNet), Chester Finn (Fordham Foundation), Kati Haycock (Education Trust), Lauren Resnick (University of Pittsburgh), William Schmidt (University of Michigan, National Research Coordinator for U.S. TIMSS), Warren Simmons (Annenberg Institute), and Marc Tucker (NCEE).[103]

Following two days of dialogue and discussion, the new "consensus" promoting education reform on behalf of government and industry agreed on priorities and pledged to continue their efforts to raise academic standards. At the end of the summit, participants adopted a five-page action plan "approved by 24 governors, 34 corporate executives, 21 state education superintendents, and the presidents of the two biggest teachers unions, among other leaders."[104] The plan included three areas of emphasis: "improving teacher quality; providing all students a fair opportunity to meet higher standards; and holding schools accountable for results."[105]

The 1999 summit was a reaffirmation of the business model for school reform, and an indication that despite some setbacks, the juggernaut of systemic reform was continuing to move forward, both state by state and nationally, led by corporate pressure and government collaboration. In 1996, only fourteen states had developed standards. However, it was projected that by spring 2000, forty-nine states would adopt at least some form of standards.[106] The 1999 summit was, depending on one's point of view, either a reassertion that the standards movement was the best way to improve America's schools, or another step in tightening the noose of standardization and control of teachers, administrators, and students by imposing a business-driven model of corporate school reform.

Gerstner, the "driving force" behind both 1990s summits, said that the 1999 summit would focus on what he called "the pain," the sting that teachers, principals, and students would feel when they realize they will be held accountable and disciplined accordingly. Gerstner was quoted in a *NYT* report:

> People are saying "Oh my God, these kids are going to fail" or "They're not going to make it, so we need to lower standards because we're going to hurt their esteem." We understand the pain. And we're going to have to deal with it. But we're not going to deal with it by backing off.[107]

Others were more critical of the reform movement. Alfie Kohn, author of *The Schools Our Children Deserve* and a progressive critic, argued that standards stunt the creativity and flexibility of the classroom teacher. "Thank God for Iowa," he said, the only state that declined to write statewide standards, deferring to districts and schools. "Because of the sensibility reflected in this conference, whole schools across the country have been transformed into giant test-prep centers, where not much thinking is going on." NEA president Bob Chase said that union members support the idea that they should be held accountable, but that "the prevailing mindset among too many politicians is something out of 'Field of Dreams': 'If we set high standards, students will magically achieve.' And they are deluding themselves."[108]

Debate on Standards and Testing

Due to the storm of controversy generated by the *National Standards for United States History*, and the controversy over OBE, the movement for uniform national standards and assessment seemed dead. By and large, the focus shifted to the states. In most areas, state and local standards were developed and by the late 1990s formed the basis for state and local assessments, mainly through standardized tests based on a traditional pattern of subject organization. The major arguments made by advocates of tough standards included:

- "Standards can improve achievement by clearly defining what is to be taught and what kind of performance is expected."
- "Standards are necessary for equality of opportunity," so that all students have equally high standards regardless of race, class, or gender.
- "National standards provide a valuable coordinating function," so that families who move will find similar curricula.
- "Standards and assessments serve as an important signaling device to students, parents, teachers, employers, and colleges," by telling everyone in the educational system what is expected of them and providing information on "how well expectations have been met."[109]

Among the most prominent advocates for standards-based accountability reform were Marc Tucker, William Bennett, Diane Ravitch, Chester Finn, Denis Doyle,

David Kearns, and a host of politicians and business leaders. Behind these arguments for educational standards was the clear and insistent emphasis of national commission reports on schooling as a lever for enhancing the position of U.S.-based multinational corporations in the international economic arena.

Arguments against Standards-Based Reform

Not everyone supported the standards movement. The first argument of many opponents of standards was that schools simply didn't need this kind of broad-brush fix. The standards movement had come to fruition through what Berliner and Biddle described as a "manufactured crisis" in education in their widely read book, *The Manufactured Crisis: Myth, Fraud, and the Attack on America's Public Schools*.[110] They argued that contrary to the myths given prominence in national commission reports and media coverage of education, for the most part our schools were doing a good job. The in-depth and longitudinal perspective on the performance of U.S. schools provided by the Sandia Report provided substantive evidence on the performance of U.S. schools and weighed against calls for accountability reform.[111]

The case against standards-based reform included arguments, from a number of perspectives, that standards would:

- reduce performance to the lowest common denominator
- narrow the curriculum, based on traditional subject matter disciplines
- harm children and distort priorities through national testing
- fail to help poor inner-city schools
- not expand equality of opportunity
- not improve achievement because most teachers would ignore them and do what they have always done
- undermine faith in public education and lead to privatization of schooling.[112]

Opposition came from those with a variety of points of view on the political and educational spectrum, including those who "cherished" local control, prioritized equitable school finance, valued diversity, questioned "the value of extensive testing in schools," and did not think "that foreign school systems were exemplary models."[113] Opposition gave rise to resistance to standards-based reform by many educators. Among the most prominent critics were Alfie Kohn, Susan Ohanian, Berliner and Biddle, Deborah Meier, and Jonathan Kozol. By the late 1990s there was a growing literature of critique from various authors, which included Alfie Kohn's *The Schools Our Children Deserve* and Susan Ohanian's *One Size Fits Few*. There was also increasing resistance from the public, parents, teachers' organizations, and students who questioned the wisdom of standards and the imposition of high-stakes testing. A few students even refused to take the tests. But most went along. In a 1998 article, critical educator Michael Apple poignantly asked, "Are

Markets and Standards Democratic?" Apple described the reform movement as "rightist, anti-school, and anti-public."[114]

In broad strokes, critics argued that behind the standards movement was a mythical manufactured crisis over the quality of schooling, combined with the image of the school as a machine, an appendage of business and industry, with the purpose of creating human capital. Beginning in the early 1980s, groups of corporate executives, worried about the lack of work skills of high school graduates, began to form business roundtables in an effort to lobby policymakers for school improvement. This led in turn to business participation in reports on schooling to proclaim the corporate world's view of what should be done. During the 1980s and early 1990s a myth was created, linking national economic problems to educational solutions. The proposed solution was to instill in students the necessary knowledge, skills, and work habits needed to make America competitive again. A "cookbook recipe for school reform" emerged, modeled on what successful businesses had done: set clear goals and standards for employees; decentralize so managers and employees who make a product decide the means; hold those managers and employees accountable; reward those who meet or exceed the goals and punish or shame those who fail, getting rid of the hopeless cases. Applying this model to schools simply meant a few changes in the wording.

Status of the Reform

By the late 1990s the movement for standards, testing, and accountability was firmly established as the new paradigm for improving schools. Gains by its advocates included development of standards and accountability testing in forty-nine states; growing numbers of charter schools, a manifestation of public school choice; and a shift toward more traditional forms of teaching focused on teacher talk, textbooks, and content, thus reinforcing the standard practices of schooling and the "grammar" of typical classroom routines.

The national focus on educational reform led to a steady stream of reports and surveys on how schools were doing in implementing standards and accountability reforms. On the whole, the reports provide a mixed picture but demonstrate that reforms were having greater impact on the day-to-day business of schooling. Several reports released in 1997 and 1998 suggested that while states and educators were "talking the talk," the standards movement "lacks teeth" and had led to little real improvement. According to the CBE, only seven states had established "very rigorous" standards in English language arts, and sixteen in math. Another report, *Quality Counts '98*, published by *Education Week*, detailed dramatic differences in achievement between urban schools, where less than half of the students reached the "basic" level, and suburban schools, where nearly two-thirds performed at the basic level or higher. Michael Casserly, executive director of the Council of Great City Schools, stated that "Gaps in student achievement, facilities, qualified teachers, funding and other resources are the results of years of national indifference."[115]

With a growing consensus of state, federal, business, and nongovernmental groups supporting the general outline of reform, many more states were implementing accountability reforms, and things were changing rapidly, at least in surface appearances. According to a progress report published by Achieve Inc. and distributed at the October 2001 Education Summit, forty-nine states had set standards, and "virtually all states" were testing students in the four core subject areas. States were increasingly adding accountability measures, "holding both schools and students accountable for performance," and creating "a host of incentives" for improvement. Achieve also noted many sources showing "trends moving in the right direction," with mathematics and reading scores on the NAEP showing general improvement in many states. On the other hand, international comparisons provided a more sobering assessment, with U.S. students below the average of participating countries in the Trends in International Mathematics and Science Study (TIMSS). "More alarmingly" the report noted, were "large gaps" between students in urban and suburban districts. American student performance in reading remained "stubbornly flat," and achievement gaps between white and minority students were large and in some cases "widening." An increasing number of states were producing or requiring "school-level report cards" (forty-four states), providing rewards for "high performing or greatly improved schools." Conversely, more states also had authority to "close or reconstitute failing schools."[116]

Public opinion surveys sponsored by the BRT, Public Agenda, ETS, and the AFT during the period showed that by the end of the Clinton administration, the standards movement had "begun to take hold in classrooms nationwide." But surveys painted a nuanced portrait of caution surrounding the use of testing data, especially in making high-stakes decisions regarding student promotion, graduation, or a teacher's professional standing.[117] The AFT report found that while standards-based reform had been "implemented in diverse ways," more states were emphasizing academic achievement and giving extra attention to students "at risk of failing to meet the standards." However, it charged that "unaligned" off-the-shelf tests were driving the reform and that states had not done the curriculum development work necessary to meet standards. The AFT report expressed concern over a "testing backlash" that had erupted in some states. According to the report, polls and newspaper articles indicated that teachers, parents, and other stakeholders generally supported standards-based reform but had reservations about how it was being implemented. In particular, the public worried about the expanded amount of testing, making high-stakes decisions on the basis of a single test, the accuracy of results, and the quality of tests.[118]

An ETS-sponsored survey of the public, educators, and policymakers, published in 2001, found that there was a "near consensus that education is a priority, that our schools are not making the grade, and that we can do better," but that respondents were hesitant to say that schools are "in crisis." Many believe that we have an "economic/education caste system," with good or excellent schools in high-income areas, fair to good schools in middle-income areas, and poor schools in low-income areas. The survey found strong support for measures to strengthen standards, testing, and accountability among the public, but mixed results from educators and policymakers. While 77 percent of the public supported the idea of testing student achievement and holding teachers and administrators responsible for student learning, "a 49% plurality of educators opposed the idea." Teachers, who made up half the educators surveyed, expressed three concerns about using testing as a means for holding teachers accountable: they worried about being "singled out" for blame; that accountability measures would "distract from the overall education experience"; and that test scores alone were "not a broad enough measure of students' or teachers' accomplishments."[119]

On testing, the ETS survey found that the public also approached the topic cautiously. While most Americans endorsed testing to measure student achievement, and most recognized the value of using testing to identify students and schools needing extra attention, they worried about too much emphasis on test scores, using tests to replace broader methods of assessment, and about "teaching to the test." Educators, on the other hand, remained "skeptical about and divided on the testing issue." Overall, the survey found that most Americans supported "a measured response to education reform" but stopped short of supporting a "complete overhaul." The survey also found that while the majority opposed tax-funded vouchers or tax credits for parents to send their children to private or religious schools, public school choice garnered much greater support.[120]

An annual report on the status of school reform published in January 2001 by *Education Week*, titled *Quality Counts 2001*, found that a majority of parents and teachers believed that efforts to raise academic standards were headed in the right direction and that the reform was beginning to change school practices:

- Almost eight in ten teachers said that the curriculum was "somewhat" or "a lot" more demanding of students.
- More than six in ten said the expectations for what students would learn were "somewhat" or "a lot" higher.
- Nearly seven in ten said students in their schools were collaborating more.
- More than six in ten said students were writing more; nearly half reported students were reading more.

Results of the teacher survey also suggested that placing too much weight on tests and their use to "drive changes in teaching and learning" may be encouraging undesirable behaviors in many classrooms. About 29 percent of teachers reported using test preparation materials a "great deal," while one-third of teachers didn't use them at all. Nearly half of the teachers reported spending "a great deal" of time preparing their students in test-taking skills. Other problems included poor alignment of tests with standards and the curriculum in many schools; the tendency of state tests to emphasize less demanding "low level" knowledge and skills in the standards; and the observation that the sheer number of state standards was too voluminous. Seven in ten teachers said that there was not enough time "to cover everything in their state standards," a problem that was more pronounced for elementary and middle school teachers.[121]

Impact on Teaching

Another study included in *Quality Counts 2001* found that while standards-based education was reaching more classrooms, not all the results were positive. It reaffirmed the finding that while some results were "positive," including a more demanding curriculum and better test scores, evidence also suggested that teachers were "being pushed to place too much emphasis on tests and test-preparation activities." Many tests focused "too much on low-level, multiple choice questions" and were poorly aligned with standards. Critics asserted that tests were "squeezing out high-quality instruction" and producing "mindless and undesirable standardization in schools." Moreover, some experts warned that test score gains could be attributed to teachers spending extra time preparing students for tests and arming them with test-taking skills.[122]

One researcher reported, "People are doing more of the content that's being tested," but found that it's much harder to get teachers "to change the ways they're teaching so that it really encourages students to think mathematically or think scientifically." While teachers reported using "hands-on materials, such as geometric solids, to teach math" on surveys, when researchers actually went into classrooms and observed, there was "a lot of basically drill and practice." Another reported that while teachers were becoming more aware of standards, they were not "moving more deeply to influence instruction."[123]

Heavy reliance on state tests to measure student learning and dole out rewards and punishments to teachers and schools had become a central feature of systemic reform. As one researcher put it, "the load-bearing wall in all of this is not the standards documents, it's the assessments." Studies suggested that teachers were changing their instruction to align it with what was being tested: increasing attention to specific topics, shifting instructional time to concentrate on topics appearing on state tests, and devising exercises that mirror test formats. As one teacher put it, "schools are changing their curriculum to teach to the test, and I think that's unfortunate because it doesn't allow for any creativity." Measurement experts noted that tests sample only a narrow range of what students should be learning rather than the broader content, and that a focus on what's tested could lead to a "bump" in test scores that does not reflect real gains in learning.[124]

In many classrooms, a specific emphasis on what was being tested served to narrow the curriculum, eliminating or minimizing use of progressive, student-centered teaching strategies and leading to greater emphasis on memorization and traditional teacher-centered approaches. Emphasis on testing and accountability and a focus on achievement meant that teachers were increasingly emphasizing activities with short-term benefits centered on memorization or technical skills. Performance-based activities and assessments that involved projects, essays, experiments, inquiry activities, or discussions were becoming less common.[125]

Conclusion

The years of the Clinton administration changed the intensity, but not the general direction, of school reform. The Clinton agenda was boosted by a major economic expansion and widening economic disparity. Both Democrats and Republicans supported what seemed a capitalist, industrialist view of reality, and extension of the nation's support for rugged individualism through schooling. Clinton's leadership on education, including Goals 2000, the IASA reauthorization of ESEA, School-to-Work legislation, and support for standards-based accountability, changed the face of federal education policy and greatly intensified efforts to implement systemic reform at the state and local levels. By the late 1990s, Clinton's leadership, combined with the continuing efforts of a rapidly growing number of businesses, nongovernmental organizations, educational reform groups, foundations, and research institutes, led to an increasingly serious standards- and accountability-driven environment in schools that would deeply influence the way many teachers, administrators, and school personnel conceived of and carried out their work with students.

Several factors contributed to these shifts and the movement toward consensus. Democrats in Congress gained increasing influence during the 1990s, with the Clinton administration, the NGA, business groups, and a cacophony of other voices convincing the public of the need for education reform. Republicans dropped proposals to abolish the DOE, and they funded most of Clinton's priorities, even adding additional funds in some years. At the state level, a business and government alliance led to increasingly tough accountability measures of academic achievement, holding schools, administrators, and teachers accountable for results as measured by standardized tests.

By the late 1990s a consensus had developed that money was a necessary ingredient but not a sufficient means for reforming schools. There was increasing pressure from minority groups and voters for meaningful reform. For its part, the Democratic Party, led by centrists and the DLC, increasingly moved away from its traditional focus on inputs and equity issues, and toward a business-driven school reform agenda combining standards-based reform, accountability, and public school choice. All of this was predicated on two key assumptions: first, that public schools were a failed monopoly, and second, that the key to improving them was through application of business principles to schools, setting clear standards and goals, measuring performance, and holding actors in the system rigorously accountable. If there was a theoretical knowledge base for the reform, it could be found in a variation of outcome-based education, drawn from the work of William G. Spady, but replacing Spady's progressive goals with a more traditional content-centered emphasis. While some states and school districts continued to pursue forms of performance assessment that were similar to what Spady proposed, the broader movement for standards-based reform concentrated on content standards and holding students, schools, teachers, and administrators responsible for specific knowledge and skills. Other key players in the reform who provided much of its intellectual backbone and contributed key leadership throughout the era, giving the reform its neoconservative patina, included William Bennett, Chester Finn, Diane Ravitch, E.D. Hirsch, Denis Doyle, Marc Tucker, Christopher Cross, and others.

The business-government consensus and state-by-state lobbying and development efforts by nongovernmental groups such as ALEC, the BRT, the CBE, and the NGA, led to the adoption of similar systemic reforms in schools in virtually every state, though there were variations. The general emphasis and direction of the reform seemed supported by the political realities of the time. Public opinion polls showed strong support for improving schools, with education as one of the top issues in national political campaigns.[126] Media reports and international comparisons continued to provide fuel for the "schools are failing" rhetoric, feeding the pressure for action at the federal, state, and local levels. Business groups, governors, and their coalition were busily carrying out their ten-year strategy to institute systemic reform, based on a commitment made at the Charlottesville Summit in 1989. According to most media accounts, the long-term strategy appeared to be working, and it morphed into what seemed a perpetual effort to improve schools.

By 2001, accountability reform in education no longer seemed controversial because many states had established reforms for seven, eight, or ten years. However, reforms remained controversial with many teachers, scholars, and educational policymakers because they were largely untested and unproven, because of their coercive and anti-progressive nature, and because of the limitations they placed on teacher freedom and creativity. The reforms represented a triumph of sorts for educational conservatives and traditionalists who had been railing against progressive education for decades. It also represented a decided triumph for a version of education focused on social efficiency with economic purposes, making the economic construction of schooling its central driving feature and centering the education of youth around human capital theory.

During the 1990s there were two important controversies focused on aspects of the larger reform—history standards and outcome-based education—each of which significantly influenced the speed and direction of reform. The battle over the history standards meant that establishing national standards in some subjects would be difficult, and it led to a strong focus on state-by-state reform under federal leadership but without national standards or national tests. It also contributed to a stronger focus on subject areas in which there was a greater chance for consensus, such as literacy, mathematics, and science, though each of these had its own internal battles. Controversy over progressive versions of outcome-based education signaled opposition to a new and stronger form of social control via a variant of education for social efficiency. This resistance was largely overcome by substituting a more conservative form of outcome-based education focused on content standards and accountability measures.

In the context of the movement for systemic school reform, social studies and citizenship education seemed largely an afterthought. With the emphasis on the economic purpose of developing human capital in the form of workers who were well prepared, progressive versions of social studies focused on issues, questions, and social transformation was seen as part of what was wrong with schools. Progressive social studies was anathema to many of the reformers, who supported approaches to social education emphasizing traditional history and geography.

The central theme of this period in the history of American schooling was increasing government involvement at previously unheard-of levels with the onset of the standards movement, and with it, the creation of a technology to enforce a neoconservative vision of schooling and American life. If the schools are thought of as a machine, then the standards movement was a runaway train, a machine in the garden of American schooling, and prospects for redirecting the movement appeared to be growing slim.[127]

The standards movement, through imposition of a technology of testing, seemed to freeze out the possibility of alternative approaches to social studies aimed at creating a thoughtful citizenry, in favor of a more narrowly conceived history and social science curriculum. The entire standards endeavor was predicated on the notion of schooling as a lever for improving the position of the United States in international economic competition. The reform was strongly influenced and enhanced by conservative interest groups such as the Heritage Foundation, the Hudson Institute, the American Enterprise Institute, the Hoover Institution, and, most notably in social studies, the Bradley Foundation, in cooperation with wealthy benefactors and business organizations. Neoliberal and neoconservative groups coalesced to lead development of a national consensus favoring standards-based reform built on dubious assumptions and activities: human capital ideology, crisis rhetoric, scapegoating of schools and teachers, the specter of self-interest, the myth of American rugged individualism, and the misuse and abuse of evidence. The reform was a house of cards built on a foundation of lies, propaganda, suppression of evidence, simplistic analyses, premature reporting, and media irresponsibility.[128]

Despite the general consensus in favor of systemic reform, there was strong opposition and resistance among many educators, and serious doubts about the wisdom of accountability reforms among many more. Schools were still reproducing inequality. Reforms seemed largely ineffectual and took attention away from underlying issues. The federal role in education had shifted from an agenda focused on equity to the creation of a testing and regulatory machine that would identify and punish failing students, teachers, administrators, and schools. Yet many voices with a stake in the battles over education policy and social studies were still present and would not go away easily. A comment by a teacher sums up what must have been a common reaction from veterans in the schools: "What infuriates me is that for decades we have had people showing us a better way of using our resources to help us develop engaged, reflective, compassionate, critical, and active citizens but special interest groups have dominated educational reform, leaving us with a public school system that, AT BEST, produces obedient worksheet completers."[129]

Notes

1. Patrick J. McGuinn, *No Child Left Behind and the Transformation of Federal Education Policy, 1965–2005* (Lawrence: University of Kansas Press, 2006); "New Orleans Declaration: Statement Endorsed at the Fourth Annual Democratic Leadership Council Conference," March 1, 1990, and "The Hyde Park Declaration: A Statement of Principles and a Policy Agenda for the 21st Century," August 1, 2000, http://www.dlc.org/print08fa.html?contentid=878.
2. Rupert Cornwell, "Bush Critics Do Their Homework on Schools," *IN*, October 1991, 16, cited in McGuinn, *No Child*, 230.
3. Jonathan Kozol, *Savage Inequalities* (New York: Crown, 1991).
4. Bill Clinton, "The Clinton Plan for Excellence in Education," *PDK* 74, no. 2 (October 1992): 131, 134–137.
5. Bill Clinton, *My Life* (New York: Alfred A. Knopf, 2004), 308; David Osborne, "Turning Around Arkansas' Schools: Bill Clinton and Education Reform," *AE* 16, no. 3 (Fall 1992): 6–17.
6. Bill Clinton for President 1992 Campaign Brochure, http://www.4president.org/brochures/billclinton1992brochure.htm; Democratic Party of the United States, "The New Covenant," *Historic Documents of 1992* (Washington, DC: Congressional Quarterly Press, 1993), 697–698; Chris Black, "Clinton Targets Schools," *BG*, May 15, 1992, 12, quoted in McGuinn, *No Child*, 80.
7. McGuinn, *No Child*, 80.
8. Will Marshall interview with McGuinn, March 27, 2003, quoted in McGuinn, *No Child*, 80.
9. Lynn Olson and Julie Miller, "Self-Styled 'Education President' Places His Record Before Voters," *EW*, February 12, 1992, cited in McGuinn, *No Child*, 82.
10. I wish to acknowledge McGuinn's use of "policy regime."
11. Mark Tucker to Hillary Clinton, November 11, 1992, *CR*, September 17, 1998, E1819–E1825.
12. National Center on Education and the Economy, *America's Choice: High Skills or Low Wages!: The Report of the Commission on the Skills of the American Workforce* (Rochester, NY: National Center on Education and the Economy, 1990).
13. McGuinn, *No Child*, 84.
14. Ibid., 85; Staff, "Democratic Leadership Council will issue 'Mandate for Change' by early December with Policy Recommendations for incoming Clinton Administration," *PS* 54, no. 045 (November 9, 1992).
15. McGuinn, *No Child*, 86.
16. Ibid., 87.
17. Ibid., 88–90.
18. *Goals 2000: A Progress Report* (Washington, DC: DOE, Spring 1995), 1, 7–8.
19. Ibid., 6, 9–10.
20. New York State Education Department (NYSED), *Federal Education Policy and the States, 1945–2009: A Brief Synopsis* (Albany: New York State Archives, 2006, revised 2009), 66–67.
21. Ibid., 67.

22. McGuinn, *No Child*, 93–94.
23. Ibid., 95.
24. William J. Clinton, "Remarks on Signing IASA," quoted in McGuinn, *No Child*, 95, 97; see also John F. Jennings, Ed., *National Issues in Education: Goals 2000 and School-to-Work* (Bloomington, IN: Phi Delta Kappa International, 1995).
25. Ibid., 97.
26. Ibid., 98.
27. Will Marshall, interview with McGuinn, March 27, 2003.
28. William G. Spady, *Outcome-Based Education: Critical Issues and Answers* (Arlington, VA: American Association of School Administrators, 1994); Spence Rogers and Bonnie Dana, *Outcome-Based Education: Concerns and Responses* (Bloomington, IN: Phi Delta Kappa Educational Foundation, 1995); Peter Schrag, "The New School Wars: How Outcome-Based Education Blew Up," *AP*, November 19, 2001, 2.
29. Richard W. Riley, "Education Reform Through Standards and Partnerships, 1993–2000," *PDK* 83, no. 9 (May 2002): 702.
30. John A. Hader, "William G. Spady, Agent of Change: An Oral History" (Chicago: Loyola University, Chicago, Doctoral Dissertation, 2011), 72.
31. Peg Luksik and Pamela Hobbs Hoffecker, *Outcomes Based Education: The State's Assault on Our Children's Values* (Lafayette, LA: Huntington House Publishers, 1995).
32. Hader, "Spady," 1–2, 87–89; David Berliner, "Educational Psychology Meets the Christian Right," *TCR* 98, no. 3 (Spring 1997): 381–416.
33. Burron, as quoted in William G. Spady, *Paradigm Lost: Reclaiming America's Educational Future* (Arlington, VA: American Association of School Administrators, 1998), ix.
34. Berliner, "Educational Psychology."
35. Hader, "Spady," 88.
36. The controversy bears striking similarities to previous controversies over schooling including the Rugg textbook controversy and the controversy over MACOS.
37. Schrag, "New School Wars."
38. Kaiser/Harvard Election Night Survey of voters conducted November 8, 1994; ABC News/*Washington Post* poll conducted October 20–23, 1994; and NBC News/*Wall Street Journal* poll conducted October 14–18, 1994, cited in McGuinn, *No Child*, 106; Richard W. Riley, "Education Reform Through Standards and Partnerships, 1993–2000," *PDK* 83, no. 9 (May 2002): 702.
39. Lamar Alexander, William Bennett, and Daniel Coats, "Local Options: Congress Should Return Control of Education to States, School Boards, and Parents." *NR* 46, no. 42 (December 14, 1994): 3.
40. Chester Finn, cited in Lynn Olson, "The Future Looks Cloudy for Standards-Certification Panel," *EW*, April 12, 1995.
41. McGuinn, *No Child*, 111–112.
42. Bill Clinton, SOU, January 23, 1995, APP.
43. Kathy Emery and Susan O'Hanian, *Why Is Corporate America Bashing Our Public Schools?* (Portsmouth, NH: Heinemann, 2004); McGuinn, *No Child*.
44. McGuinn, *No Child*, 119.
45. H. Dellios, "Battle Over History May Itself Prove Historic," *CT*, October 30, 1994, 2C.
46. Lynne V. Cheney, "The End of History," *WSJ*, October 20, 1994.
47. Diane Ravitch to Charlotte Crabtree, undated fax, and Gary Nash to Diane Ravitch, June 17, 1994, "History Standards, 1994" folder, Box 50, Ravitch Papers.
48. Rush Limbaugh television show, October 28, 1994.
49. Dellios, "Battle Over History," 4; Cited in Theresa Johnson and Patricia G. Avery, "The Power of the Press: A Content and Discourse Analysis of the United States History Standards as Presented in Selected Newspapers," *TRSE* 27, no. 4, 457.
50. PBS, "Standards—Are We There Yet? Testing Our Schools," *Frontline*, http://www.pbs.org/wgbh/pages/frontline/shows/schools/standards/bp.html, page 3.

51. NCHS, *National Standards for United States History: Exploring the American Experience*, Grades 5–12 (Los Angeles: NCHS, 1994).
52. Gary Nash, Charlotte Crabtree, and Ross E. Dunn, *History on Trial: Culture Wars and the Teaching of the Past* (New York: Knopf, 1997), 175.
53. Howard Zinn, *A People's History of the United States* (New York: Harper and Row, 1980).
54. Gary B. Nash and Ross E. Dunn, "History Standards and Culture Wars," *SE* 59, no. 1 (January 1995): 6.
55. Ibid., 5, 7.
56. Linda Levstik, chair, *NEH History Standards: Report to the NCSS Board of Directors* (Washington, DC: NCSS Focus Group, 1994), 3.
57. Arthur Schlesinger, Jr., "History as Therapy: A Dangerous Idea," *NYT*, May 3, 1996.
58. National Center for History in the Schools, *National Standards for History, Basic Edition* (Los Angeles: National Center for History in the Schools, 1996). See also Robert Cohen, "Book Review of *History on Trial*," *SE* 62, no. 2 (February 1998), 116–118.
59. Diane Ravitch, "Better Than Alternatives," *Society* 34, no. 2 (January/February 1997): 29–31.
60. Nash, Crabtree, and Dunn, *History on Trial*; Lynda Symcox, *Whose History? The Struggle for National Standards in American Classrooms* (New York: Teachers College, 2002).
61. Minutes of NCSS Board of Directors Meeting, July 25–26, 1992, NCSS Papers.
62. Center for Civic Education, *National Standards for Civics and Government* (Calabassas, CA: National Center for Civic Education, 1994).
63. Geography Education Standards Project, *Geography for Life: National Geography Standards, 1994, What Every Young American Should Know and Be Able to Do in Geography* (Washington, DC: National Geographic Research and Exploration, 1994).
64. *CUFA*, Fall 1993, 4. Resolution proposed by Ron Evans, seconded by Jack Nelson.
65. NCSS, *Expectations of Excellence: Curriculum Standards for Social Studies* (Washington, DC: NCSS, 1994).
66. Michael Hartoonian, "National Standards: A Common Purpose," *SE* 58, no. 1 (January 1994), 4.
67. C. Frederick Risinger and Jesus Garcia, "National Assessment and the Social Studies," *The Clearing House* 68, no. 4 (March/April 1995): 227. See also Stephen Buckles and Michael Watts, "National Standards in Economics, History, Social Studies, Civics, and Geography: Complementarities, Competition, or Peaceful Coexistence?," *JEE* 29, no. 2 (Spring 1998), 157–166.
68. McGuinn, *No Child*, 119–126.
69. Ibid., 128. "Policy window" is John Kingdon's term from his multiple streams model for understanding the public policy process. See John W. Kingdon, *Agendas, Alternatives, and Public Policies*, 2nd edition (New York: Longman, 1995).
70. William J. Clinton, "Address Before a Joint Session of Congress on the State of the Union," February 4, 1997, APP; DOE, *Raising Standards for American Education: A Plan for Improving American Education*, 1997, "Plan for America's Schools" folder, 1–29, Box 93, Reed Collection.
71. Ibid.
72. Bruce Reed and Mike Cohen to the President, "Strategy for Implementing Your Call to Action for American Education," February 24, 1997, "Strategy" folder, 78–81, Box 95, Reed Collection.
73. Bruce Reed and Michael Cohen to the President, "Meeting on Educational Standards," March 4, 1997, "Standards (1)" folder, Box 94, Reed Collection.
74. "Clinton's School Testing Plan," *WP*, November 23, 1997, "Testing (3)" folder, Box 96, Reed Collection.
75. Bruce Reed and Mike Cohen to the President, February 17, 1997, "Strategy" folder, 87–122, Box 95, Reed Collection.

76. Bruce Reed, Gene Sperling, Mike Cohen, and Bob Shireman to the President, "Education Strategy," March 15, 1998, "Strategy" folder, 1–9, Box 95, Reed Collection.

77. Chester Finn quoted in Romesh Ratnesar, "A Tempest Over Testing," *TM*, September 22, 1997, 168.

78. Bill Goodling to Colleagues, "Stop the Run-away Train: Co-Sponsor the Goodling Resolution to Put the Brakes on National Testing," August 6, 1997, "Testing (1)" folder, 115, Box 95, Reed Collection; Bill Goodling, "More Testing Is No Solution," August 13, 1997, *WP*, "Testing (3)" folder, 182, Box 96, Reed Collection. Opponents included the Christian Coalition, Eagle Forum, Family Research Council, and other conservative and New Right groups.

79. William Bennett and Chester Finn, "National Tests: A Yardstick to Learn By," *WP*, September 15, 1997, "Testing (3)" folder, 116, Box 96, Reed Collection. Supporters of Clinton's proposal included mainstream groups such as the BRT, AFT, NEA, CCSSO, NAESP, and NSBA.

80. McGuinn, *No Child*, 134.

81. William J. Clinton, "Address Before a Joint Session of Congress on the State of the Union," January 27, 1998, APP.

82. David Hoff, "Clinton's 100,000 Teacher Plan Faces Hurdles," *EW*, February 4, 1998.

83. The Editors, "An Education Primer," *ND*, March 1, 1998.

84. Jennifer Marshall, interview with Patrick McGuinn, March 26, 2003, quoted in McGuinn, *No Child*, 139–140.

85. McGuinn, *No Child*, 140.

86. NYSED, *Federal Education Policy*, 72.

87. Bob Sweet interview with Patrick McGuinn, April 30, 2003, quoted in McGuinn, *No Child*, 144.

88. NYSED, *Federal Education Policy*, 71–72; Kathy Emery, "The Business Roundtable and Systemic Reform: How Corporate-Engineered High-Stakes Testing Has Eliminated Community Participation in Developing Educational Goals and Policies" (Doctoral Dissertation, University of California, Davis, 2002); Emery and O'Hanian, *Bashing*.

89. The Fordham Institute began publishing ratings of standards in the 1990s. See, for example, Sheldon M. Stern, *State Standards for U.S. History* (Washington, DC: Fordham Institute, 2003).

90. NYSED, *Federal Education Policy*, 72.

91. Louis V. Gerstner, Jr., Roger D. Semerad, Denis P. Doyle, and William B. Johnson, *Reinventing Education: Entrepreneurship in America's Public Schools* (New York: Dutton, 1994), 256; See also Louis V. Gerstner, *Who Says Elephants Can't Dance: Inside IBM's Historic Turnaround* (New York: Harpers, 2002).

92. Louis V. Gerstner, Jr., "Public Schools Need to Go the Way of Business," *USAT*, March 4, 1998, "Business" folder, Box 88, Reed Collection.

93. PBS, "Standards—Are We There Yet?," 3.

94. Sybil Eakin, "Forum: National Education Summit," *TQ* 5, no. 2 (Summer 1996), 3, http://www.ait.net/technos/tq_05/2eakin.php.

95. *A Review of the 1996 National Education Summit*, 3, www.achieve.org/summits.

96. Peter Applebome, "Governors and Business Leaders Gather to Map Route to Elusive New Era of Education," *NYT*, March 26, 1996.

97. Adapted from *A Review of the 1996 National Education Summit*, 3, www.achieve.org/summits.

98. William J. Clinton, "Remarks to the NGA Education Summit in Palisades, New York," March 27, 1996, APP.

99. Eakin, "National Summit," 2.

100. PBS, "Standards—Yet?," 3; Ellen T. Hayden, "Standards Mean Business: 1996 Education Summit," *SCBJ* 15, no. 4 (May 1996), 6; Nelson Smith, *Standards Mean Business* (New York: National Alliance of Business, 1996).

101. Chris Pipho, "The Standards Parade," *PDK* 77, no. 10 (June 1996), 701.
102. Achieve, Inc., *1999 National Education Summit* (Washington, DC: Achieve, Inc., 1999), 3.
103. Ibid., 16.
104. Jacques Steinberg, "Course of Action," *NYT*, October 2, 1999, 10.
105. *1999 National Education Summit*, 10.
106. Jacques Steinberg, "Educators Focus on 'Pain' of Standards," *NYT*, September 30, 1999.
107. Ibid.
108. Ibid.
109. Diane Ravitch, "The Case for National Standards and Assessments," *CH* 69, no. 3 (January/February 1996): 134–135.
110. David Berliner and Bruce J. Biddle, *The Manufactured Crisis: Myths, Fraud, and the Attack on America's Public Schools* (Reading, MA: Addison-Wesley, 1995).
111. Huleskamp, "Perspectives on Education in American Society," *PDK* 75 (May 1993), 718–721.
112. Diane Ravitch, *National Standards in American Education: A Citizen's Guide* (Washington, DC: Brookings Institution Press, 1995), 18–25.
113. M. Gittell, "National Standards Threaten Local Vitality," *CH* 69, no. 3 (1996): 148–150.
114. Michael Apple, "Are Markets and Standards Democratic?," *ER* (August/September 1998), 27.
115. Tamara Henry, "Schools Failing on Tough Standards," *USAT*, January 8, 1998.
116. Achieve, Inc., *2001 National Education Summit Briefing Book* (Washington, DC: Achieve, Inc., 2001), 11–17.
117. Public Agenda and Education Week, "Public Agenda: Reality Check 2001," *EW*, February 21, 2001.
118. AFT, *Making Standards Matter 2001* (Washington, DC: AFT, 2001).
119. ETS, *A Measured Response: Americans Speak on Education Reform* (Princeton, NJ: ETS, 2001), 2, 4, 15–16.
120. Ibid., 2, 4, 17.
121. "Executive Summary: Seeking Stability for Standards-Based Education," and Lynn Olson, "Balancing Act: Finding the Right Mix," in *Quality Counts 2001, EW*, January 11, 2001, 8–9, 12–13.
122. Olson, "Balancing Act," *EW*, January 11, 2001, 12–13.
123. Ibid., 14–15.
124. Ibid., 15–16.
125. Ibid.; Sharon Beder, *This Little Kiddy Went to Market: The Corporate Capture of Childhood* (New York: Pluto Press, 2009), 89–90; Larry Cuban, *The Blackboard and the Bottom Line: Why Schools Can't Be Businesses* (Cambridge, MA: Harvard University Press, 2004).
126. McGuinn, *No Child*.
127. Leo Marx, *The Machine in the Garden: Technology and the Pastoral Idea in America* (London: Oxford University Press, 1964), 227–229.
128. Berliner and Biddle, *Manufactured Crisis*; David C. Berliner and Gene V. Glass, *50 Myths and Lies That Threaten America's Public Schools* (New York: Teachers College, 2014).
129. Phillip Kovacs review of William G. Spady, *Paradigm Lost: Reclaiming America's Educational Future* (Washington, DC: AASA, 1998), as quoted on Amazon.com.

6

NO CHILD LEFT

The passage of the No Child Left Behind Act (NCLB) of 2001 transformed the movement for school reform from a largely voluntary attempt at improvement to a mandatory top-down program with a focus on tough new accountability measures. The federal role, seemingly overnight, went from a focus on inputs to the measurement of outputs with high stakes attached. The assumptions that had guided the reform up to this point continued: the educational system as a failed monopoly; improvement by borrowing business management techniques to sanction performance; and imposition of content standards and accountability testing. NCLB was the logical culmination of a reform movement and an educational system rooted in the paradigm of industrial-era education that had begun in the late nineteenth century and that had seemed, to many observers, impossible to change. Movement toward a bipartisan, compromise federal policy on education made significant progress during the Clinton administration. Given the rise of education to the top of voters' lists of concerns and the constant pressure of business groups, to some observers, at least, it seemed inevitable that the nation would strike some sort of "grand bargain" on school policy—increases in funding and greater flexibility for the promise of rigorous accountability—in the effort to institutionalize systemic reform. But the details of such a compromise were yet to be worked out. As we shall see, the election campaign and the first year of the Bush administration would answer remaining questions and stay the course on school reform in a direction encouraged by many constituents and interest groups.

The 2000 Election Campaign

For the first time in the nation's history, education was the leading issue in a presidential campaign. The candidates from both major parties developed detailed education reform plans and chose to emphasize the topic in their campaigns. Perhaps even more remarkable, both George W. Bush, the Republican candidate, and Al Gore, the Democratic nominee, agreed on support for an expanded federal role in education. As one observer noted during the campaign, "the contrast with recent political history is impossible to miss. No one is arguing over whether the federal government has any business sticking its nose into local schools. The argument is over how best and how far to stick it in."[1] Both candidates agreed that the focus of education policy should be improving schooling for all students.

Both candidates ran as moderates, and education became the most prominent issue in what was frequently described as a "race to the center." Both Gore and Bush seemed to draw on Clinton's centrist playbook. Moreover, a series of budget surpluses during the Clinton years made it possible for both candidates to advocate new programs and spending in their domestic proposals, including education.[2]

Advisors to both candidates urged attention to education and federal policy on schooling because public opinion polls placed education at the top of voters' concerns in 1999 and 2000. A poll conducted in August 2000 reported that more than 90 percent of respondents said the issue of K–12 education was either very important or extremely important in determining their vote.[3] Given the prominence of education in opinion polls, there was pressure on the candidates to propose a strong federal role in education reform. Both candidates embraced a similar set of centrist education reform proposals—standards and testing, accountability, increased funding, and improved teacher training—that "appeared to target the median voter."[4]

Though Democrats usually benefited from voter concerns over education, Bush's leadership on education reform in Texas gave him a strong selling point on the issue. Bush and his advisors believed that running a conservative campaign would likely lead to the same outcome as in 1996, and they proclaimed throughout the campaign that he was a new and different breed, a "compassionate conservative," borrowing a phrase coined by Marvin Olasky.[5] In a speech in Indianapolis on July 22, 1999, Bush began describing the tenets of this new brand of government activism that both "knows its limits and shows its heart." This represented a clear break, at least in rhetoric, with the limited-government philosophy of traditional conservatives such as Ronald Reagan.[6]

This strategy also allowed him to highlight his experience with education reform as governor of Texas, and to tout what he claimed were significant improvements in student performance, especially among black and Latino students in urban areas, despite controversy over the so-called "Texas miracle," which was hotly debated by the Gore campaign and the media. A few reputable scholars reviewed test score gains and found problems with the claim. A study completed at the Center for the Study of Testing at Boston College found that the dropout rate in Texas increased after implementation of reforms, especially among minority students, and suggested that schools were "pushing large numbers of kids out" in order to raise average scores. A researcher at Harvard found that the standards on the reading test had been lowered each year between 1995 and 1998, in effect producing a miracle on paper only.[7] Despite the controversy, the education proposals that Bush promoted during the campaign appeared to be built upon the reforms he had championed in Texas, including standards, testing, accountability, and choice.[8]

In developing his education plan, Bush and his staffers also borrowed ideas from the New Democrat's Progressive Policy Institute (PPI), thus co-opting moderate ideas developed by centrists from the opposition party and claiming the middle ground. On policy, this approach became all but impossible for Gore and the Democrats to refute. Their plans were so similar that PPI president Will Marshall stated, "I can't criticize [the Bush] plan because it's ours."[9] Gore's stance on education was very similar, though he did propose significantly more spending than Bush. His policy proposals were essentially a continuation of the Clinton agenda. Both Bush and Gore ran as "education candidates" and put forward centrist education reform plans, advocating a stronger federal role though higher academic standards, increased federal funding, broadened support for charter schools and public school choice, and stronger performance measures through rigorous testing and accountability.

In the end, despite losing the popular vote, Bush eked out a narrow victory in the electoral college in a contested election in which the U.S. Supreme Court intervened to interpret voting results from Florida, with the outcome resting on hanging paper chads. The close election, and Bush's victory, came partly because of Bush's appeal on education. He had a strong reputation as an educational reformer in Texas, despite critiques, and made education the centerpiece of his campaign.[10] The convergence of Bush and Gore on increased spending, standards, accountability, and choice prepared the context for a bipartisan compromise on reauthorization of ESEA, and led to a new federal policy regime in education.[11]

No Child Left Behind

Three days after President Bush's inauguration, on his second full day in office, Bush sent his education proposal to Congress. The "No Child Left Behind Act" was based on his campaign proposals and offered a plan similar to what he had implemented in Texas. The proposal, which would eventually result in passage of a federal law more than six hundred pages in length, was brief, only twenty-eight pages. It was advanced to the Republican-controlled House and Senate in outline form, with an invitation to Congress to join in a bipartisan effort to craft the legislation.[12] The decision to seek a bipartisan reauthorization of ESEA was a wise and logical choice. The Republican majority was slim, particularly in the Senate. With a bipartisan compromise on school reform, Bush could begin his presidency with a potent symbol of his centrist "compassionate conservatism" that fit perfectly with the systemic school reform promoted by business groups over the past decade. His strong support for accountability was based in part on his experience as a Major League Baseball team owner, which he described as "a world where accountability was a daily reality." Where any citizen can "open the newspaper, analyze your performance in a box score, and demand change."[13]

At a meeting held at the Governor's Mansion in Austin, Texas, before his inauguration, Bush invited a number of Democratic leaders on education policy to attend. Among these were Rep. George Miller (D-CA), a liberal who supported accountability measures, and centrist senators Joseph Lieberman (D-CT) and Evan Bayh (D-IN), who's "Three R's" plan from the previous Congress was similar to Bush's campaign proposals. Sen. Ted Kennedy (D-MA), who was the leading liberal voice on education and a supporter of the equity regime, was not invited. Gradually, Bush's advisors became convinced that support from centrist New Democrats such as Lieberman and Bayh would not draw sufficient Democratic support. For his part, Kennedy gradually began to realize that it would take more than money to improve the schools, and he started to reconsider his longstanding opposition to testing and accountability reform. Bush's early talks with Lieberman and Bayh led Kennedy to recognize that he could be shut out of participating in what was looming as the most important education bill in nearly half a century. In a January 2001 meeting at the White House, one day prior to release of Bush's NCLB proposal, Bush and Kennedy agreed to work together on education reform, with Kennedy telling reporters, "there are some areas of difference, but the overwhelming areas of agreement and support are very, very powerful."[14] So, instead of demonizing liberals such as George Miller and Ted Kennedy, Bush co-opted them by seeking compromise, publicly committing only to general principles, and retaining flexibility on specific legislative language.

Bush's NCLB proposal called for annual tests of all students in grades three through eight in reading and mathematics; grants to expand school choice; a new "Reading First" grants program; flexibility for states and districts; accountability measures including financial rewards and punishments for states that made progress or failed to meet objectives; and encouragement of efforts to improve teacher quality. Though the proposal identified key areas of emphasis and contained many of the ideas that would be part of the final legislation, its brevity and focus on general principles meant that it could serve as a useful starting point in negotiations.[15]

Bush's proposal combined key elements from two major proposals from the 106th Congress, the Three R's plan introduced by Lieberman and Bayh and the Straight A's block grant proposal from Republicans."[16] Differences centered on vouchers, the amount of funding increase, and targeting poorer schools. As in the 1990s, debate over NCLB revealed four factions in Congress when it came to education policy: liberal Democrats, New Democrats, conservative Republicans, and moderate Republicans. For moderate Republicans and centrist Democrats, the Bush proposal was very similar to their own policy proposals, but conservative Republicans and liberal Democrats were another story. They would have to be courted, and compromise would be necessary to gain their support.[17] Democrats who had long resisted testing and accountability saw that the Republican majority in the House and Senate could mean a conservative bill and made the decision that it was better to be involved and have some influence rather than oppose the whole thing.

Negotiation and Compromise

The Bush plan contained elements that each faction could support. Democrats were generally supportive of its call for increased federal spending, while Republicans supported its increased flexibility for states and stronger accountability. On the other hand, the NCLB proposal had elements that each party opposed. Democrats voiced opposition to the plan for private school vouchers and the charter agreements proposal, which was criticized as a block grant that would eliminate important safeguards for disadvantaged students. Bush's call for federally mandated testing in grades three through eight brought concerns from Democrats over their impact and how tests would be structured, and from Republicans who were wary about such a major expansion of federal power over schools. Though negotiations went on for nearly a year, and the outcome was far from certain, in the end, leaders from both parties compromised on their longstanding opposition to many elements of the bill.

The legislative process by which NCLB was finally approved was deeply contentious and involved a number of trade-offs. Conservative Republicans and groups including the Family Research Council, James Dobson's Focus on the Family, Phyllis Schlafly's Eagle Forum, and the Traditional Values Coalition saw Republican majorities and control of the White House as an historic opportunity to pass voucher legislation. However, moderate Republicans and Democrats were strongly opposed. Bush's desire for a bipartisan victory led to the early removal of the voucher proposal and compromise on other aspects of the legislation including increased funding.

Testing Controversy

Despite a bipartisan approach and negotiated deals on several planks, there was little compromise on testing. The centerpiece of Bush's NCLB proposal, mandated testing in grades three through eight in reading and mathematics, encountered resistance from both left and right. Liberal Democrats and many educators argued that tests were being overused and that their results would be unfair to minority and disadvantaged students. Conservatives held their perennial view, that federal testing requirements were the first step on a slippery slope to a national curriculum, ending local control. During the House Education Committee markup session, several members spoke in favor of an amendment, from Rep. Betty McCollum (D-MN), to completely remove the testing provisions from the bill, though it was defeated on a voice vote. When it reached the House floor, the testing provision was challenged again, this time by an alliance of liberals and conservatives led by Rep. Peter Hoekstra (R-MI), a conservative, and Rep. Barney Frank (D-MA), a liberal, though their amendment to remove the testing provision was defeated 173–255 on May 23, 2001.[18]

The testing provision was saved under pressure from the left and right by a combination of "heavy White House lobbying," and the efforts of leaders in Congress, notably Boehner and Miller in the House and Kennedy and Judd Gregg (R-NH) in the Senate. Attempts by liberals and conservatives to water down or delete provisions on standards, testing, and accountability were also countered by heavy lobbying and public support for the bill from business groups such as the NAB, the BRT, Achieve Inc., and the BCEE. In addressing the Hoekstra-Frank amendment, the BRT called on its members to ask Congress to defeat any attempts to eliminate NCLB's testing provisions. In a variety of venues, including interviews with the media, private meetings with senators and representatives, and testimony on Capitol Hill, business leaders stressed support for the legislation and its importance for the nation's economy.[19] Direct lobbying and vocal support during negotiations was more than matched by the BRT's ten-year plan of bringing business-oriented accountability reform to schooling.

Negotiations were also influenced by polls that showed strong public support for the plan by more than a three-to-one margin. Support was strong for several key proposals in NCLB, with 77 percent supporting greater flexibility for states in deciding how funds would be used, and 75 percent supporting holding schools accountable for student learning. Support for increased use of standardized tests to measure achievement was less strong, but positive nonetheless at 55 percent. Though many Republicans became disillusioned with the lack of privatizing and decentralizing elements they had originally wanted, most voted for it so as not to weaken Bush's somewhat tenuous position. As Rep. Mark Souder (R-IN) remarked, the president had "a very narrow [election] win, and we don't want to jeopardize his number one initiative. But that doesn't mean we like it."[20]

The bill passed both houses of Congress by huge margins, the House on May 23, 2001, by 384–45, and the Senate on June 14 by a vote of 91–8, after which it went to the conference committee whose task it was to find common ground between the House and Senate versions. Among the key individuals involved in negotiating the compromise were Senators Kennedy and Gregg, Representatives Boehner and Miller, and Bush advisors Margaret Spellings and Sandy Kress. The House and Senate versions called for different levels of funding increases but also contained important differences on accountability. In its provisions on "adequate yearly progress" (AYP), the House version set unobtainable goals for improvement. Moreover, accountability language in the Senate version was regarded as too complex. Disagreements over the legislation had become public, and educational interest groups redoubled their efforts to derail the legislation.

An Act of War

On September 11, 2001, President Bush was at an elementary school promoting NCLB when he learned the news of airplanes hitting the World Trade Center. Though it is difficult to evaluate the impact of the attacks on any one piece of legislation, the events of 9/11 did create a sense that passing a major bipartisan education bill could provide a symbol of national unity, evidence of a functioning government, and a sense that the nation would return to a semblance of normalcy. As one legislator noted, "it strengthened the resolve of both Congress and the administration to proceed with the business of the people."[21] In mid-October, Bush called the leaders of the conference—Boehner, Miller, Kennedy, and Judd—to the Oval Office and urged them to pass the legislation to show that an act of terrorism would not stop the nation from moving forward. Following the meeting, the factions of the conference committee made the necessary compromises leading to passage of NCLB. They agreed on a 20 percent increase in funding, and they reached a compromise on accountability, allowing states to design their own tests and set their own definitions for student "proficiency" but requiring adequate yearly progress for all students in twelve years.[22]

The final version of NCLB that came out of the conference committee was approved by overwhelming bipartisan margins in both the House (381–41) and Senate (87–10). Crafting the legislation required both sides to make major concessions. Republicans dropped their voucher proposal and most of the block grant proposals from Straight A's, while Democrats accepted new mandates on testing and accountability. Though it was an omnibus bill, with voluminous sections prescribing the federal role in governing and awarding money to schools, its central new feature was the requirement that all states adopt systemic reform by developing academic standards and a testing and accountability system meeting specific federal guidelines. Though most states had already developed standards and some testing requirements, NCLB raised both the frequency and the stakes. It required annual testing in reading and mathematics in grades three through eight; a "highly qualified teacher" in each classroom; and escalating sanctions for schools that did not reach performance objectives. It encouraged use of "scientific, research-based" approaches to teaching with documented effectiveness, and expanded federal support for charter schools.

Passage and implementation of NCLB represented the single largest expansion of federal power over the education system in the nation's history. Approval of the legislation occurred for several important reasons. It represented the culmination and logical extension of trends that had been in motion for some time: an educational system that had existed for more than a century, and a reform movement that had been seeking to improve it for two decades. NCLB built on previous reform activities centered on excellence and accountability from *A Nation at Risk*, to *America 2000* and Goals 2000. It built upon an expanding federal role in education that had begun to grow in profile and power since passage of the NDEA in 1958 and ESEA in 1965. It was also instigated by what many perceived as slow progress in the implementation of national goals after passage of Goals 2000 and the IASA in 1994. Though forty-eight states had standards and testing in place by 2000, only thirteen were testing in reading and mathematics every year from third through eighth grade, and fewer still had established strong accountability measures with high stakes attached.

NCLB would not have passed without the election of George W. Bush and Republican majorities in Congress. Had Gore won the disputed election, an education bill reauthorizing ESEA might have been enacted, but with much different provisions, especially on testing and accountability. Bush came to Washington, in part, basing his qualifications for the Oval Office on what appeared to be a successful model of school accountability in Texas. Though a few scholars had warned that the Texas miracle was not real, that rising test scores were a direct result of a soaring dropout rate, most in Washington did not heed the warning. Under different circumstances the protracted battles over funding, expansion of federal power over schooling, heavy emphasis on testing, and extreme and often punitive forms of accountability might have delayed or derailed the legislation. However, the events of 9/11 had a profound effect on the mood of the nation, and NCLB was approved by a very large bipartisan consensus.

Another key influence was the business lobby. NCLB was first and foremost a culmination of business-led pressure for reform. From the 1970s business groups grew increasingly organized and formed endless pressure groups, foundations, and other nongovernmental organizations in an effort to promote education reform. Business activists consistently supported systemic reform and called for rigorous application of business principles including standards, accountability, and choice to rescue an educational system they viewed as a failed monopoly. Their efforts to improve schooling found strong collaborators among the nation's governors, selected scholars, and others. Moreover, business groups pushed for passage of NCLB by exerting public and private pressure during congressional deliberations.[23]

The Law

In passing NCLB, Congress approved a national program that was similar to the Texas model. NCLB, "An act to close the achievement gap with accountability, flexibility, and choice, so that no child is left behind," was large and highly complex. What had been introduced as a 28-page blueprint was now some 670 pages of fine print.[24] Its plan for school reform included increased accountability via "annual statewide assessments in reading and mathematics in grades three through eight by the 2005–2006 school year"; test results "disaggregated by poverty, race, ethnicity, disability, and limited English proficiency" so that each group is monitored and none left behind; "academic proficiency" for all students within twelve years; and testing in science three times during K–12 schooling. The law also included sanctions requiring "adequate yearly progress (AYP) for every subgroup" in Title I schools, with gradual but increasingly severe "corrective actions" such as replacing staff or turning over operations to the state or a private management firm. Additional provisions offered "choice" to attend a better public or charter school in the district; "flexibility" in use of grant money; support for grants applying "scientific, research-based" approaches in reading programs; requirements for "highly qualified" teachers; support for charter schools; and grant programs to improve instruction in American history and civics.[25] With its requirements for testing and accountability, the law created a new federal policy regime in which guidelines required states to implement the kind of bottom-line systemic reform for which business groups and reformers had long been clamoring.[26]

Business Influence

Business and other interest groups had a profound influence on negotiations to pass NCLB as well as on the general direction of reform. Intense lobbying by business and other interest groups preserved the testing and accountability provisions of NCLB at a time when there was still uncertainty about the final shape of the legislation. Lobbyists helped defeat the Hoekstra-Frank amendment, which would have removed the portion of the bill requiring tests in reading and mathematics for students in grades three through eight.[27] Behind the lobbying effort was an extensive network of business organizations supporting systemic reform. Since their pledge to support systemic reform at the 1989 Charlottesville Summit, business leaders helped create an interlocking corporate-government-foundations-nonprofits network to make their "ten-year plan" for systemic reform a reality. Without this background network, NCLB would not have become law.

Corporate support for school reform was rooted in the same rationale expressed during the 1980s, "because the well-being of their companies and every American is at stake." In an education policy paper from Brookings Institution, Milton Goldberg and Susan Traiman summarized the rationale:

> If the United States is to compete effectively in the demanding international economy, and if each person is to contribute to and benefit from the nation's economic success, the most potent weapons in its competitive arsenal are skill and intelligence. The country cannot rely on history of good luck to provide these tools to the work force. They must be developed, nourished, and honed by the education system. Students need to know what the modern world expects them to know and be able to do, in clear, unequivocal statements.[28]

According to Goldberg and Traiman, successful application of standards-based education included "grade by grade standards, with textbooks and curricula aligned to the standards; the expectation that all students will meet the same standards; statewide assessments closely linked to the standard; accountability linked to assessment results, with rewards and sanctions for performance; deregulation and increased local flexibility; achievement data used for continuous improvement; and, reallocation of resources to schools with more disadvantaged students."[29]

The business network supporting systemic reform and leading to NCLB included an ever-expanding list of new organizations but appeared rooted primarily in the work of the BRT, the NAB, the NGA, and the U.S. Chamber of Commerce. The Business Coalition for Education Reform (BCER) included each of these groups as well as the Business-Higher Education Forum, the Conference Board, the National Association of Manufacturers, and Achieve Inc. Moreover, leading groups in the network were involved in partnerships with the DOE, the AFT, and the NEA.[30] In addition, in the 106th and 107th Congress a set of "newly influential" interest groups was exerting pressure on key congressional representatives that cast key swing votes on NCLB. Among these were mainstream groups such as the Education Trust, the centrist PPI, and the NGA, but also more conservative groups such as the Education Leaders Council (made up of state schools chiefs), the Heritage Foundation, the Fordham Foundation, and the EXPECT Coalition. Though representing a range of perspectives on other issues, these newly influential groups were united in their support for stronger systemic reform and high-stakes accountability.[31]

Though their work at the national level was higher profile, much of the momentum for reform came at the state and local levels through state business roundtables and business-led education coalitions, supported by donations from a who's who of corporate America.[32] From the 1980s, state and local business roundtables and organizations had lobbied for standards-based education reform. Their activities were ramped up by the 1989 Charlottesville Summit and development of the BRT's ten-year plan. Almost every state had some activity on this front, and by 2000, virtually all had developed state standards and adopted new accountability measures, though the level of implementation varied widely. Groups like the BRT and ALEC lobbied for passage of state-by-state education reform and built momentum and support for a stronger federal role.

By the mid- to late 1990s, Edward Rust, CEO of State Farm Insurance, had became one of the leading figures in the business push for standards-based accountability and served as chair of the BRT Education Task Force, co-chair of the BCEE, and on the board of the NAB, CED, Achieve Inc., and AEI. Business leaders developed intimate relationships with governors and other state officials that helped make progress on systemic school reform possible.[33] Rust provided testimony before the House Committee on Education and the Workforce on March 8, 2001, in which he called for increasing the intensity of accountability by "aligning assessment systems to standards, . . . annual state testing," and "basing state accountability on increased student performance with clear rewards for increasing achievement and consequences for persistently failing schools."[34] As a central figure in the BRT push for systemic education reform, Rust was appointed to President-elect Bush's White House Transition Advisory Team Committee on Education.[35]

The BRT also built bipartisan support for its agenda through state-by-state public relations campaigns. Alliances with publishers sought "front page" newspaper coverage, while concerns over increased testing were met with speakers' bureaus to build public support. Rising opposition led to an extensive media and community outreach campaign that included workshops for editorial writers and Chambers of Commerce to build support.[36] Overcoming resistance to the new accountability agenda was a key part of BRT strategy. Many of the twenty-four governors who gathered at the Palisades Summit in October 1999 acknowledged that the new reforms had produced "demoralizing effects, which Gerstner described as 'the pain.'"[37] In the spring of 2001, as NCLB was debated in Congress, the BRT published a booklet titled *Addressing the "Testing Backlash."* It provided a range of strategies for "handling" parents and teachers who opposed the new testing regime. Its nostrums included: "Anticipate organized opposition," "Keep the focus on student learning, not testing," and "Take advantage of the superior organization and resources of the BRT network." These recommendations were combined with other strategies to deflect meaningful opposition and avoid penetrating questions.[38]

Lest we think that these strategies were only the extreme policies propagated by a few at the top of the power pyramid, Achieve Inc. received financial support from a who's who of mainstream, corporate-sponsored foundations and philanthropies.[39] Achieve Inc., in cooperation with the NGA, sponsored summits in 1999, 2001, and 2005. The 2001 National Education Summit was wide ranging and included a focus on many of the same topics as the 1999 summit, with more emphasis on addressing the "testing backlash" and other implementation issues. The 2005 summit, held in Washington, DC, focused on high schools, with the implication that higher education would come next. It recommended "An Agenda for Action" that would ensure all graduates are prepared for postsecondary education and work, and put forth a comprehensive plan for states to "redesign the American high school" by improving academic standards, curricula, and teachers. It called for holding "high schools and colleges accountable for student success by setting meaningful benchmarks, intervening in low-performing schools and demanding increased accountability of postsecondary institutions."[40]

Foundations

Another important source of corporate influence came through a new influx of money for school reform paid for and directed by a "billionaire boys club" made up of foundations determined to remake and improve education by applying business- and market-driven reform ideas. During earlier decades philanthropic foundations contributed to school improvement projects. The Carnegie Corporation, the Rockefeller Foundation, the Ford Foundation, and the Annenberg Challenge funded a variety of school and curriculum improvement projects with varying degrees of success. In most cases, foundations reviewed and funded grant proposals submitted by schools, states, and local educational agencies.[41]

With the change to the new millennium, there was a major upheaval in the source and type of foundation funding. During the 1990s much of the funding for school improvement came from traditional philanthropic foundations that existed partially to serve as a tax shelter for the extremely wealthy, who would use some of their money to support good causes such as public libraries, nonprofits, and educational improvement, most often to fund locally designed projects and activities. By 2002 the top two philanthropies were the Bill and Melinda Gates Foundation and the Walton Family Foundation, soon joined in education by the Eli and Edythe Broad Foundation. What was different was not only the concentration of enormous wealth in a few key foundations but their approach to what came to be called "venture philanthropy," in which organizations targeted certain kinds of education reform that were expected to produce "measurable results" or a "return on investment." The trifecta of the Walton, Gates, and Broad foundations supported market-driven reforms consonant with key assumptions of corporate school reform, strategies that reflected their own experiences including choice, incentives, deregulation, and similar business-like approaches. The Walton Family Foundation, established in 1987 by Sam Walton, founder of Walmart, awarded millions to support charter schools, charter school chains, and voucher programs. The Waltons focused their giving on alternatives to public education emphasizing choice, competition, and privatization, rooted in the notion that the private sector would provide better services.

The Gates Foundation—established by Bill Gates, creator of Microsoft and the world's richest man—has used its fortune to address some of the world's most serious problems. Beginning in 2000 it supported education programs aimed at boosting high school graduation and college entrance rates from urban areas, and it did so by supporting small schools initiatives in which larger high schools were broken into smaller units, often with themes, to make the experience of schooling more personal and relevant for students. However, small schools experiments produced mixed results. By 2005, the Gates Foundation shifted its focus to increase funding for advocacy groups, from $276,000 in 2002 to $57 million in 2005. Grants were given far and wide, and recipients included Achieve Inc., the Council of Chief State School Officers (CCSSO), the Education Trust, the NGA, the PPI, the Fordham Institute, and other organizations that were playing a prominent role in efforts for systemic reform.[42] Among the biggest grantees were charter schools and developers of redesigned high schools. In recent years the Gates Foundation has focused more of its giving on charter schools and teacher effectiveness, judged primarily on the basis of test data.

The Broad Foundation, built on the success of Eli Broad's home-building business and other investments, focused its grant funding on programs emphasizing efficient management, competition, choice, deregulation, measurement, data, results inspired by incentives, and sanctions tied to performance. Broad's "investments" in school reform have focused on the redesign of schools so that they function like corporations, and have embraced the notion that school leaders can be business managers with little need for knowledge of education.[43] Together, these foundations and others have pursued strategies aimed at replacing neighborhood schools with an array of market-driven choices, leading inexorably toward the privatization of schooling.[44] Beyond these philanthropic organizations were conservative political foundations and groups that were even more explicitly aimed at influencing policy.[45]

The administration also lent support to efforts for privatization. In December 2005 President Bush signed into law a program to aid victims of Hurricane Katrina that included vouchers to pay for students to attend parochial schools in New Orleans. A number of cities including Cleveland and Washington, DC, also developed voucher programs, which were declared constitutional by a 2002 Supreme Court decision in which Chief Justice William Rehnquist found that the Cleveland voucher program did not "constitute the establishment of religion" and was instead part of "a general and multifaceted undertaking by the State of Ohio to provide educational opportunities to the children of a failed school district."[46]

Was NCLB a privatization "conspiracy," as some have argued? Though there are many charges and countercharges in the discourse, evidence on this point is rather inconclusive. Though there were a number of influential groups, much of their collusion is open to public scrutiny. Collusion is not the same as conspiracy.[47] A conspiracy might have exacted stronger privatization measures. However, the law did contain provisions supporting charter schools, public school choice, and a stronger role for private companies and religious organizations in a move toward privatization. Although NCLB and Bush administration policies supporting choice and privatization may not have been the "conspiracy" to destroy public education that some critics claimed, the administration and NCLB definitely set the nation on a course toward parental choice of a wider mix of schools.[48] Moreover, many of the activities of the coalition behind school accountability reform have taken place behind closed doors with many untold, secretive elements.[49]

A more plausible explanation is offered by Kathy Emery, who suggests that corporate leaders have seized control of public school goals in order to meet their need for new categories of workers due to a fundamental realignment in the U.S. economy. The BRT effort to transform the American school system was not a conspiracy because there was "nothing hidden about the BRT's motives, intentions, and strategies."[50] Since at least the late 1980s, BRT leaders have consistently argued that public education must be "fundamentally transformed" and have worked diligently to align support for their vision across a wide variety of government leaders, nongovernmental organizations, and private-sector leaders in keeping with their ten-year plan to improve schooling. As Edward Rust argued in 1999, the BRT created

> The Business Coalition for Education Reform [BCER], now a 13-member group that serves as a unified voice for the corporate community, and in developing a Common Agenda for reform endorsed by the business community. . . . Roundtable companies are at the forefront of a national effort by businesses to stimulate academic progress by aligning their hiring, philanthropic and site location practices with our education reform agenda.[51]

As part of this larger effort, governors were "socialized" to promote high-stakes testing through the efforts of the ECS and other groups. Emery writes, "Current evidence, when placed in its historical context, suggests the BRT wishes to transform not destroy public schools—create a new tracking system (college prep and prison prep) administered by a leaner and meaner bureaucracy."[52] She views the educational reform movement as an effort by business leaders to control the goals of education and transform the system so as "to sort the nation's children" into new job categories and "socialize them to accept these arrangements."[53]

There is little doubt that the BRT and its allies have sought to transform the nation's school system through their support for high-stakes accountability measures. They are the driving force behind current reforms. The question remains whether the sorting of children into categories such as college prep, prison prep, and a range of other outcomes is intentional or a consequence of hubris combined with naïveté and a disturbing ignorance of educational theory and practice. The sorting function of schooling is certainly nothing new, but it has become more openly acknowledged in the schools I visit, where the line between "proficient" and "needs improvement" is more clearly and publicly drawn than ever before. More likely, the sorting function is the unintended consequence of naïve educational reformers acting in what they believe is the nation's best interest, on core assumptions running through the reform movement: that schools are a business and can be improved by application of business management techniques; that education scholars and teachers unions are largely to blame for the "unacceptable" performance of American students; and that educators must either be co-opted or bypassed to create and implement meaningful reform.

In the end, a combination of business, government, and nongovernmental organizations formed a powerful coalition in support of NCLB and systemic reform efforts, almost guaranteeing market-based reforms. They effectively marginalized critics, parents, school administrators, and teachers unions that had long played a key role in education policy and that ultimately had a more intimate investment in the state of our schools than did many of the reformers. Though other interest groups did play a role in both the negotiations over NCLB and in its implementation, the role of the NEA and the AFT was less prominent than in previous reauthorization debates.

"A Rising Tide of Opposition"

The night after Bush signed NCLB into law, Secretary of Education Roderick Paige met with thirty state chief education officers warning them that they would be held to the letter of the law and that the administration would not grant waivers or allow noncompliance. Paige warned that the DOE was developing tough and detailed regulations to support implementation of NCLB and would threaten to withhold federal funds from states that failed to comply.[54] After passage of NCLB, the Bush administration went into promotional mode, launching a new website to provide information and a "No Child Left Behind Tour Across America," in which Paige and the DOE conducted a twenty-five-city promotional tour highlighting key provisions of the law and drumming up support for its implementation.[55]

Despite a positive spin, threats over compliance, and the administration's promotional efforts, opposition to standards-based education had been mounting for some time. The new law and its more rigorous accountability measures led to a rising chorus of protest from educators. Perhaps the most vociferous critics were educational progressives who argued that NCLB, with its emphasis on state-mandated standards and testing, had greatly reduced the freedom of individual teachers to provide meaningful classroom experiences. In the years immediately following passage of NCLB, a small cottage industry producing books critical of the reform was born. There were books from progressive critics such as Alfie Kohn, whose book *Education, Inc.: Turning Learning into a Business* critiqued business and market influences on education and whose many other books and essays offered a thorough and penetrating critical perspective on the school reform movement; Susan O'Hanian, who coauthored, with Kathy Emery, *Why Is Corporate America Bashing Our Schools?*, detailing corporate organizations and the reform's influence on schools. There were books from longtime critics such as Jonathan Kozol (*Shame of the Nation: The Restoration of Apartheid Schooling in America*) and Gerald Bracey (*The War Against America's Public Schools*). There were books from critical educators such as Wayne Ross and Rich Gibson (*Neoliberalism and Education Reform*), Shirley Steinberg and Joe Kinchloe (*What You Don't Know About Schools*), Michael Apple (*Educating the "Right" Way: Markets, Standards, God, and Inequality*), and an anthology of key critical work by Bill Bigelow and the folks at Rethinking Schools, titled *Rethinking School Reform: Views from the Classroom*. In these works and other volumes, educators took on the standards and testing regime furthered by NCLB. They traced and critiqued its origins, exposed the underlying forces behind the reform, questioned its assumptions, and examined its impact on schools, children, teachers, and teaching.[56]

There were also critical books from other well-known educators such as Deborah Meier, who co-edited a collection of essays titled *Many Children Left Behind: How the No Child Left Behind Act Is Damaging Our Children and Our Schools*, and Larry Cuban, who authored a penetrating analysis and critique of the history of business-driven reforms in *The Blackboard and the Bottom Line: Why Schools Can't Be Businesses.* There were also books from longstanding critics of the reform such as David Berliner who coauthored a book with Sharon Nichols detailing the impact of NCLB titled *Collateral Damage: How High-Stakes Testing Corrupts America's Schools.* The book described the ways in which high-stakes testing was undermining both the validity of testing and the integrity of the education system and described numerous cheating scandals.[57] There were also many articles, books, and reports detailing the impact of the new regime on schools from a host of highly regarded researchers such as Linda Darling-Hammond, Gary Orfield, Marilyn Cochran-Smith, and others. Their findings were mostly negative: the reform was not closing the achievement gap; it was leading to a higher dropout rate; and it was having a negative impact on the quality of teaching.[58] As the reform progressed, there were also critiques from insiders who had participated in and/or supported standards-based reform and NCLB. Among these was an interesting work by Frederick M. Hess and Chester Finn whose edited volume was titled *No Remedy Left Behind: Lessons from a Half-Decade of NCLB* and offered a sobering assessment of how NCLB was "working—and not working."[59]

Interestingly, a major though mostly behind the scenes player in the standards-based reform effort, William G. Spady, the most well-known advocate of OBE, offered a critique of NCLB in 2007 titled "The Paradigm Trap," published in *Education Week.* Spady described NCLB as "the natural extension of a paradigm that has defined, shaped, and sustained our public education system for over a century." It was a paradigm that embodied the leading ideas of the late nineteenth-century industrial age: "a subject-structured curriculum, an age-based grade-level grouping and promotion structure, a time-based and time-defined form of organization, and a decidedly uniform pace of instruction" mimicking factory assembly lines. The model became so "institutionalized, legalized, internalized, and reinforced" that it is "virtually impossible to change." What we know simply as "school" are

> Huge boxes . . . that placed literal boundaries around the thinking and actions of educators, parents, policymakers, and the students themselves . . . These tightly bounded and self-constraining "boxes" of school included the content-subjects box, the grade-level box, the time box, the requirements box, the role box, the grading box, the credentialing box, the opportunity box, the classroom box, and (now ascendant) the test-score box—all intertwined in a web of mutually reinforcing boundaries and limits, something we know today as a closed system.
>
> Hence, the boxes have become the way we think, talk, and act whenever we deal with "schools." . . . That's the paradigm trap we've fallen into, because its all that most of us have ever experienced about education. I call it "educentrism"—a closed-system mind-set that views and treats these boxes as givens and then bases and defines everything else, including educational

change, on and around them, as if no other alternatives are possible. The No Child Left Behind law simply represents educentrism at its extreme, with a very heavy dose of threat, coercion, control, and punishment piled on top.[60]

Spady went on to briefly trace the development of "the great regression" from *A Nation at Risk*, which set the course for the reform centered on the subject-centered "new basics" and built on the premise, "If it doesn't work, keep doing what you've always done, only harder, longer, better." That was followed by the content-standards bandwagon of the 1990s, which defined excellence as "advanced content and concepts" valued by experts as "essential" for every student. The next natural step, paper-pencil tests linked to high stakes, took the "great regression" to its lowest and narrowest point, reducing a child's value to a set of numbers. Finally, Spady pointed to "frightening evidence" of the effects on schools: lower "motivation and morale" among teachers; "loss in droves of talented and creative educators"; "a severe narrowing of curriculum offerings; major increases in student stress, dysfunctional behavior, failure rates and dropout rates; and the wholesale suppression of nontraditional educational approaches."[61]

Perhaps the most well-known critic of NCLB to emerge in the latter portion of the Bush administration was a neoconservative critic of progressive education and a longtime advocate of standards-based reform, educational historian Diane Ravitch, who had served as deputy secretary of education during the George H.W. Bush administration.[62] Ravitch supported accountability reforms and other conservative and essentialist approaches to education from at least the middle of the 1980s, and she was a strong supporter of NCLB until she attended a Fordham Foundation conference examining how the reforms were faring, leading to a sea change in her views. In *The Death and Life of the Great American School System*, Ravitch wrote that NCLB was not working, and no amount of tinkering was likely to fix it. Its assumptions were flawed. Testing and accountability were ruining schooling and hurting children and teachers. Choice and privatization were undermining neighborhood schools. Market-driven reforms were largely inappropriate and should not be applied to schooling, where teachers and students, too often treated as widgets, are motivated by other, more intrinsic matters, closer to the heart.[63]

Teachers unions were also questioning NCLB. The AFT and NEA split in their stance during congressional negotiations leading to passage of NCLB, with the AFT largely supportive, and the NEA questioning.[64] In July 2003, the NEA announced that it would file a lawsuit to challenge the new law as an unfunded mandate. NEA efforts "to get the law killed" led to a confrontation with DOE secretary Rod Paige in February 2004, who called the NEA a "terrorist organization." Paige later apologized in a *Washington Post* editorial, but he still critiqued the union's "obstructionist scare tactics."[65]

By that time, both teachers unions were calling for adjustments to the law and greater flexibility for educators. The NEA insisted that parents be given the right to exempt their children from state-mandated tests, launched an "aggressive lobbying effort" to stop implementation of the law, and was trying to enlist states in a lawsuit against the federal government to stop the law.[66] By July of 2004, both unions were critical of NCLB, and the NEA was demanding alternative approaches that would promote greater "flexibility . . . ensuring that students, teachers, and schools are evaluated on more than test scores alone." While recognizing NCLB's "laudable" goals, the NEA argued, "the law presents obstacles to helping students and strengthening schools" by focusing on punishments, mandates, and privatization. The AFT, a group that had supported the law's passage, now found "serious flaws in the law," arguing that its AYP mandates were "too confusing and inaccurate" and that interventions in schools labeled "in need of improvement" were "not based on scientific research" and were "not constructive."[67]

Critics argued that the accountability provisions of the law and resulting sanctions were punitive and would do more harm than good; choice provisions were largely a mirage, with few real choices for most; clauses demanding "scientific" and "research based" teaching strategies were too narrowly constructed; claims of improved student test scores were based on faulty data, on states adjusting their definitions for "proficiency" and lowering standards; and provisions requiring schools to give military recruiters student contact information and other access were inappropriate. Critics argued that the law's implementation led to a narrowing of the curriculum to focus on skills in reading, writing, and mathematics, subjects seen as most important for student economic success, at the expense of other subject areas that were not part of NCLB's accountability standards. They pointed out that schools were reducing instructional time in history, art, languages, and music in order to give more time to mathematics and English, and that programs for the gifted and talented were being neglected or eliminated because of the focus on basic skills. Most disconcerting, the law's unrealistic goals and punitive sanctions created incentives for schools to lower expectations so that more students would pass mandated proficiency tests. Moreover, its system of rewards and punishments created a strong motivation for schools, districts, and states to manipulate test results.[68] Finally, and most persistently, critics complained that the law amounted to an unfunded mandate by placing additional demands on local school districts and states, thus creating additional expenses, but not providing necessary funds.

Critics

By 2004, criticism of the law seemed a "rising tide of opposition." By 2005, large numbers of schools were classified as "in need of improvement." In all, this amounted to some six thousand, or 13 percent of all Title I schools. During 2004, legislatures in a number of states debated resolutions declaring that NCLB was a violation of states' rights, that it was "inadequately funded," or that it was being implemented in an "inflexible" or "unworkable" manner. Several states passed resolutions prohibiting schools in their states from spending state or local funds to implement the law.[69] Moreover, a number of media reports found that public opinion was beginning to turn against NCLB.[70]

Because of all the criticism from educators, difficulties with implementation, and activity in legislatures and courtrooms, the opposition succeeded in gaining some level of flexibility with implementation, but was far from overturning the law. Governors in only three states signed bills critical of NCLB (Utah, Maine, and Vermont), and only Utah declared that it would not follow NCLB provisions that conflicted with state education goals. The DOE responded to widespread concerns over the law by sending representatives around the country to deliver a two-part message: "NCLB is here to stay, so stop complaining and start complying"; states that do not comply "will forfeit your state's share of federal funds." States found it difficult to turn down federal funds, even with strings attached, because even though it was less than 10 percent of their funding, it often added up to hundreds of millions of dollars used to fund supplemental programs that stakeholders had come to expect.[71] In 2005, the state of Connecticut challenged the legality of NCLB in court (the law was later upheld in this and other court challenges).[72]

A good deal of the concern about NCLB was centered on flexibility of enforcement. In March 2004, Bush and his education advisors met with the chief state school officers of thirty-five states in a two-hour meeting to air concerns. A few days after that meeting, and in subsequent months, the DOE changed the rules on test-participation rates, allowing greater flexibility for states so that more schools could meet AYP requirements.[73] At the start of his second term, Bush replaced Secretary of Education Paige with Margaret Spellings, a former domestic policy advisor. Spellings introduced more changes early in 2005, announcing "a new commonsense approach" granting new flexibility to states in reaching the desired goals, and noted, "it is the results that matter, not the bureaucratic way that you get there." She announced that the DOE would introduce greater flexibility in testing requirements for students with learning disabilities and would examine alternative models for calculating AYP.[74] Spellings called the new guidelines "a comprehensive approach to implementing the law" but reiterated that "the bright lines" of the statute—such as "annual testing to determine student achievement, reporting results by student subgroups and highly qualified teachers—were not up for negotiation."[75] Even with new flexibility in implementation, the central emphasis of NCLB and virtually all of its key provisions remained intact. Within a month of the changes in implementation policy, three states (Michigan, Texas, and Vermont) joined with the NEA in filing suit against the federal government over NCLB on the grounds that it was an "unfunded mandate."[76]

Despite all the controversy, and claims that opposition was growing, a number of opinion polls showed that public support for NCLB, though mixed, remained a supporting factor. Polls found that NCLB continued to be viewed more favorably than unfavorably (24 to 20 percent), and a majority of respondents believed that NCLB would help improve student achievement. One poll found respondents evenly split on the law. Another found that 37 percent believed NCLB had a positive effect on schools while 21 percent believed it had a negative impact.[77]

Even with criticisms, concerns, minor adjustments in implementation, and significant erosion in public support, the bipartisan coalition that passed and supported NCLB remained largely intact. Bush administration officials and congressional Republican leaders remained steadfast in their support of the law. Though Democrats criticized what they called "inadequate funding," and called for more flexibility, key liberals continued to support the law's general principles and approach to reform.[78] Kennedy, when introducing legislation in 2004 that would provide states and districts more flexibility in implementation, was careful to comment, "It's important to acknowledge what this bill does not do. It does not make fundamental changes to the requirements under No Child Left Behind. Those reforms are essential to improving our public schools."[79]

After five years of NCLB implementation, a number of important questions began to take shape that would need to be addressed in discussion of the law's next reauthorization, due in 2007, but not undertaken by Congress by the end of the Bush administration. Was this major new federal education strategy focused on standards, assessment, and accountability succeeding? Was student performance improving? Were the schools, and the nation, better off than before? If there were unintended negative consequences of the law, what were they and how could they be addressed? If the overall strategy was flawed, what would replace it?

Social Studies under Siege

As we have seen in previous chapters, developments in social studies over the last two decades of the twentieth century included continued attempts to replace social studies as a broad and progressive field of study with a more traditional form of social education centered on traditional history, geography, and civics. The period from 2001–2008 represented a culmination of much of what had transpired during the previous quarter of a century, from at least the time of the MACOS controversy, the tumultuous conflict in Kanawha County, West Virginia, and other 1970s controversies inspired by the new and newer social studies.

The revival of history struck a nerve among historians, the public, and many teachers. Part of the reform agenda included a return to the basics and a reemphasis on traditional teaching methods, pushed along by neoconservatives and the New Right. During the standards-based reform era, there were regular reports of state-by-state battles over the social studies curriculum, frequently involving revision of state curriculum frameworks and guidelines from a more progressive "social studies" framing in which disciplinary boundaries were crossed, to a reworking of curriculum documents to focus on "history and the social sciences."[80] Often, this relabeling carried implications for the kinds of content studied; whether it would emphasize history and disciplinary content or broader, interdisciplinary

themes and issues; multiculturalism or monoculturalism; thinking or memorization; socialization or counter-socialization; imposition or questioning.

The culmination of more than two decades of effort by historians and history education researchers to improve the teaching of history and simultaneously degrade social studies, which was portrayed by many as the nemesis of
good history education, was having an impact. There was less attention to broad
field interdisciplinary social studies across the curriculum. At the elementary level,
schools often left out social studies and history because it was seldom included
in state-mandated tests.[81] This trend could be seen as collateral, unintended damage from the emphasis on systemic reform and its focus on learning that was
deemed critical to student economic success. Middle schools and junior high
schools often de-emphasized social studies courses, especially for students needing
additional instruction in the basics and more time focused on reading, writing,
and mathematics.

Just as standards and testing regimes were being implemented in more and
more states, history educators were "quietly celebrating" signs that their efforts
to revive and improve the teaching of history in schools were having an impact.
According to a 2003 *Education Week* article, policymakers were increasingly pushing for improvements in the teaching of history. "This is a high point for history,"
exclaimed Elaine Wrisley Reed, executive director of the National Council for
History Education, formed in 1990 by historians who were part of the Bradley
Commission. "Never has there been so much attention placed on the teaching
and learning of American history," Reed stated. On the other hand, scholars in
social studies were less than excited about the trend. "They've made a scapegoat
out of social studies," argued Ronald W. Evans. "The historians in the rhetorical
war have the upper hand right now," Evans said. "Things are moving toward a
narrowing of the curriculum."[82]

There were clear indicators that the revival of history was making a dent in
schools and policy discussions. One sign of history's "rising dominance" could be
seen in legislation authorizing the Teaching American History Grants Program,
which received $100 million in the 2001 federal budget, and half a billion dol-
lars by 2006, with the aim of promoting the teaching of history "as a separate
academic subject (and not as a component of social studies)."[83] The legislation
that authorized the first set of Teaching American History Grants specifically
excluded social studies projects from funding.[84] In announcing the program,
Sen. Robert C. Byrd (D-W.Va.), sponsor of the legislation, specifically blamed
the blending of history with other subjects as a contributor to declining student
knowledge. "Too many schools today are lumping history together with other
subjects and offering them as courses broadly titled 'social studies,'" Byrd said.
"This conglomeration certainly does not provide the kind of focused study that
history deserves and requires."[85]

Others were even more forthright. Kay Hymowitz, writing for the *Weekly
Standard*, a publication of the conservative Manhattan Institute, aimed "scathing

criticism" at social studies, and the NCSS as its chief proponent, for promoting what she described as "a betrayal of the Founders' view of education" by promoting "a critical view of the nation's history" and contributing to "a woeful ignorance of their American heritage." She argued that education should instead emphasize "a love of America and its guiding principles" through the teaching of traditional history and government. Hymowitz offered seething critiques of NCSS and social studies advocates, citing their calls for restraint in the aftermath of 9/11 and the need to "de-exceptionalize" the United States. She claimed that states using the NCSS guidelines as their model required "no history at all."[86]

Another, similar criticism of the 1994 NCSS social studies standards came from Paul Gagnon, who complained that the NCSS standards de-emphasized history because "They are not organized by subject (history, geography, economics, civics) but under ten abstract, over-lapping themes."[87] Gagnon and Horowitz were countered by Phipps and Adler, who stated that critics failed to understand "the critical distinction between content standards and curriculum standards." They argued that NCSS curriculum standards were intended to be used "in concert" with content standards, to develop a focus on thinking and decision making while teaching the specified content.[88]

Much of the growth of history education in the schools could also be attributed to the influence of conservative foundations that were increasingly lobbying for a return to traditional history as an antidote to what they viewed as the progressive influence of social studies. Conservative and right-wing groups engaged in the rhetorical "war" on social studies included the Lynne and Harry Bradley Foundation, the Fordham Foundation, the Heritage Foundation, the Manhattan Institute, and the Gilda Lehrman Institute. Other contributors on a lesser scale included the American Enterprise Institute, the Olin Foundation, and the Hudson Institute.[89] These groups contributed a steady stream of reports, documents, and opinion pieces critiquing social studies and promoting history education, especially traditional history. They also contributed funding to support key organizations and people active in the siege.[90]

The Teaching "Traditional" American History Grant Program

Given that the revival of history was one of the dominant trends in social studies, government support for improving the teaching of history was a critical element and developed late in the Clinton administration due to the leadership of Senator Robert C. Byrd. The Teaching American History (TAH) grants program began with an amendment to the education appropriation budget from Sen. Robert C. Byrd (D-W.Va.) on June 30, 2000, providing $50 million "to develop, implement and strengthen programs to teach American history (not social studies) as a separate subject within school curricula." Byrd went on to expand on the program's rationale by warning readers of a "hybrid called 'social studies' [that] has taken hold in our schools." The purpose of Byrd's proposed "Teaching Traditional

American History" program (the word "Traditional" was later cut) would be to restore history to its rightful place in the curriculum, thus insuring that "our Nation's core ideals—life, liberty, justice—will survive."[91] Congress approved and funded the legislation three months later. Within a year, the TAH grant program was approving and supporting projects with its initial allocation of $50 million. By 2009, the program had funded some nine hundred grant projects at a cost of approximately $838,172,000.[92] This was by far the largest federal incursion into the social studies curriculum since the era of the new social studies, and its explicit intent was to counteract progressive versions of the field.

The program supported competitive grants to local education agencies for the purpose of promoting and improving "the quality of history instruction by supporting professional development for teachers of American history." The central underlying thesis of the TAH program was that "in order to teach history better, teachers need to know more history." So the program focused on improving teachers' knowledge of history, rather than emphasizing a particular pedagogical approach or some other goal.[93] Grants were typically designed to "assist schools in implementing scientifically based research methods" aimed at improving the quality of history instruction, professional development, and teacher education. Local educational agencies carried out their activities in partnership with a college or university, a nonprofit history or humanities organization, a library or museum. According to the DOE, the goal was "to demonstrate how school districts and institutions with expertise in American history" could collaborate over three years "to ensure that teachers develop the knowledge and skills necessary to teach traditional American history in an exciting and engaging way."[94]

Despite a good deal of hype surrounding the program, an early DOE evaluation was quite critical. Its authors found that 91 percent of the projects used self-report data in evaluations, that projects may have failed to reach those teachers "considered most in need" of professional development, and that experiences provided didn't always match "research-based definitions of effective professional development."[95] Moreover, a prominent history educator, Sam Wineburg, wrote that while the program had "breathed new life into history teaching" and had likely made contributions to teacher knowledge, there was little proven connection between all the professional development efforts and "verifiable gains in student learning."[96]

In a speech before an audience of the OAH, Wineburg, in effect, wondered whether the program was a billion dollar "boondoggle," with its weakly focused assessment of project outcomes via multiple-choice testing of student and teacher knowledge of basic facts from American history. What teachers needed, he said, was not facts, but how to put facts into "productive classroom use," citing a 2005 study in which teachers received nearly perfect scores when asked factual questions, but "when they were asked to do history—drawing up lesson plans relating cause and effect and the significance of events—scores dropped by half."[97] Wineburg's comments underscored flaws with the "traditional history" framework under-girding much of the TAH work, the complexity of educating teachers, and the program's support for the "anti-social studies" coalition that was the emphasis of policymakers. Other scholars also wondered about the program's efficacy and found little evidence that "two decades of promoting history and attacking social studies" had led to improvement in teaching. Moreover, NAEP U.S. history scores provided evidence of "only minor improvements" in students' "historical understanding" since 1994. A subsequent evaluation study led to the end of program funding.[98] In sum, although the TAH grant program created renewed interest among historians in the teaching of the field, generated a good deal of excitement among its advocates, and may have engaged many teachers in thoughtful in-service activities, there is little evidence that it improved the teaching of history in schools. Moreover, its framing borrowed heavily from the coalition that had been attacking social studies for nearly a quarter century, while its emphasis on traditional history meant that it was doubtful that the program did much to improve the broader social understanding of the nation's youth.[99]

Where Did Social Studies Go Wrong?

The continuing effort by conservative groups to replace social studies with traditional history, a back-to-basics curriculum, and a more traditional emphasis continued with James Leming's edited volume, *Where Did Social Studies Go Wrong?*, published in 2003 by the Fordham Foundation. The book was the product of a group of self-described "contrarians" within the social studies field, in cooperation with longtime critics of social studies such as Chester Finn and Diane Ravitch, and originated with a conversation between Lucien Ellington and Ravitch a few years earlier.[100] The book's thesis was that social studies theory and research is dominated by ideologues who have laden teachers in the field with an emphasis on issues and process over the learning of factual content, contributing to the field's regrettably poor condition. The book's preface, by Chester Finn, blamed the "deterioration of social studies in U.S. schools" on the "lunatics" who have "taken over the asylum," who are imparting "ridiculously little knowledge" to students, who possess "no respect for Western civilization," and who are inclined "to view America's evolution as a problem for humanity rather than mankind's last, best hope."[101] In their introduction, the editors asserted that social studies is in "deep trouble" because of the "politically correct . . . belief systems of the social studies education professoriate" who train future teachers, a philosophy at odds with most Americans that has resulted in a field that "eschews substantive content and subordinates a focus on effective practice to educational and political correctness." Moreover, they argued, "politicized" topics and issues such as "peace studies, the environment, gender equity issues, multiculturalism, and social and economic justice" dominate the curriculum, leading to neglect of academic content.[102] Diane Ravitch contributed an essay on the history of social studies that was brief and biased, depicting social studies as a bastard form of "extreme utilitarianism," far inferior to the traditional academic history she favored and promoted. She portrayed the field as "rife with confusion" and argued that it "invites capture by ideologues and by those who seek to impose their views on the classroom."[103] There were chapters critiquing the "collapse of standards," a "global education ideology," radical multiculturalism, and a host of other progressive sins. There were other chapters promoting "direct instruction," traditional "teacher-centered instruction," and critiquing the professoriate's desire to use social studies as a "vehicle for promoting social change."[104]

A review by Ronald W. Evans charged that the volume suffered from "inflammatory rhetoric," and "scapegoating social studies as an entire field" to further a traditionalist agenda. He wrote that the authors were "aiming to destroy social studies as a broad and multidisciplinary field and replace it with a narrower curriculum" in consonance with other recent critics.[105] A review by Ross and Marker framed the volume as an argument for the "citizenship transmission" model of social studies that promotes "student acquisition of certain American or democratic values through the teaching and learning of discrete, factual pieces of information" drawn from Western culture.[106] Alan Singer cast the volume as the product of a coalition of conservative groups, funded by well-heeled foundations, that had been "making war on social studies" for at least two decades.[107]

A New Civic Climate?

Along with a continuing stream of critics attacking progressive versions of social studies and championing a return to traditional teaching methods, there were other significant developments impacting the social studies field and citizenship education broadly. There were new initiatives and discourse on the need to improve civics education, though they came at the field from a range of perspectives. NCLB contained a provision funding grants for improvement of civic education. In particular, it funded We the People, a program of the Center for Civic Education. We the People received funding in the range of $12 to $17 million each year from 2001 through 2006 and was part of a broad effort to revive and renew the teaching of civics in U.S. schools.[108] This was a mainstream and bipartisan effort begun in 1987 to improve civic education that reached as many as 30 million students and 90,000 educators.[109]

In addition, there was "The American History and Civics Act of 2004," an act to establish summer academies for teachers and students of American history and civics, based on a bill introduced by Senator Lamar Alexander (R-TN) to combat "civic illiteracy." In his remarks introducing the legislation, Alexander addressed the program's neoconservative intent and said it was time to "put the teaching of American history and civics back in its rightful place in our schools so our children can grow up learning what it means to be an American." He lamented, "Our children do not know what makes America exceptional," claimed that American history had been "watered down," and noted that civics was "often dropped from the curriculum entirely." He blamed "so called reforms" of the 1960s that resulted in widespread elimination of required classes.[110]

Beyond We the People and the American History and Civics Act of 2004, there was also a new initiative funded by the Carnegie Corporation and CIRCLE, the Center for Information and Research on Civic Learning and Engagement, and involving a wide array of educators, civic education agencies, and others as described in the 2003 report, *Guardian of Democracy: The Civic Mission of Schools.* The report provided a comprehensive look at the role civic learning plays in maintaining our democracy. It examined major problems confronting civic learning, "proven practices," and provided recommendations for policymakers, educators, and citizens.[111] However, as the decade wore on, there were increasing concerns that, despite these efforts, the civic mission of schools was being undermined by NCLB and assessments, using multiple-choice tests, that "focus primarily on memorizing information, rather than demonstrating civic skills." Research suggested that during the decade after NCLB, states shifted educational resources away from social studies toward subjects that appeared on statewide assessments, which most often emphasized reading and mathematics and less frequently tested students on social studies. A CIRCLE study found that most states do not emphasize civic education, which includes "learning about citizenship, government, law, current events and related topics."[112]

During the Bush administration there were also "Faith-based Initiatives" sponsored by NCLB, which provided new forms of access for religious groups to schools and gave additional support for private religious schools, as part of the larger trend toward privatization. Faith-based initiatives were a part of the broad and more conservative kinds of citizenship education championed by the Bush administration. The inclusion of faith-based initiatives was important to President Bush, who issued an executive order several days after taking office in 2001 to establish a White House office to "expand opportunities for faith-based and other community organizations and to strengthen their capacity to better meet the needs in American communities."[113] Though there was not a voucher plan included in the final draft of NCLB, the law contained several sections giving religious organizations the opportunity to play a more active role in the public schools, purportedly as a way to contribute to the education of children. NCLB made specific grant funds available for religious groups "to provide tutoring and other academic enrichment services for eligible low income students." Funds could be used to help with "reading, language arts, and mathematics," and programs could take a variety of forms including after-school literacy offerings, mentoring programs, or technology education. Guidelines provided by Secretary Paige provided clarification to school administrators regarding student prayer in schools, organized prayer groups, meetings of religious clubs, and so on. Unmistakably, the new faith-based initiatives allowed access for religious groups to public schools, along with student expression of religious faith.[114] This combined with the administration's support for "abstinence only" sex education programs gave the larger arena of civic education a decidedly conservative and "patriotic" tone.

Damage in Classrooms

The impact of NCLB, as the latest phase of standards-based reform, was damaging to social studies practice in schools. It included deliberate efforts to promote traditional teaching based on "effective schools" research, and caused collateral damage to the field by imposing a new and more extreme phase of accountability. The emphasis on content standards and testing in social studies led to classroom emphasis on drill and practice with a focus on memorization from textbooks to prepare students for standardized tests. More than ever, the emphasis was on socialization rather than counter-socialization.[115] While there was increased disciplinary focus on history, it was often without the conceptual moorings that could be built by student learning that was centered in materials, concepts, and ideas from political science, geography, sociology, and other areas of study. Though advocates of the revival of history as the core of social studies suggested that content from the other social sciences would be built into narrative history, there was little evidence that this was done effectively.[116]

The DOE and a few observers claimed that the new testing and accountability measures mandated under NCLB led to improvement in student achievement, along with a wealth of new and helpful data on how schools were performing.[117] Students in the nation's schools were definitely spending more time on reading and mathematics. Other impacts often cited as positives included increased attention to aligning curriculum and instruction with content standards and assessments; use of testing data to modify instruction; more intensive focus on helping low-achievers; emphasis on the needs of low-income racial and ethnic minority students; addressing the achievement gap; and helping English language learners and special needs students.[118] However, there were also warnings early on from a number of respected scholars that emphasis on testing and accountability would lead to unintended consequences.[119]

Doubts about NCLB's Impact

Evidence on the impact of NCLB suggests that the law did not accomplish its central stated aim of raising the level of achievement of American students. Though student scores on state achievement tests were rising, most states had adjusted their definition for "proficiency" to allow a higher pass rate, in effect relaxing standards to a somewhat more realistic level. NAEP scores in reading and mathematics showed little or no real gains, especially as compared with growth in previous years. Dropout rates, push-outs, and exclusions from testing had increased, along with labeling of students and schools.[120] Though there was a great deal more time and energy devoted to testing, the achievement gap continued. Accounting for dropouts, it worsened.[121] Moreover, the extreme emphasis on testing and the pressure it created for rising scores led to collateral damage in the form of widespread cheating and corruption, eroding the validity of any claims of improvement and distorting the integrity of the system.[122]

There were also grave doubts about the efficacy of NCLB provisions on AYP and its systemic reform accountability provisions, the rewards for improvement and sanctions for schools failing to make the grade. Increasing numbers of schools were sanctioned as "failing," and critics labeled the system "unrealistic" and "the most toxic flaw" in a compliance-driven system that "re-creates the very pathologies it was intended to solve."[123] According to reliable research, restructuring simply wasn't working. In most "failing" schools the restructuring process could best be described as remodeling by shuffling, relabeling, and shifting personnel, leading to cosmetic makeovers making little real difference in student outcomes as schools and states pretended to meet AYP goals.[124] Mainstream and conservative observers agreed that "Choice," while producing a few hopeful signs in some schools, was not working as hoped. Most parents and students were given few choices; fewer still were taking advantage of the supplemental private tutoring that schools were required to provide. Furthermore, evidence on the quality of charter schools was mixed, at best.[125]

In terms of the impact of NCLB on educators and their craft, there was growing evidence that reforms led to disregard for the scholarly community in education, and privileged neoconservatives and others who supported the systemic reform model. It had a negative impact on teachers' morale, de-professionalizing teachers, many with advanced degrees, by wresting professional judgment from experienced practitioners, who were now often required to follow scripted, teacher-proof lessons purchased from textbook companies as part of reading, math, or science curriculum packages.[126] It also led to "teaching to the test" and huge amounts of classroom time devoted to test preparation. As one researcher noted, these changes "oversimplifie[d] the process of teaching," research, and practice, and left teachers "void of agency."[127]

Curriculum Narrowing

A major consequence of NCLB and imposition of high-stakes testing was a widely noted "narrowing" of the curriculum that reduced time devoted to subjects that were not the main focus of testing. Social studies, history, geography, the social sciences, the arts and humanities, and even science were all marginalized by NCLB requirements, especially in elementary schools.[128] Moreover, teaching was more frequently focused on drill and practice in low-level skills most often measured by high-stakes tests, with less attention to the needs of gifted students. In social studies this meant a redesign of instruction that emphasized memorization, quizzes, and traditional forms of teacher-centered instruction, and severely limited assignment of essays, projects, or other thought-provoking or motivational activities.[129] Studies showed that the intrinsic motivation that often encouraged students to learn was much less when a system of rewards and sanctions was used, and that it resulted in lower levels of critical thinking. High-stakes tests often "decreased student motivation" and led to higher student dropout rates.[130] The impact of testing was especially negative in social studies classrooms. Numerous studies showed that when it wasn't tested, social studies was shunted to the side in elementary schools. When it was taught and tested there was increased attention to regurgitation of facts, along with lower levels of critical thinking.[131]

Standards-based education, the accountability mandates of NCLB, the conservative restoration, and the revival of traditional history all combined to have a profound impact on classrooms and teaching practice across the nation. Though there was variation from state to state and school to school, in the typical social studies or history classroom, there was less attention to creating a deliberative process—less discourse, more teaching to the test, more teaching from the textbook, more memorization, and more emphasis on traditional forms of teaching that had been the bulwark and seemingly unchangeable grammar of social studies for years: teacher talk, textbooks, commercial instructional programs, lecture, and PowerPoint. Most of the time, the banking approach was dominant, with emphasis on depositing discrete, often fragmented, bits of knowledge into students' minds.[132]

Increasing numbers of elementary school teachers were being asked to follow scripted lessons in which every teacher move was dictated by a teacher's guide from a package of materials created by a publisher who closely followed standards, and who had won a contract for purchase of materials with the local district or state. Moreover, the curriculum was monitored by administrators who would regularly check classrooms for adherence to the standardized curriculum, look for written standards posted on a chalkboard or bulletin board, or impose a "pacing guide" to keep classes on schedule, in strict adherence to the curriculum and textbook. In short, standards, accountability, and textbooks came to dominate teaching in unprecedented ways in many classrooms across the nation. To add to the mix, emphasis on "scientific" and "effective schools" research meant a de-emphasis on the qualitative, historical, and philosophical discourse needed for teachers to reflect on their aims and purposes and develop meaningful ways of implementing theory into practice. The new watchword, it seemed, centered on what "works," promoting basic teaching truisms and social efficiency-driven practices supported by correlation and process-product research. This generally served to reify traditional teaching methods that focused on imparting content for students to memorize, and did little to promote either disciplined inquiry or issues-centered study.

Unfortunately, given the mandates of the NCLB era, and the rush through the textbook that it seemed to produce, there was less room for teachers' creativity to flourish. Reports found that teacher morale had reached a new low. The reform was anti-progressive, anti-teacher, and anti-child in tone and aims, leading to fewer child-centered and interest-building activities—the kinds of things that motivate teachers and students and that can make school enjoyable. There were fewer critical thinking activities that could intrigue the mind and make school interesting. There was a shift away from the intrinsic motivation that such activities often created, and an extreme focus on extrinsic rewards alone.[133]

Though this description is accurate for most mainstream public schools, there were exceptions. Some charter and experimental schools had a focus on innovative teaching. For example, an alliance of charter schools connected with Theodore Sizer's "Coalition of Essential Schools" network, such as High Tech High in San Diego, focused on project-based learning or other thoughtful approaches.[134] Schools in wealthier areas could afford to pay less attention to test results because their scores were high, and teachers were afforded greater freedom to use interactive approaches to learning.[135] Unfortunately, such schools were few and most students attended traditional neighborhood schools that were deeply impacted by the reform and seemingly had to focus on test scores even to survive.

Questioning Assumptions

Dismal evidence on the consequences of the new test and punish regime imposed under NCLB caused a number of observers to question the basic assumptions underlying the reform. Scholars questioned the notion that the schools were broken; that testing could motivate educational achievement; that socioeconomic status and the gritty realities of poverty could be overcome by raising the bar, measuring results, and imposing tough accountability; that fear and coercion would bring results; that business principles drawn from market capitalism could be successfully applied to schools.[136] Some questioned whether the school system as presently configured, based on industrial-age assumptions, could be improved without a major paradigm shift. For many critics, it was a system rooted in the cult of efficiency. Under NCLB and the testing regime, it was now an industrial-age system on steroids, multiplying the severity and unintended consequences of problems with schools that critics of the sixties pointed to with disdain: its coldness, its inhumanity, its sorting and labeling of children, preparing them to work in the industrial and war machines.[137] For many critics, the framework of the business model raised questions about the entire approach to school reform embodied in standards-based education and a regime focused on accountability. It also raised questions about who, in fact, was benefiting from the new system, other than testing companies, operators of charter school chains, educational management companies, and businesses that gained increased access to schoolchildren.[138]

Conclusion

NCLB represented a major expansion of federal authority on education, but questions remained about the wisdom of its strong-armed application of accountability mandates to schooling. The political center in support of a stronger federal role in education grew enough for the law to pass, applying the Texas model to all public schools in the United States, not just the most troubled or endangered. Implementation of NCLB mandates proved to be a messy, contentious, top-down, and forcible imposition of accountability.

The larger context of growing corporate influence upon American society, mirrored in growing disparities in wealth, income, and power, meant that school reform based on application of business principles drawn from market capitalism was part of a larger shift toward rule by an oligarchy. It meant that the power of wealth over commonplace American institutions such as schools was on the rise.[139] Stubborn refusal to fund schools equitably masked an underlying and growing financial inequality in the nation.[140]

Critics have argued, based on substantive evidence, that although the NCLB law claimed to be a step toward improving schools and establishing equal opportunity for all, it was actually harming those it was most intended to help, stigmatizing students and schools attended by children of the poor, channeling them into remedial programs, labeling them as "not proficient" and "in need of improvement," and leading many to drop out or be pushed out. Moreover, the political landscape of the nation, and the movement toward market-based solutions for social and economic problems, was eroding trust in public institutions, leading to disinvestment from public education and contributing to the movement toward privatization.

Core assumptions of the school reform movement were still operating: the notion of schools as a failed monopoly; the idea that application of business principles and competition will lead to reform and improvement; the premise that reform strategies embracing a potent mix of standards, measurement, accountability, and sanctions, known as "systemic reform," would improve schooling. The paradigm of school reform was rooted in industrial-era assumptions, rugged individualism, and the eighteenth-century philosophy of Adam Smith, as adapted to the modern era by Milton Friedman, whose 1955 essay, "On the Role of Government in Education," outlined a market-based approach to schooling eerily similar to what has transpired.[141] In this approach to schooling, with every teacher, student, and school acting in their own self-interest, the "invisible hand" of free market competition will guide the system to serve the best interests of all. Reforms were based on the notion that teachers, administrators, and students can best be motivated through bottom-line accountability, in which the strong survive and prosper and the weak either adapt or drop out. The reform centered on motivation through hope and fear, using sanctions of reward and punishment. This was an economic construction of educational purposes and practice. Others, especially teachers and scholars, saw flaws in the reform and questioned whether actors in the educational system were motivated primarily by economic factors. They argued that teachers, students, and administrators could best be motivated through interest in subject matter and its relevance to life, by the intrinsic rewards that come through teaching and learning, through inquiry, discovery, and child-centered forms of learning, directed by caring adults.[142]

NCLB put business leaders, or their mentality, literally "in charge" of the school system. Even though it had seemed for years that no one was really in charge of the vast and uncoupled school system, under NCLB, that began to change.[143] The new federal policy regime gave unprecedented power to the DOE in administering schools, with power to impose requirements, directives, rewards, and punishments. With the new reforms, an unholy alliance of business and government meant that entrepreneurial, capitalist, free market approaches to school reform were the new law of the land, and for a time, the schools were reeling from the change.

On balance, were NCLB and standards-based accountability helpful or harmful to schools and children? Its advocates pointed to benefits. They argued that with accountability we now had clear evidence on how schools were doing; performance targets meant that schools were now working toward measurable goals. However, it was less clear whether the reforms were assisting the at-risk students they purported to help. Evidence of rising student achievement and performance, based largely on state tests, was questionable, at best. The strongest indicators, NAEP scores, showed little substantive improvement. Moreover, dropout rates were rising, suggesting that rather than helping, reforms were actually creating schools that rejected the most "at risk" students.

In social studies, the results were devastating. A field that had long played second fiddle to literacy and mathematics was relegated to endangered status in the elementary school, and to a lower profile in secondary schools. The broad and comprehensive goals of schooling that included basic skills and preparation for citizenship had clearly been rearranged to focus on economic aims and the training of human capital. This redefinition had an impact on pedagogy and the curriculum. Reading, writing, mathematics, and to a lesser extent science were elevated to primary status, while the curricula of social studies was now of secondary importance. A curriculum emphasizing broad inclusion of social studies concepts, knowledge from history and the social sciences, and in many classrooms, an emphasis on inquiry and critical thinking, had shifted toward a new emphasis on traditional history and geography as the citizenship education of choice. Pedagogically, with NCLB's mandated emphasis on "scientific" and "evidence-based practice," there was a new emphasis on the highly questionable findings of "effective schools research" that showed test score gains for classrooms that used traditional teaching approaches dominated by teacher talk, textbooks, and lecture. In practice, this meant more emphasis on traditional teaching, less student discourse, and fewer meaningful learning activities that could be described as democratic forms of education. It meant more authoritarian teaching, more memorization of textbook content, and less problem posing and questioning. It meant more emphasis on socialization, and less attention to counter-socialization or questioning. In sum, it meant that new and old variants on education for social efficiency had run amok—and were now running the schools. It meant that citizenship education was largely redefined as citizen-worker training as a form of human capital development. It meant that now, more than ever, students were being schooled for work.

Notes

1. Donald Kettl, "Schoolhouse Tango," *GM*, December 1999, 12, quoted in Patrick J. McGuinn, *No Child Left Behind and the Transformation of Federal Education Policy, 1965–2005* (Lawrence: University of Kansas Press, 2006), 146.
2. CNN/*USA Today* polls, August 4–5, 7–9, 24–27, 2000, and PDK/Gallup poll, 2000, cited in McGuinn, *No Child*, 148; Kathleen Frankovic and Monika McDermott, "Public Opinion in the 2000 Election: The Ambivalent Electorate," in Gerald Pomper, Ed., *The 2000 Election* (New York: Chatham House, 2001), 89.
3. CNN/*USA Today* poll, August 4–5, cited in McGuinn, *No Child*, 148.
4. Melissa Marshall and Robert McKee, "From Campaign Promises to Presidential Policy: Education Reform in the 2000 Election," *EP* 16 (January/March 2002): 110, cited in McGuinn, *No Child*, 150.
5. See Marvin Olasky, *The Tragedy of American Compassion* (Washington, DC: Regenery Gateway, 1992), and Marvin Olasky, *Compassionate Conservatism: What It Is, What It Does, and How It Can Transform America* (New York: Free Press, 2000).
6. McGuinn, *No Child*, 152.
7. William Hayes, *No Child Left Behind: Past, Present, and Future* (Lanham, MD: Rowman and Littlefield, 2008), 14; Walt Haney, "The Myth of the Texas Miracle in Education," *EPAA* 8 (August 19, 2000): 41; Stephen P. Klein et al., "What Do Test Scores Tell Us?" *RAND Issue Paper IP-202* (Santa Monica, CA: RAND, 2000), 2, 9–13.
8. As cited in Michael Kinsley, ". . . And His Wise-Fool Philosophy," *WP*, September 5, 2000, A25.
9. Eric Pooley, "Who Gets the 'A' in Education?" *TM*, March 27, 2000, 38; Jack Jennings interview, January 15, 2003, quoted in McGuinn, *No Child*, 157.
10. McGuinn, *No Child*, 163–164.
11. Ibid.
12. White House, *Transforming the Federal Role in Education So That No Child Is Left Behind*, http://georgewbush-whitehouse.archives.gov/news/reports/no-child-left-behind.html.
13. George W. Bush, *Decision Points* (New York: Crown, 2010), 274.
14. Susan Crabtree, "Changing His Tune, Kennedy Starts Work with Bush on Education Bill," *RC*, January 25, 2001, quoted in McGuinn, *No Child*, 167.
15. Joetta L. Sack, "Bush Unveils Education Plan," *EW*, January 23, 2001.
16. David Nather, "Broad Support Is No Guarantee for Bush's Legislative Leadoff," *CQW*, January 27, 2001, 221, quoted in McGuinn, *No Child*, 168.
17. David Winston interview with Patrick McGuinn, May 9, 2003, quoted in McGuinn, *No Child*, 170.
18. McGuinn, *No Child*, 174.
19. Keith Bailey, "Testimony before the Committee on Education and the Workforce, U.S. House of Representatives," March 29, 2001, quoted in McGuinn, *No Child*, 175.
20. David Nather, "Compromises on ESEA Bills May Imperil Republican Strategy," *CQW*, May 5, 2001, 1009, quoted in McGuinn, *No Child*, 175.
21. Donald Payne (D-NJ), a member of the House Education Committee, in Donald Payne, "Reflections on Legislation: Reauthorization of ESEA, Challenges Throughout the Legislative Process," *SHLJ* 315 (2003): 26, quoted in McGuinn, *No Child*, 176.
22. McGuinn, *No Child*, 176.
23. George W. Bush, "Remarks on Signing the NCLB Act of 2001 in Hamilton, Ohio," January 8, 2002, APP.
24. "No Child Left Behind Act of 2001" Public Law 107–110, Jan. 8, 2002, p. 1425, http://www2.ed.gov/policy/elsec/leg/esea02/index.html.
25. Adapted from "No Child Left Behind Act of 2001" Public Law 107–110, Jan. 8, 2002, p. 1425, http://www2.ed.gov/policy/elsec/leg/esea02/index.html; "The No Child Left Behind Act of 2001: Executive Summary," January 7, 2002, http://www2.ed.gov/

nclb/overview/intro/execsumm.html; and "An ESEA Primer," *EW*, January 9, 2002, http://www.edweek.org.

26. This overview of NCLB provisions is drawn from the "NCLB Act of 2001," "NCLB Executive Summary"; *NCLB, A Desktop Reference*; and other sources.

27. Frankie J. Petrosino, "The NAACP and Congress," *The Crisis*, September–October 2002, 60; McGuinn, *No Child*, 174.

28. Milton Goldberg and Susan L. Traiman, "Why Business Backs Education Standards," *BPEP*, no. 4 (2001): 75.

29. Ibid., 97.

30. Kathy Emery and Susan O'Hanian, *Why Is Corporate America Bashing Our Public Schools?* (Portsmouth, NH: Heinemann, 2004), 209–210.

31. Elizabeth H. DeBray, "Partisanship and Ideology in the ESEA Reauthorization in the 106th and 107th Congresses: Foundations for the New Political Landscape of Federal Education Policy," *RRE* 29 (2005): 42–44.

32. Emery and O'Hanian, *Bashing*, 210–211.

33. BRT, *A Business Leader's Guide to Setting Academic Standards* (Washington, DC: BRT, 1996).

34. Quoted in Emery and O'Hanian, *Bashing*, 38.

35. Ibid., 34.

36. BRT, *Building Support for Tests That Count* (Washington, DC: BRT, 1998); Emery and O'Hanian, *Bashing*, 38–42.

37. Jacques Steinberg, "Academic Standards Eased as a Fear of Failure Spreads," *NYT*, December 3, 1999.

38. BRT, *Addressing the "Testing Backlash": Practical Advice and Current Public Opinion Research for Business Coalitions and Standards Advocates* (Washington, DC: BRT, 2001).

39. Achieve, Inc., *National Education Summit on High Schools Briefing Book* (Washington, DC: Achieve, Inc., 2005), 2–4.

40. Achieve, Inc., *An Action Agenda for Improving America's High Schools* (Washington, DC: Achieve, Inc., 2005), 5.

41. Diane Ravitch, *The Death and Life of the Great American School System: How Testing and Choice Are Undermining Education* (New York: Basic Books, 2010), 195–222.

42. Ibid., 210. See also Erik W. Robelen, "Gates Learns to Think Big," *EW*, October 11, 2006; Phillip E. Kovacs, *The Gates Foundation and the Future of US "Public" Schools* (New York: Routledge, 2010).

43. Ibid., 212–217.

44. Among the many nonprofit foundations contributing to school reform efforts are the Broad Foundation, the Carnegie Corporation of New York, the Carnegie Foundation for the Advancement for Teaching, the Ford Foundation, the Gates Foundation, the Charles Stewart Mott Foundation, the Lilly Endowment, the Pew Charitable Trusts, the Rockefeller Foundation, the Smith Richardson Foundation, the Soros Foundation, the Stuart Foundation, and the Spencer Foundation. All seem to support the current framework for reform, though they may vary on some of the particulars.

45. DeBray, "Partisanship and Ideology in ESEA Reauthorization," 42–44; Alan Singer, "Strange Bedfellows: The Contradictory Goals of the Coalition Making War on Social Studies," *TSS* 95, no. 5 (September–October 2005); Ronald W. Evans, *The Tragedy of American School Reform: How Curriculum Politics and Entrenched Dilemmas Have Diverted Us from Democracy* (New York: Palgrave Macmillan, 2011).

46. Hayes, *NCLB*, 119; Linda Greenhouse, "Supreme Court, 5–4, Upholds Voucher System That Pays Private Schools' Tuition," *NYT*, June 28, 2002.

47. A dictionary definition for conspire reads "1 a: to join in a secret agreement to do an unlawful or wrongful act or to use such means to accomplish a lawful end."

48. Alfie Kohn, "Test Today, Privatize Tomorrow," *PDK* 85, no. 8 (April 2004), 568–577; Ravitch, *Death and Life*.

49. Kim Phillips-Fein, *Invisible Hands: The Making of the Conservative Movement from the New Deal to Reagan* (New York: W.W. Norton, 2009); Lee Fang, *The Machine: A Field Guide to the Resurgent Right* (New York: New Press, 2013).

50. Kathy Emery, "Corporate Control of Public School Goals: High-Stakes Testing in Its Historical Perspective," *TEQ* 34, no. 2 (Spring 2007): 29.

51. Ibid., 30; Edward Rust, "No Turning Back: A Progress Report on the Business Roundtable," (Washington, DC: Business Roundtable, 1999), as quoted in Emery, "Corporate Control of Public School Goals," 30.

52. Emery, "Corporate Control of Public School Goals," 38. Others have expressed concern about the school to prison pipeline. See, for example, *Federal Policy, ESEA Reauthorization, and the School-to-Prison Pipeline* (A joint position paper of Advancement Project, Education Law Center—PA, FairTest, the Forum for Education and Democracy Juvenile Law Center, NAACP Legal Defense and Educational Fund, Inc., March 2011, Revised).

53. Ibid., 25.

54. McGuinn, *No Child*, 183.

55. "NCLB Update: Tour and New Web Site Launched," *ERV*, April 12, 2002, http://lobby.la.psu.edu/_107th/132_Math_Science_Funding/Agency_Activities/Dept_Ed/Dept_of_Ed_Archived_ED_Review_04_12_02.htm; "Fact Sheet: President Joins 'No Child Left Behind Tour Across America,'" May 2, 2002, APP.

56. Alfie Kohn and Patrick Shannon, *Education, Inc.: Turning Learning into a Business* (Portsmouth, NH: Heineman, 2002); Emery and O'Hanian, *Bashing*; Jonathan Kozol, *Shame of the Nation: The Restoration of Apartheid Schooling in America* (New York: Three Rivers Press, 2005); Gerald Bracey, *The War Against America's Public Schools: Privatizing Schools, Commercializing Education* (Boston: Allyn and Bacon, 2002); E. Wayne Ross and Rich Gibson, *Neoliberalism and Education Reform* (Cresskill, NJ: Hampton Press, 2007); Shirley Steinberg and Joe Kinchloe, *What You Don't Know About Schools* (New York: Palgrave Macmillan, 2006); Michael Apple, *Educating the "Right" Way: Markets, Standards, God, and Inequality* (New York: Routledge Falmer, 2001); Linda Christiansen and Stan Karp, *Rethinking School Reform: Views from the Classroom* (Milwaukee, WI: Rethinking Schools, 2003); Susan O'Hanian, "Capitalism, Calculus, and Conscience," *PDK* 84, no. 10 (June 2003), 736–747; Kathy Emery, "The Business Roundtable and Systemic Reform: How Corporate-Engineered High-Stakes Testing Has Eliminated Community Participation in Developing Educational Goals and Policies" (Doctoral Dissertation, University of California, Davis, 2002).

57. Deborah Meier and George Wood, *Many Children Left Behind: How the No Child Left Behind Act Is Damaging Our Children and Our Schools* (Boston: Beacon Press, 2004); Larry Cuban, *The Blackboard and the Bottom Line: Why Schools Can't Be Businesses* (Cambridge, MA: Harvard University Press, 2004); Sharon Nichols and David Berliner, *Collateral Damage: How High-Stakes Testing Corrupts America's Schools* (Cambridge, MA: Harvard Education Press, 2007).

58. Gary Orfield, *Losing Our Future: How Minority Youth Are Being Left Behind by the Graduation Rate Crisis* (Cambridge, MA: Civil Rights Project at Harvard University, 2007); Linda Darling-Hammond, "No Child Left Behind and High School Reform," *HER* 76, no. 4 (Winter 2006): 642–667; Linda Darling-Hammond, "Race, Inequality, and Educational Accountability: The Irony of 'No Child Left Behind,'" *REE* 10, no. 3 (September 2007): 245–260.

59. Frederick M. Hess and Chester E. Finn, Jr., *No Remedy Left Behind: Lessons from a Half-Decade of NCLB* (Washington, DC: AEI Press, 2007); Ravitch, *Death and Life*.

60. William G. Spady, "The Paradigm Trap," *Education Week*, 2007.

61. Ibid.

62. See Ravitch Papers. Diane Ravitch received support from the Olin Foundation during several years leading up to her role in the Bush administration. EEN and NCHE also

received foundation funding. Both the war on social studies and accountability reform received strong backing from well-heeled conservative interest groups.

63. Diane Ravitch, *Death and Life*. Though there are differences, it is tempting to draw a parallel linking Spady and Ravitch with previous reformers such as John Dewey and Jerome Bruner, who eventually became critics of the reforms they helped spawn.

64. New York State Education Department (NYSED), *Federal Education Policy and the States, 1945–2009: A Brief Synopsis* (Albany: New York State Archives, 2006, revised 2009), 76.

65. Robert Pear, "Education Chief Calls Union 'Terrorist,' Then Recants," *NYT*, February 24, 2004.

66. Fox News, "NEA Seeks to Undo No Child Left Behind," February 28, 2004, http://www.foxnews.com/story/2004/02/28/nea-seeks-to-undo-no-child-left-behind/.

67. Wendy C. Lecker, "Teachers' Unions Critical of NCLB, Offer Other Approaches," July 22, 2004, National Access Network, Teachers College, Columbia University, http://www.schoolfunding.info/news/federal/7-22-04Teachers.

68. Cheating scandals have proliferated in recent years.

69. Patrick McGuinn, "The National Schoolmarm: No Child Left Behind and the New Educational Federalism," *PB* 35, no. 1 (Winter 2005): 57–60.

70. Erik Robelen, "Opposition to School Law Growing, Poll Says," *EW*, April 7, 2004.

71. McGuinn, "National Schoolmarm," 60.

72. NYSED, *Federal Education Policy*, 77.

73. McGuinn, "National Schoolmarm," 61; "Changing the Rules," *EW*, March 24, 2004.

74. Sam Dillon, "New U.S. Secretary Showing Flexibility on 'No Child' Act," *NYT*, February 14, 2005; "Secretary Spellings Announces More Workable, 'Common Sense' Approach To Implement No Child Left Behind Law," Press Release, April 7, 2005, http://www2.ed.gov/news/pressreleases/2005/04/04072005.html; "Raising Achievement: A New Path to NCLB," http://www2.ed.gov/policy/elsec/guid/raising/new-path-long.html.

75. "Secretary Spellings Announces."

76. McGuinn, "National Schoolmarm," 62.

77. Rose and Gallup, 36th Annual Phi Delta Kappan/Gallup Poll, 2004; Educational Testing Service, "Equity and Adequacy: Americans Speak on Public School Funding" http://ftp.ets.org/pub/corp/2004summary.pdf; "Attitudes on No Child Left Behind Law," *EW* 21 (January 2004): 29; "State Views on No Child Left Behind Act," *EW*, February 4, 2004; McGuinn, "National Schoolmarm," 65–66.

78. Ibid., 63–64.

79. Ibid.; NYSED, *Federal Education Policy*, 80.

80. Stephen J. Thornton and Keith C. Barton, "Can History Stand Alone? Drawbacks and Blind Spots of a 'Disciplinary' Curriculum," *TCR* 112, no. 9 (September 2010): 2483; see also S.G. Grant, *Measuring History: Cases of State-Level Testing Across the United States* (Greenwich, CT: Information Age, 2006); S.D. Brown and J. Patrick, *History Education in the United States: A Survey of Teacher Certification and State-Based Standards and Assessments for Teachers and Students* (Washington, DC: Organization of American Historians, 2006).

81. James Schul, "Unintended Consequences: Fundamental Flaws That Plague the No Child Left Behind Act," http://nau.edu/uploadedFiles/Academic/COE/About/Projects/Unintended%20Consequences.pdf.

82. Kathleen Manzo Kennedy, "History Invading Social Studies' Turf in Schools," *EW* 22, no. 19 (January 22, 2003): 1.

83. Ibid.

84. Thornton and Barton, "Can History Stand Alone?" 2482.

85. Kennedy, "History Invading Social Studies."

86. Kay S. Hymowitz, "Anti-Social Studies," *WS*, May 6, 2002.

87. Paul Gagnon, *Educating Democracy: State Standards to Ensure a Civic Code* (Washington, DC: Albert Shanker Institute, 2003).

88. Stuart Phipps and Susan Adler, "Where's the History?" *SE* 67, no. 4 (September, 2003): 296–297.

89. Singer, "Strange Bedfellows"; Vincent Stehle, "Righting Philanthropy," *NAT*, June 30, 1997, 15–20; Evans, *Tragedy*; Ravitch, *Death and Life*. See also the Thomas B. Fordham Foundation Papers, Hoover Institution.

90. See Ravitch Papers and Finn Papers.

91. Cary D. Wintz, "Teaching American History: Observations from the Fringes," in Rachel G. Ragland and Kelly A. Woestman, Eds., *The Teaching American History Project: Lessons for History Educators and Historians* (New York: Routledge, 2009), 301–318.

92. Sam Wineburg, "The Teaching American History Program: A Venerable Past and a Challenging Future," in Ragland and Woestman, *The TAH Project*, ix–xii; Rachel G. Ragland and Kelly A. Woestman, "Preface," *The TAH Project*, xiii–xviii.

93. Ragland and Woestman, "Preface," xiii–xviii.

94. Ibid., xiv.

95. Daniel C. Humphrey, Christopher Chang-Ross, Mary Beth Donnelly, Lauren Hersh, and Heidi Skolnik, *Evaluation of the Teaching American History Program* (Washington, DC: DOE and SRI International, 2005).

96. Wineburg, "The Teaching American History Program," xi.

97. Rick Shenkman, "OAH 2009: Sam Wineburg Dares to Ask If the American History Program Is a Boondoggle," *HNN*, April 19, 2009, http://hnn.us/articles/76806.html.

98. Thornton and Barton, "Can History Stand Alone?" 2484; M.S. Lapp, W.S. Grigg, and B.S. Tay-Lim, *The Nation's Report Card: U.S. History 2001*, NCES 2002–483 (Washington, DC: OERI, DOE, 2002); J. Lee and A. Weiss, *The Nation's Report Card: U.S. History 2006* (Washington, DC: NCES, DOE, Publication No. 2007–474).

99. Maurice P. Hunt and Lawrence E. Metcalf, *Teaching High School Social Studies: Problems in Reflective Thinking and Social Understanding* (New York: Harper & Brothers, 1955, 1968).

100. James S. Leming, Lucien Ellington, and Kathleen Porter, Eds., *Where Did Social Studies Go Wrong?* (Washington, DC: Thomas B. Fordham Foundation, 2003). Beyond contributing to a network of educators pushing for systemic reform and attacking progressive shibboleths such as social studies, the Fordham Foundation also awarded annual prizes for contributions to education. The list of nominees reads like a who's who of neoconservative accountability reformers. See Boxes 15–19, Fordham Papers.

101. Chester E. Finn, Jr., "Foreword," in Leming et al., *Where Did Social Studies Go Wrong?*, i–vii.

102. James S. Leming and Lucien Ellington, "Passion Without Progress: What's Wrong with Social Studies Education?" in Leming et al., *Where Did Social Studies Go Wrong?*, i–vi.

103. Diane Ravitch, "A Brief History of Social Studies," in Leming et al., *Where Did Social Studies Go Wrong?*

104. Leming et al., *Where Did Social Studies Go Wrong?*

105. Ronald W. Evans, "The Social Studies Wars Revisited: Book Review of Leming, Ellington, and Porter, Eds., *Where Did Social Studies Go Wrong? TRSE* 31, no. 4 (Fall 2003): 525, 538.

106. E. Wayne Ross and Perry M. Marker, "Social Studies: Wrong, Right, or Left? A Critical Response to the Fordham Institute's *Where Did Social Studies Go Wrong?*," *TSS* 96, no. 4 (July/August 2005): 139, 141. See also articles contained in the two-part special section of *The Social Studies* responding to *Where Did Social Studies Go Wrong?* in *TSS* 96, no. 4 (July/August 2005) and no. 6 (September/October 2005).

107. Alan Singer, "Strange Bedfellows."

108. "We the People" Funding Status, Ed.Gov, http://www2.ed.gov/programs/wethepeople/funding.html; Donovan R. Walling, "The Return of Civic Education," *PDK*

89, no. 4 (December 2007): 285–289. Walling lists sixteen national organizations involved in the move to revitalize civic education, but does not list NCSS.

109. "We The People: The Citizen and the Constitution," http://new.civiced.org/wtp-the-program.

110. Senator Lamar Alexander, "Remarks of Senator Lamar Alexander on the introduction of his bill, The American History and Civics Education Act, March 4, 2003," http://www.congresslink.org/print_expert_amhist.htm.

111. Carnegie and CIRCLE, *The Civic Mission of Schools: A Report from Carnegie Corporation of New York and CIRCLE* (Washington, DC: CIRCLE and Carnegie Corporation of New York, 2003). CIRCLE was founded in 2001 with a grant from Pew Charitable Trusts.

112. "Civics Education Testing Only Required in 9 States for High School Graduation: CIRCLE Study," *HP*, October 12, 2012, http://www.huffingtonpost.com/2012/10/12/circle-study-finds-most-s_n_1959522.html.

113. Hayes, *NCLB*, 114.

114. Ibid., 114–117.

115. Shirley H. Engle and Anna S. Ochoa, *Education for Democratic Citizenship: Decision Making in Social Studies* (New York: Teachers College Press, 1988).

116. Thornton and Barton, "Can History Stand Alone?"

117. DOE, *A Nation Accountable: Twenty-Five Years after a Nation at Risk* (Washington, DC: DOE, 2008).

118. Jack Jennings and Diane Stark Rentner, "Ten Big Effects of the No Child Left Behind Act on Public Schools," *PDK* 88, no. 2 (October 2006): 110–113.

119. Lorrie Shepard, "The Hazards of High-Stakes Testing," *IST* 19, no. 2 (Winter 2002–2003): 53–58; Audrey L. Amrein and David C. Berliner, "A Research Report: The Effects of High-Stakes Testing on Student Motivation and Learning," *EL* 60, no. 5 (February 2003); Audrey L. Amrein and David C. Berliner, *An Analysis of Some Unintended and Negative Consequences of High-Stakes Testing* (East Lansing, MI: Great Lakes Center for Educational Research and Practice, 2002); and William J. Mathis, "No Child Left Behind: What Are the Costs? Will We Realize Any Benefits?" (Washington, DC: EDRS, ERIC, 2003).

120. Orfield, *Losing Our Future*; Darling-Hammond, "No Child Left Behind and High School Reform"; Darling-Hammond, "Race, Inequality, and Educational Accountability."

121. Ravitch, *Death and Life*; Darling-Hammond, "No Child Left Behind and High School Reform," 642; Darling-Hammond, "Race, Inequality, and Educational Accountability," 245; Jennings and Rentner, "Ten Big Effects."

122. Nichols and Berliner, *Collateral Damage*; Schul, "Unintended Consequences"; there have been frequent media reports on cheating scandals.

123. Ravitch, *Death and Life*; Caitlin Scott, *Managing More Than a Thousand Remodeling Projects: School Restructuring in California* (Washington, DC: Center on Education Policy, 2008); Frederick M. Hess and Chester E. Finn, Jr., Eds., *No Remedy Left Behind: Lessons from a Half-Decade of NCLB* (Washington, DC: AEI Press, 2007), 327–328.

124. Caitlin Scott, *A Call to Restructure Restructuring: Lessons from the No Child Left Behind Act in Five States* (Washington, DC: Center on Education Policy, 2008); Jennings and Rentner, "Ten Big Effects"; John Cronin, Michael Dahlin, Deborah Adkins, and G. Gage Kingsbury, *The Proficiency Illusion* (Washington, DC: Thomas B. Fordham Institute, 2007).

125. David C. Berliner and Gene V. Glass, *50 Myths and Lies That Threaten America's Public Schools* (New York: Teachers College, 2014), 22–26.

126. Marilyn Cochran-Smith and Susan L. Lytle, "Troubling Images of Teaching in No Child Left Behind," *HER* 76, no. 4 (Winter 2006): 668–697; Kozol, *Shame of the Nation*; Schul, "Unintended Consequences."

127. Cochran-Smith and Lytle, "Troubling Images of Teaching"; Shepard, "Hazards of High-Stakes Testing"; Ravitch, *Death and Life*.

128. Jennifer McMurrer, *Choices, Changes, and Challenges* (Washington, DC: Center on Education Policy, 2007); Jennifer McMurrer, *Instructional Time in Elementary Schools* (Washington, DC: Center on Education Policy, 2008); Patricia V. Pedersen, "What Is Measured Is Treasured: The Impact of the No Child Left Behind Act on Non-assessed Subjects," *CH* 80, no. 6 (July/August 2007), 287–291; Schul, "Unintended Consequences"; Jennings and Rentner, "Ten Big Effects"; Kelly V. King and Sasha Zucker, *Policy Report: Curriculum Narrowing* (New York: Pearson Education, 2008); Cochran-Smith and Lytle, "Troubling Images of Teaching."

129. Shepard, "Hazards of High-Stakes Testing"; Darling-Hammond, "No Child Left Behind and High School Reform"; Darling-Hammond, "Race, Inequality, and Educational Accountability"; Barbara Knighton, Carol Warren, Rachel Sharpe, Bruce Damasio, Sue Blanchette, Timothy J. Tuttle, "No Child Left Behind: The Impact on Social Studies Classrooms," *SE* 67, no. 4 (September 2003): 291–295.

130. Amrein and Berliner, "Effects of High-Stakes Testing."

131. Pedersen, "What Is Measured Is Treasured"; Elizabeth R. Hinde, "The Tyranny of the Test: Elementary Teachers' Conceptualizations of the Effects of State Standards and Mandated Tests on Their Practice," *CIE* [online] 6, no. 10 (May 27, 2003); S.G. Grant, *History Lessons: Teaching, Learning, and Testing in U.S. High School Classrooms* (New York: Routledge, 2003); CIRCLE, 2012.

132. Paulo Freire, *Pedagogy of the Oppressed* (New York: Continuum, 1970).

133. Schul, "Unintended Consequences"; Sharon Beder, *This Little Kiddy Went to Market: The Corporate Capture of Childhood* (New York: Pluto Press, 2009); Cuban, *Blackboard*; Evans, *Tragedy*; Amrein and Berliner, "A Research Report: The Effects of High-Stakes Testing"; CIRCLE, "Civics Education Testing Only Required in 9 States"; Kozol, *Shame of the Nation*; Lorrie Shepard, "Hazards of High-Stakes Testing"; Marguerite Clarke, Arnold Shore, Kathleen Rhoades, Lisa Abrams, Jing Miao, and Jie Li, *Perceived Effects of State-Mandated Testing Programs on Teaching and Learning: Findings from Interviews with Educators in Low-, Medium-, and High-Stakes States* (Boston: National Board on Educational Testing and Public Policy and Boston College, 2003).

134. Coalition of Essential Schools; High Tech High School, San Diego, California.

135. Shepard, "Hazards of High Stakes Testing."

136. John Marsh, *Class Dismissed: Why We Cannot Teach or Learn Our Way Out of Inequality* (New York: Monthly Review, 2011); Ravitch, *Death and Life*; Cuban, *Blackboard*; Theoni Soublis Smyth, "Who Is No Child Left Behind Leaving Behind?" *Clearing House 81,* no. 3 (January-February 2008): 133–137.

137. John Taylor Gatto, "Against School," *HA*, September 2003; Spady, "The Paradigm Trap"; see works by Kozol, Illich, Postman, and Weingartner, and other "new wave" critics of schooling during the 1960s and 1970, as cited in Evans, *Tragedy*, 35–46.

138. Alfie Kohn and Patrick Shannon, *Education, Inc.: Turning Learning into a Business* (Portsmouth, NH: Heineman, 2002); Alex Molnar, *Giving Kids the Bu$iness: The Commercialization of America's Schools* (Boulder, CO: Westview Press, 1996); Ravitch, *Death and Life*.

139. Kevin Phillips, *Wealth and Democracy: A Political History of the American Rich* (New York: Broadway Books, 2002); G. William Domhoff, *Who Rules America? Power and Politics, and Social Change* (Boston: McGraw Hill, 2006); G. William Domhoff, "Wealth, Income, and Power," http://www2.ucsc.edu/whorulesamerica/power/wealth.html (2006, updated 2013); Oxfam, *Working for the Few: Political Capture and Economic Inequality* (Oxford, UK: Oxfam International, 2014).

140. Hayes, *NCLB*; Marsh, *Class Dismissed*; Kozol, *Shame of the Nation*.

141. Adam Smith, *An Inquiry into the Nature and Causes of the Wealth of Nations* (London: W. Strahan, 1776); Milton Friedman, "The Role of Government in Education," in Robert A. Solo, Ed., *Economics and the Public Interest* (Newark, NJ: Rutgers University

Press, 1955), cited by 989 books and articles according to Google Scholar: an indication of widespread influence.

142. John Dewey, *Democracy and Education* (New York: Macmillan, 1916); Jerome S. Bruner, *The Process of Education* (Cambridge, MA: Harvard University Press, 1960); Alfie Kohn, *The Schools Our Children Deserve: Moving Beyond Traditional Classrooms and Tougher Standards* (Boston: Houghton Mifflin, 1999); Nel Noddings, *Caring: A Feminine Approach to Ethics and Moral Education* (Berkeley: University of California Press, 1984).

143. Frederick M. Wirt and Michael W. Kirst, *Schools in Conflict: The Politics of Education* (Berkeley, CA: McCutchan, 1982).

7

RACE TO NOWHERE?

In the 2008 presidential election, Barack Obama, a first-term Democratic senator from Illinois, lawyer, community organizer, and stirring speaker, was elected
as the first African-American and the first biracial president. For many citizens,
his election seemed to prove that Americans could still be inspired to have hope
for the future. In spite of a great deal of rhetoric and controversy on all sides
over Obama's politics and personal heritage, his first term in office proved him
to be a moderately progressive pragmatist and a capable leader in many ways.
The dominant issues in the 2008 election centered on approaches to domestic
policy, the economy, and how to end U.S. involvement in two protracted conflicts in the Middle East. Despite a good deal of attention to domestic policy
issues, education was no longer at the top of the list of Americans' concerns.
Yet, the topic did receive a good deal of attention during the primaries and the
general election.

Barack Obama unveiled his education platform and ideas in a speech on
November 20, 2007, in Manchester, New Hampshire, when he presented a
detailed, three-part plan to reform U.S. public schools. Though he supported the
general goals of NCLB, including "more accountability" and "higher standards,"
he critiqued many specifics and its implementation and called for changes to correct what he saw as longstanding problems with the reform. In his speech that
day, Obama charged that Bush and Congress had sabotaged the reform when
they "left the money behind," failed to provide the financial resources and qualified teachers necessary, and when they labeled schools as "failures" then walked
away. His speech included a litany of the problems that had been aired since the
law's inception. He critiqued the overuse of standardized tests, the narrowing of
the curriculum, and the demoralizing impact on students and teachers in struggling schools. The three main parts of Obama's plan included "providing quality,
affordable early childhood education"; to "recruit, support, and reward teachers

and principals" while treating teaching "like the profession it is" by instituting a "career ladder initiative" that rewards the best teachers for mentoring others; and new forms of assessment that can help improve achievement by "including the kinds of research, scientific investigation, and problem-solving that our children will need to compete in a 21st century knowledge economy."[1]

Obama's speech was accompanied by a fifteen-page campaign document and policy brief providing details of a "comprehensive" plan.[2] The speech and the policy statement provided a vision of a forward-looking overhaul of NCLB, addressed many of the complaints and critiques of educators, and aimed at giving the accountability system a more positive spin, an approach that "supports schools to improve, rather than focuses on punishments." The Obama plan retained most of the key and controversial provisions of the law, including its mandate for accountability testing in grades three through eight in reading and mathematics. However, it did call for "a broader range of assessments that can evaluate higher-order skills." This would include assessing student's ability to "use technology, conduct research, engage in scientific investigation, solve problems, and present and defend their ideas," along with providing "immediate feedback" so that teachers can "improve student learning right away."[3]

While Obama's plan, released during the buildup to primary season, called for a more typical Democratic approach to reform, it retained the core ideas of NCLB and the central assumptions of business-driven standards-based reform. It appeared to be a somewhat revised continuation of the Bush plan. During the primaries, Obama's sternest competition came from former first lady and New York senator Hillary Rodham Clinton. Clinton's plan for education called for a much different approach, and an explicit vow to end NCLB. Clinton believed that NCLB had proven "too rigid and unworkable" for teachers, principals, and children. She stated that "it's time to end this one-size-fits-all approach to education reform, and start a new beginning that prepares every child to succeed in our global economy." Though she went further than Obama in her rhetoric against NCLB, Clinton offered many remedies to improve schooling that were similar to Obama's including increased funding for schools, standards directly aligned with "college-prep needs" with the goal of preparing to move students toward the ultimate goal of college, and improved efforts to "recruit and retain outstanding teachers, especially in urban and under-resourced areas."[4]

During the 2008 presidential campaign, candidates from both parties supported NCLB's provisions for high standards and school accountability in a general sense. However, they offered a range of opinions on what to do. As we have seen, Hillary Clinton said she would "end" NCLB because it was "just not working." Barack Obama called for a "fundamental" overhaul, retaining the basic outline for reform. Democratic candidate John Edwards criticized its overemphasis on testing, and stated, "You don't make a hog fatter by weighing it." Republican presidential candidate Mike Huckabee, like a number of Republican lawmakers, objected to NCLB's intrusion on states' rights, and said he preferred that states develop their own standards and accountability systems.

Republican nominee John McCain's education platform was not as detailed as Obama's, but called for a more conservative Republican approach on education. McCain was supportive of a litany of conservative positions regarding schools, including school prayer, vouchers for private school choice, and states' rights in determining use of federal funds through unrestricted block grants.[5] On NCLB, he argued that the law was adequately funded, but called for doing away with the "sanctions" forcing schools that don't improve to offer tutoring or enrollment at another school. He supported providing "immediate access" to federally funded tutoring with private companies marketing directly to parents and stated that he might change the target date for 100 percent proficiency in reading and mathematics from 2014 to a later deadline.[6]

Partly due to pressing concerns over the nation's economy and wars in Iraq and Afghanistan, education was not one of the headline issues in the campaign. Because NCLB had become a "dirty word," both candidates seemed to stay away from making extensive comments about the law.[7] Mostly on the basis of factors other than federal education policy, Obama won a November 4 election in which a record 131.3 million votes were cast, or 63 percent of eligible voters. In an election marred by controversies over vote suppression and media bias, Obama won 52.93 percent of the popular vote compared to McCain's 45.65 percent, and an electoral college landslide. Though education was not as prominent an issue as it had been in some previous campaigns, the general orientation of the parties and the candidates on education may have played some role in the voters' decision.[8]

The Obama Plan

Much of the attention of the public and the Obama administration during the early months of his presidency focused on economic recovery. Nonetheless, the administration took steps to include education spending and significant policy planks in its first major act, the economic stimulus bill, officially known as the American Recovery and Reinvestment Act, signed into law on February 17, 2009.[9] The determination to include education reform in the economic stimulus bill was a "policy improvisation" made "on the fly" during the December work of the Obama transition team, made while many governors were pleading for federal help to prevent layoffs during the economic crisis. The transition team was led by Linda Darling-Hammond, a professor of education at Stanford University and a longtime advocate of systemic reform but a critic of NCLB implementation flaws.[10] On January 7, 2009, prior to Obama's inauguration, Arne Duncan, the former Chicago school superintendent and appointee as secretary of education, announced the administration's intent to channel billions in stimulus funds to the states in exchange for governors' pledges to "double down on education reform."[11]

The stimulus money, totaling $831 billion, with $100 billion to education, saved many teachers' jobs, especially in states with budgets deficits.[12] Clues to the Obama administration's new direction on education reform were contained in the fine print of the stimulus law. To receive emergency education funds, governors had to make four assurances: improve the quality of standardized tests; raise standards; and assign the most effective teachers "equitably to all students, rich and poor." A final provision gave Duncan control over $5 billion in a "Race to the Top Fund" that he could use to reward states for making progress "lining up behind this agenda."[13]

As Obama's plan for education reform began to unfold, clues suggested that Obama and Duncan would use incentives and bureaucratic regulations linked to funding to toughen requirements. The administration appeared to be preparing remedies for what it viewed as NCLB's most serious defects. However, its gradually emerging policy plans were disappointing to critics who had hoped for a sharper break with the Bush-era law. One observer remarked, "Obama has given Bush a third term in education policy."[14] A report in *Education Week* noted the similarities and observed that while Obama had campaigned on a "message of change," in K–12 education he "appears to be walking in the footsteps of his recent predecessors," by sounding themes of accountability based on standards and assessments, performance-based pay for teachers, and expansion of charter schools.[15]

As superintendent of Chicago Public Schools, Duncan had established a strong track record of business-driven systemic reform, in cooperation with the Commercial Club of Chicago. As one observer noted, "Obama chose Arne Duncan for a reason, and part of that reason is the experimentation that Duncan has done in Chicago and his real attention to data and outcomes." Another predicted, "I expect that experimentation to continue on a national scale."[16]

On the other hand, critics of Duncan's efforts in Chicago viewed his leadership as part of a plan supporting privatization, arguing that the emphasis on reopening "failing" public schools as charter schools amounted to "shaving off" large segments of the education system and giving it over to private providers.[17] Critics cited *Left Behind*, a 2003 Commercial Club report arguing that the root of the problem with the city's schools was that it was a public monopoly and recommending that it be broken by turning schools over to market forces, fostering competition and innovation.[18] Michael Apple saw the trend toward privatization in Chicago and other major cities as an instance of democracy being "transformed into a wholly economic concept" through voucher and choice plans fostered by neoliberal politics, masking the increasing influence of capital to govern daily life.[19]

Critics suggested that for many neoliberal politicians, the goal of education reform was to convert the education system into markets, and, as much as possible, privatize educational services. This goal received the support of conservative foundations for many years, and privatization was an underlying and often explicit aim of many corporate leaders involved in education reform. Milton Friedman, among others, had argued in favor of taking steps toward the privatization of education and many other government services, and supported vouchers as a way "to transition from a government to a market system."[20]

Race to the Top

The heart of the Obama education reform plan took form in a competitive grant program titled Race to the Top (RTT) through which states could submit proposals. Specifics of the program were not publicly released until a speech on July 24, 2009. Obama and Duncan announced that states that were "leading the way on school reform" would be eligible to compete for Race to the Top grants to "support education reform and innovation in classrooms" worth a total of $4.35 billion.[21] Touted as the "centerpiece of the Obama administration's education reform efforts," the RTT fund aimed to "highlight and replicate effective education reform strategies" in four areas:

- Adopting internationally benchmarked standards and assessments that prepare students for success in college and the workplace;
- Recruiting, developing, rewarding, and retaining effective teachers and principals;
- Building data systems that measure student success and inform teachers and principals how they can improve their practices; and
- Turning around our lowest-performing schools.[22]

According to Duncan, "The $4.35 billion Race to the Top program that we are unveiling today is a challenge to states and districts. We're looking to drive reform, reward excellence and dramatically improve our nation's schools." In addition to RTT funds, the DOE also planned to award more than $5.6 billion in competitive grants through programs that supported the administration's priorities. Among these were "research-based" innovative programs to close the achievement gap; the "Teacher Incentive Fund" to support "performance pay and teacher advancement"; data systems to track students' achievement and link it to teachers and principals; turnaround models for the lowest-performing schools; and educational technology grants. A portion of RTT funds was also set aside to fund development of common assessments.[23] The administration announced that in order to be eligible to receive RTT funds, at the time of application "there must not be any legal, statutory, or regulatory barriers at the State level to linking data on student achievement" to teachers' and principals' evaluations, a requirement that led to changes in the law in all but two states.[24]

The program gave "Absolute Priority" to states developing a "comprehensive" approach to reform aimed at increasing student achievement, decreasing the achievement gap, and upping graduation rates. It also gave priority to states emphasizing Science, Technology, Engineering, and Mathematics (STEM) and those emphasizing innovations for improving early learning outcomes, expanding longitudinal data systems, improving program alignment, and providing "flexibility and autonomy" in educational innovation.[25] Program guidelines included detailed selection criteria making it clear that the administration would play hardball, awarding RTT funds only to states that complied with its specifications and priorities on a range of issues, from use of test data in teacher evaluations and performance pay, to school turnarounds, opening more charter schools, emphasizing STEM, and reforming teacher education.

The net effect of the Obama education reform program under RTT and other competitive grants was to persuade states to rewrite education laws via the aggressive use of economic stimulus money. The program provoked heated debates over the proper federal role in education and the use of standardized test scores, renewing controversies that flared frequently during the George W. Bush administration. The rules guiding application for RTT funding made standardized achievement testing more powerful by linking student scores to teacher evaluations, and led to an outpouring of complaints. One administrator from Virginia wrote that proposed regulations were "overly burdensome. They give the impression that stimulus funds provide the federal government with unbridled capacity to impose bureaucratic demands" and would lead to worsening "test frenzy."[26] Ironically, the RTT program and rules surprised many educators who had hoped that Obama's call for an overhaul of NCLB would mean a reduced federal role and less emphasis on standardized testing.[27] Supporters called RTT "bold and revolutionary leadership" aimed at "opening up the traditional top-down monopoly" of a "broken" school system. Critics called for the administration to "respect the requirements of federalism" rather than "mandating policies" from the top.[28]

During 2009 and 2010, by dangling RTT grant money Duncan secured a commitment from forty-eight states and the District of Columbia to participate in national common standards. Two states, Delaware and Tennessee, were awarded RTT grants after the first round of competition, and nine more states received awards after the second round.[29] Several states did not submit applications for either round. In announcing his state's plans not to participate, Texas governor Rick Perry stated, "We would be foolish and irresponsible to place our children's future in the hands of unelected bureaucrats and special interest groups thousands of miles away in Washington."[30]

Critics asserted that the reforms were unproven, had been unsuccessful in the past, and were "not working."[31] Others detected a "geographic bias" favoring the East Coast and urban areas.[32] The NEA expressed concerns about use of a competitive grant program to fund education, creating a culture of winners and losers, and argued that the program might prevent resources from getting to the schools and children that needed them most. Still other critics complained that the program was not based on sound education science, rewarding the "fads of the moment."[33] Another observer thought that RTT was "fundamentally about two things: creating political cover for state education reformers to innovate and helping states construct the administrative capacity to implement these innovations effectively."[34]

Others viewed RTT as a "profoundly flawed" reform plan that increased "standardization, centralization, and test-based accountability." Joseph Onosko spoke for many educators when he charged that common national standards would homogenize classroom teaching and learning; undermine and de-professionalize teaching; further privatization; and inflict greatest harm on poor and minority students.[35]

In its most salient features, the RTT plan was a continuation of systemic and business-driven reform, built on the same assumptions that underlay reform through two decades: public schools as a failed monopoly, remedies based on application of business principles including standards, measurement, rigor, competition, and choice. It increased support for charter schools and raised competition to a new level, fostering competition among states to "innovate" according to administrative guidelines. It used bureaucratic muscle and incentives to force change, rather than offering a consistent theory of education other than application of pressure.[36] It also raised the level of social efficiency and control in education—contradicting the freedom necessary for classroom innovation. Moreover, it continued the sorting of children into categories—basic, below basic, proficient, advanced—all based on the "needs" of the twenty-first-century economy.

The Blueprint for Reauthorization

President Obama's initial foray into educational reform focused on grant programs supported by stimulus money partly because it was apparent to all concerned that a reauthorization of NCLB-ESEA would be difficult. This was especially so given a divided Congress, other pressing priorities, and the decision to seek health care reform. By 2010, the administration decided that it was time to advance a reauthorization proposal. In late January, while preparing its budget request, the administration announced that it would seek an extensive rewrite of NCLB including revamping its frequently criticized system for rating schools' AYP based on test scores.[37]

In March 2010, the Obama administration called for a "broad overhaul" of NCLB, proposing major changes yet retaining key features of the law, including annual testing in reading and mathematics in grades three through eight. There were far-reaching changes proposed for other areas, including flexibility in exchange for compliance on key policies. On Monday, March 14, the administration sent to Congress *A Blueprint for Reform: The Reauthorization of the Elementary and Secondary Education Act*, outlining its plans for reform of NCLB, a forty-five-page document that outlined a "re-envisioned" federal role. A preface to the *Blueprint* reiterated the administration's goals and underlying rationale:

> America was once the best educated nation in the world. A generation ago, we led all nations in college completion, but today, 10 countries have passed us. It is not that their students are smarter than ours. It is that these countries are being smarter about how to educate their students. And the countries that out-educate us today will out-compete us tomorrow.[38]

The *Blueprint* focused on four main areas: teacher and principal effectiveness; using data for improvement; college and career-ready standards; and improving achievement in the lowest-performing schools. In each area, the *Blueprint* offered high-sounding and forward-looking goals, applying its version of a business-modeled reform to make NCLB more workable and addressing its most well-publicized flaws regarding AYP, teaching to the test, and curriculum narrowing. The *Blueprint* was heavy on incentives and competition, extending the approach from RTT.[39] A key feature of the plan divided schools into several groups, with a focus on the ten thousand failing or struggling schools that would require some form of state intercession. This replaced NCLB's punitive sanctions and shaming with vigorous interventions. The proposed plan aimed to end NCLB's unrealistic mandate of full proficiency in reading and math for every child by 2014, which Obama administration officials had labeled "utopian," and replace it with a new target that all students should graduate from high school prepared for college and career, a goal stated in less unrealistic language.[40]

Reactions

Responses to the plan were mixed. Teachers unions found the plan disappointing. One union leader said its emphasis on testing and competition for resources meant a continued focus on "winners and losers." On the other hand, a BRT spokesperson called it "a really positive step forward" in helping all students graduate from high school ready for college and career. Senator Tom Harkin (D-IA) called the plan a "bold vision" that could "help fix the problems" with NCLB.

A Heritage Foundation blogger argued that the *Blueprint* offered "more lip service to reform and flexibility" and that the "choice to adopt common standards" was becoming "less and less voluntary" and would reduce choice for parents and students.[41] A Fordham Foundation blogger argued the new proposed federal role would be "more targeted, less prescriptive," for the vast majority of schools.[42] Another critic expressed concern about the school-to-prison pipeline making "criminalization and incarceration" more likely and "high-quality education less likely." Schools indirectly pushed students into the pipeline through practices making them likely to drop out.[43] A scholarly review focused on research summaries used as the evidentiary base for the plan and found "a disturbing set of patterns" including oversimplified solutions, flawed logic, a lack of peer-reviewed research, and "misused or misinterpreted research evidence." The reviewers called it "a partisan" text that "starts with a conclusion" and "finds evidence to support it."[44] Despite all the attention to the *Blueprint* and the Obama administration's push for comprehensive reauthorization, prospects for its passage were slim. Republican control of the House meant that the political climate for reauthorization was not favorable.[45]

Waivers

Given the difficulty it was encountering in seeking ESEA reauthorization and its success with using administrative power to enforce its education policies, the Obama administration sketched an outline of its plan for introducing waivers in June 2011. Then, in August of that year, Secretary Duncan announced that he would unilaterally override the centerpiece requirement of NCLB, that 100 per-cent of students be proficient in math and reading by 2014. Duncan told reporters that he was acting because Congress had failed to act to rewrite NCLB, which he described as a "slow-motion train wreck."[46]

It seemed that something had to be done to make adjustments to NCLB. Many educators were hoping for extensive changes that would roll back the frenzy of standards and high-stakes testing reform. By 2010, about 38 percent of the nation's public schools were falling short of their test score targets, and Secretary Duncan predicted that the number would rise to 80 percent in 2011, because of the unrealistically steep annual increases in performance required by the law. Though skeptics countered that Duncan's predictions were exaggerated, "a huge number of schools were falling short under the AYP system." In Florida, for example, 89 percent missed federal testing targets.[47]

In a conference call with reporters, Duncan and Melody Barnes, director of the Obama Domestic Policy Council, said the DOE would issue guidelines invit-ing states to apply for waivers. For a waiver to be approved, states would need to demonstrate that they were adopting higher standards by which students would be "college and career ready" upon graduation, were working to improve teacher effectiveness by implementing teacher evaluation systems based on student test scores, were implementing turnaround plans for the lowest-performing schools, and were adopting new school accountability systems. The requirements for waiv-ers were very similar to those applied in the RTT grant competition.[48] Though the waiver program would not be a competition, it did serve as another lever for the Obama administration to influence states to go along with its policy proposals.

As of this writing, thirty-four states and the District of Columbia have gained approval for ESEA flexibility, "regarding specific requirements of the No Child Left Behind Act of 2001 (NCLB) in exchange for rigorous and comprehensive State-developed plans designed to improve educational outcomes for all students, close achievement gaps, increase equity, and improve the quality of instruction." The DOE reviewed requests for waivers from forty-four states, the District of Columbia, Puerto Rico, and the Bureau of Indian Education (BIE).[49] As of Janu-ary 2013, eleven states, including the BIE and Puerto Rico, had an ESEA Flex-ibility Request under review.[50]

A list of the peer reviewers for the waivers program offers some clues to the direction of the Obama/Duncan education directorate. Reviewers included Kati Haycock, founder and president of the Education Trust; Daria L. Hall, direc-tor, K–12 Policy Development, the Education Trust; selected administrators and policy advisors from several state departments of education, research insti-tutes, and universities; and other players in the standards-based reform move-ment, including key representatives from Delaware and Tennessee, the two states that had gained approval for RTT funds in the first round of competition. In a few cases, the reviewers' titles revealed a distinct orientation: "Research Scien-tist . . . Value-Added Research Center." Value-added was a numerical gimmick for determining a teacher's contribution to student growth, as measured by standardized test scores, and was highly dependent upon the validity of educational success as measured by a test.[51] By 2012 it had become the subject of intense controversy in places where it had been used to derive teacher ratings, which were released to the public despite broad concerns about their validity.[52] In Los Angeles, one teacher committed suicide after his test scores appeared in the *Los Angeles Times*.[53]

Response

The waivers program drew a range of reactions. One critic challenged its "legal authority." Another called it "a backdoor Round 3 of Race to the Top," a "dramatically broad reading of executive authority," and "a troubling precedent," suggesting that when the current waivers expire in 2014–2015, the next administration would use waiver authority to impose its preferred reforms. Others saw waivers as the best available alternative due to the impasse in Congress over reauthorization.[54]

When waivers recipients were announced, Obama proclaimed, "After waiting far too long for Congress to reform No Child Left Behind, my Administration is giving states the opportunity to set higher, more honest standards in exchange for more flexibility." Duncan touted the reforms as "plans crafted in the states." Despite administration rhetoric, each of the states securing waivers had to develop a DOE-approved plan for reform, including adoption of "college and career ready" standards (i.e., Common Core); new systems for evaluation of teachers and principals making use of student test data; and development of aggressive intervention plans for low-performing schools.[55]

The waivers drew the ire of conservative commentators. One pundit lamented that states would give up federal rules supported by Congress for another set "approved by unaccountable bureaucrats in Washington," providing "temporary relief" in exchange for "new long-term handcuffs."[56] Another viewed the policy as "dangling waivers in front of states thirsting for relief," in exchange for "national standards and tests," labeling it "yet another federal overreach into education."[57] In essence, Obama used waivers as a backdoor route to support the creation of national standards and tests in two core subjects, along with ancillary movement in other subjects, thus making real progress toward a goal that the business community had held for years. Like RTT, waivers were a way of using funding and executive muscle to push through a divisive program.[58]

Pundits, historians, legal scholars, educators, and citizens have taken drastically different positions on Obama. Historian James Kloppenberg views Obama as a "true intellectual" and a "philosopher president," guided by "pragmatism" embracing "open-minded experimentation."[59] Others agree that he serves in the "modern democratic pragmatist tradition,"[60] but argue that his education plan was largely a continuation and refinement of his predecessor's.[61] Another views the "central dynamic" of Obama's presidency as "more active government," using federalism "in service of progressive policy."[62]

Critics on the left viewed Obama as a "tragic failure" who had not fulfilled the promise of progressive change, while the right viewed him as "a frightening success" who "transformed" the role of the federal government, "ruined the economy," and brought a new and unwelcome level of federal interference in schooling. Many conservatives labeled him a "socialist" and used terms like "radical," "socialist," and "totalitarian" to describe Obama's philosophy.[63] While some pundits lamented an unprecedented expansion of the federal role, others argued that his approach reflected the influence of a dominant elite and was not working.[64]

Origins of the Common Core

The next phase of accountability reform brought coalescence around the notion of common standards, a revised version of the unsuccessful push for national standards during the 1990s. The story of how the nation moved from state-by-state reform to a focus on common standards is interesting and troubling. It is a story, once again, of business and government collaboration, strongly influenced by wealth and power. However, this time around leading groups of educators were enlisted to support the effort. Obama's approach to education reform was deeply influenced by a broad coalition of business and government groups that had been directing education reform for some time, and supported a "national" approach. Among these groups were the BRT, the BCER, the CED, the National Center on Education and the Economy (NCEE), their allies in the NGA and CCSSO, and their subsidiary organizations and projects such as Achieve Inc. and the American Diploma Project (ADP). The core of this agenda received the backing of the major lobbying groups of American business including the U.S. Chamber of Commerce, the National Association of Manufacturers, and others.

One indication of the general direction of reform supporting new "world class standards" came in a 2007 report from a blue-ribbon group known as the New Commission on the Skills of the American Workforce (NCSAW) led by Marc Tucker, longtime architect of systemic reform in education and president of NCEE. Based upon two years of research and two decades worth of policy positions, the commission put forth a ten-point program designed to prepare students for the workforce of the twenty-first century, arguing that international trends in economic globalization and education meant that the United States was falling behind in the percentage of its population that was graduating from high school ready for college and career. It meant that our economic competitors were steadily gaining on us, while "getting more education, their young people are getting a better education," with the United States placing from the middle to the bottom of the pack in comparative studies of student achievement in mathematics, science, and literacy. In 2007 the commission wrote:

> The core problem is that our education and training systems were built for another era, an era in which most workers needed only a rudimentary

education. It is not possible to get where we have to go by patching that system. . . . We can get where we must go only by changing the system itself.[65]

The NCSAW's ten-point program included a system of Board Exams beginning at the end of tenth grade, to determine whether students should go to community college, technical school, or stay in high school to prepare for a selective college or university, mirroring the European system. It also included other major systemic changes such as recruiting a stronger teaching force by raising pay and recruiting from the top third of college graduates; high-quality preschool education for all; resources and support for disadvantaged students to succeed; and new standards and assessments that go beyond content acquisition, and focus instead on creativity, innovation, and other key qualities. It also called for a high-performance management model with schools operated by independent contractors, many owned and run by teachers; a strong and wide-ranging data system; a "wide range of performance incentives"; choice for parents and students among all available contract schools; and high-quality universal early childhood education.[66] Several of these recommendations were included in the Obama plan for school reform, notably those centering on upgrading standards and assessments, expanding choice, and making college accessible.

The report of the commission made the cover of *Time* magazine and received a great deal of media attention, along with a good deal of criticism.[67] It was funded by the Annie E. Casey Foundation, the Bill and Melinda Gates Foundation, the William and Flora Hewlitt Foundation, and the Lumina Foundation for Education. By this time, what was emerging was an interlocking directorate in support of systemic school reform comprised of a business and government elite with collaboration from several academic and community leaders and groups.

Achieve Inc. and the ADP

The major business architect for school reform, whose recommendations were largely adopted by the Obama administration, was the American Diploma Project (ADP) and the American Diploma Project Network (ADPN), sponsored by Achieve Inc. Achieve Inc. was "the entity" created at the 1996 Palisades Summit and charged with shepherding the process of setting and implementing standards. The central aim of the ADPN for American K–12 schools was "College and Career Readiness," the theme trumpeted by Obama in his education plan and heralded in most of his related policy initiatives. The ADPN was created at the 2005 Achieve Summit on the High School, and it built upon developments in systemic reform to that point. The 2005 National Education Summit was held in Washington, DC, with forty-five governors, CEOs from some of the nation's largest businesses, and education leaders from K–12 and higher education in attendance.

The 2005 summit was sponsored by Achieve Inc. and the NGA, with support from Prudential Financial, Washington Mutual, State Farm, Intel Foundation, and IBM Corporation. It received additional support from the Bill and Melinda Gates Foundation. The leaders gathered at the summit "confronted alarming statistics" about the preparation of American students in "an increasingly competitive global economy," including troubling high school graduation rates, college remediation, and the increasing education and skills needed in new and growing occupations. At the end of the summit, Achieve Inc. and the governors of thirteen states, with more than one-third of the nation's students, said they were forming a coalition aimed at improving high schools by "adopting higher standards, more rigorous courses and tougher examinations." They launched the ADPN, making a commitment to closing the expectations gap and instituting "college- and career-ready policies."[68] By the close of the summit, six foundations offered $23 million to help states revamp their high schools, with the largest grant, $15 million, coming from the Gates Foundation.[69]

Governors and education officials at the summit said they would "raise high school standards" to reflect "the skills and knowledge needed to succeed," "restore the value of a high school diploma" by requiring all students to take "rigorous courses" that would help prepare them for college and the workforce, and that they would "test students regularly" to measure progress in meeting tougher state standards.[70] The four "pillars" of the ADPN program included:

- Aligning high school academic content standards in English and mathematics with the demands of college and careers;
- Establishing graduation requirements that require all students to complete a college- and career-ready curriculum;
- Developing statewide high school assessment systems anchored to college- and career-ready expectations; and
- Creating comprehensive accountability and reporting systems that promote college and career readiness for all students.[71]

The push for college and career readiness and raising expectations for all students "spurred" the Common Core State Standards (CCSS) Initiative. As of this writing, due to a combination of corporate, community, and public support, significantly enhanced by federal pressure, forty-five states have adopted the CCSS, and others have revised or developed their own standards for college and career readiness.[72] This was the latest focus of business-driven reform, led by an interlocking directorate consisting of Achieve Inc., the BRT, the NGA, the ADPN, and Bill Gates and the "billionaire boys club," in cooperation with government. The general assumptions guiding business-driven systemic reform remained present, but this time business and government leaders managed to get substantial buy-in from key groups of educators in developing and implementing revisions. The lure of participation by educators, the promise of a new generation of tests, the availability of grant money, and the potential for profit were undoubtedly appealing to many who participated.

Preceding the ADPN, the ADP was launched in 2001 as a joint project sponsored by Achieve Inc., the Education Trust, the Thomas B. Fordham Foundation, and the NAB. As noted in one policy report:

> Achieve, Education Trust and the Thomas B. Fordham Foundation launched ADP to help states restore the diploma's value by anchoring high school graduation standards to those of jobs and colleges. Toward that end, ADP moves beyond the kinds of standards that reflect experts' consensus view of what is *desirable* for students to learn, to expectations linked directly to the *essential* demands faced by students preparing for college, work and citizenship.[73]

The following passage is a description of the benchmarking process conducted by ADP as described by Achieve Inc.:

> The American Diploma Project (ADP) commissioned leading economists to examine labor market projections for the most promising jobs—those that pay enough to support a small family and provide real potential for career advancement—to pinpoint the academic knowledge and skills required for success in those occupations. ADP then surveyed officials from 22 occupations, ranging from manufacturing to financial services, about the skills they believe are most useful for their employees to bring to the job. Following those conversations, ADP worked closely with two- and four-year postsecondary leaders in the partner states to determine the prerequisite English and mathematics knowledge and skills required for success in entry-level, credit-bearing courses in English, mathematics, the sciences and the humanities. The resulting ADP Benchmarks reflect an unprecedented convergence in what these employers and postsecondary faculty say are needed for new employees and freshmen entering credit-bearing coursework to be successful.[74]

Released in 2004 and published by ADP as *Ready or Not: Creating a High School Diploma That Counts*, the ADP Benchmarks were the "culminating report of the original ADP," and became the precursor to the CCSS. The ADP was a "multi-year research project" based on "statistical analysis of employment data" and "extensive research involving over 300 faculty members" from postsecondary institutions and high schools that led to development of the ADP Benchmarks, "end-of-high school expectations" in math and English language arts.[75] Support for the ADP project came from its partner organizations, Achieve Inc., the Education Trust, and the Thomas B. Fordham Foundation, all key players in the systemic reform movement.[76] The goal, according to the report, was to "identify the skills and knowledge required for success after high school." Its authors "found that all students, whether they are heading to college or embarking on a meaningful career, need the same rigorous academic foundation." They "identified a series of policies states could enact to increase the chances that students would be taught and would learn those essentials," centering on a common set of new, more rigorous standards.[77]

The efforts of ADP and ADPN represented a second wave of systemic reform, extending the standards movement vertically, K–16, and aligning it with postsecondary needs in an effort to "build constituencies and develop policies to support a coherent K–16 system." In a general sense, it was not unlike reforms aimed at college and school alignment during the 1890s. The ADP was originally working with a small consortium of several states including Indiana, Kentucky, Massachusetts, Nevada, and Texas. By 2006, the ADPN had grown into "a coalition of 26 states dedicated to aligning K–12 curriculum, standards, assessments and accountability policies with the demands of college and work."[78] Much of this activity was part of a long-standing effort by business groups to position education as the key factor in the nation's economic competitiveness and global leadership, strongly linked to national security.

The ADP job skill survey and benchmarking process seemed eerily similar to a federal government program from the 1940s known as "Life-Adjustment Education," in which the curriculum was linked to specific life and job skills in what could only be described as an orgy of social efficiency. Subsequent changes to curriculum documents and some school programs led to scathing reports in the media, and, subsequently, to the discrediting of progressive education reform during a deluge of criticism in the 1950s. The most obvious difference was that the focus of the ADP was primarily on the economic arena and work-related skills rather than broader life-adjustment. Another major difference was that the ADP initiative was launched during an era of accountability and had the support of a "Billionaire Boys Club," school reform partnerships with Gates, Broad, Walton, and Mott, giving specific individuals and their associates, many of whom had little firsthand knowledge of education or its complicated history, a dominant role in the direction of school reform.

Touching the Third Rail

A "third rail" pushing for common standards began with a small group gathered in a June 2006 meeting in Raleigh, North Carolina, put together by former North Carolina governor James B. Hunt, Jr., to talk about the possibility of developing national standards. This was followed by a September 2006 meeting in Washington, DC, behind closed doors, led by Hunt and bringing together leaders of national education policy organizations such as the Aspen Institute, the Education Trust, and the Thomas B. Fordham Institute.[79] Discrepancies in state performance, widely differing levels of student "proficiency," and the "unintended consequences" of NCLB provided a good deal of the impetus for reform toward common standards and tests. Evidence from international comparisons showed that high-performing countries had common benchmarks for student performance and national standards. Hunt proved a persuasive advocate for common standards, which he saw as "essential to improving the economy," and said that his concern came from "involvement in the worldwide economy."[80]

Hunt pursued national standards with cooperation of the Hunt Institute for Education Leadership and Policy board members including Diane Ravitch, Kati Haycock, and Governor Mitch Daniels of Indiana. SBE was "not working as it was intended to" in many states, focusing on "the pressure" and giving little "guidance and support for teachers."[81] Based on National Research Council (NRC) findings, in June 2008 the Hunt Institute developed a strategy for developing common standards. Their report, *Common Standards for K–12 Education?*, said, "If states are to develop a set of rigorous standards in common, guidance can be derived from the NRC's recent research and deliberations. If ever there were a time to build a better mousetrap, now is the time."[82] The fact that other groups were simultaneously discussing the idea of common standards, and had been for some time, meant that the possibility of widespread support for common standards by the states was very real. The Hunt Institute joined a growing chorus calling for common standards that would be comparable across states, along with a new generation of improved assessments.

In January 2009, the NGA and Council of Chief State School Officers (CCSSO) formalized the project at a forum held in Washington, DC, to develop the Common Core State Standards (CCSS) Initiative. Formal partners included Achieve Inc., the Alliance for Excellent Education, the Hunt Institute, the National Association of State Boards of Education (NASBE), and the BRT. In April 2009, in an effort to gauge the level of state support for common standards, the NGA and CCSSO arranged a meeting at the Chicago Airport Hilton and found that "support was overwhelming."[83] Organizers then developed a "memorandum of agreement" to participate in "development and adoption of a common core of state standards" along with common assessments. By June 2009, all but four states—Alaska, Missouri, South Carolina, and Texas—had signed the agreement, and by August, forty-eight states had agreed to participate.[84]

Behind what seemed a swift movement toward common standards was more than $200 million from the Bill and Melinda Gates Foundation to support development of CCSS and bankroll political support across the nation. According to one report, "Bill Gates was de facto organizer," spreading money across the spectrum, enlisting support for the CCSS initiative from groups on the left and right, many of whom had been at odds for years, including the AFT, NEA, the U.S. Chamber of Commerce, ALEC, and the Fordham Institute. Gates's money also went to states and local groups to help build consensus. Moreover, the Obama administration "was populated by former Gates Foundation staffers and associates."[85]

The Common Core Standards Initiative was officially announced on June 1, 2009. One year later, standards were released for mathematics and English on June

2, 2010. The math standards require that students explain how they got answers and learn multiple ways to solve problems. The English standards call for students to back up oral and written arguments with evidence and emphasize nonfiction. The CCSS are not a curriculum but focus instead on skills, with content, materials, pedagogy, and implementation left to states, local school districts, and teachers.[86]

During 2010, with federal pressure, including incentives from RTT competitive grants, the number of states committed to the CCSS rose to forty-five, with most of the remaining states choosing to develop their own versions of standards that would meet the new and higher expectations. So what started in 2001 as an effort by a small group of five states expanded at the 2005 Achieve Summit to thirteen states. The effort then expanded again in 2006 to include twenty-six states as more signed on to the ADPN, and it expanded again in 2009 and 2010, with establishment of the CCSS and RTT incentives, to eventually include a peak of forty-six committed states. Given the fate of previous attempts to develop national standards in the 1990s, this was a remarkable development.

Alongside movement for CCSS was a continuing effort to privatize education. This effort found its strongest support in efforts to expand charter schools during the Bush and Obama administrations, and through the work of groups such as ALEC in state-by-state efforts to privatize schools through voucher-system experiments, creation of new private charter schools with public funds, and private online schools. ALEC-sponsored legislation allowed schools to loosen certification requirements for teachers and administrators, exclude students with disabilities or special needs, escape collective bargaining agreements, and experiment with merit pay. A typical means by which ALEC and its well-heeled backers curried influence was through secretive meetings with state legislators at vacation resorts, such as the one in 2012 at the Ritz-Carlton on Amelia Island, Florida. Closed to the press and public, the event was billed as a conference addressing issues in school reform including "charter schools accessibility, accountability and transparency, standards for teacher excellence, open enrollment, vouchers, tax credits, and blended learning options."[87]

The continuing national focus on education reform was also fueled, in part, by attention from independent filmmakers during 2010 depicting the current state of schools and offering perspectives, cautions, and simplistic solutions. *The Cartel* documented the "failure" of New Jersey's education system and blamed teachers unions, overpaid administrators, and patronage—a system that could be broken, according to the film, only by vouchers and charter schools.[88] *The Lottery* followed four families with children seeking admission into the Harlem Success Academy, founded and run by Eva Moskowitz and known as one of the best charter schools in Harlem. What is most disturbing about the film is that admission is based on "blind luck" and the non-winners were forced into rundown neighborhood public schools.[89]

Waiting for Superman, the most widely viewed film, looked at the journey of promising students through a system of schooling that limits their growth and potential. *Superman* offered a broad indictment of the nation's schools, made teachers unions the culprit, and offered charter schools as the savior. The film was criticized for its simplistic portrayal of charter schools, heroization of reformers such as Michelle Rhee, and villainization of unions. A critic commented, "By siding with a corporate reform agenda of teacher bashing, union busting, test-based 'accountability' and highly selective, privatized charters, the film pours gasoline on the public education bonfire."[90]

Race to Nowhere offered an alternative perspective. The film portrayed young people pushed to the brink and educators worried that teaching to the test was undermining education.[91] It focused mainly on the stress that kids, families, and teachers experienced as a result of the policies supporting the education "race" and its unintended consequences.[92] Each of these films raised important questions about systemic school reform, but few provided real insights into the nature of the reform movement or its impact on teachers and children. *Race to Nowhere* stands alone as a significant exception.

The Social Studies Wars Revisited

During the first term of the Obama administration, two controversies involving social studies instruction would claim widespread media attention. In essence, both controversies, in Texas and Arizona, focused on state and local battles in the larger culture wars. The first, in Texas, became the butt of jokes and wonder across the nation and around the world as citizens, the media, and scholars from both sides of the aisle wondered what those folks in Texas were up to. The second, centered on Tucson, brought to the surface deep concerns about censorship, free speech, and the politicization of schooling. In both cases, underling differences over multiculturalism and the purposes of education played out before a national audience.

Sideshow in Texas

Ignoring the pleas of college history professors and other content experts, curriculum specialists, and teachers, in May 2010, the Texas State Board of Education (SBOE) approved a set of controversial curriculum standards that gave a conservative spin to standards that had been previously developed by a panel of experts. The standards would decide which historical figures and events, and which social science concepts, Texas's 4.8 million public school students would study for the next decade. In a story that attracted media coverage from across the nation and around the world, it was widely feared that the decision could impact the way the subject is taught in other states.[93]

The story had its beginnings in 2008 when the SBOE selected review committees to revise and update the state curriculum standards for each subject area, a process that takes place every ten years. Review committees were made up of four to nine members each and included teachers, district administrators, and college professors. The board also appointed six "expert reviewers," several of whom were ministers. The "expert reviewers'" report was made public in July 2009, just a few weeks before release of the first draft of new curriculum standards by the social studies review committee on July 31. The eleventh grade U.S. history committee accepted most reviewer recommendations, ignoring some. The culture war began to flare in Texas, inflamed by media reports detailing lists of names in or out, combined with inflammatory language from some of the reviewers. Discussion on the board and in the media shifted to questions of balance rather than a focus on nuance, context, historical reasoning, or critical thinking. So long as the mentioning of names struck a balance that could satisfy opposing sides in the culture wars, the process could move forward. In the fall of 2009, the board invited public comment on the July draft of the review committee and announced that it would hear public testimony at each of its meetings in January, March, and May of 2010, also inviting written reviews.

Texas Education Code grants the SBOE "statutory authority" over the standards, meaning that after the three public hearings, the standards carried force of law. The board approved approximately one hundred amendments to the proposed standards in January, one hundred more in March, and additional changes in May. None of the amendments were subject to further review by either the review committee or "expert" reviewers.[94] Changes to the standards at the March meeting drew the loudest responses from the media, as journalists, historians, educators, and late-night comedians made comments on "removing" Thomas Jefferson, replacing "capitalism" with "free enterprise system," and failing to note the presence of Latinos at the Alamo.

Media stories reported after the March meeting that "three days of turbulent meetings" led to approval of a social studies curriculum that "put a conservative stamp on history and economics textbooks, stressing the superiority of American capitalism, questioning the Founding Fathers' commitment to a purely secular government and presenting Republican political philosophies in a more positive light." The elected board gave preliminary approval to the standards by a 10–5 vote along party lines, with all the Republicans on the board supporting it. Because Texas is one of the largest buyers of textbooks, many believed the vote would have influence beyond Texas. "The books that are altered to fit the standards become the bestselling books, and therefore within the next two years they" end up in other classrooms, said Fritz Fischer, chairman of the National Council for History Education. "It's not a partisan issue, it's a good history issue."[95]

However, in the digital age, the influence of large-state adoptions, like Texas and California, may have diminished to some extent, because it is easier to tailor books to particular state standards. Moreover, the economics of selling textbooks to a national market for a profit "argue otherwise," as one seasoned observer noted. Nonetheless, because of the well-documented tendency for teachers to rely on textbooks, a trend reinforced by content standards and emphasis on high-stakes testing, many believed the changes could have a significant impact beyond Texas.[96]

The conflict over social studies standards mirrored a 2009 battle over science standards between conservatives on the board who questioned Darwin's theory of evolution and the science of global warming, and a handful of Democrats and moderate Republicans who fought to preserve mainstream approaches to those topics.[97] Don McLeroy, a dentist and leader of the conservative faction on the board, said, "We are adding balance. History has already been skewed. Academia is skewed too far to the left." Attempts by some board members to include more Latino figures as role models were consistently defeated, leading one member, Mary Helen Berlanga, to comment, "They can't just pretend this is a white America and Hispanics don't exist. They are going overboard, they are not experts, they are not historians," she said. "They are rewriting history, not only of Texas but of the United States and the world."

Conservative members countered that they were trying to correct a liberal bias, and they made dozens of changes challenging concepts such as separation of church and state and the secular nature of the American Revolution. Conservatives also included a plank that would insert "the conservative resurgence of the 1980s and 1990s, including Phyllis Schlafly, the Contract with America, the Heritage Foundation, the Moral Majority and the National Rifle Association." McLeroy put through an amendment to the civil rights movement to ensure that students study not only the nonviolent philosophy of Dr. Martin Luther King, Jr., but also the violent philosophy of the Black Panthers. He also added a plank that would mention Republican support in Congress for civil rights legislation, saying, "Republicans need a little credit for that. I think it's going to surprise some students." Another conservative member, Mr. Bradley, gained approval for a change calling for students to study the "unintended consequences" of the Great Society legislation, affirmative action, and Title IX. Discussions also included amendments calling for President Reagan to get more attention and for president of the Confederacy Jefferson Davis's inaugural address to be studied alongside President Abraham Lincoln's, both of which were approved.

In economics, revisions to the standards added Milton Friedman and Friedrich von Hayek, champions of free market economic theory, to the usual list of economists studied. They also replaced the word "capitalism" with "free-enterprise system" throughout the standards, mirroring a change in wording promoted by a 1930s propaganda campaign led by the National Association of Manufacturers. "Let's face it, capitalism does have a negative connotation," said Terri Leo, a conservative member. "You know, 'capitalist pig!'" In sociology, conservative member Barbara Cargill put through an amendment that required teaching "the importance of personal responsibility for life choices" in a section on teen suicide, dating violence, drug use, and eating disorders. "The topic of sociology tends to blame society for everything," Cargill said. Another conservative member managed to cut Thomas Jefferson from a list of historical figures that inspired revolutions in the late eighteenth and early nineteenth centuries. Jefferson was not well liked by conservative Christians on the board because he coined the phrase, "separation between church and state."[98] Historians said the founding fathers had a variety of approaches to religion, and that some, like Jefferson, were quite secular.[99]

At its May meeting, the SBOE approved more than one hundred additional amendments during marathon sessions leading up to its vote. The board approved changes to the standards, on a 9–5 party-line vote, with many of the changes putting a "conservative spin" on a curriculum proposal that had been prepared by a panel of history and social studies experts. By the time of the vote, more than twenty thousand people had submitted public comments during a thirty-day period while the document was posted online. Among those who testified against the standards during the May meeting were Benjamin T. Jealous, president of the NAACP; Rod Paige, former U.S. secretary of education; and Diane Ravitch, former deputy secretary of education. In his testimony, Paige requested that the board delay its vote, and commented, "We have allowed ideology to drive and define the standards of our curriculum in Texas."[100]

Among the harshest critics of the new standards were six of the nine members of the original review panel appointed by the board, who released a two-page statement expressing their "collective disgust" with the changes to their proposal, which "distorted" their work. "We feel that the SBOE's biased and unfounded amendments undercut our attempt to build a strong, balanced and diverse set of standards," the statement read. "Texans should be outraged" at the revisions made "without regard to standard historical interpretations."[101] The American Historical Association also submitted a letter to the board in the days before its May meeting, calling on the board to reconsider its amendments to the standards, to delay a vote, and to undertake "further review."[102]

After the media attention ended, memories of the battles were celebrated, condemned, or otherwise judged. The fact that Phyllis Schlafly's name was added to beef-up portrayal of the conservative resurgence of the 1980s and 1990s was celebrated at an awards ceremony held by the Eagle Forum. In December 2010, a coalition of civil rights groups filed a complaint in federal court alleging discrimination in the board's final product. In February 2011, the Fordham Institute awarded the Texas history standards a grade of D, describing them as a "political distortion of history."[103] As a result of the controversy and media frenzy, the real-world impact on the standards was to increase their length. Culture war "balance" found resolution primarily in adding more words, names, and phrases to appease various constituencies. As a result, the standards grew unevenly, and they took on a more conservative spin. Perhaps the most significant problem, related to the system of review, was that the standards became a laundry list of names rather than a statement of expectations that students would "read, think, solve problems, and communicate" and engage in critical thinking. When one commentator raised the concern before the board at its May 2010 meeting that the standards section devoted to social studies skills such as problem solving, analysis, and decision making was too brief and inadequate, and was repeated verbatim for every grade level from K–12, the concern was dismissed by a board member, who said, in essence, "We leave that to the classroom teachers."[104]

As time went on the episode received a good deal of comment and attention from a variety of perspectives. Diane Ravitch decried the standards for mandating patriotism and promoting ignorance; historian Jonathan Zimmerman critiqued the standards while calling for greater attention to balance and multiple perspectives.[105] Later, one group of scholars addressed the episode as an attempt to undermine and undo multiculturalism. Another group of scholars, many of whom were participants, described it as an attempt to unravel the tenets of quality scholarship and good teaching.[106] Seemingly left out of the discussion was the fact that textbooks had a long history of glorifying our nation's history, presenting corporate America's version of our past, "sculpted and sanded down" so as not to offend, in order to bring profits to the publishers.[107] The question of who benefits from the typical textbook, standard routinized teaching, and lack of meaningful discourse on our national story and the many difficult or troubling questions that it raises was also largely left out.

The Tucson Controversy

Another conflict over social studies teaching that had been simmering for some time in Arizona exploded onto the national scene in January 2012, when the Tucson Unified School District (TUSD) voted to suspend its Mexican American Studies (MAS) classes to avoid losing more than $14 million in state money. The controversy had its origins in April 2006, when a guest speaker, Dolores Huerta, appeared at Tucson High Magnet School during Cesar Chavez Week. One of the comments Huerta made was that "Republicans hate Latinos."[108] The school put a statement from the speech on its website, and the incident attracted the attention of Tom Horne, state superintendent of schools. A few weeks later, Margaret Garcia-Dugan, a Republican and the state's deputy superintendent of instruction, was brought in to speak at the school before an assembly of students. Garcia-Dugan addressed the importance of considering "both sides of an issue, making your own decision and avoiding stereotypes." Students who wanted to ask questions of the speaker were told by Horne to write the questions down and that he would pick out questions to be asked. Many students felt they were being censored, and put tape over their mouths. Other students displayed "pro-Latino" T-shirts reading, "You can silence my voice but not my spirit," "Prop 203 is anti-Latino," and "English only is anti-Latino." Other students turned their backs or raised their fists in the air. The protesting students subsequently "walked out of the assembly after Garcia-Dugan stopped speaking."[109]

Following the incidents at Tucson High Magnet School, there were a number of exchanges between TUSD and the state, leading to passage of a state law, while Horne was state superintendent, aimed at challenging the Tucson ethnic studies program, which the Arizona legislature passed in spring 2010. Horne wrote the measure, and it was signed into law by Governor Jan Brewer in May of that year, amid raging protests over the state's crackdown on illegal immigration. The state law banned classes primarily designed for a particular ethnic group or that "promote resentment toward a race or class of people." In January 2011, after being elected state attorney general, Horne officially declared the Tucson district's Mexican American Studies Program to be in violation, shortly after the new law went into effect. He gave the district sixty days to comply. About a year later, after protest efforts by teachers and others, and some wrangling over the matter in the courts, the TUSD board voted, in January 2012, to suspend the program in order to avoid losing more than $14 million in state aid.[110] Critics of the program, led by State Schools Chief John Huppenthal, who had helped write and pass the law, said that framing historical events in racial terms "to create a sense of solidarity" was promoting "victimhood." Program advocates said that the MAS classes teach neglected topics in America's cultural heritage, focusing on Latino perspectives on literature, history, and social justice, and pointed out that the classes inspired many Latino students to become successful.

When asked in an interview about the origins and rationale for the law, Huppenthal stated that tracing it to the 2006 incident was an "oversimplification" and that the law was "also based on the information that was flowing out of the Mexican-American studies classes" in Tucson. When asked to discuss parts of the Tucson program that caused him the most concern, citing a journal article written by leaders of the Tucson MAS program, he replied,

> They said they were going to racemize(ph) the classes using a Paulo Freirean(ph) philosopher—and he's a writer of the book "Pedagogy of the Oppressed," and he, right in his book, talks about that word oppressed comes right out of "The Communist Manifesto." And he talks about having a Marxist structure where the entire history of mankind is the struggle between the oppressed and the oppressor . . . So the racemizing of the class was to imbue a sense that the oppressed are Hispanic kids and the oppressor is a white Caucasian power structure . . . To tell kids that the whole deck—that they can't get ahead, that they're victims in, you know, a country in which Barack Obama is president, it defies what we know.[111]

The one member of the Tucson board who voted to continue the program, despite possible loss of millions in state aid, was Adelita Grijalva, who said in an interview that an initial district audit of the program found that it was in compliance with the law. In response to the charge that the courses created "a sense of victimization" and spurred resentment among Mexican American students toward their white peers and society at large, she said,

I feel, on the contrary, the courses teach our students that they can rise up over any obstacle, over any form of oppression. It discusses what the Mexican American experience has been in our history. The students leave basically believing that they can not only change their lives, but they can change the world. . . . I wonder how you teach some of these parts of our history without being one sided. I mean, how do you talk about the fact that there is a sign that is in one of our picture books that students can no longer access that says, No Mexicans or Dogs Allowed. . . . Unfortunately, we're moving in the direction in this country that we're rewriting history and eliminating or downplaying the parts that we don't want to remember.[112]

Among the seven books that were removed from classrooms and placed in storage were *Rethinking Columbus* from Rethinking Schools, Paulo Freire's *Pedagogy of the Oppressed*, and several histories of the Mexican American people.[113] Following the vote of the TUSD board to comply with the law and remove the books, there was a good deal of anger, frustration, and confusion among teachers and others. From one MAS teacher's perspective, enforcement of the law meant that a culture of oppression had been created in Tucson classrooms. Teacher Curtis Acosta wrote:

What I can tell you is that TUSD has decreed that anything taught from a Mexican American Studies perspective is illegal and must be eliminated immediately. Of course, they have yet to define what that means, but here's an example of what happened to an essay prompt that I had distributed prior to January 10th.[114]

The passages showed innocuous explanations edited from an assignment by district officials because they were "found to be too leading toward a Mexican American Studies perspective." The passages were declared "illegal and out of compliance" according to Acosta's letter. Included were brief quotes from a great literary figure, playwright Luis Valdez saying, "Chicano playwright Luis Valdez once stated that his art was meant 'to inspire the audience to social action. Illuminate specific points about social problems. Satirize the opposition. Show or hint at a solution. Express what people are feeling.'" The passage was placed immediately before a writing prompt for students, who were to discuss a novel by Ana Castillo related to the Valdez quote. The writing prompt was not edited.[115]

A semester after the Tucson program was discontinued, many students and teachers were still heartbroken over the decision, saying that the course had provided them with a sense of empowerment. However, it was the strident nature of some of the classes, exacerbated by teacher quality issues and the slippery slope of critical pedagogy, that apparently led Horne and Huppenthal to push for the law. They found an unlikely ally in Loretta Hunnicutt, a liberal Democrat from Tucson who had been involved in school reform efforts for thirty years. "I came out in defense of the classes," she said. "That's how I got pulled into this whole situation." After talking with teachers and parents she began to rethink her opinion, and said the class had become very political, with little emphasis on culture or history. "It seeped into every single one of the class offerings, unfortunately . . . even when you had really conscientious teachers, it couldn't help but become political in nature." Controversy over Mexican American Studies was picking up at around the time when the Arizona legislature introduced Senate Bill 1070, aimed at curtailing illegal immigration, based on ALEC model legislation. The Latino community felt like it was under siege.[116] Both of these major controversies suggested to many that social studies in the schools was rife with a troubling ideological bias, the kind of charge that had long haunted the field, and that it needed to be reformed if not jettisoned entirely.

A Continuing Struggle

As the controversies in Texas and Arizona illustrate, social studies could still be highly contentious, even when it was being devalued in schools. Meanwhile, the various ideological camps in social studies continued to struggle over a preferred vision for the field. Occasional battles continued to be fought between advocates of traditional history and progressive social studies. For example, an article by Michael Knox Beran published in the Manhattan Institute's *City Journal* in 2012 called for schools to "abolish" social studies as a "pseudo-discipline" rife with ideological bias that had "outlived its usefulness." Appealing to a golden age of schooling during which schools used the "resources of the culture" to develop each child's individual potential, Beran lamented that social studies "seeks to adjust him to the mediocrity of the social pack." To support his point, Beran cited a litany of progressive social studies advocates including Harold Rugg, George Counts, and Paul Hanna, along with more recent theorists, whom he castigated for attempting to mold young minds to collectivist ideology. Moreover, he critiqued modern elementary social studies textbooks as "doing too little to acquaint children with their culture's ideals of individual liberty and initiative" while promoting the "socialization of the child" at the expense of the "development of his own individual powers." Beran concluded that despite its social idealism, social studies offered an "insipid approach to the cultivation of the mind" contributing to the "progress of dullness," and should be abolished.[117]

One notable change from which the field was still reeling was the continuing influence of money through the work of politicized foundations, think tanks, and interest groups on both rhetoric and practice. As part of their attempt to replace progressive social studies with a more traditional academic approach to the field, several groups began regularly reviewing history and social studies standards. The Heritage Foundation, the Fordham Institute, and the CBE all conducted state-by-state reviews of history standards, in each case with the not-so-hidden agenda of furthering their own preferred version of the field, heavy on traditional history and geography and aimed at moving the field away from a broader progressive version of social studies.[118]

In another change, funding for the Teaching American History grant program, which had supplied more than $1 billion over a decade, was reduced for fiscal year 2011, cut from $119 to $46 million, and was no longer included at all in the fiscal year 2012 budget.[119] The administration planned to replace it with a humanities grant program that would include history education as part of a broader program aimed at "Effective Teaching and Learning for a Well Rounded Education," linked to ESEA reauthorization. The administration did not make a request for resuscitating TAH in its 2013 budget proposal, instead emphasizing "accountability and flexibility" for states, rather than fielding specific grants.[120] As of this writing, ESEA reauthorization was at a stalemate, and the plan had not led to funding. While the TAH grant program may have contributed to improving instruction in history, at least in some classrooms, its overall impact was questioned by many, including an evaluation study and a leading figure in history education, who intimated that it was a billion dollar boondoggle. However, the program did contribute support to ongoing efforts from neoconservatives and others to replace a broad approach to social studies and civic education with a history as core structure, in state curriculum frameworks, and in practice, especially at the lower levels.

One of the most devastating critiques of the TAH program came in a DOE-funded evaluation study published in 2011 that found both positives and negatives, but concluded that case studies "did not find associations between TAH practices and outcomes." While evaluators found that program practices were "aligned with principles of quality professional development," they also reported that TAH grants often "lacked active support" from school administrators and were "not well integrated at the school level." In short, while self-reports from teachers indicated that the program "had a positive impact on the quality of their teaching," including more "use of primary sources" and better lesson plans that "engaged students in historical inquiry," grantee evaluations "lacked rigorous designs" and "could not support a meta-analysis to assess the impact of TAH on student achievement or teaching knowledge."[121] The end of funding brought the end to a sustained period during which history educators and allied researchers benefited from the neoconservative revival of history in schools, and during which TAH boosted attention to history, while subtly undermining social studies, the social sciences, and civics.

On a parallel track, civic education initiatives continued, with perhaps the most prominent being the Civic Mission of Schools led by Sandra Day O'Connor and others. The Civic Mission of Schools developed a program known as iCivics, an expanded online program aimed at middle school students. iCivics included free curriculum materials and lesson plans linked to standards and promoted public service. O'Connor launched the project that became iCivics in 2006, the same year she retired as a U.S. Supreme Court justice. Civics, which was once a commonplace offering at the junior high level, had all but disappeared from the nation's schools, and with it, a substantial amount of civic learning. Also, civics and social studies were not emphasized under NCLB, and so, schools that had once included social studies as part of their basic curriculum often reduced attention to the subject. According to advocates of iCivics, civic education included explaining the structure of government, the meaning of the U.S. Constitution and its evolution over time, as well as encouraging students to engage in the democratic process. Some critics feared a "narrow indoctrination into traditional mores that deserved to be questioned," while others perceived "a bias toward liberal activism."[122] Supporters included the Center for Civic Education, CIRCLE, and a long list of interest groups and foundations focused on improving civic education.[123]

Despite these initiatives, social studies educators seemed beaten down, discouraged by the general lack of attention to the field in the national reform movement.[124] For most of two decades, social studies had been the forgotten link, the subject most often left out in discussions of school reform. The broader field of social studies was also under siege from the neoconservative revival of traditional history and was the subject of continuing attacks that served to submerge attempts to resuscitate the field.

The second-tier status of the social studies field was the subject of an open letter to President Obama from C. Frederick Risinger, a former NCSS president, who wrote to express his concerns about the increasing emphasis on mathematics, science, and reading/language arts, while a fourth area—social studies—was "being marginalized by lack of funding and reduced interest" from the DOE, state departments of education, and the CCSS movement. Risinger made a strong case on the need for effective citizenship education, citing "inability to work together, name-calling, and extreme political polarization" as part of an increasing unwillingness to "enter into discussions of issues." He cited one study that found in K–6 classrooms, nearly 32 percent of students were receiving "only 25 minutes of social studies/citizenship education" per week, because it was not tested. He also cited a recent meeting of national organizations sponsored by NCSS and the Civic Mission for the Schools to discuss working on common standards as a hopeful sign, but cautioned,

> If we do not teach our young citizens about history, geography, economics, civics and other social studies areas, our nation will lose its national bearings . . . it will lose its soul.[125]

He called for Obama to appoint a Presidential Commission on Citizenship Education "to thoroughly review the role of citizenship education in America's schools" and to "make recommendations for its improvement" so as to return social studies to its former status as "one of the core curriculum areas in preK–12 education."[126]

Secretary of Education Arne Duncan answered Fred Risinger's plea, albeit somewhat indirectly, in an article published in *Social Education* in May/June of

2011. Duncan acknowledged that social studies teachers "live with the unintended consequences" of NCLB and its "flawed incentives" that lead to curriculum narrowing and leave out core subjects "essential to a well-rounded curriculum, including social studies." He characterized the marginalization of social studies "for the sake of reading and math" as "educational neglect" and called the field a "core subject, critical to sustaining an informed democracy and a globally competitive workforce." Duncan also used the opportunity to promote Obama's blueprint for ESEA reauthorization, calling it a plan that is "fair, flexible, and focused on the schools most at risk." He also echoed the administration's call for better assessments that go beyond "mediocre fill-in-the-bubble tests of today." And he acknowledged the difficulty of testing students "to see whether or not they are becoming curious and informed participants" in our democratic society. Duncan lauded the efforts of the Connected Learning Coalition and encouraged teachers to work with states to include social studies in their accountability systems, "as proposed by the President's plan."[127] Duncan's article was accompanied by reflections from five longtime leaders of the NCSS, each of whom had served as president. As a group, they endorsed Duncan's paean to social studies but pointed out contradictions and critiqued administration policies. Two described RTT as an extension of NCLB and said that it was continuing a policy of curriculum narrowing. Others called for broader application of authentic assessments already in existence. As a group, they called for enactment of policy changes that would support Secretary Duncan's rhetoric.[128]

The Connected Learning Coalition (CLC), mentioned by Duncan and at least one of the respondents, is a group comprised of educational subject matter organizations including the NCSS, NCTE, NCTM, and NSTA, representing some 250,000 content area teachers, administrators, educational technology experts, and others. The CLC was formed when the executive directors of six groups came together with common concerns about improving assessments, which had been "sidetracked in recent years by the demands of accountability."[129] Apparently initiated by the Association for Career and Technical Education (ACTE), the coalition supported greater use of "authentic" and formative assessment, and endorsed six "Principles for Learning" centered on "helping students grasp new ideas, solve problems, collaborate, and use their imaginations to pursue challenging questions" and develop "a habit of inquiry."[130]

The group stated in a paper that it was deeply concerned that the pressure for a "new accountability system" combined with the push for Common Core Standards in 2014 "may provoke a rush to a system that reduces time for teaching and learning and homogenizes curricula and teaching methods in order to preserve comparability across school systems." It stated that it sought a transition from "over-emphasis on testing to effective assessment practices that support student learning and school improvement."[131] Given the damaging impact that standardized testing and accountability were having on classroom processes and instruction, their concerns and goals seemed very reasonable.

Cause for Hope?

In most ways, Barack Obama's record on education reform rivals George W. Bush at playing the game of test, sort, discipline, and punish. Bush passed NCLB, which gave the DOE and recent presidential administrations greater power over the states and schools. Obama largely continued in the same direction, while tinkering with the details. Because of the slim prospects for legislative reauthorization of NCLB, Obama used funding and competitive pressure to "prod states and school districts into embracing the administration's vision for education policy," which is "voluntary" only for states willing to forgo millions in federal funding.[132] This was a brilliant but deeply flawed strategy, continuing much of the top-down NCLB program uninterrupted.[133]

Defining his RTT program as a "race" was politically astute, encapsulating the achievement-oriented, competitive, and business-driven ethos of the entire reform era, with a host of both positive and negative ramifications. For most schools and teachers, it meant more of the same—more top-down direction of the curriculum; more pressure to raise test scores; more mandates to follow; and continued limits on the freedom to make professional judgments over what and how to teach. For students, the Obama administration's agenda continued to focus schooling on the economic purposes of education, at the expense of other needs. The reform agenda continued to operate on virtually all of the same basic assumptions: schools as a failed monopoly; use of a business-like system of standards and measurement for improvement; sanctioning schools with rewards and punishments; increasing teacher accountability; and support for charter schools. Modifications during the Obama administration included greater emphasis on competition among states and districts; a focus on improving the lowest-performing schools; rhetoric espousing greater flexibility for states and districts; use of incentives, carrots rather than sticks; expanded support for charter schools; and development of CCSS and a new generation of "smarter" tests.

While these shifts have led to changes, continuity with policies established under NCLB and the movement for systemic reform is still their most striking feature. While the bulk of schools are now viewed as doing well, and the administration has backed off from strict enforcement of many NCLB mandates, all schools are still subject to the testing requirements of NCLB. Though standards and testing appear to be undergoing significant revision under the CCSS initiative that will likely improve their palatability and create greater freedom and flexibility for teachers to innovate, it remains to be seen whether new requirements will lead to genuine improvement, continued compliance, or new forms of resistance.

To the Obama administration's credit, they did address several of the key flaws in NCLB, offering greater flexibility and increased funding to states in exchange for going along with the administration's agenda in support of common standards, development of a new generation of tests, expansion of charter schools, and use of test scores in teacher evaluation. However, it is unclear at this point whether these changes in policy will help relieve the curriculum narrowing that has made social studies a second-tier subject, or provide teachers with the freedom and support necessary to develop reflective and highly interactive approaches to instruction. Despite rhetoric aimed at addressing concerns about declining attention to social studies in schools, very little has changed. The CCSS initiative focuses primarily on mathematics and English language arts, but includes only modest integration of history. For most students, despite the attention to fixing NCLB, the policies of the Obama education plan have meant continuation of a test-driven, competitive school climate where education for social efficiency, excessive focus on test preparation, sorting students by test scores, and labeling students will continue for the foreseeable future.

The CCSS movement is establishing what will likely become a virtual national curriculum with tests in mathematics and English language arts, a process that is mirrored in development of common core like social studies standards and assessments by a smaller but significant group of states.[134] As of this writing, it is too early to judge the impact that the Common Core standards and assessments will have on social studies or on schools writ large. Though many educators are hopeful that it will lead to improvement, giving a boost to meaningful learning, others are skeptical and fear that it may lead to continuing curricular narrowing and further privatization.[135] Despite the potential for improvement, it is important to recognize that while the common standards movement may bring some refinement and greater flexibility, it is built on the same assumptions as the larger movement of which it is part.

Why was this movement for national standards succeeding where others had failed? There were several possible reasons. It was described by proponents as coming from the states, though its origins were from national interest groups and business influence. The CCSS movement also involved a few key educational organizations in the process, giving it a more collaborative feel. It promised to include greater attention to inquiry, critical thinking, and meaningful learning. It was pushed by a powerful combination of business and government groups and, ultimately, by federal policy muscle and incentives. It received large amounts of private financial support from philanthropic foundations and policy advocacy groups ranging from the Gates Foundation and Charles Steven Mott Foundation to the Fordham Institute and others—creating a consensus of bipartisan support. The CCSS also offered a rhetoric of flexibility and stopped short of spelling out the specific content that should be taught, letting states and local districts adapt their content standards to the CCSS. It received buy-in from major groups of educators including the Association for Supervision and Curriculum Development (ASCD) and CCSSO in the development process. The buy-in later snowballed, as more groups such as the NCSS joined in the effort and participated in developing common standards for other subject areas.

A number of thoughtful educators view the CCSS as a worthy cause and are hopeful that they will bring relief to the "unintended consequences" of NCLB and accountability reform, such as curriculum narrowing, excessive test preparation, and a decline in inquiry and discussion.[136] Others are skeptical, ranging from those who see it as unproven and untested "nonsense," to those who see it as yet another way in which the business community is seeking to push school reform via ever more pressure, by creating comparability and competition among states.[137] Some critics see it as a thinly veiled federal power grab. Others view it as part of a larger move toward privatization, with benefits for Pearson and other test and textbook publishers. Still others have raised concerns about data collection and privacy issues. There is little doubt that the CCSS are a major step toward national standards and testing. Moreover, CCSS embodies the same human capital mindset and business principles applied to schooling as previous reforms. It is an untested reform being applied to virtually all the states without proper pilot study or field-testing. These attributes and conditions understandably raise a caution flag.

Many educators would likely agree that the CCSS are "much better than the state standards they replace because they focus on analysis, understanding concepts, and skills, more than specific content."[138] Though the CCSS offer the possibility of movement toward schooling that goes beyond a curriculum focused on drill and practice, many questions and uncertainties remain. Even with a new set of standards and assessments, would standards and test-driven control of the CCSS developed by a consortium of states and corporate-backed NGOs be substantially different from control by the federal government? Would it lead to greater flexibility or a new generation of scripted lessons aimed at higher performance on "smarter" assessments? Would it lead to better teaching and learning than under NCLB? Would it inspire a new wave of innovation, creativity, and classroom thoughtfulness or impose bland uniformity? Would it allow greater intellectual freedom in schools or constrain meaningful discussion of contentious issues? How much difference would CCSS make without OTL standards aimed at eradicating the glaring educational inequalities that condemn millions of low-income, minority, and immigrant youth to live in poorer communities and attend substandard schools? Finally, can teachers, who are historically resistant to change and tend to rely on low-level instructional patterns, learn to teach the new standards?

As of this writing, there are increasing signs of pushback against the accountability movement and the testing machine. Movement to roll back the CCSS is occurring in several state legislatures.[139] Moreover, many individual educators, and several organized groups, have been speaking out against systemic reform since its inception. Despite what seems a rising tide of challenges to the CCSS and the systemic reform agenda, instances of teachers, parents, or students actively challenging the accountability reform movement remain isolated and sporadic. Moreover, significant numbers of educators have hitched their hopes for an improved and more reasonable climate in schools by supporting the CCSS movement. How this will all play out, whether the CCSS will be a "better mousetrap," or whether increasing resistance in state legislatures will lead to its undoing, is rather unpredictable. Yet it seems that for many, a window of hope for genuine improvement may have opened.

Notes

1. Deborah White, "Obama's Education Plan to Reform Schools and Reward Teachers," February 12, 2012, http://usliberals.about.com/od/education/a/ObamaEdPlan_5. html; Barack Obama, "Press Release—In Major Policy Speech, Obama Announces Plan to Provide All Americans with a World-Class Education," November 20, 2007, APP.
2. Obama '08, BarackObama.com, "Barack Obama's Plan for Lifetime Success Through Education," Obama Campaign Document, http://www.elementarysciencecoalition. org/PreK-12EducationFactSheet.pdf.
3. Ibid., 2.
4. "Hillary Clinton on Education," Education.com Magazine [online], 2008 http://edu cation.com/magazine/article/Hillary_Clinton/ (accessed February 12, 2013; no longer in service); Connor P. Williams, "In 2016, Democrats Have Good Reason to Run Against Obama's Education Record," *New Republic,* June 3, 2014, http://www.newrepublic. com/article/117989/hillary-clintons-education-policy-other-implications-2016.
5. Justin Quinn, "Arizona Sen. John McCain's Education Platform," undated, http:// usconservatives.about.com/od/johnmccainontheissues/a/McCainEducation.html.
6. Gregg Toppo, "Where They Stand: McCain, Obama Split on Education," *USAT,* October 14, 2008; Quinn, "McCain's Platform."
7. Toppo, "Where They Stand."
8. Patrick J. McGuinn, *No Child Left Behind and the Transformation of Federal Education Policy, 1965–2005* (Lawrence: University of Kansas Press, 2006).
9. "The American Recovery and Reinvestment Act of 2009: Saving and Creating Jobs and Reforming Education," http://www2.ed.gov/policy/gen/leg/recovery/imple mentation.html.
10. Nanette Asimov, "Stanford Professor Leads Obama Transition Team," *SFC,* November 22, 2008.
11. Sam Dillon, "Education Standards Likely to See Toughening," *NYT,* April 14, 2009, A12.
12. "The American Recovery and Reinvestment Act of 2009."
13. Dillon, "Standards Toughening."
14. Ibid.
15. Erik W. Robelen, "Obama Echoes Bush on Education Ideas," *EW,* April 18–19, 2009, 1.
16. Maria Glod, "Chicago School Reform Could Be a US Model," *WP,* December 30, 2008, http://articles.washingtonpost.com/2008-12-30/news/36790173_1_gay-friendly-high-school-arne-duncan-school-systems.
17. David Hursh, *High-Stakes Testing and the Decline of Teaching and Learning: The Real Crisis in Education* (Lanham, MD: Rowman & Littlefield, 2008), 105.
18. Civic Committee of the Commercial Club of Chicago, *Left Behind: A Report of the Education Committee of the Civic Committee* (Chicago: Commercial Club of Chicago, 2003).
19. Michael Apple, *Educating the "Right" Way: Markets, Standards, God, and Inequality* (New York: Routledge, 2006), 39.
20. Milton Friedman, "Public Schools: Make Them Private," Cato Briefing Paper No. 23, http://www.cato.org/pubs/briefs/bp-023.html; Milton Friedman, "The Role of Government in Education," in Robert A. Solo, Ed., *Economics and the Public Interest* (Newark, NJ: Rutgers University Press, 1955); Jonah Goldberg, "Public Schools Flunk Every Course," *DC,* June 5, 2007, A-12, and R.M. Eberling, "It's Time to Put Public Education Behind Us," Future of Freedom Foundation Commentaries, cited in Hursh, *High-Stakes Testing,* 87.
21. "President Obama, U.S. Secretary of Education Duncan Announce National Competition to Advance School Reform," Press Release, July 24, 2009, http://www2.ed.gov/news/pressreleases/2009/07/07242009.html.
22. DOE, *Race to the Top Program Executive Summary* (Washington, DC: DOE, November 2009), 2.

23. "President Obama."
24. Ibid., 4.
25. Ibid., 4–5.
26. Sam Dillon, "Dangling Money, Obama Pushes Education Shift," *NYT*, August 17, 2009.
27. Ibid.
28. Ibid.
29. "Race to the Top Phase I Final Results," March 4, 2010, http://www2.ed.gov/pro grams/racetothetop/phase1-applications/score-summary.pdf; "Race to the Top Phase II Final Results," August 24, 2010, http://www.siue.edu/ierc/pdf/Race_to_the_Top_ Phase_2_Results.pdf.
30. "Press Release—Governor Perry: Texas Knows Best How to Educate Our Students; Texas will not apply for Federal Race to the Top Funding." February 13, 2010, http:// governor.state.tx.us/news/press-release/14146/.
31. Diane Ravitch, "The Big Idea: It's Bad Education Policy," *LAT*, March 14, 2010.
32. Kevin Hart, "Critics See East Coast, Urban Biases in Race to the Top Awards," *NEAT*, August 26, 2010.
33. Frederick M. Hess, "National Review: Race to the Top Limps to a Finish," *NPR*, August 31, 2010.
34. Patrick McGuinn, "Stimulating Reform: Race to the Top, Competitive Grants and the Obama Education Agenda," *EP* 26, no. 1 (2012): 136–159.
35. Onosko, "Race to the Top Leaves Children and Future Citizens Behind," *DE* 19, no. 2 (2011): 1–3.
36. Alyson Klein, "Obama Uses Funding, Executive Muscle to Make Often-Divisive Agenda a Reality," *EW* 31, no. 35 (June 26–28, 2012), 1.
37. Sam Dillon, "Administration Outlines Proposed Changes to 'No Child' Law," *NYT*, February 1, 2010.
38. DOE, *A Blueprint for Reform: The Reauthorization of the Elementary and Secondary Education Act* (Washington, DC: U.S. DOE, 2010), 1.
39. Ibid., 6.
40. Sam Dillon, "Obama Calls for Major Change in Education Law," *NYT*, March 13, 2010.
41. Lindsey Burke, "ESEA Reauthorization Blueprint: Another Federal Overreach," *FHF*, March 15, 2010, http://blog.heritage.org/2010/03/15/esea-reauthorization-blueprint- another-federal-overreach/.
42. Fordham Foundation, http://www.edexcellence.net/blog-types/flypaper.
43. Juvenile Law Center, "Federal Policy, ESEA Reauthorization, and the School-to-Prison Pipeline," March 2011, http://www.jlc.org/resources/publications/federal-policy-e sea-reauthorization-and-school-prison-pipeline.
44. Casey D. Cobb, "A Review of *The Obama Education Blueprint: Researchers Examine the Evidence* by William Mathis and Kevin Welner," *DE* 19, no. 1 (2011), 30; William J. Mathis and Kevin G. Welner, Eds. *The Obama Education Blueprint: Researchers Examine the Evidence* (Charlotte, NC: Information Age, 2010).
45. Barbara Michelman, "The Never-Ending Story of ESEA Reauthorization," *PP* 18, no. 1 (Spring 2012): 3.
46. Sam Dillon, "Overriding a Key Education Law," *NYT*, August 8, 2011.
47. Ibid.
48. Ibid.
49. ED.gov, "ESEA Flexibility" February 14, 2013, http://www2.ed.gov/policy/elsec/ guid/esea-flexibility/index.html.
50. ED.gov, "States with ESEA Flexibility Request under Review (including BIE and PR)," updated January 11, 2013, http://www2.ed.gov/policy/elsec/guid/esea-flexibility/ index.html.
51. "U.S. Department of Education ESEA Flexibility Peer Reviewers," December 2011– October 2012, http://www2.ed.gov/policy/elsec/guid/esea-flexibility/index.html.

52. Alexandra Zavas and Tony Barboza, "Teacher's Suicide Shocks School," *LAT*, September 28, 2010.

53. Ibid.

54. Michelman, "ESEA Reauthorization," 3; Jenna S. Talbot and Rachel V. Gibson, "Don't Hold Your Breath: Waivers and ESEA Reauthorization," February 8, 2013, *WA*, http://www.whiteboardadvisors.com/news/don't-hold-your-breath.

55. Sean Cavanaugh, "Ten States Get NCLB Waivers, New Mexico Has to Wait," *EW*, February 9, 2012.

56. Rory Cooper, "Morning Bell: Obama Circumvents Congress on Education Policy," *FHF*, September 26, 2011, http://blog.heritage.org/2011/09/26/morning-bell-obama-circumvents-congress-on-education-policy/.

57. Lindsay Burke, quoted in Cooper, "Obama Circumvents Congress."

58. Klein, "Obama Uses Funding, Muscle."

59. Patricia Cohen, "In Writings of Obama, a Philosophy Is Unearthed," *NYT*, October 27, 2010; James T. Kloppenberg, *Reading Obama: Dreams, Hope, and the American Political Tradition* (Princeton, NJ: Princeton University Press, 2011).

60. Rogers M. Smith, "The Constitutional Philosophy of Barack Obama: Democratic Pragmatism and Religious Commitment," *SSQ* 93, no. 5 (December 2012): 1251.

61. Eric Robelen, "Obama Echoes Bush on Education Ideas," *EW* 28, no. 8 (April 8, 2009): 1, 18–19.

62. Gillian E. Metzger, "Federalism Under Obama," *WMLR* 53 (2011): 569, 591–592, 597.

63. Norman J. Ornstein, "Obama: A Pragmatic Moderate Faces the Socialist Smear," *WP*, April 14, 2010, A19.

64. See works of Apple, Giroux, Wayne Au, William Ayers, Ravitch, and Darling-Hammond.

65. New Commission on the Skills of the American Workforce, *Tough Choices or Tough Times* (Washington, DC: National Center on Education and the Economy, 2007), 8

66. Ibid., 9–20.

67. See Ravitch and others.

68. Achieve Inc. and NGA, *2005 National Education Summit on High Schools* (Washington, DC: Achieve and National Governors Association, 2005);

69. Robert Pear, "Governors of 13 States Plan to Raise Standards in High Schools," *NYT*, February 28, 2005.

70. Ibid.

71. Achieve Inc., *Closing the Expectations Gap: 50-State Progress Report on the Alignment of High School Policies with the Demands of College and Careers* (Washington, DC: Achieve Inc. and the ADPN, 2011), 7.

72. Ibid.

73. Achieve Inc., *Achieve's Comparison of the American Diploma Project (ADP) English Benchmarks with the Rhode Island High School Grade-Span Expectations (GSEs) for Reading, Writing, and Oral Communication for Grades 9–10, 11–12* (Washington, DC: Achieve Inc., 2006).

74. Ibid.

75. ADP, *Ready or Not: Achieving a High School Diploma That Counts* (Washington, DC: Achieve Inc., 2004).

76. Ibid.

77. Ibid., 7.

78. "American Diploma Project," according to one school district report, drawing on sources from the Education Trust and Achieve Inc., http://www.sandhills.edu/academic-departments/english/teaching/adp.html.

79. Robert Rothman, *Something in Common: The Common Core Standards and the Next Chapter in American Education* (Cambridge, MA: Harvard Education Press, 2011), 53. Rothman, a participant in the systemic reform movement and a senior fellow at the Alliance for Excellent Education, argues that support for national standards, long seen as the "third rail" of education policy—like the third rail on subways, touch it and you die—was no longer so dangerous.

80. Ibid., 55–56.

81. National Research Council, *Common Standards for K–12 Education? Considering the Evidence: Summary of a Workshop Series* (Washington, DC: National Academies Press, 2008), 70–71.

82. Rothman, *Something in Common*, 57.

83. Ibid.

84. Ibid., 62–63.

85. Lindsay Layton, "How Bill Gates Pulled Off the Swift Common Core Revolution," *WP*, June 7, 2014.

86. CCSS Initiative, *Common Core State Standards for English Language Arts and Literacy in History/Social Studies, Science, and Technical Subjects*, http://www.corestandards.org.

87. Dustin Beilke, "ALEC Education 'Academy' Launches on Island Resort," PRWatch.org, February 2, 2012, http://www.prwatch.org/news/2012/02/11272/alec-education-academy-launches-island-resort.

88. Mark Phillips, "Education Docs: No Chide Left Behind," *GCD*, June 22, 2010.

89. Ibid.

90. Stacy Teicher Khadaroo, "'Waiting for "Superman"': A Simplistic View of Education Reform," *CSM*, September 24, 2010.

91. *Race to Nowhere*, http://www.racetonowhere.com.

92. Ronald W. Evans, Panel Discussion, *Race to Nowhere* screening, San Diego, California, 2010.

93. Katherine Mangan, "Ignoring Experts' Pleas, Texas Board Approves Controversial Curriculum Standards," *CHE*, May 23, 2010.

94. Keith A. Erekson, Ed., *Politics and the History Curriculum: The Struggle Over Standards in Texas and the Nation* (New York: Palgrave Macmillan, 2012).

95. Michael Birnbaum, "Historians Speak Out Against Proposed Texas Textbook Changes," *WP*, March 18, 2010.

96. Gilbert T. Sewall, "Are Texas's Social Studies Standards Really So Bad?" *WP*, September 16, 2010.

97. James C. McKinley, Jr., "Texas Conservatives Win Curriculum Change," *NYT*, March 12, 2010; Michael Birnbaum, "Historians Speak Out"; Mangan, "Ignoring Experts."

98. McKinley, "Texas Conservatives Win Change."

99. Birnbaum, "Historians Speak Out."

100. Editor, "Texas School Board Approves Controversial Textbook Changes," *Need to Know on PBS*, May 23, 2010.

101. Mangan, "Ignoring Experts."

102. AHA, "AHA to the Members, Current and Elected, of the Texas State Board of Education," May 18, 2010, http://www.historians.org/press/2010_05_18_Texas_State_Board_of_Education.html.

103. Keith A. Erekson, "Social Studies Circus: Moving Beyond the 'Culture War' Model," in Erekson, *Politics and the History Curriculum*, draft, 33, n. 17.

104. Ibid., 29, n. 21.

105. Diane Ravitch, "'T' is for 'Texas Textbooks,'" *DB*, March 14, 2010; Jonathan Zimmerman, "History, By the Book," *LAT*, March 17, 2010.

106. Sundiata K. Cha-Jua, "Obama, the Rise of the Hard Right, Arizona and Texas and the Attack on Racialized Communities Studies," *BS* 40, no. 4 (Winter 2010), 2–6; Erekson, *Politics and the History Curriculum*.

107. Frances Fitzgerald, *America Revised: History Schoolbooks in the Twentieth Century* (New York: Vintage Books, 1980); James E. Loewen, *Lies My Teacher Told Me: Everything Your American History Textbook Got Wrong* (New York: New Press, 1995).

108. Spiff, "Marxist Agitator Dolores Huerta Speaks at Tucson High School, 'Republicans Hate Latinos,'" *Free Republic*, April 6, 2006, http://www.freerepublic.com/focus/f-news/1610739/posts; Eric Sagara, "'Hate-Speak' at School Draws Scrutiny," *TC*,

April 13, 2006, http://tucsoncitizen.com/morgue/2006/04/13/9256-hate-speak-at-school-draws-scrutiny/; Eric Sagara, "'Equal-Time' Talk Fuels Protest," *TC*, May 13, 2006, http://tucsoncitizen.com/morgue/2006/05/13/12461-equal-time-talk-fuels-protest/.

109. Sagara, "Equal-Time."
110. Stephen Cesar, "Tucson Students Confront Loss of Their Chicano Studies Class," *LAT*, January 11, 2012, http://articles.latimes.com/2012/jan/11/nation/la-na-ethnic-studies-20120112.
111. Michael Martin, "Mexican American Studies: Bad Ban or Bad Class?" January 18, 2012, *NPR*.
112. Michael Martin, "Ethnic Studies: Teaching Resentment or Pride?," *NPR*, January 19, 2012.
113. Roque Planas, "7 Mexican American Studies Books Banned From Tucson, Arizona Classrooms," *HP*, October 5, 2012.
114. Curtis Acosta, "To my friends and all our supporters," reprinted in "Banning Critical Teaching in Arizona: A Letter From Curtis Acosta," January 23, 2012, *RSB*, http://rethinkingschoolsblog.wordpress.com/2012/01/23/banning.
115. Ibid.
116. Al Letson, "A Year Without Mexican-American Studies in Tucson," *NPRW*, June 24, 2012; Lee Fang, *The Machine: A Field Guide to the Resurgent Right* (New York: New Press, 2013), 213–214.
117. Michael Knox Beran, "Abolish Social Studies," *CJ*, Autumn 2012.
118. See surveys of state standards by conservative groups, Box 12, Fordham Papers.
119. Erik W. Robelen, "Federal History-Grant Program Takes Budget Hit for Fiscal 2011," *EW* 30, no. 28 (April 20, 2011), 22.
120. Staff, "President Obama's Proposed FY '13 Budget Request to Congress," National Coalition for History, Blog Archive, February 15, 2012, http://historycoalition.org/2012/02/15/president-obamas-proposed-fy-13-budget-request-to-congress/.
121. DOE, *Teaching American History Evaluation: Final Report* (Washington, DC: DOE, 2011), xi.
122. Howard Blume, "Building the Case for Civics Lessons," *LAT*, December 27, 2011, AA1, AA4.
123. See Donovan R. Walling, "The Return of Civic Education," *PDK* 89, no. 4 (2007): 285–289.
124. Mark Previte, chair of NCSS Issues Centered Education Community, personal communication.
125. C. Frederick Risinger, "An Open Letter to President Barack Obama from C. Frederick Risinger, August 26, 2010," *SE* 74, no. 2 (November/December, 2010): 338–339.
126. Ibid., 339.
127. Arne Duncan, "The Social Studies Are Essential to a Well-Rounded Education," *SE* 73, no. 3 (May/June 2011): 124–125; see Connected Learning Coalition: A Foundation for Transforming K–12 Education, https://www.acteonline.org/clc/#.VA4rBYUxLMA.
128. Steve Goldberg, Syd Golston, Michel M. Yell, Gayle Thieman, and Peggy Altoff, "The Essential Role of Social Studies: Reflections on Secretary Arne Duncan's Article," *SE* 73, no. 3 (May/June 2011): 126–130.
129. CLC, "Connected Learning Foundation: Transforming K–12 Education," Transcript, August 27, 2012.
130. "About Us," Connected Learning Coalition, https://www.acteonline.org/clc/#.VA4rBYUxLMA; CLC Transcript, August 27, 2012.
131. CLC "Assessment: A Fundamental Component of Learning," policy paper, (Washington, DC: Connected Learning Coalition, November, 2011).
132. Klein, "Obama Uses Funding, Muscle"; McGuinn, "Stimulating Reform."

133. Onosko, "Race to the Top Leaves Children Behind."

134. NCSS, *Social Studies for the Next Generation: Purposes, Practices, and Implications of the College, Career, and Civic Life (C3) Framework for Social Studies State Standards* (Silver Spring, MD: NCSS, 2013).

135. S.G. Grant, Kathy Swan, and John Lee, "Lurching Toward Coherence: An Episodic History of Curriculum and Standards Development in Social Studies," paper presented at the annual meeting of the American Educational Research Association, Vancouver, British Columbia, April, 2012. See NCSS, *Social Studies for the Next Generation: Purposes, Practices, and Implications of the College, Career, and Civic Life (C3) Framework for Social Studies State Standards* (Silver Spring, MD: NCSS, 2013).

136. Grant, Swan, and Lee, "Lurching Toward Coherence."

137. See for example, Diane Ravitch, "Why I Oppose Common Core Standards," *WP*, February 26, 2013; Alan Singer, "Is Pearson Education in Serious Financial Trouble?" *HP*, April 25, 2014.

138. Ronald A. Wolk, "Common Core vs. Common Sense," *EW*, December 5, 2012.

139. Teresa Watanabe, "Standardized Testing Becomes the Great Divide in Schools Policy," *LAT*, March 3, 2013; Indiana, South Carolina, and Oklahoma have withdrawn from the CCSS, choosing to develop alternatives.

CONCLUSION: SOCIAL STUDIES
LEFT BEHIND

School reform in the twenty-first century is haunted by ghosts. By the ghosts of Adam Smith and Milton Friedman, of T.H. Bell and Ronald Reagan, David Kearns and Sandia Labs, of William Chandler Bagley and Michael J. Demiashkevich, and by the ghosts of John Dewey and Harold Rugg. I began this book with a description of instruction in social studies, contrasting a high-level, reflective vision of social studies teaching and the typical classroom dominated by teacher talk, textbooks, and low-level classroom practices. Frank Ryan's description of the typical social studies classroom and his comparison with a dynamic "new social studies" classroom still resonates, even though it was written in 1973.[1] Miera Levinson's more recent description of "speeding" through the curriculum to cover the content on state standardized tests captures the state of the field under NCLB's extreme accountability: a race through the textbook with little time for in-depth attention to inquiry or issues.[2]

This dilemma is one of a handful of key long-term problems facing the social studies field and civic education writ large. A second major dilemma is the influence of curriculum politics. Debate over schooling is, in part, a debate over competing visions of the American future. It is a struggle among competing interest groups with differing definitions of the worthy society.[3] Perhaps more than any other subject area, social studies is impacted and constrained by bitter struggles among polarized interest groups.

In recent years we have seen two major shifts in education that have had an important and largely detrimental impact on social studies instruction. The first is connected to the rising influence of business on schools. The business lobby has supported a model of education as competition, using business ideas to improve schooling. The essential elements of this model are captured in a few key assumptions: the public schools are a failed monopoly, and they can be fixed by applying free market business principles to the entire system. Schools can be improved if we treat them as a business: set standards, measure results, and hold everyone in the system accountable; competition among students, teachers, and schools will lead to improvement; and privatization through public school choice and experimentation with vouchers will help fix what's wrong with the public schools.

The second major change has been a somewhat less publicized shift in the dominant philosophy of education. Despite rhetorical support for "innovation," a major emphasis of reformers has centered on increasing curriculum requirements to develop a more rigorous school experience—and raise standards. Behind this shift is an essentialist philosophy of education that emphasizes the importance of content and gives short shrift to questions of pedagogy. Though the philosophy of education behind the reform is a little harder to discern than the broad outlines of business-driven accountability, there is a persistent strain in the rhetoric of excellence and accountability reform that is strongly anti-progressive and supportive of more conservative approaches favoring educational essentialism and effective schools research. The work of Diane Ravitch and Chester Finn, two of the key intellectual architects of the reform, has especially emphasized this strand. Moreover, the brand of essentialism they promoted is consonant with the development of school accountability, imposition of more rigorous requirements, and educational measurement centered on standardized testing. So, while students are spending more time in required courses, the approach to teaching supported by the reform has emphasized traditional teacher-centered approaches, with less time for in-depth inquiry and less frequent use of democratic practices involving discussion and critical thinking. While CCSS shifts this emphasis to some degree, increasing the possibility of greater depth, flexibility, and a more inquiry-oriented focus, its influence is still uncertain. Moreover, the reform retains the superstructure of accountability via testing and sanctions.

In social studies, the reform has emphasized courses rooted in traditional university-based disciplines such as history, geography, and economics. It has led to the decline or elimination of social studies as a broad and interdisciplinary field, as reflected in courses that meld more than one discipline, that focus on issues and civic education, and that allow students and teachers choice of elective content and the time and space for in-depth inquiry. It has also meant less time for connecting the curriculum to student interests, fewer opportunities for meaningful learning, and emphasis on socialization over counter-socialization. In the larger struggle over the purposes of education, between social control and schooling for intellectual freedom, schools today are caught up in what could best be described as "an orgy of efficiency." While some may point to increased course taking, more rigorous requirements, and claims of a higher graduation rate as evidence of better preparation for college and career, this shift was accompanied by a regrettable loss of teacher and student autonomy and intellectual freedom, key elements of meaningful learning.[4]

Education as a competition and emphasis on content to the detriment of process are signs of a reform movement out of balance. The process of education conceived as a competition lessens the purpose and lowers the aims. In the current school reform, emphasis on competition is overdone. Education is not a business, nor is it a game. It is a process of growth and acculturation that should be guided by the joy of discovery and the motivating force of wanting to know and understand. Some students respond to competition and do well. Others do not. As Jerome Bruner wrote in 1960, "the rebel," "the misfit," and "the late bloomer" are frequently ignored, shunted aside by a system focused on competition.[5]

A focus on content, with little attention to how students learn, breeds dissonant, fragmented classroom teaching. Anti-progressive in orientation, it ignores the basic problems of how we learn and grow, along with other key questions at the heart of the educational process. It ignores the needs and interests of the child. It ignores the question of motivation. Progressive educational reformers believed that childhood has value. Educational reformers need to pay attention to process as well as content. Which kind of classroom do you want for your child? Do you want a classroom that is sterile, focused on memorization, or one that is dynamic, that transforms learning into an exciting and engaging intellectual thrill ride?

In this book I have sought answers for a few key questions: Why did the shift toward accountability and more traditional teaching occur? Where did it originate? What impact has it had on classroom practice in social studies and civic education broadly? Context is one key for understanding the era of accountability reform. All of the interest groups that have been fighting over education for a century are still present. But the dominant trends in recent years have been shaped by a few key groups. Accountability reforms have been framed and driven by business groups in collaboration with government and neoconservative educators.[6] Context is a key determinant of which vision of reform holds court among multiple alternatives. The context that gave rise to accountability reforms was one in which it was argued that schools were failing and had to be improved if our nation was to compete effectively in the international economic arena.

The United States is a capitalist society, a world leader in economic and military might. We are also a society with a long history of white, Anglo-Saxon, Protestant dominance. We are a society in which the dominant narrative of our history as presented in schools and in the media is one of American exceptionalism. That is, our nation is different than others, with a higher purpose of creating a truly democratic society in which altruistic motives are most prized. However, underlying this veil of exceptionalism is the truth of a society dominated by competition, rugged individualism, and increasing social isolation.[7] We are an achievement-oriented culture, a society in which power, wealth, and income combine to form a power pyramid in which elites hold a dominant position of hegemony.[8] A reflection of our nation's economic power, we are also the dominant military power in the world. While our rhetoric reflects the goal of furthering democracy, many of our actions have supported neocolonialism, our nation as an empire. Behind the positive image of a powerful and democratic society are multiple contradictions. We are a society in which two Americas exist, one rich and the other poor. While most Americans find these contradictions troubling, they are largely accepted as just the way things are.

We are a society in which values are often contradictory. We value economic growth but worry about its impact on the environment. We celebrate wealth, and express concern about the poor. Recent school reform is situated in the larger context of a corporate move for power, seeking more influence on policy and control over workers.[9] The Powell memo, the founding of the BRT, decades of influence peddling, and schooling as a lever for creating worker-citizens are strong evidence of the rising corporate domination of American life.[10] We live in a society in which the greater good is increasingly defined by the agenda of corporate leaders. It is a society in which technology is increasingly used to make education into a marketable commodity, controlled by the corporations designing and developing educational materials.[11] Who benefits from this state of affairs? The economic elite and upper middle classes benefit the most, at the expense of low-wage workers.[12] As Harold Rugg wrote in 1941, it is still a battle of "Me vs. We."[13]

Overview

The origins of accountability reforms in schools can be found in a confluence of interests: business, government, conservative and neoconservative politicians and educators, and the religious right. These groups combined to lead development of a mainstream consensus in support of accountability reform, fueled by pervasive myths about public schools as a failed monopoly and business principles as the solution. They have developed a one-dimensional schooling for human capital. It is an approach to schooling framed by standards and testing, a systemic reform that repels alternatives such as schooling for democratic citizenship and the deep questioning, intellectual freedom, and human potential that go with it.

Schooling in the United States has long embodied a cult of efficiency by which advocates of scientific management in education have attempted to engineer social improvement. Several trends of the 1970s led to calls for changing and improving schools. Among these were neo-efficiency trends such as minimum competency testing, the back-to-basics movement, a growing conservative reaction to trends of the 1960s, and a series of academic freedom battles over what was taught in schools and how it would be taught. These trends, combined with growing concerns over U.S. performance in international economic competition and declining test scores on college entrance exams, led to calls for school reform.

Critics suggested that schools were dominated by Deweyan educational ideas that were leaving students ignorant and unskilled. During the Reagan administration, *A Nation at Risk* and other reports sounded the alarm and called for raising standards, a return to a core of "new basics" and to traditional approaches to teaching. Business groups clamored for more effective development of human capital and called for higher standards and a system of measurement. Neoconservative educators and interest groups trumpeted an essentialist vision for education focused on the traditional academic disciplines and the classics. In social studies, this meant an emphasis on traditional history and geography. Gradually, business groups, government, neoconservative educators, and systemic education reformers joined forces to create a national consensus centered around the notion that schools were a failed monopoly and that the solution lay in setting standards, measuring results, and holding students, teachers, administrators, and schools accountable, while at the same time supporting public school choice, development of charter schools, and other efforts toward privatization. The BRT developed a ten-year plan to improve schooling.

Government and business leaders held a series of summit meetings, beginning in 1986, in a collaborative effort to improve school performance by imposing higher standards and accountability. The election of George H.W. Bush and the 1989 Charlottesville Summit marked a key turning point after which the nation appeared set on moving toward imposition of serious accountability reform measures. During the Clinton administration, a series of controversies over outcome-based education, national standards for U.S. history, and proposals for national testing led to delays in federal legislation and a focus on state-by-state development of systemic reform. By the end of the 1990s, as a result of continuous lobbying from business groups combined with federal pressure, most of the states had adopted systemic school reform measures including statewide content standards and achievement testing.

The 2000 election marked a high water mark for concern over education and led to passage of the No Child Left Behind Act, with strong bipartisan support, which mandated standardized testing in language arts and mathematics in grades three through eight, making systemic reform the official federal government policy, though it would continue to be implemented by the states. Concerns over a lack of flexibility in implementation led to modifications during the Obama administration, including use of administrative incentives to induce states to join the movement for common core standards.

In schools and classrooms, systemic reform under NCLB meant a more rigorous, more uniform curriculum and increased use of traditional teacher-centered teaching practices focused on textbooks, basic skills, teacher talk, and memorization. It meant reduction in the use of progressive or democratic forms of education such as open forum discussion, student projects, making connections, deep understanding of concepts, curriculum integration, cooperative learning, critical thinking, and analytical reasoning. It meant that teaching became more traditional and less progressive. This was combined with a decline in teacher autonomy and increasing imposition of scripted lessons, often draining the "joy" from teaching and learning.

Evidence on course taking from transcript studies conducted by the NCES showed that more graduates were completing a "challenging" or "rigorous" curriculum, with graduates' average total Carnegie units up from 21.58 units in 1982 to 27.15 units by 2009. In social studies, students were completing more courses, up from 3.16 units in 1982 to 4.19 units in 2009, illustrating a similar increase in course taking. However, there was little evidence that the increased course taking was making much difference in student outcomes. There was no improvement in twelfth-grade NAEP scores, casting doubt on the authenticity of achievement gains. Moreover, the school reform movement and revival of traditional history led to changes in social studies content, with dramatic increases in world history and significant increases in economics and a few other social sciences. Course taking in more progressive social studies offerings such as global studies, civics, and social problems declined sharply.

Over its history, accountability reform has had a significant impact on classroom teaching, leading to more emphasis on traditional, teacher-centered approaches to teaching in most schools and in most states, though there was a good deal of variability and exceptions in some charter schools. It led to less use of progressive, child-centered, interactive, and interest-building practices. Thus, the net effect was the reification of a standard grammar of schooling, with increased emphasis on low-level classroom practices reinforced by standards, tests, textbooks, scripted lessons, and pacing guides.

Reformers point to the positives: more data on the condition of education; media attention to school reform; test scores as a reflection of school and teacher quality; and more course taking as evidence of improvement. Negatives include the misplaced use of data, which is largely redundant; a punitive atmosphere dominated by fear, restrictions, and constraint; less room for the creativity of teachers to flourish, a concern that matters, because creativity is at the heart of great teaching; reduced teacher and student autonomy; too little attention to student motivation; little attention to the needs and interests of children, except as defined by adults; and few choices for students—a prescribed curriculum. Unfortunately, many of these reforms were consciously designed to kill off any vestiges of progressive educational pedagogy. During the NCLB era, they largely succeeded.

An Interpretation

As we have seen, the evidence presented in this history of school accountability reform reflects an approach that has reified industrial-era patterns of schooling. The thinking has been, as William G. Spady suggests, if it isn't working do more of the same, only longer and harder, and with more consequences attached, including large does of shame and humiliation.[14] Competition and market-driven approaches dominate school reform, with emphasis on winners and losers and the inevitable reproduction of social stratification that results. This has led to the alienation and oppression of both labor (teachers and administrators) and many students. This system of school reform has an impact on self-image, positive for some, but negative for many others. Moreover, it is largely destructive of community. Somehow, the rising number of school shootings seems related to the disintegration of community, to the increasing emphasis on bowling alone, and to a society and school system that increasingly champions rugged individualism.[15]

What has motivated the reformers? Most accountability reformers have limited school experience and lack insider knowledge of education. They have focused on systemic reform with an approach aimed at "making schools a business," set on making over the system in their own image. What was already a factory model, based on capitalist, industrial-era patterns, is now a factory-modeled system on steroids. Greed and ambition are driving forces; money, position, and control are paramount, thinly hidden by a rhetoric of caring and closing the achievement gap, a rhetoric that has brought little real change. Reformers have imposed a one-dimensional schooling for the development of human capital. They have strengthened and shored up the worst aspects of schooling—as dehumanizing institutions driven by achievement and rugged individualism, sorting children into a class-based meritocracy. They imposed a curriculum favoring memorization and control, with too little room for questioning. These dehumanizing aspects are, historically, some of the most troubling characteristics of schools, critiqued and condemned by new-wave critics of the 1960s and 1970s such as Jonathan Kozol, Herb Kohl, Postman and Weingartner, and others.[16] School accountability reform has been largely anti-democratic and anti-community, with emphasis on development of human capital to produce corporate workers. Moreover, as Kathy Emery points out, top-down, business-driven reform has reduced community participation in determining educational goals and practices.[17]

There were several important factors leading to these changes, including back-to-basics and neoconservative rhetoric, media frenzy over declining test scores in international comparisons, a powerful business lobby backed by wealthy individuals and corporations, and a coalition of interest groups and conservative foundations supporting accountability reform and a shift to more traditional forms of education.[18] The bottom-line result was a pendulum swing to the right, reinstitution of essentialist educational practices, and a decline in progressive, interdisciplinary, child-centered, and issues-centered approaches to learning. With the advent of CCSS, this may be changing, with a shift toward more inquiry-oriented approaches to teaching and learning and emphasis on "thinking deeply," "integrating learning," and "making connections," though the impact and sustainability of this new direction remain uncertain.

Perspective on the Reform

It may be instructive to compare this reform to other reform attempts. Previous reforms still have some influence on the rhetoric and practices of educators—though they have largely been shelved. Progressive education reform was rooted in the philosophy of John Dewey and the notion that education should balance subject matter and traditional school learning with the needs and interests of the child. Deweyan pedagogic progressives such as Harold Rugg and William H. Kilpatrick emphasized active learning, inquiry, issues, and school as an embryonic community.[19] Inquiry-oriented reforms of the 1960s were pedagogically similar in that they emphasized active learning and questioning, though mostly within a discipline-based framework. Jerome Bruner and others emphasized discovery learning, curiosity, and inquiry, and tapped student motivation as a key element in learning.[20] In contrast to these previous reforms, the current accountability reform seems quite shallow.

Advocates trumpet the benefits of increasing amounts of data on student performance. "Now we have data" is the common refrain. Trouble is, we've had similar data for decades. Moreover, much of the data being collected on state tests is misused to reward and punish schools and teachers based on questionable assumptions—that test scores are an accurate reflection of the quality of teaching; that accountability and a system of rewards and punishments will lead to improved performance. Another frequently cited positive is that as a society we are more attuned to questions of educational performance and quality. The rhetoric of "No Child Left Behind" sounds good. However, the reform has done little to change entrenched patterns of school funding and operation that provide much higher-quality educational services to children in some neighborhoods than to others, based on the relative wealth of the area.

According to many critics, accountability reform has failed, even by its own standards.[21] It has led to a "one size fits all" approach to education and a focus on content acquisition. It has led to support for traditional teacher-centered approaches to teaching based on an essentialist philosophy and dubious use of research. It has occurred during a context of increasing economic and social stratification, a context that leads to inequality in educational resources and treatment that reformers have largely ignored. It has been divisive, with most educators on one side, and most businesspeople on the other. The reform has also led to widespread cheating.

Critics charge that core assumptions of the reform are deeply flawed. They argue that the reform is built on the assumption that schools are a business and can be reformed via a top-down command model. Critics argue that reformers have assumed that *all* the schools are failing and that *all* schools need systemic reform. Reformers have applied concepts drawn from free market business principles to schooling in a simplistic and heavy-handed way, assuming that this would effectively reform the institution of schooling. However, schools are not businesses. While they may have some business-like features and functions, their purposes, many would argue, should center on developing human potential in a democratic society. The reform has largely submerged the historic aims of democratic education, under the rhetoric and reality of systemic reform with emphasis on education as preparation for work.

Critics argue that students are intelligent beings and should not be subject to such crass manipulation for the profit and personnel needs of the military-academic-industrial complex. Critics suggest that schooling in the United States is an increasingly inhumane system in which there are few alternatives for those whom it rejects.[22] The child is not a widget or a product. The business metaphor ultimately breaks down on the fact of our humanity. The child has a will and a personality, enthusiasms and interests, creative impulses and curiosity. Education at its best is focused on tapping into the needs and interests of the child. It seeks to develop the child's fullest potential. This was the mantra of an earlier generation of educators with a progressive philosophy. The problem with an essentialist approach to learning is that by focusing on content, it largely omits the needs and interests of the child. While the Common Core Standards have shifted greater emphasis to the learning process, their impact and outcomes remain uncertain.

Education and Democracy

Over its history, accountability reform has not worked if the goal is improvement in teaching and learning. It has only worked if the goal is to impede freedom, to manage, to control, to sort, and to drill. Jules Henry once wrote that schools exist for "drilling children in cultural orientations." He described the typical pattern of social studies instruction as an exercise in "learning to be stupid," in which children learn myths about their nation and the world and are seldom asked to confront the sometimes troubling realities.[23] Continuation of accountability reform only makes sense if the reification of these cultural purposes makes sense. Or, to put it more forcefully, I would like to quote Jack Barnes, who wrote, on the eve of the 2000 election, just as rhetoric on education reform was peaking:

> Most everything else we are taught in school, especially the so-called social sciences and related "disciplines" are things we need to unlearn. Civics courses, social studies courses, these are all obfuscation . . .
>
> [Bush and Gore] share the same underlying dog-eat-dog assumption: that education is about ensuring that your family's children have the best shot at the lifetime struggle of each against all.
>
> The purpose of education in class society is not to educate. It is to give "the educated" a stake in thinking they are going to be different than other people who work all their lives . . . [Schools are] not institutions of learning but of social control, aimed at reproducing the class relations and privileges of the prevailing order.[24]

From a critical perspective, the primary underlying goal of schooling in a capitalist society is to produce obedient workers and thus reproduce class relations, the privilege of elites, and the established social order.[25]

Accountability reform is not working if our aim is to improve education for democracy. Democracy in America is at risk.[26] Democratic education is at odds with the context of corporate control of schooling and American life. To keep alive the possibility of improvement, we need to resurrect progressive social studies and civic learning as a democratic form of education emphasizing inquiry, issues, interactive learning, and questioning. To the extent that CCSS and accompanying modifications move classroom teaching in this direction, we may benefit, though it is far too soon to tell.

Little by little the look of the country changes because of who we admire and to what we aspire. The approach we take to education matters. Educational methods contain a message—I call it the content of the form—that imparts important value lessons to the student. Traditional methods tend to impart the underlying truth that the teacher, the book, the school, or the boss is the authority, to be obeyed, not questioned. For teachers and students, obedience is the order of the day.[27] On the other hand, reformers of the past, calling for alternative methods, believed that the teacher, the book, the school, the boss, and knowledge itself are socially constructed. They are human creations and inherently flawed. Questions of the approach to education go right to the heart of our deepest beliefs about the nature of knowledge and knowing, to epistemology, and to our beliefs about the nature of man.

During their history, accountability reforms have damaged citizenship education and education for democracy. The context of accountability reform is one key to understanding why this has occurred. An overarching focus on the economic construction of education and development of human capital as its central overriding purpose is at the heart of the reform. Since the beginnings of accountability reform, a capitalist, business-driven framework has been its dominant underlying feature. Accountability reform corresponds to the continued development of a power pyramid in American society, with an increasing shift of money and power to the top.

Accountability reform has led to more influence for conservative and neoconservative groups, wealthy individuals, and their ideas. It reflects growing corporate influence in American society and around the globe, inspired in part by the Lewis Powell memo and the 1970s decision by corporate leaders to fight back against unions and liberal interest groups by organizing the Business Roundtable, the Heritage Foundation, ALEC, and similar groups and to fight for more favorable policies. In this context, education is an arena in which business groups have successfully organized and asserted a broad and compelling influence. Greater knowledge and awareness of these realities may be an important step toward undoing the damage.

Notes

1. Frank L. Ryan, "Implementing the Hidden Curriculum of the Social Studies," *SE* 37, no. 7 (November 1973).
2. Meira Levinson, *No Citizen Left Behind* (Cambridge, MA: Harvard University Press, 2012), 250–253.

3. Herbert M. Kliebard, *Struggle for the American Curriculum, 1893–1958* (Boston: Routledge and Keegan Paul, 1986); Ronald W. Evans, *The Social Studies Wars: What Should We Teach the Children?* (New York: Teachers College, 2004).

4. See Nancy C. Patterson, "What's Stopping You? Classroom Censorship for Better or Worse," *SE* 74, no. 6 (Nov/Dec 2010): 326; Jack L. Nelson, "The Need for Courage in American Schools: Cases and Causes," *SE* 74, no. 6 (Nov/Dec 2010): 298.

5. Jerome S. Bruner, *The Process of Education* (Cambridge, MA: Harvard University Press, 1960).

6. Kevin Kumashiro, *The Seduction of Common Sense: How the Right Has Framed the Debate on America's Schools* (New York: Teachers College Press, 2008).

7. Geoffrey Mohan, "Social Isolation Increases Risk of Early Death, Study Finds," *LAT*, March 26, 2013, A9.

8. G. William Domhoff, "Wealth, Income, and Power," http://www2.ucsc.edu/whorulesamerica/power/wealth.html (2006, updated 2013); Oxfam, *Working for the Few: Political Capture and Economic Inequality* (Oxford, UK: Oxfam International, 2014).

9. Alana Semuels, "How the Relationship Between Employers and Workers Changed," *LAT*, April 7, 2013, A1.

10. Lewis F. Powell to Eugene B. Snydor, "Confidential Memorandum: Attack on American Free Enterprise System," August 23, 1971, 1, 11, 25–26, Powell Papers.

11. Alex Molnar, *Giving Kids the Bu$iness: The Commercialization of America's Schools* (Boulder, CO: Westview Press, 1996); Jonathan Kozol, *Shame of the Nation: The Restoration of Apartheid Schooling in America* (New York: Crown, 2005).

12. Jacob S. Hacker and Paul Pierson, *Winner-Take-All Politics: How Washington Made the Rich Richer—And Turned Its Back on the Middle Class* (New York: Simon and Schuster, 2010).

13. Harold O. Rugg, *That Men May Understand: An American in the Long Armistice* (New York: Ginn, 1941).

14. William G. Spady, "The Paradigm Trap," *Education Week*, January 10, 2007.

15. Robert Putnam, "Bowling Alone: America's Declining Social Capital," *JD* 6, no. 1 (1995): 65–78.

16. Ronald W. Evans, *The Tragedy of American School Reform: How Curriculum Politics and Entrenched Dilemmas Have Diverted Us from Democracy* (New York: Palgrave Macmillan, 2011), 37–44.

17. Kathy Emery, "The Business Roundtable and Systemic Reform: How Corporate-Engineered High-Stakes Testing Has Eliminated Community Participation in Developing Educational Goals and Policies" (Doctoral Dissertation, University of California, Davis, 2002); Kathy Emery and Susan O'Hanian, *Why Is Corporate America Bashing Our Public Schools?* (Portsmouth, NH: Heinemann, 2004).

18. Lee Fang, *The Machine: A Field Guide to the Resurgent Right* (New York: New Press, 2013); Kim Phillips-Fein, *Invisible Hands: The Making of the Conservative Movement from the New Deal to Reagan* (New York: W.W. Norton, 2009).

19. Evans, *Social Studies Wars*; C. Gregg Jorgensen, *John Dewey and the Dawn of Social Studies* (Charlotte, NC: Information Age, 2012); Ronald W. Evans, *This Happened in America: Harold Rugg and the Censure of Social Studies* (Charlotte, NC: Information Age, 2007). It is important to distinguish pedagogic progressives from administrative progressives, many of whom promoted somewhat similar social efficiency-oriented reforms and could be thought of as forerunners of systemic school reformers. See David Tyack, *The One Best System: A History of American Urban Education* (Cambridge, MA: Harvard, 1974).

20. Peter F. Dow, *Schoolhouse Politics: Lessons from the Sputnik Era* (Cambridge, MA: Harvard, 1991).

21. Kenneth J. Saltman, "What (Might) Happen When Teachers and Other Academics Connect Reason to Power and Power to Resistance?" Rouge Forum Conference, April 2012, Vancouver, BC; Kenneth J. Saltman, *The Failure of Corporate School Reform* (New York: Paradigm Publishing, 2012).

22. Sandy Banks, "Troubled Youth Deserve More Effective Discipline Than Suspension," *LAT*, May 17, 2013.

23. Jules Henry, *Culture Against Man* (New York: Random House, 1963), 283–284, 320–321.

24. Jack Barnes, *The Working Class and the Transformation of Learning: The Fraud of Education Reform Under Capitalism* (New York: Pathfinder Press, 2000), 21, 24, 26, in Box 43, Pathfinder Papers.

25. On lessons from school reform, see David Tyack and Larry Cuban, *Tinkering Toward Utopia: A Century of Public School Reform* (Cambridge, MA: Harvard University Press, 1995); see also recent work by W. James Popham, Diane Ravitch, Sharon Beder, and David Hursh.

26. Jeffrey Gates, *Democracy at Risk: Rescuing Main Street from Wall Street* (Cambridge, MA: Perseus, 2000).

27. Paulo Freire, *Pedagogy of the Oppressed* (New York: Continuum, 1970); Hayden White, *Tropics of Discourse: Essays in Cultural Criticism* (Baltimore: Johns Hopkins, 1978).

LIST OF ABBREVIATIONS

Organizations, Committees, Commissions, etc.

Adequate Yearly Progress	AYP
American Association of School Administrators	AASA
American Diploma Project	ADP
American Diploma Project Network	ADPN
American Educational Research Association	AERA
American Enterprise Institute	AEI
American Federation of Teachers	AFT
American Historical Association	AHA
American Legislative Exchange Council	ALEC
Association for Career and Technical Education	ACTE
Association for Supervision and Curriculum Development	ASCD
Business Coalition for Education Reform	BCER
Business Coalition for Excellence in Education	BCEE
Business-Higher Education Forum	BHEF
Business Roundtable	BRT
Center for Information and Research on Civic Learning and Engagement, The	CIRCLE
Committee for Economic Development	CED
Common Core State Standards	CCSS
Connected Learning Coalition	CLC
Council of Chief State School Officers	CCSSO
Council on Basic Education	CBE
Democratic Leadership Council	DLC
Department of Education (United States)	DOE
Education Commission of the States	ECS
Educational Consolidation and Improvement Act	ECIA
Educational Excellence Network	EEN
Educational Testing Service	ETS
Elementary and Secondary Education Act	ESEA
Excellence for Parents, Children, and Teachers	EXPECT

Improving America's Schools Act	IASA
Life Adjustment Education	LAE
Man: A Course of Study	MACOS
Mexican American Studies	MAS
National Advisory Council on Educational Research and Improvement	NACERI
National Alliance of Business	NAB
National Assessment of Educational Progress	NAEP
National Association of Elementary School Principals	NAESP
National Association of Manufacturers	NAM
National Association of State Boards of Education	NASBE
National Center for Education Statistics	NCES
National Center for History in the Schools	NCHS
National Center on Education and the Economy	NCEE
National Commission on Excellence in Education	NCE
National Council for History Education	NCHE
National Council for the Social Studies	NCSS
National Council of Teachers of English	NCTE
National Council of Teachers of Mathematics	NCTM
National Council on Education Standards and Testing	NCEST
National Defense Education Act	NDEA
National Education Association	NEA
National Education Goals Panel	NEGP
National Education Standards and Improvement Council	NESIC
National Endowment for the Humanities	NEH
National Governors Association	NGA
National Institute of Education	NIE
National Research Council	NRC
National School Boards Association	NSBA
National Science Foundation	NSF
National Science Teachers Association	NSTA
New Commission on Skills of the American Workforce	NCSAW
New York State Education Department	NYSED
No Child Left Behind	NCLB
Office of Educational Research and Improvement	OERI
Office of Management and Budget	OMB
Opportunity to Learn	OTL
Organization of American Historians	OAH
Outcome-Based Education	OBE
Parent Teachers Association	PTA
Partnerships in Education	PIE
Problems of Democracy	POD
Progressive Policy Institute	PPI
Race to the Top	RTT
Scholastic Aptitude Test	SAT
Science, Technology, Engineering, and Mathematics	STEM
Standards-Based Education	SBE
State Board of Education (Texas)	SBOE
State of the Union Address	SOU
Teaching American History Project, The	TAH
Trends in International Mathematics and Science Study	TIMSS
Tucson Unified School District	TUSD
United States Office of Education	USOE

Journals, Periodicals, and Media Sources

American Economic Review	AER
American Educational Research Journal	AERJ
American Educator	AE
American Prospect, The	AP
American Scholar, The	ASCH
American Spectator	AS
Atlantic Monthly	AM
Black Scholar, The	BS
Boston Globe	BG
Brookings Papers on Educational Policy	BPEP
Change: The Magazine of Higher Learning	CHG
Chicago Tribune	CT
Christian Science Monitor	CSM
Chronicle of Higher Education	CHE
City Journal	CJ
Clearing House, The	CH
Congressional Quarterly Weekly	CQW
Congressional Record	CR
CUFA Newsletter (College and University Faculty Assembly, NCSS)	CUFA
Current Issues in Education	CIE
Curriculum Inquiry	CI
Daily Beast, The	DB
Democracy and Education	DE
Democrat and Chronicle	DC
Detroit News	DN
Economics of Education Review	EER
Education Policy Analysis Archives	EPAA
Education Review	ERV
Education Week	EW
Educational Forum	EF
Educational Leadership	EL
Educational Policy	EP
Educational Researcher	ER
Elementary School Teacher	EST
Fortune	FT
Foundry, The: Heritage Foundation	FHF
Governing Magazine	GM
Green Cine Daily	GCD
Harper's	HA
Harvard Education Review	HER
History News Network	HNN
Huffington Post	HP
Independent	IN
International Journal of Social Education	IJSE
Issues in Science and Technology	IST
Journal of American History	JAH
Journal of Curriculum Studies	JCS
Journal of Democracy	JD
Journal of Economic Education	JEE
Journal of Educational Research	JER
Journal of Political Economics	JPE

Los Angeles Times	*LAT*
Monthly Review	*MR*
Nation, The	*NAT*
National Public Radio	*NPR*
National Public Radio Weekend Edition	*NPRW*
National Review	*NR*
NEA Today	*NEAT*
New Democrat	*ND*
New Republic	*NRP*
New York Review	*NYR*
New York Times	*NYT*
New York Times Magazine	*NYTM*
Newsweek	*NW*
Peabody Journal of Education	*PJE*
Phi Delta Kappan	*PDK*
Pink Sheet, The	*PS*
Policy Priorities	*PP*
Public Opinion Quarterly	*POQ*
Publius	*PB*
Race, Ethnicity, and Education	*REE*
Rethinking Schools Blog	*RSB*
Review of Research in Education	*RRE*
Roll Call	*RC*
San Francisco Chronicle	*SFC*
School Administrator	*SA*
Seton Hall Legislative Journal	*SHLJ*
Social Education	*SE*
Social Policy	*SP*
Social Science Quarterly	*SSQ*
Social Studies Review	*SSR*
South Carolina Business Journal	*SCBJ*
Teacher Education Quarterly	*TEQ*
Teachers College Record	*TCR*
Technos Quarterly	*TQ*
The Social Studies	*TSS*
Theory and Research in Social Education	*TRSE*
Time	*TM*
Tucson Citizen	*TC*
USA Today	*USAT*
Wall Street Journal	*WSJ*
Washington Post	*WP*
Washington Times	*WT*
Weekly Standard, The	*WS*
Whiteboard Advisors	*WA*
William and Mary Law Review	*WMLR*

LIST OF MANUSCRIPT COLLECTIONS ABBREVIATED IN NOTES

American Presidency Project, University of California, Santa Barbara
    Presidents' Public Papers   APP

Dolph Briscoe Center for American History
    NCSS Manuscript Collection   NCSS Papers
    Definition of Social Studies Papers submitted
    by Margit McGuire, NCSS President, 1991–1992,
    NCSS Manuscript Collection   McGuire Papers

George H.W. Bush Library
    WHORM Subject Files, Education   Bush Papers
    Rae Nelson Files   Nelson Files
    President's Public Papers   Bush Public Papers

George W. Bush Library
    George W. Bush Public Papers   GW Bush Papers

William Jefferson Clinton Library
    Education Series, Bruce Reed Collection   Reed Collection

Hoover Institution Archives
    Chester E. Finn, Jr., Papers   Finn Papers
    Education Subject Collection   Hoover ESC
    Thomas B. Fordham Foundation   Fordham Papers
    Bruno Manno Papers   Manno Papers
    Pathfinder Press Papers   Pathfinder Papers
    Diane Ravitch Papers   Ravitch Papers

Lyndon Baines Johnson Library
    White House Central Files   LBJ Papers
    LBJ Public Papers   LBJPP
    Douglass Cater Files   Cater Files

National Archives and Records Administration II
    RG 441, General Records DOE
        Commissioner's Office Files   Bell Papers
        NACERI Files   NACERI

Richard M. Nixon Library
    Nixon ED Files (Education)   Nixon Papers

Ronald Reagan Presidential Library
    WHORM Subject Files [ED (Education) Series]   Reagan Papers

Washington and Lee University School of Law
    Powell Archives
        Lewis F. Powell, Jr., Papers   Powell Papers

INDEX